Reaper Leader

Reaper Leader

The Life of Jimmy Flatley

Steve Ewing

NAVAL INSTITUTE PRESS

Annapolis, Maryland

Naval Institute Press
291 Wood Road
Annapolis, MD 21402

Library of Congress Cataloging-in-Publication Data
Ewing, Steve.
Reaper leader : the life of Jimmy Flatley / Steve Ewing.
        p. cm.
Includes bibliographical references and index.
ISBN 1-55750-205-6 (alk. paper)
    1. Flatley, Jimmy, 1906–1958. 2. United States. Navy—Officers—Biography.
3. Admirals—United States—Biography. 4. Fighter pilots—United States—
Biography. 5. World War, 1939–1945—Aerial operations, American. 6. World
War, 1939–1945—Naval operations, American. 7. World War, 1939–1945—
Campaigns—Pacific Area. I. Title.
V63.F53 E95 2002
940.54'5973'092—dc21

                                                          2002004273

Printed in the United States of America on acid-free paper ∞
09 08 07 06 05 04 03 02   9 8 7 6 5 4 3 2
First printing

Contents

Foreword

The first six months of World War II encompassed one of the most baleful periods in American history. The shock of the disaster at Pearl Harbor was quickly followed by the loss of Guam, the surrender of the Philippines, the capture of Wake Island, the defeat in the Java Sea, and the invasion of the Aleutians. At Midway on 5 June 1942, the American navy did achieve a great victory. It decisively defeated the Japanese, but in this action, the U.S. Navy lost one of its three available carriers; and due to incomplete information at that time regarding Japanese carrier construction, the extent of the devastating damage inflicted upon the Japanese carrier navy was not immediately known in the United States.

Excuses could be made for our failures: the surprise at Pearl Harbor; the remoteness of Guam, Wake, the Java Sea; the overwhelming enemy numbers at Bataan; and the superiority of the Japanese Zero in all of the air actions. Then in August 1942, in a night action at Savo Island, the Americans lost four heavy cruisers to a Japanese force of comparable size, with only minor damage to the enemy ships, and the U.S. Navy had to temporarily abandon the marines just put ashore on Guadalcanal. This time there could be no excuses other than a lapse in leadership at all command levels. Again the Imperial Japanese Navy seemed invincible. If the United States were to avert defeat in the Pacific, sweeping improvements in equipment, tactics, and leaders had to occur—and time was the critical factor.

Naval aviation was the newest arm of the fleet and presumably the most modern and operationally advanced. However, the carrier forces, like the rest of the navy, had also suffered from the previous decade of peacetime budgets and public lassitude. The U.S. Navy's combat aircraft in many cases had proved to be inferior to their Japanese counterparts. Some first-line carrier planes like the Brewster Buffalo fighters and the TBD Devastator torpedo planes were no more than death traps for their crews when they engaged in combat with the Japanese.

It became patently clear in the first days of the war that more aircraft with significantly improved performance, flown by better-trained pilots using smarter tactics, were essential just to halt the inexorable Japanese advance—much less to win the war in the Pacific. It soon became equally apparent to the admirals in Washington that none of these improvements in equipment, training, and tactics could happen without changes in leadership at all levels in the fleet and the shore establishment. New leaders—vigorous, bold, wise, and courageous—would have to be identified and moved into positions of influence and authority. But there was little time to make these changes. Already our losses in the Pacific were enough to dismay the strategic planners and discourage the fighting forces.

In this time of national crisis our system of government worked. Although our ethos as a democracy may have encouraged isolationism and stifled an incentive to rearm in peacetime, the U.S. Army and Navy, drawing on the resources of an all-out national mobilization, worked effectively within the framework of their own expanded organizations. Military leaders competent to fight a war almost immediately emerged, their professional ability to command quickly lifting them high above the pack. As national leaders such as Marshall, King, Eisenhower, MacArthur, and Nimitz assumed the top responsibilities, other capable flag officers were moved into the operating forces to relieve the on-site commanders who were exhausted and demoralized by the nightmarish events of the opening months of the war. The new leaders, such as Spruance and Halsey, would command the fleets, translating national strategy into workable operational plans. Carrier aviation needed to be transformed into a force that could carry out the complex operations of the Third and Fifth Fleets in a vast oceanic theater against a formidable foe. To direct that transformation, a cadre of talented officers was required at the level of unit commander, who could personally lead the combat in the air. But only a handful of naval aviators had become serious students of carrier air warfare during the peacetime years and had, through their professional diligence, earned the right to command and the privilege of constructive criticism.

Jimmy Flatley was among that handful. When the shooting started, it was inevitable that his service reputation would propel him into positions of leadership and command, and to him would fall a major share of the responsibility for evolving the air warfare doctrines of the U.S. Navy.

Jimmy Flatley had spent his apprenticeship as a naval aviator in the years of the 1930s when the battleship was both the symbol and the measure of naval superiority. But by the later period of his career, when he was senior enough to be assigned command responsibilities, he had already demonstrated a professional maturity marked by a solid intellect and refreshing degree of imagination. It was fortunate that the blossoming of his career as a naval aviator came at a time when his contributions were most needed, and under the circumstances where he could exert a tangible influence on the changes taking place in the U.S. Navy. The service was at the eve of one of its seminal transformations, comparable to the transition from sail to steam and from wood to steel.

In a brief period of time between 1941 and 1944, the world powers came to acknowledge the importance of air power at sea. The Japanese were among its initial protagonists. The United States had to learn the hard way. America's first battle of World War II was Pearl Harbor, in which the Japanese, using carrier-based air power alone, defeated the U.S. Pacific Fleet in an engagement where the ships of the two opposing sides never were in visual contact or exchanged a shot during the entire battle. Less than a week later the Royal Navy was shocked at the sinking of two British battleships, HMS *Prince of Wales* and *Repulse* off Singapore, to Japanese land-based bombers. No Japanese warships were involved in that engagement and the battleships had no fighter protection.

This new era of war-fighting at sea began with Japan's entry into World War II, and the U.S. Navy had to undergo a wrenching change of direction—in weapons, tactics, and strategy—in the shortest possible time under the most difficult of circumstances, while actually fighting a war in which the survival of the fleet was at stake. By the end of that war the aircraft carrier had emerged as the principal ship of the fleet and the centerpiece of fighting at sea.

In the early 1930s the carrier had been looked upon as primarily a reconnaissance platform to provide scouting aircraft as the eyes of the fleet, whose mission was to bring the battleships of the line into gun range of the enemy battleships. The Second World War was the beginning of the epoch of naval aviation, as the aircraft carrier became the sine qua non of sea power for the United States and changed the very concept of fighting a war at sea, both for that conflict and in the Cold War that followed.

From a humble collection of only seven fleet carriers of various designs and sizes on 7 December 1941, carrier force levels increased to more than a hundred flat-topped commissioned ships designated as aircraft carriers of all types and missions by the war's end. Although the United States continued to construct destroyers, cruisers, and battleships and to deploy these surface combatants to the war in considerable numbers, their principal roles became shore bombardment and escorting carriers for close-in defense in the screen of a carrier task force. Following the fighting off Guadalcanal in 1942, in only one subsequent battle of the war did U.S. Navy forces win a major engagement between surface forces of two fleets in which no aircraft were involved: the Battle of Surigao Strait at Leyte Gulf. All of the other major naval victories in the Pacific involved aircraft carriers as the main components.

The offensive capability of the U.S. Navy, the means by which America was to control the seas to enable the U.S Army and Marines to move across the Pacific in an unbroken series of successful amphibious landings, was through carrier-based aircraft. As the fleet air operations evolved, the mission capabilities of the carrier dramatically expanded. Initially focused on fighting a war at sea to destroy the Japanese ships and aircraft opposing the American advance, carrier planes soon demonstrated their ability to provide support for our engaged troops ashore. Originally a tactical function to which the navy's first-line aircraft were committed, close air support in the Pacific became the principal mission of the smaller escort carriers, which lacked the speed and staying power of the fleet carriers, the twenty-seven-thousand-ton *Essex*-class and eleven-thousand-ton *Independence*-class cruiser conversions. These fleet carriers were capable of a speed of thirty knots and were organized into fast carrier task groups with their escorting destroyers, cruisers, and battleships. By 1943 these fast carrier striking forces had enlarged their mission capabilities to a new and major strategic function that provided a significant contribution to the Pacific campaign. These were the deep-interdiction strikes against enemy airfields and facilities far behind the most forward lines of advance of our occupying ground forces. Subsequently this role of projecting power ashore became a primary mission of the carrier battle groups of the Cold War and the operative element of our forward collective strategy which achieved its ultimate success with the collapse of the Soviet Union.

The foundations of this metamorphosis in the U.S. Navy can be attributed to a small number of naval aviators who had the vision, wisdom, aggressiveness, and leadership to make it happen. Jimmy Flatley was one of the architects of the sweeping changes. Along with a handful of others—Jimmie Thach and Butch O'Hare were among the most prominent—Flatley fought the war on several fronts. Leading his fighter squadron in successful combat against the acknowledged superiority of the Japanese Zero, he established his credentials for passionate but articulate battles with the bureaucrats in the shore establishment and the entrenched staff officers. In most cases their professional stubbornness in resisting change was due to a lack of combat experience, which Jimmy Flatley had in vast amounts. Yet Flatley differed from many others of his combat-experienced contemporaries. He spoke out, but when he did, he was temperate, practical, and reasonable. Flatley was smart enough to realize when something was wrong, astute enough to know whether it could be corrected, and wise enough to propose the solution. Then he would muster the boldness to pursue his convictions with gritty persistence. Perhaps most important of all, Jimmy Flatley had credibility. He had earned the respect of his policy-making seniors by his brilliant combat record and the demonstrated validity of the changes he espoused.

It was fortuitous that Flatley was a visionary in the practical sense. Change was needed, but the changes had to be the right ones the first time around. There was not the luxury of exploring tactical theories in the benign environment of peacetime maneuvers. This was a war, and the United States was not winning it. Changes in material could not undergo exhaustive flight-testing. Planes and equipment were needed in the fleet. Once design changes were decided upon, new models would immediately move down the production line. There was no time for prototyping. It took bold decisions to commit to new ways of waging war, and irrefutable arguments to change the professional mind-set. It was largely through the initiative of Flatley, and others like him, and their determination to be heard, that naval aviation was able to overcome its initial immaturity to grow to enormous power by the end of World War II, as evidenced by the Okinawa campaign and the carrier strikes on the Japanese home islands.

Yet, as one reflects on Jimmy Flatley's broader legacy, it must not be forgotten that he was the consummate fighter squadron commander. Training his men and then personally leading them in combat against a skilled enemy, he demonstrated even in the early days of the war a remarkable success and effectiveness that belied the Japanese superiority in aircraft and edge in experience. He was a naval hero in every sense of the word.

Adm. J. L. Holloway III, USN (Ret.)

Preface

On 30 November 1944 Cdr. Robert E. "Bob" Dixon wrote a letter from his desk in the Navy Department Bureau of Aeronautics, Washington, D.C., to Cdr. James Henry Flatley Jr., who was then Task Force Fifty-eight operations officer for Vice Adm. Marc A. Mitscher in the Pacific. As Flatley read the letter on board the admiral's flagship, his light-blue eyes squinted at the neatly typewritten pages and then widened as he quickly digested the contents.

In November 1944 Dixon was head of the military requirements section at the Bureau of Aeronautics. Years later, having advanced to the rank of rear admiral, he would return as chief of the bureau. But in November 1944 he was better known to Jimmy Flatley as a fellow naval aviator who had fought with him in the world's first carrier-versus-carrier encounter, the May 1942 Battle of the Coral Sea. And it was Dixon who had sent the gleeful message, "Scratch one flattop," announcing the sinking of the Japanese carrier *Shoho*.

The major thrust of Dixon's 30 November letter required no reading between the lines. "We are having a most difficult time trying to gaze into the crystal ball. A seemingly pressing requirement in the Fleet one day appears to become a matter of no import the next . . . progress is upset by the semi-experts who have been with you a few days for their total war experience and come back with all the dope. This is mainly a plea to you to insure [*sic*] that the real dope gets back to us. If you . . . want increased performance [in aircraft], you had better ask for it and often because we hear constantly that 'what we have will win the war.'

Again let me stress that it is extremely difficult to sell new articles [aircraft] here unless we get some backing from you out there."

Dixon's letter to Flatley is a prime example of a middle-grade officer in position to influence decision makers at high levels in Washington, sharing critical information with another middle-grade officer in position to influence decisions at high levels in combat. Leaders at the top of the command chain such as Mitscher in the Pacific and many flag officers in Washington were removed in time from direct association with recent advances in naval aircraft, ordnance, and tactics. And for the most part they had not experienced combat in the new war. Consequently, those few successful middle-grade officers who had combat experience in the latest planes and had witnessed first hand the capabilities of ordnance and tactics against the enemy were placed in position to exert influence well beyond what might have been expected in earlier wars. Advances in technology were flooding forth at a rapid pace. Application to both matériel and tactics required the best advice possible to properly prosecute the war.

Of course not all middle-grade officers who had experienced combat were successful. Indeed, some had failed to adequately use the technology available, while others were too narrowly focused on the immediate concerns of daily combat to view the larger picture. Soon after the war began, flag officers in the Pacific and Washington were anxious to incline an ear to those few who had demonstrated not only valor and success in combat but who also had the ability to visualize the larger scope of requirements and potential. Too, it helped when such a middle-grade officer could offer recommendations in a cogent manner, both orally and in writing.

One of the few was Jimmy Flatley. In old air group or squadron photographs it was never difficult to locate him except when he was sitting or kneeling, as the eye flows rapidly to the shortest man in the group. Although he was the shortest man in nearly every squadron to which he was assigned (Flatley was five foot six)—during World War II many others in those photographs considered him a giant. "Everything that followed only verified what we had learned at the start, that Flatley was a giant among men," said Hampton Barnes, an intelligence officer on *Enterprise* in 1942 (as he was quoted in the *Congressional Record*, July

1958, 14779). Rear Adm. Martin D. "Red" Carmody also offered the same thought in a 26 March 1996 letter to this writer. Even now, over forty years after leaving this world, Jimmy Flatley's stature in naval aviation has not diminished.

As a World War II fighter pilot, squadron leader, and air group commander, Flatley enjoyed considerable success. And as a middle-grade officer during the war he held significant billets affecting both the tactical and strategic prosecution of the war. Many of the significant events, battles, and contributions pertaining to Vice Admiral Flatley have already been recounted in numerous books and articles on the Pacific War. However, his leadership evolution has not been treated. Nor has there been a discourse attempting to analyze his command experience, even though he is remembered for his distinctive manner of leadership by those in naval aviation who knew him best. Thus, the purpose of this biography is to trace Flatley's leadership evolution while at the same time reliving air combat and the tribulation of command through his eyes, actions, sure steps, and the inevitable missteps. Where possible, Flatley's words and those of his contemporaries are used to ensure accuracy in interpretation.

Many have earned success in part by being mentors, the wise and trusted counselors who set positive goals and provide examples of how to teach others. Jimmy Flatley evolved into a mentor long before the term enjoyed common use, and long before the undertaking became a stated goal for naval officers, civic leaders, and individuals who could serve as role models for others. Even though focus herein is on Jimmy Flatley's leadership evolution—from a troubled early career, through increased responsibilities and influence far beyond his relatively modest rank, to commanding officer and flag rank—it is acknowledged that his experience is not necessarily applicable as a formula for others.

No other publication to my knowledge has treated the role and responsibilities of a task force operations officer with the same depth as this volume. Flatley's activities as Admiral Mitscher's operations officer are traced in detail from the October 1944 Battle of Leyte Gulf through the 1945 battles for Iwo Jima and Okinawa. The day-to-day experiences of navy life are also included. Drills, routine, and some of the problems and joys of port calls are covered to a greater degree than in many other naval books. But there is another component to Jimmy Flatley's navy career in the Pacific. He was a fighter pilot and lived in the world of military heroes "where bullets fly." Jimmy did fire many shells and see plenty of tracers fired at him in the battles of the Coral Sea, Santa Cruz, Rennell Island, and off the Philippines, Iwo Jima, and Okinawa. Yet the significance of this book does not rest on his duels in the sky. Through time, Jimmy Flatley's legacy of leadership has equaled, if not surpassed, the numerous individual combat exploits of the little giant, who was better known to his Guadalcanal campaign fighter squadron pilots as "Reaper Leader."

Acknowledgments

Many individuals have contributed to this book. The family of Vice Adm. James H. Flatley Jr. invited me to write the book, offered all the resources at their disposal, and did not request editorial influence or review. Other than seeing a draft of the first chapter, no member of the family saw the text before publication. Consequently, any and all errors of fact or interpretation rest solely with me.

Having written several books on World War II naval history, particularly on the USS *Enterprise* (CV-6) in 1982, it was my privilege to meet and know many of the officers and men who served with Jimmy Flatley when he was commanding officer of Fighting Squadron Ten, the "Grim Reapers." And having been employed at Patriots Point Naval and Maritime Museum since 1987, with an office aboard the museum ship USS *Yorktown* (CV-10), it has been my privilege to meet many former members of the crew who served with Jimmy when he was the "Fighting Lady's" first air group commander. This background, and the opportunity to work with numerous other Flatley fellow warriors and friends in the course of serving Patriots Point as curator and historian, made possible the opportunity to record the life of this luminary of naval aviation.

Not long after Admiral Flatley's untimely death at age fifty-two on 9 July 1958, a house fire burned some family treasures, but many of the admiral's files and papers survived. In the following years the family, primarily sons Rear Adm. James H. III and David, acquired additional documents from the several depositories (noted in the bibliography) to learn as much as possible about the father they had too little time to know. These extensive sources in addition to others I acquired during the writing process served as the foundation for the project.

In addition to myself, a number of authors have for many years requested and received assistance from the Flatley family. Among those who utilized the Flatley papers was John Lundstrom (my co-author for *Fateful Rendezvous: The Life of Butch O'Hare*) for his books *The First Team* and *The First Team and the Guadalcanal Campaign*. Another was Clark Reynolds for *The Fast Carriers* and *The Fighting Lady*. Both of these personal and professional friends read the manuscript of *Reaper Leader* and offered significant recommendations. Other friends who have made notable contributions to naval aviation history assisted by offering documents and suggestions. Among these were Robert J. Cressman, Mark Gatlin, Hill Goodspeed, Robert L. Lawson, Barrett Tillman, and Larry Sowinski. Dr. George Lowry, Catherine Lowry, Diane Brown Palmer, and Dr. Paul Turner offered welcome and salient perspectives from their respective academic disciplines.

Superb assistance was forthcoming from the staff of the Naval Institute Press, particularly Thomas J. Cutler, senior acquisitions editor, and Rebecca E. Hinds, managing editor. Naomi Grady provided invaluable insights in addition to magnificently handling all the usual duties of a copy editor.

Fellow members of the Patriots Point Museum family generously offered support for this book. Don Bracken crafted the maps; Jim Vickers designed the cover and assisted with the photographs; Julia Hammer, Laura Langston, and Eleanor Wimett rendered administrative assistance. David Burnette, David A. Clark, Sam Derrick, Waring "Butch" Hills, and Charles G. Waldrop offered encouragement, a gesture always appreciated.

I am also grateful to the veterans who served with Jimmy Flatley a half century ago. Without their sharing spirit offered in conversations, interviews, and correspondence, this book would have been much more difficult to write and far less complete, devoid of many facts, interpretations, and insights. The names of these men are listed in the bibliography; and it is with considerable sadness that for too many of them, I now have only their letters, their voices on audio tape, and memories of the enjoyable hours we shared together, often over lunch or dinner.

Occasionally, they themselves brought up the subject of their inevitable demise. When they discussed their passing, one theme always seemed to be included. They believed that subsequent American generations would find sufficient numbers of men who would understand devotion to duty and who would successfully meet future challenges to our national life. And they held these views in the waning days of their lives when it seemed to them that most Americans had forgotten them, their contributions, and all that they placed on the altar of sacrifice.

Reaper Leader

I

A Little Rogue

SOCIAL SCIENTISTS have centered primary attention on deviant behavior, especially that which threatens order and stability within a society. Considerably less attention has been devoted to the behavioral characteristics and attributes evident in the formative years of fighter pilots. In retrospect some of naval aviation's most celebrated World War II fighter pilots displayed examples of deviant behavior as well as examples of courage and proficiency in combat. Leading aces such as David McCampbell (naval aviation's top ace with thirty-four kills), Tommy Blackburn (of VF-17 "Skull and Crossbones" fame with eleven kills), and Gregory "Pappy" Boyington (marine leader of the VMF-214 "Black Sheep" Squadron with twenty-four kills plus four probables) were renowned for their prodigious consumption of alcohol.[1] All three acknowledged their problems in later years. Perhaps the most poignant acknowledgment was Blackburn's account that the navy knew better than to promote him to rear admiral with all attendant responsibilities when he had demonstrated he could not control his own appetite for alcohol and the deleterious actions that sometimes followed.[2] Certainly, Boyington's memoirs reveal a man not only brutally honest about his problems but also a person of considerable introspection.[3] Of course, not all successful fighter pilots were alcoholics, suffered through multiple divorces, or were free spirits; but something in the mind of any fighter pilot would seem to be different. Arguably, a love for speed and a need for excitement are factors since both satisfy the inner person, whether or not anyone else takes notice.

In their youth McCampbell, Blackburn, and Boyington experienced a love for speed and excitement. In his teens Jimmy Flatley expressed his proclivity for speed and excitement by driving the family automobile fifty miles per hour over ice-covered roads, a challenge for the engine of the Model T Ford, but no challenge in the cold environment around Green Bay, Wisconsin. On one occasion his speed was too fast even for him to contemplate stopping at a railroad crossing, and a locomotive brushed the bumper of his car. The event thrilled him: his female companion, with colorful and adamant eloquence, expressed other emotions.

In contemporary Green Bay, Jimmy's life is commemorated by Flatley Park located downtown on the Fox River, rather than by a cemetery marker resulting from his dangerous childhood driving habits. The first of six children (Dorothy, Emmett, Mary, Ruth, and John) born to Irish descendants James ("John") Henry and Joan Nash Flatley, James Henry Junior, entered this world on 17 June 1906. Growing up in a comfortable neighborhood that surrounded the family's two-story, eight-room home at 806 South Quincy Street, he attended St. John's Evangelist Elementary School. His childhood was normal until age thirteen when he suffered a severe hip injury while playing sandlot football. A larger lad fell on him, and at first Jimmy paid little attention to the pain. However, in the following weeks it became more difficult to meet the demands of his paper route and by Christmas 1919 he could no longer stand on one leg. The diagnosis of local doctors was tuberculosis of the hip, and he was sent to Chicago for orthopedic surgery. From there he was moved to the Mayo Clinic. The injury and subsequent surgery resulted in nearly a year in traction: a cruel fate for any thirteen-year-old boy.

For the longest year of his life, Jimmy could do little but look through his bedroom window at the change of seasons and wonder whether or not he would again know a life of normal health and pursuits. Despite constant visits by his three sisters and two brothers—and neighborhood boys and girls whose path to his bed was more often through a window rather than the front door—loneliness became an abiding companion. Hope was sustained by dreams—dreams that someday he could again run and play football, a sport that was a passion to him long before it became equally so to Green Bay Packer fans; dreams that someday he could enter into all the activities of his friends; and dreams that someday he could travel to the other side of the clouds he stared at through his window. The Great War had just ended in Europe, and the names of American aerial aces Eddie Rickenbacker, Frank Luke, and others were household names. Prized toys for Jimmy were paper models of biplanes that had fought over Flanders' fields. Particularly prized were the stories of combat in the sky, a new frontier in both concept and reality. Often supplying such literature to Jimmy was his mother's cousin, Gerald F. "Gerry" Bogan. Bogan, who had graduated from the Naval Academy in 1916, served aboard surface ships during and immediately after World War I; he entered naval aviation in 1924 and would eventually rise to the rank of vice admiral. Years later Jimmy credited Bogan for supplying not only his first ride in an airplane as a youth but also inspiring him to seek a career in naval aviation.[4]

Another inspiration to young Jimmy was former president Theodore Roosevelt, who died during the same year of Jimmy's protracted affliction. (In speeches during the 1940s and 1950s, Jimmy spoke of Roosevelt's leadership, the adult Flatley's many tributes to the late president relating Roosevelt's early health problems and how he overcame them by sheer determination and fortitude.) Joan Flatley tutored her son during his illness, her academic lessons facilitating his continuing formal education, and her reminders of Roosevelt's example helped water the seed the former president's words and deeds had planted. Encouragement also was offered by a neighbor, Kenneth Hoeffel, a 1917 Naval Academy graduate who later became a war hero and rear admiral.[5]

Encouragement alone was not enough to overcome a debilitating handicap. Too young to comprehend theories of motivation, Jimmy nonetheless understood that he wanted to rise, walk, run, and live life. Finally released from traction and bed, he began a Roosevelt-inspired regimen of calisthenics and exercise, especially biking, to rebuild strength in his injured leg. By age sixteen Jimmy showed no evidence of limp or disability, and varsity football eluded him only because of size (at the time Jimmy was under the five foot five, hundred pounds minimum). Still not fully appreciating the implications of his teenage tribulation, he had nonetheless affected much of his future personality by beginning to learn that a sense of purpose was crucial for success in any significant endeavor.

Before graduating in 1925 from St. Norbert's High School, an all boy's Catholic school, in nearby De Pere, Wisconsin, Jimmy consciously made up for lost time. Having "lost" a year of his life, he was propelled to reach deeper into everyday experiences. On 27 July 1923 the seventeen-year-old high school student enlisted in the U.S. Naval Reserve following the interest Gerry Bogan and Ken Hoeffel prompted. Joining others on a subchaser moored in the Fox River, he and his fellow reservists searched for imaginary U-boats from the mouth of the river into Lake Michigan, drank illegal booze, learned the pleasures of smoking ciga-rettes, and in general just had great fun. Jimmy's father, however, had a different perspective of the Naval Reserve. Although a hard-working man who operated a gas station and sold coal, fuel oil, cement, and building supplies, he did not necessarily want to see his oldest son deliver coal and oil to homes by sled in winter and by wagon or truck in summer. With a large family and a small business—and with many hands reach-ing for its minimal profits—John Flatley envisioned the Naval Reserve as a first step toward a free college education for his son. John and Joan Flatley made a place in their budget to help Jimmy through prep school prior to entrance into the Naval Academy, but they could not afford to attend his academy graduation.

Equal to his interests in sports and the navy was his interest in girls, a pervasive interest so apparent that the 1929 Naval Academy yearbook, the *Lucky Bag*, reported, "As for the femininity, the only trouble that 'Jimmee-ee-ee' has is in staying clear of them. He falls for them, just as fast as he is encouraged, and he couldn't get enough time to answer all encouragements." And Jimmy's youngest brother recalls that he was "a good looking young man, [but] he had a number of misfires with the fairer sex." Although Jimmy was destined to become a leader of men, too often in his youth he was a follower of women. On one occasion he impetuously gave a ring to a girl at a Chicago dance hall, evidently implying he intended to marry her. The family learned of this distressing episode when the ring-wearing damsel tracked him to Green Bay (perhaps this is when the future fighter pilot learned never to underestimate persistence, and that distance is not necessarily sanctuary). In high school Jimmy was constantly in violation of his mother's curfew when returning from dates, and his record at Annapolis was littered with demerits for the same offense. At St. Norbert's although Jimmy did well in his studies, he had a reputation as "a little rogue."[6] At graduation from the Naval Academy in 1929 remembrance in the *Lucky Bag* was more positive. "With numberless friends, he's a man, a good roommate, and a priceless friend. May the gods smile down on his service career."

On 6 June 1929 Jimmy graduated from the academy and took the oath as an ensign. Graduating near the bottom of a class of 240, he took solace in the fact that 130 who started with him did not graduate and in the knowledge that class rank did not always serve as an indication of future success. Even so, his class standing did influence at least one important future assignment, and it impacted his place on housing lists for years to come, much to the discomfort of his future wife.

Sailor and Pilot

Graduates of the academy reported to the fleet soon after graduation. First assignments for the new junior officers were usually to battleships, cruisers, and destroyers. After a period of time, usually one to two years, a young academy graduate could chose special training such as aviation or submarine duty. Knowing he would apply for flight training as soon as regulations permitted, Jimmy was especially pleased to receive orders on 15 May 1929 to one of only three aircraft carriers then in the United States Navy, USS *Saratoga* (CV-3). Traveling by train, he first visited the family in Green Bay and then made his way to Spokane, Washington, before catching up with the carrier in San Pedro, California. The 3,009-mile journey netted the new ensign a total of $122.79 as portions of the trip allowed eight cents a mile and the remainder three cents. Although a princely sum in 1929, it was hardly enough to pay for all the required uniforms, which in a short time amounted to over two thousand dollars, and Jimmy's lifelong struggle with finances began in earnest. As a new ensign his base salary was $125: his subsistence allowance was considerably less, and nothing was paid for quarters if he was living in the bachelor officers quarters (BOQ) or aboard ship. Not helping was the onset of the Great Depression that began three months after he reported aboard *Saratoga*. Soon he began sending a $25 monthly allotment to his parents to help with household expenses as the family business declined.

Reporting aboard his large floating home on 13 July 1929, Jimmy was assigned quarters and duty as communication watch officer, assistant radio officer, junior officer of the deck, plus boxing and wrestling officer. His battle station was the number three 5-inch gun group, an assignment much different in 1929 than it would be thirteen years later when he would ride carriers during wartime conditions. Other than perhaps the *Lexington* (CV-2), Jimmy's first months of active duty could not have been spent on a better ship to facilitate his own entry into naval aviation. Two early pioneers of naval aviation were aboard. The flag chief of staff was Capt. Ken Whiting, Naval Aviator No. 16 (the number assigned for completion of flight training), and the executive officer (XO) was Cdr. Albert C. Read, Naval Aviator No. 24. Also aboard in 1929 and early 1930 were several future aviation notables. The flight deck officer was Lt. Cdr. Arthur W. Radford, who would rise to flag rank during World War II and eventually become chairman of the Joint Chiefs of Staff. The flag secretary was Lt. Forrest P. Sherman, a future chief of naval operations. The torpedo squadron commanding officer, Lt. Cdr. Alfred E. Montgomery, later became a World War II carrier division commander. And fighter pilot Lt. (jg) Clarence Wade McClusky, who would make one of the most critical combat decisions of World War II during the Battle of Midway, was developing his skills as a pilot. The significance of their presence aboard *Saratoga* in 1929 to Jimmy Flatley was their example and encouragement for him to pursue his goal of becoming a pilot.

Less than two weeks after reporting aboard the carrier, Jimmy had temporary duty orders for a three-week course of instruction in eliminative flight training at Naval Air Station (NAS) San Diego. The course was the first big hurdle to weed out those grossly unfit for further flight training. On 6 August he reported to San Diego and on 8 August he was in the air for an hour-and-fifteen-minute orientation flight.[7] Except for the two weekends he was in the air every day accumulating twenty hours of flying time. All twenty hours were logged in a Consolidated NY-1 primary trainer biplane, student and instructor seated in tandem in open cockpits, that had a top speed of only ninety-eight miles per hour. Literally and emotionally the high point came on 26 August, the last day of training, when he made his first solo flight. On 29 August the young ensign was back aboard ship, not too anxious to tell all he ranked tenth in a class of twenty, but quite anxious to tell all he had passed the course. Two days later his formal request for flight training at Pensacola, Florida, was endorsed and forwarded to the Bureau of Navigation. The only tense moments in the process came in late February 1930 during his physical examination when he had to explain the large surgical scar from his 1919 hip operation. As he showed no negative effects from the surgery, a positive recommendation was forthcoming. On 29 March 1930 a letter from the Bureau of Navigation arrived detaching him from *Saratoga* effective 25 April and ordering him to NAS Pensacola for a year long course in heavier-than-air instruction effective 23 May.

After settling in the BOQ at NAS Pensacola, on 29 May Jimmy was again in the familiar NY trainer and progressing satisfactorily until 26 June when he was admitted to the hospital with respiratory problems, missing two months of training. Returning to duty on 2 September, he continued in the land and seaplane versions of the NY, the Vought O2U (similar in appearance to the NY but faster at 150 mph). Then he flew the Curtiss F6C (a single pilot fighter with a top speed of 155 mph), and the Martin T4M1 (a two-man, scout-torpedo-bomber with a top speed of 110 mph) recording 220 hours of dual and solo flights, plus formation and night flying. Just before completing training in late May 1931 as Naval Aviator No. 3806, he experienced his first catapult shot, not from a carrier but from the shore along Pensacola Bay.

Nothing during his training at Pensacola signaled greatness, as his fitness reports indicated satisfactory but not distinguished progress. Indeed, the duty recommendation of the commandant at Pensacola was "Observation Plane Squadron." Jimmy's first choice for assignment was any fighter squadron on the West Coast. To his surprise and great satisfaction orders directed him to a highly coveted billet; Fighting Squadron Five-B (VF-5B), the "Red Rippers." The B denoted assignment to the

Battle Force (rather than the Scouting Force), a designation used to identify the two components of the United States Fleet until June 1937.

Arriving at NAS San Diego on North Island in San Diego Bay on 25 June 1931, Jimmy was welcomed into the squadron by Lt. (jg) A. B. Vosseller, who within days turned over command to Lt. David Rittenhouse. On 30 June Jimmy went aloft in the navy's best fighter, the Boeing F4B-1, for two familiarization flights. This was what it was all about for Jimmy Flatley: twenty-five years old, a member of an elite navy fighter squadron, and a pilot of the navy's best fighter. Retained aboard carriers into 1937, the F4B-1 and F4B-2 fixed-gear models carried only a pilot, two fixed forward-firing .30-caliber machine guns, and they were capable of 176 mph with the 450 hp Pratt and Whitney R-1340-8 engine. The open cockpit Boeing was highly maneuverable and fun to fly, and Jimmy enjoyed section and squadron tactics, cross-country flights, night flying, navigation, and carrier landings. In early August the squadron flew from North Island to land on its floating base, the *Lexington,* for gunnery drills with towed targets and bombing practice. Although primarily a fighter the F4B carried bomb racks. Just as the immediate and future utilization of the navy's three carriers were not fully understood or completely defined, the function of the carrier fighter was also evolving. And there was a real need for such evolution as Japan, seeing the Western world mired deep in the Great Depression, invaded Manchuria in September 1931. The days of flying for fun were nearing an end.

Development as an Officer

Happy as he was in the role and routine of a navy fighter pilot, the period from September 1930 to January 1933 was for Ens. Jimmy Flatley a period of very deep lows and exceptional highs. On 4 September 1931 after flying high, he dove into a major low when he crashed an F4B-1 on the then unpaved Rockwell Field, the army's side of North Island. His subsequent fitness report noted that he "used very poor judgment in allowing the plane . . . to run out of gasoline unnecessarily." The commanding officer of the *Lexington,* Capt. Ernest J. King, who would command all naval forces during World War II, was no happier than

Jimmy. Planes cost money, naval appropriations were paltry, and Captain King was a perfectionist.

The crash of the F4B-1 kept Jimmy out of the air for only ten days but other "crashes" marked him emotionally for a more protracted period. On 15 July 1932 he received a letter from the Bureau of Navigation informing him that he was deficient in the subject of Marine Engineering and would have to be reexamined before again being considered for promotion to lieutenant (junior grade). On 17 August he passed and promotion followed 4 October, to date from 6 June 1932. Before the smile could fade from his face for this success, a second letter arrived on the day of his promotion notification. This letter from his commanding officer ordered him to immediately reply to a claim from Lion Clothing Company in San Diego that he was past due on a clothing account. Lion Clothing noted their reluctance to offer credit to the young officer as he had been slow to pay on accounts at two other stores, and despite a signed promissory note, Jimmy was over three months past due on a $45 obligation. The money was sent in a 10 October letter, but the personal embarrassment was compounded as copies of the letter were required to be forwarded not only to his commanding officer but also to the Bureau of Navigation. While not offering details Jimmy wrote in his letter to Lion Clothing that "the delay was due to urgent financial obligations which I have had to meet during that period."

The "urgent financial obligations" were in part the result of gambling and yet another "misfire" with a woman, but this time there was a repercussion well beyond embarrassment. Words from a golden throat across a silver tongue lubricated by Prohibition-quality liquor fell upon a comely face with receptive ears. Although the pulchritude of his listener did not diminish as the intoxicating effects of the libation wore off, the emotional excitement dissipated, and it was soon obvious to both that they regretted the brief relationship; but divorce was not an option for a life-long Catholic who had once served as an altar boy, had an aunt who was a nun, and who was a distant relative of several priests. The tenets of the Catholic Church had never been questioned in the Flatley's Green Bay home. For the entire family: Mass was always attended, confession was a matter of routine, and the teachings of the Bible—as interpreted by priests, parochial school teachers, and nuns—were the foundation of norms for individual life, family life, social life, and public life. Over time, however, Jimmy had allowed his religion to become peripheral, the "cares of the world" parable (Matthew 13) having overtaken him. For the first time since contemplating the meaning of life and soliciting the church's assistance during the year of his hip injury, he again turned to a priest. The need to heal the body in 1919 now seemed a small challenge: this time the soul was in danger.

Preoccupied at varying levels of his consciousness, Jimmy continued his flying duties. In the air there was enough to think about to keep his personal problems distant, but upon return to earth his burden awaited. While an exact measurement of his personal trauma is not possible, his 9 April 1932 fitness report noted, "He suffers some from the irresponsibility of youth." In the same report he was rated lowest, although still satisfactory, on Force ("with reference to moral power possessed and exerted in producing results") and Leadership. While personally embarrassed to receive an average rating for Force, it was professionally embarrassing to be judged relatively low in Leadership—as that was and is the essence of being a naval officer. Adding to his distress was an unfavorable 30 September fitness report stating he had been inattentive to duty as a landplane duty officer, for which he was punished by being suspended from duty for five days. Mitigating the offense was the written comment by squadron commander Lt. Cdr. W. M. "Dutch" Dillon that "inexperience rather than an inherent personal characteristic" caused the lapse.

Officially, the ill-fated marriage lasted until early January 1933, the process of annulment requiring several months of work by lawyers, in part because Jimmy procrastinated on starting the paperwork. The financial cost was heavy, but not as heavy as the emotional burden. Long discussions with priests centered on Jimmy's attitudes and conduct that contributed to the unfortunate result. Answers to the problem of the unwanted marriage were welcomed, but as important as these answers were, the excruciating experience put in place, for Jimmy, a foundation for responding to personal and professional crisis management in the future. The few individuals allowed to share his distress seemed to understand his distress, and the process of a person stepping into the hurt, fears, and confusion of another provided him with compassion and direction. It was a lesson of effective leadership Jimmy never forgot.

Turning Point

By the late spring of 1932 the interrelationship between Jimmy's personal and professional life had been painfully apparent. One affected the other. Alcohol played a role in his brief marriage (the next morning he could not remember the ceremony). The annulment plus gambling contributed to economic hardship, and the result was recorded on both his fitness reports and letters in his official file. Although aware of the impact of his recent conduct upon his chosen profession and his religion, he did not quit drinking. However, he knew his limit and resolved not to surpass it. Ironically, though, the most significant factor contributing to the turning point in his life began with a journey to a bar.

Prohibition was still in force in the summer of 1932, and aviators based at North Island jumped into their cars on Wednesday and Saturday afternoons to head south of the border to Tijuana, Mexico, or further south to Caliente. In Mexico open liquor and beer sales were quite legal. A few select Mexican bars became de facto officers clubs as nearly all navy and marine aviators could be found within on Wednesdays and Saturdays. While inside Caesar's Bar in late June 1932, Jimmy spotted a lovely, petite young lady in the company of a marine officer and his wife. Spotting turned to long looks and finally a stare, a stare so obvious that marine captain John "Toby" Munn—class of 1927 and Jimmy's friend from Naval Academy days—asked his wife's friend if she would like an introduction to the naval officer who could not take his eyes off her. "Might as well," responded Dorothy "Dotty" McMurray. The introduction went well, and Jimmy and Dotty saw each other every day for the next six weeks.

Twenty-four-year-old Dotty, a Florida native, had come to Coronado to visit her college friend, Leah Chalker, who had recently married Captain Munn. Dotty's father was a medical doctor and her mother a nurse, who died when Dotty was a year old. Her father remarried, and only five years later typhoid fever took his life. Raised by her stepmother, Dotty was taken to Illinois to live before yet another family tragedy led to her return to Florida. Graduating from high school in Daytona, Dotty then attended and graduated from an all-girls college (an institution that has since evolved into Florida State University) where she earned a bachelor's degree in education. Dotty had just completed her second year of teaching before her vacation journey to California. Within two weeks of her meeting Jimmy, he was talking marriage. He wanted to get married "right now," the slow process of the annulment notwithstanding. Dotty, then, faced three major dilemmas. First, she had signed a contract to return to her Florida teaching position in September. Second, she was already engaged to a young lawyer, a dream seemingly come true as she had grown up in a family of professionals and anticipated marriage to a doctor or lawyer. Third, she knew almost immediately she would marry Jimmy: "I had never felt such a surge of affection. When he talked to me he was really with me, and he was so warm . . . everything I could have ever wanted."[8]

Much of the courtship from late June through July and into early August was conducted at Toby Munn's house. More than once, Jimmy insisted Dotty ride out to North Island so he could show her the Boeing F4B fighter. Whether at Toby's, North Island, Caesar's, or anywhere else, Jimmy interspersed words of love for Dotty with words of his other love, flying. While sometimes not intrinsically interested in Jimmy's aeronautical discourses, Dotty was nonetheless impressed with his enthusiasm and dedication to his profession. When she could get in a word edgewise, Dotty attempted to tell Jimmy that she was not a Catholic, and that although her family might like him, they would not be happy about a wedding in California.

By late 1932 Jimmy's adult personality was approaching the maturity that would sustain him to the end. The combination of his strict but loving family, his teenage illness, training at the Naval Academy, and unbridled enthusiasm culminating with an annulment—all contributed significantly to his personality. Raised in a family that valued love, compassion, and generosity, it was not difficult for him to appreciate empathy. And from his own struggle to overcome a year in bed, he understood the Biblical example of that one "purpose in his heart" (Daniel 1:1–8 and Genesis 39), which could enable him to achieve an ultimate goal. In mid-1932 he understood that with his immature attitude and conduct, he had hurt himself and others.

Fitness reports from June 1932 into early 1933 reveal a man of budding promise, and his abilities in the air gradually increased from good to excellent, aerial gunnery drawing special notice. In a 31 March 1933 fitness report Commander Dillon wrote that "Flatley's previously reported improvement in industry and attention to duty has continued. . . . His performance of duty as Assistant Matériel officer and as Assistant Gunnery Officer has been highly satisfactory. During the past year [he] has settled and matured and is now, in the opinion of the Commanding Officer, an excellent and reliable officer."

In mid-August Dotty returned to Florida and the classroom, but resigned in December. Early on 7 January 1933 Jimmy was in his F4B-2 for squadron experimental bombing flights before driving his Ford coupe to Yuma, Arizona. With the annulment paperwork complete, he and Dotty married. As Dotty was a Protestant, the wedding was not in a church, but a second ceremony soon followed in a church. After a one week honeymoon the couple returned to Coronado, and Jimmy said goodbye to his new bride as his squadron prepared to fly aboard *Lexington* on 21 January for Fleet Problem XV (a tactical combat training exercise). On 24 March he was back in Coronado, and the newlyweds moved into the two-bedroom white stucco house formerly occupied by the Munns. The cute little house where they had courted quickly became a home.

Although the Flatley's trips into Mexico continued on Wednesdays and Saturdays, the Flatley home also became a social center once a week. The usual guest list included one or two other couples and at least one bachelor to eat steaks, roast beef, or leg of lamb. Jimmy and most of his aviator friends built their diets around steak and potatoes, with bourbon and water before and after the evening repast. Conversation centered on flying among the men while the women separated into their own group to discuss anything but flying. Small gatherings at the Flatley home resembled the larger squadron parties as the men and women separated before dinner but rejoined during and after the meal.

In Mexico, at his new home, or at other settings where most of the squadron would gather, Jimmy was very much in his element. Whether he was host or guest, he was quite comfortable living in a very social situation. At first it was not as comfortable for Dotty. Playing host and hostess once a week was expensive over the course of time, and Dotty was constantly writing home for money as Jimmy's meager salary didn't stretch very far. Arriving in California in January, it was too late for Dotty to find a teaching job; and before school began again in the fall, she knew a child was due near the date of her first wedding anniversary. She never taught again.

Further contributing to Dotty's early discomfiture were the expectations placed on her as a new wife in the squadron. Like it or not, she too was in the navy. Dutch Dillon was an effective, serious-minded squadron commander on duty, but when he was off duty, he was noted for his informality. His wife, Mary, was likable but more formal. Mary wasn't Dotty's problem: the problem was the new social structure and attendant expectations. The wives were close, especially when the squadron was away at sea, but squadron life still pervaded and prevailed. "Young wives must learn protocol," Mary counseled Dotty, adding "it is your job to support your husband and the Navy." In time Dotty realized that the lessons learned from Mary Dillon plus the squadron executive officer's wife and other wives had a positive function. "Proper conduct and knowing one's place" were necessary to operate effectively within a structured system wherein rules were not written, but failure to comply had definite consequences. Once oriented Dotty embraced her new role, particularly after realizing the value of facilitating her husband's career. The interaction with other squadron wives was especially appreciated, and in time she understood that being at the bottom of the squadron social system was a learning process that eventually would help her assist other women new to the U.S. Navy.

Looking back, Dotty recalls the period as "beautiful times." And they were. New friends, a new home, new challenges, and a loving husband who was earning recognition as a competent and responsible officer. Although he was not ready for a leadership role, never again after January 1933 did anyone think of Jimmy Flatley as "a little rogue."

2

Flying in the Depression-Era Navy

Fighter Pilot (1931–1934)

FOR THE first three years of the Great Depression, Jimmy Flatley and nearly everyone else in the United States Navy were pleased to be in the service. For many, military life was much better than life in the civilian economy. The major effects of the Depression, with its consequent significant military appropriations cuts, did not occur until 1933. Complaints among officers and men increased—especially over proposals to cut flight pay—but appreciation for their relative economic standing remained. Throughout the Depression, however, there were always shortages, and probably no situation in naval aviation served as a more salient reminder of the economy than the paucity of bullets available for live firing. Camera guns that simulated gunfire were highly effective for analyzing mock air combat in squadron training, and they also saved ordnance. The temptation for neighboring squadrons at North Island and other aviation installations to "borrow" live ammunition was omnipresent. In the first months of World War II a high price was paid for the lack of training with sufficient live ammunition as guns jammed and deteriorated ordnance did not explode.

Still, not all effects of the Depression were deleterious to the navy. As part of the New Deal legislation proposed by new president Franklin D. Roosevelt, the June 1933 Vinson-Trammell Act authorized two new aircraft carriers, USS *Yorktown* (CV-5) and USS *Enterprise* (CV-6), and USS *Wasp* (CV-7) the following year. Roosevelt, who had earlier served as assistant secretary of the navy during World War I, sought in 1933–34 to build up the navy at least to treaty strength while providing employment to spur the domestic economy during the darkest days of the Depression.

Desire for peace after World War I and a propensity to cut military budgets led to the Washington Naval Conference of 1922 and the London Treaty of 1930. The Washington Treaty established a five to five to three capital ship ratio for naval powers Great Britain, the United States, and Japan, respectively. Until 7 December 1941 diplomats and many naval officers believed the battleship would determine victory at sea. Proponents of aircraft carriers actually benefited from these treaties as 135,000 tons was allotted in 1922 to the United States and Great Britain with Japan allowed 83,000. Some hulls then available or under construction could be converted to aircraft carriers. The United States converted two battle cruisers, *Saratoga* and *Lexington,* while Japan converted a battle cruiser, *Akagi,* and battleship, *Kaga.* These carriers proved great advances over the first experimental carriers (USS *Langley* CV-1 and Japan's *Hosho,* both completed 1922). The Royal Navy was well ahead of both the United States and Japan in carrier construction and development, their first carrier HMS *Argus* having been completed in 1918 with three others in service several years before "Sara," "Lex," *Akagi,* and *Kaga.*

Laid down soon after World War I, *Saratoga* was commissioned 16 November 1927 and *Lexington* on 14 December 1927. Along with *Langley* the three converted hulls comprised the entire U.S. Navy carrier fleet, and the quest began for the optimum use of carriers. Officers whose careers had been spent in aviation were well ahead in understanding its potential, but there had not yet been enough time for aviators to work their way into the upper echelons of the naval hierarchy. The majority opinion among naval commanders was that the priority function of U.S. Navy aircraft carriers was to scout and support the battle line. Vested career interests of surface officers and the small number of aircraft carriers available in the early 1930s also influenced this genuine disagreement favoring the big guns of battleships and cruisers. A few visionaries, such as Rear Adm. J. M. Reeves, Rear Adm. Harry Yarnell, and Capt. (later Adm.) John Towers, could foresee independent offensive carrier tactics in the late 1920s, and in some fleet problems soon after their commissioning, *Saratoga* and *Lexington* demonstrated carriers' offensive potential. Still, the pioneer period for carrier development was over, the basics understood by aviators. Ahead was a multitude of technical and tactical innovations with strategic application, and it would fall to a second generation of naval aviators to build upon the foundation of theory and practices established by the mid-1930s. Jimmy Flatley had no difficulty appreciating naval aviation's past and was more than anxious to be a meaningful part of its continuing development.

In a manner of speaking, Jimmy had to be a part of the future of naval aviation since it had few officers and enlisted men in the early 1930s. In 1931 the U.S. Navy counted a total of 1,204 aircraft with 776 designated for combat. By the summer of 1934 when Jimmy left VF-5B, the count was 1,347 and 950, respectively.[1] Whether to their advantage or disadvantage, naval aviators in the early and mid-1930s could not help but know many others in their small, exclusive fraternity. Although they did not belong to the same squadron, one acquaintance from the early North Island days impacted Jimmy's life and career more than anyone else. Lt. Cdr. Joseph James (nicknamed "Jocko" at the beginning of World War II) Clark had graduated from the Naval Academy in 1918, completed flight training in 1925, and commanded Fighting Squadron Two (VF-2B). In that time he came to know Jimmy and was impressed with his potential, not only as a pilot but also as an officer meticulous in writing reports.[2] Writing reports was not a favorite endeavor with many pilots whether they were good at it or not. Jimmy could write, but equally important to higher-ranking officers, he would do so without complaint. While not much thought of future association crossed the minds of either Flatley or Clark during the early days of their acquaintance, their respective careers were greatly enhanced by working together several times in later years.

In all his three-year experience with VF-5B from 1931 into mid-1934, no single training event became more meaningful to Jimmy in later years than his participation in Grand Joint Exercise Number Four.

Bold lettering in his log book for Sunday 7 February 1932 reads, "Dawn Attack On Oahu." Although some umpires seemed unrealistic in their judging of the exercise, the Japanese Navy did not miss the significance of the mock attack on Pearl Harbor.[3] The tactical exercise continued on 9 and 10 February with Jimmy flying over eight hours of attacks in his F4B-1 on U.S. Army installations (7 and 9 February) and engaging Army bombers on 10 February. Like many others who participated in the same exercise he was later considerably disturbed that the significance of the 1932 Sunday morning attack was lost on his own navy until 7 December 1941. Years later Gerry Bogan, Jimmy's cousin, and Clark felt the same consternation as Bogan, then a lieutenant commander, had led the fast attack group during the 1932 exercise, and Clark, then also a lieutenant commander, had led the protective fighters.

The First Grumman Fighter

The vast majority of Jimmy's flight time from 1931 through May 1934 was in the Boeing F4B-1 and F4B-2. The small single-seat biplane was the navy's best fighter into 1933, but it was apparent with the final version, the F4B-4, that the plane had reached its optimum performance level. One significant factor limiting future performance improvement was drag created by the fixed landing gear. The fledgling Grumman Aircraft Engineering Corporation had formed in late 1929 and experienced its first official contact with the navy in 1930, contracting to build an all-metal stressed-skin amphibious float with retractable wheels and a carrier arresting hook. The successful float led the navy to inquire whether Grumman could incorporate retractable landing gear into the Boeing aircraft. Determining this proposal unfeasible, Grumman did advise the navy that the corporation was designing a two-seat fighter that would have space for recessed wheels. Grumman's first plane was the experimental XFF-1, Bureau Number (BuNo.) 8878 nicknamed "Fifi." The inaugural flight was made 29 December 1931 by the corporation, and soon after "Fifi" was turned over to the navy for testing. After more than a year of demanding tests, twenty-seven FF-1s were accepted for production with delivery to VF-5B scheduled for June 1933. (In the spring of 1934, thirty-three similar SF-1 scouts were assigned to VS-3B, also attached to *Lexington*.) The experimental BuNo. 8878 arrived earlier than the production models, allowing Jimmy an opportunity to fly her for two and a half hours on 17 March 1933.

"Fifi," with her seven-hundred-horsepower Wright Cyclone R-1820-78 engine, proved to be about ten miles per hour faster than the F4B and had greater range, but there was no meaningful improvement in climb or service (altitude) ceiling. At 3,250 pounds it was slightly over a thousand pounds heavier than the Boeing and side by side, the larger dimensions of the Grumman were obvious. On balance, Jimmy wondered aloud whether or not "Fifi" was the better fighter. The Boeing fighter seemed to have been built just for diminutive Jimmy. Larger men like J. J. Clark and Lt. Leslie E. Gehres—a future commanding officer of USS *Franklin* (CV-13) and pilot extraordinaire with the "High Hats" at the 1929 Cleveland Air Races—had some difficulty fitting into the small cockpit. The Grumman fighter had a larger cockpit for the pilot —even though it was extended aft—and accommodation for a backseat observer/gunner. For the first time the pilot was protected from the weather and colder temperatures at altitude. But what mattered most to Jimmy, and other fighter pilots aboard *Lexington,* was combat performance and there seemed little or no improvement for that one paramount consideration.

As both the Boeing and Grumman products were biplanes, a pilot's vision was still obstructed by the upper wing. Forward fixed firepower was not improved—still two guns—but "Fifi" did offer a .30-caliber flexible rear mount. This, however, was not necessarily an advantage to a fighter pilot who might value speed and maneuverability more than defensive potential as the greater weight of another man, gun, and ordnance did not aid performance. Additionally, the arrangement of guns seemed to indicate the Grumman FF-1 was a defensive fighter instead of the offensive weapon Jimmy and most other VF-5B pilots desired. For the last half of 1933 Jimmy logged about as many hours in the F4B as he did in the FF-1, but from January 1934 until reassignment in May, nearly all hours were in "Fifi." By late 1936 when Jimmy returned to fighters, the debate pertaining to the two planes was moot as neither were then front-line aircraft. Still, Jimmy would enjoy many more hours in the Boeing F4B before depending upon the Grumman descendants of the FF-1 to carry him into combat.

By March 1934 Jimmy had orders and knew he would be leaving *Lexington* and fighter planes for assignment to patrol planes. He would miss fighter squadron life, but development as an officer and aviator required broad experience. In the last days of his first major naval aviation assignment, he embraced carrier life for all it was worth. May 1934 was little different than earlier months of the year; nearly every day he was involved in either division or squadron tactics. Jimmy was always alert when landing his aircraft aboard a carrier, but in May while lining up his landings, he dropped his head over one side of his FF-1 and then the other just a little earlier than usual to get maximum enjoyment from the last seconds before touchdown. Then, after the always tense but professional routine of landing planes, he joined the other officers dressed in white uniforms for dinner in the wardroom. Jimmy appreciated the good food and good company even more during this last month; and even though he enjoyed the after-dinner movie as much as anyone, he would not have objected to its absence in favor of more time for wardroom camaraderie.

The fighter squadron experience had been very rewarding intrinsically, and in May 1934 the navy added to Jimmy's satisfaction with a letter of commendation from Rear Adm. C. A. Blakely, the commander of aircraft in the Battle Force, to all the pilots of VF-5B. The admiral wrote in a 24 May 1934 letter, "Never before in the history of aviation have carriers and their Squadrons operated as extensively and efficiently as in the past Problem [XV]." And Jimmy was particularly gratified with a 27 October 1933 fitness report that noted, "He is calm and even tempered and exceptionally cool headed in trying situations. He is a superior fighting plane pilot, aerial gunner and bomber. His piloting of the FF-1 airplanes in experimental test flights were [*sic*] superior."

Patrol Aircraft (1934–1936)

On each Report on the Fitness of Officers form, officers were given an opportunity to express a preference for their next duty, one choice for sea duty, the other for shore duty. Throughout his time with VF-5B Jimmy's first choice was to remain with aircraft squadrons attached to the Battle Force or assignment to the lighter-than-air (LTA) USS *Akron* (ZRS-4) or USS *Macon* (ZRS-5). An assignment to one of the dirigibles, or "aircraft carriers in the sky," would allow him to continue flying planes similar to the Boeing F4B. The Curtiss F9C Sparrowhawk attached to the large airships greatly resembled the F4B in appearance and was nearly as much fun to fly. However, the crash of the *Akron* on 4 April 1933 that took the lives of seventy-three including Rear Adm. William A. Moffett, chief of the Bureau of Aeronautics, ended the LTA possibility (*Macon* was also lost 12 February 1935). Jimmy did not request a patrol squadron or Hawaii, but that is what he got. When unofficially told about impending orders in February 1934 he was "plenty griped but I don't know of anything I can do about it. Honolulu will be wonderful for the baby [James Henry III born 9 January 1934], but that is the only thing in its favor."[4] In April 1934 Dorothy and baby "Jimboy" traveled to Florida to visit her family, and in early June Jimmy traveled to Green Bay for a brief visit with his parents. On 23 June Jimmy sailed to Honolulu aboard the Matson Liner *Malolo* arriving on the twenty-eighth. Dotty and son followed from California aboard the same ship on 7 July.

At Pearl Harbor Jimmy reported to Patrol Squadron Four-F (VP-4F). The patrol planes were literally "flying boats": many flights that fell short of their destinations proved the seaworthiness of the hulls. The paramount purpose of the flying boat was to find an enemy ship or submarine before it could attack the U.S. coast or units of the fleet. During World War I German U-boats were the main object of patrol plane searches. That role continued in World War II but was greatly expanded.

For the two years that Jimmy was assigned to VP-4F, over 90 percent of his flight hours were logged in two patrol aircraft, the Douglas PD-1 and the Consolidated P2Y. The Douglas PD-1 was a derivative of the PN-12 series built by the Philadelphia-based Naval Aircraft Factory, the PN dating from 1924 and the PD-1 from 1929. Equipped with two 575 hp Wright R-1750 Cyclones, the PD-1 could fly up to fifteen hundred miles but not at its top speed of 121 mph. For attack it could carry over nine hundred pounds of bombs or depth charges, and for defense two flexible guns could be mounted. The later P2Y, mounting a series of improved engines just below the upper parasol wing and capable of carrying more than double the amount of ordnance, was built by Consolidated Aircraft Company and entered U.S. Navy service in early 1933.[5] In January 1934 six P2Y-1s with their five man crews flew from San Francisco to Pearl Harbor in a little over twenty-four hours, a distance of twenty-four-hundred miles. Jimmy regretted not having an opportunity to fly the Consolidated PBY Catalina monoplane that entered service in March 1935 and earned a multitude of laurels during World War II. The large patrol planes he did fly while assigned to VP-4F (PD-1, P2Y-1, P2Y-2, and P2Y-3) were all relegated to training roles just prior to U.S. entry into the war.

Training in VP-4F consisted of squadron and division tactics, instrument and night flying, navigation, gunnery, bombing, scouting problems, photographic flights, and, most important, search missions. Most of these functions were put to good use in May 1935 when the squadron participated in early advanced base operations at French Frigate Shoals and Midway Island as part of Fleet Problem XVI. Although Jimmy's PD-1 made the seven-hour flight from Pearl to Midway on 11 May without difficulty, he saw three of the forty-eight patrol planes return to Pearl with engine trouble. Within a week two other patrol planes made water landings and one was lost. On the seventeenth the main base for the patrol planes was surprised by an "attack" from cruiser aircraft—the attack not expected for another twenty-four hours, and to compound matters the patrol planes could not overtake the cruisers, which had headed into the wind. Late on 22 May two more patrol planes were down, both from Squadron Six. One aircraft, 6-P-10, was safe in the water, but the second, 6-P-7, was lost. Jimmy and his crew flew over nine hours on the twenty-third before the wreckage was located. Surprisingly, perhaps, it was the first fatal accident for patrol aircraft in two years. The experience gained in this and previous war games, including the loss of life, were to pay considerable dividends for Jimmy during World War II.[6]

While his primary assignment was patrol planes, Jimmy did manage to find a few occasions to slip back into an F4B fighter to tow targets or fly administrative flights. Despite his love for fighters, evidence of his maturity as a man and as a naval officer became apparent in his patrol plane work. Serving as engineering officer for the squadron, he was directly involved in the assembly of planes arriving in Hawaii by ship as well as being directly involved with maintenance, overhaul, and upkeep of the aircraft. Lt. Cdr. Harold J. Brow—the November 1923 holder of the world's speed record—served as commanding officer of VP-4F for all but the last two months of Jimmy's two years with the squadron. His remarks on Jimmy's fitness reports record not only duties and industry but also the first manifestations of leadership and leadership potential. After Jimmy's first three months with the squadron, Brow had rated him a "very good *average* young officer" who "has not yet developed any outstanding characteristics," and graded him 3.4 as a pilot and 3.3 for all duties.[7] A year later, Brow's opinions were considerably different as he marked Jimmy 3.9 as a pilot and 4.0 for all duties stating, "Lt. (jg) Flatley is outstanding in every respect. Too much cannot be said for his efficiency, industry and tireless devotion to his duties as Engineer Officer." Brow went on to highlight Jimmy's "ingenuity and resourcefulness" and accorded him the highest mark possible for leadership and most other qualities on the fitness report.[8] Not the least important consideration in Brow's view was the exceptional interest and talent Jimmy applied to directing assembly of the new P2Y-3s. "In analyzing and correcting the numerous structural and engineering defects encountered . . . he has demonstrated ability and initiative far beyond that usually expected."[9] Genuine interest and hard work brought recognition, and this peer appreciation brought higher and continuing expectations from within Jimmy. It was not a new or unique formula but for him it was a new plateau.

A plateau, no matter how high, is still level. There was room for growth in Jimmy's professional life, and probably no other assignment guaranteed that growth more than the next. By 10 April 1936 he had orders transferring him back to fighters. Detached 22 May 1936 with a princely $366 advance of two months pay Jimmy, Dotty, two-year-old Jimboy, and six-month-old Ray Patrick (born 6 January 1936) boarded the transport U.S. *Grant* headed for San Francisco.

Fighters Again (1936–1937)

On 25 June 1936 Jimmy again reported for duty with his old squadron, VF-5B. The squadron was still based in San Diego but was now operating from USS *Ranger* (CV-4), the first U.S. Navy carrier built from the keel up as an aircraft carrier. This was temporary duty as the basic orders received in April directed him to report in December 1936 to the fitting-out fighter squadron VF-7B. That squadron would go aboard *Yorktown* (CV-5), which was still being built, scheduled to be commissioned 30 September 1937 and based at Naval Operating Base, Norfolk, Virginia. In the interim Jimmy and family set up again in Coronado, a stay that would last a full year rather than the expected six months.

There was no way Jimmy and Dotty could make long-range plans upon their return to San Diego. Within the first week back with VF-5B, Jimmy received orders for temporary duty with VF-3B, also based at San Diego, effective 29 July through 8 September 1936 in connection with that squadron's participation in the National Air Races. Appointed assistant flight officer he also served as a pilot in the regular tactical organization of the squadron. U.S. Army fliers in the mid-1920s had initiated the idea of a demonstration team, but not until 1927–28 did navy fliers modify and improve their engines to perform in like manner. The "Three Sea Hawks," flying the F2B-1 in the 1928 National Air Races, and the "High Hats," who flew in the 1929 Cleveland Air Races, formed the foundation of what eventually became the Blue Angels. Jimmy was tasked to assist VF-3B in developing their flying routine and the tactics to be used during the races that were being staged in Los Angeles for that year on 4–7 September. Mock dive-bombing and dogfighting, long since deleted from Blue Angel programs in the contemporary jet age, were crowd favorites. Jimmy did his job well and received a letter of commendation for his six-week temporary duty. The commendation letter dated 14 September helped ease Jimmy's embarrassment of crashing on 31 August. A one-hour navigation flight from San Diego to Los Angeles was completed without incident. But while returning he set down at Long Beach Airport with part of his mind on navigation and the other part in a fixed gear Boeing F4B. Unfortunately, he was in a Grumman F2F-1 and he forgot to lower his landing gear. So much for the new technology and part of his upper right eyelid!

Jimmy's favorite mount to that point in time, the F4B, was no longer the squadron's principal fighter. On his first day back in VF-5B he was in the air for two hours familiarizing himself with the new Grumman F3F-1. Jimmy's *Ranger*-based VF-5B and *Saratoga*'s VF-6B were the first fighter squadrons to receive the F3F-1s beginning in early 1936. After 1 July 1937, VF-5B became VF-4, *Ranger*'s hull number, while VF-6B became VF-3, *Saratoga*'s hull number. In the continuing evolution of the early Grumman biplane fighters that began with the FF-1 ("Fifi"), fifty-four production models of the F2F-1 were delivered to the navy in mid-1935, followed finally by the F3F series (-1-2-3) comprising a total of 162 production planes.[10] The F2F-1 differed from "Fifi" by being a single seat fighter, smaller, lighter, and faster (231 mph vs. 207). Larger than the F2F, but not as large as "Fifi," the F3F series was faster (264 mph in the F3F-3 versus 231) with the most powerful engine used being the F3F-3's 950 hp Wright R-1820-22. All the Grumman biplanes were highly maneuverable and improved with each model, but firepower was still the same twin .30 fixed guns synchronized to fire through the propeller. Initial climb improved through each succeeding model of the series, but appreciation for increase in absolute performance, especially in climb, was tempered by recognition that this factor could not be fully valued until the relative performance of an enemy was known. Even though some pilots in Jimmy's squadron expressed some concern for the bellicose actions of Japan—in Manchuria since 1931—and current stirrings in Germany, the potential of Japanese and German aircraft was unknown in 1936. Consequently, the fighter pilots of the U.S. Navy continued to concentrate on dogfighting each other.

Dogfighting, or "individual combat" as worded in Jimmy's flight logs and those of other fighter pilots, comprised only a small portion of flight time in squadron-training schedules. During his first full month back in fighters, only one hour of the twenty-six logged was devoted to individual combat, emphasis being on section and squadron tactics. In the following months individual battle practice (IBP in log books) for gunnery and bombing received considerably more time with instrument flying, navigation, night flights, and formation tactics accounting for the remainder of flight time. When not in the air, they always had administrative paperwork and a never-ending stream of papers to read. Bureau of Aeronautic newsletters were of particular interest to pilots, not only for news relating to other segments of naval aviation but also for the latest findings in safety. In those days as in later, studies of crashes—both fatal and non-fatal—emphasized pilot error. The key to pilot error into

1937 appeared to be faulty judgment: (1) attempting to reach a destination despite bad weather and disregard for weather reports; (2) choosing to fly over rugged terrain; and (3) maneuvering at high speed and low altitude for no useful purpose. Technical problems at the head of the list were carburetor icing, malfunctioning fuel gauges, improper fuel mixture control, taking off with the gasoline system taking suction from an empty tank, and failure to fully extend retractable landing gear. These problems were of special interest to Jimmy as he was VF-5B's assistant engineering officer before moving up to engineering officer. While the errors could apply to pilots of any type plane, Jimmy and his fellow fighter pilots took particular notice of practices pertaining directly to them and placed special emphasis on (1) changing position in formation and cutting off others' wings and tails; (2) dogfighting at low altitude; and (3) dogfighting with excessive reality and fallible judgment.[11] In February 1932 over Pearl Harbor both army and navy fighter pilots —including Jimmy—were admonished for too much realism; but no amount of admonition brought cessation because excessive reality was the essence of being a fighter pilot. As will be seen later, Jimmy made little effort to curtail such conduct among his men when he became a squadron commander.

Jimmy's flight time in fighters was actually more than time logged with patrol planes. Throughout his prewar fighter squadron experience, the Depression appeared to have little effect on flight time consistency. Whether the year was 1931, '32, '33, '34, '35, '36, or '37, flight time in fighters was normally about twenty-six hours a month. As with patrol planes, hours went up considerably during fleet problems or other major exercises.

Although the heart of the Depression years was in peacetime, naval aviation nonetheless prepared for war. While squadron and division tactics dominated over individual dogfight training, there was a specific manner in which such combat was practiced, doctrine being codified for the United States Fleet in chapter 3 of USF-13. The basic principles for success in aerial combat were (1) superiority of firepower (then defined as having more planes than a potential enemy as opposed to mounting more and larger caliber guns as was done in the World War II era) and (2) superiority of position.[12] It was understood that fighter pilots would develop techniques of their own and that those basic principles could not guarantee success. But failure was assured to those who totally disregarded them.[13] The first sign that one might have to enter individual combat was the sighting of another single seat aircraft (only fighters had one seat). The primary objective was to get headed in the same direction, turn in such a manner to give the opponent no chance to turn back, and be in a position above and slightly behind, always staying on the outside of the opponents turns and not turning too slowly.[14]

Interestingly there appeared to be two schools of thought in 1937 concerning the future of carrier aircraft combat. One believed the day of the dogfight was over, finished with World War I. Thinking was "that all operations in the future will be VF squadron[s] or group[s] versus VB or VS [scout] squadron[s] or groups, with opposing fighters passing each other with a friendly wave of the wings."[15] These enemy squadrons would not engage each other but continue on their way to attack each others' fleet. Apparently this school of thought was in the majority as fighter squadron training—well documented by the flight logs of Jimmy Flatley and other fighter pilots of the period—concentrated on squadron and division tactics.

This debate aside, for individual combat training (dogfight) two fighters ascended together with one taking an altitude advantage of one thousand feet, and the fight began when they passed on opposite courses.[16] The objective was to get right behind the opponent, or "saddle" position, a desirable tactic given the relatively short range of the two .30-caliber Brownings available to carrier fighters of the day.[17] After the first encounter and kill, the positions of the two planes were reversed. If the skill of the two pilots were equal, whoever had the altitude would usually win unless the two were willing to go into a scissors tactic—the plane in the defensive position constantly turning toward the attacker—resulting in a tie at the end.[18] Indeed, if the pilot who started on the bottom could avoid being "killed" he had done well.[19] One of Jimmy's dogfight opponents in the summer of 1937 was Ens. John J. Hyland, fresh from Pensacola. Hyland recalled that although a neophyte, he was not a plumber (a poor pilot), but it made no difference how he and Jimmy started as Jimmy always won and "in very short order." At that time to Hyland and many other fighter pilots, Jimmy's name was synonymous with skill.[20]

Deflection shooting was a known and practiced tactic in U.S. naval aviation since the 1920s, but it was not necessarily favored by other air forces in part due to limited ordnance range and the relatively great maneuverability of 1930s era biplanes. Still, a position slightly above or below in the dogfight potentially required a deflection shot even it the angle was only 15 to 20 degrees (a quarter deflection). Full deflection, a 60 to 90 degree angle, became more popular later due to the higher speeds of aircraft and increased defensive firepower. But whether prewar or during World War II one principle remained firm, not to fire until the target filled the gun sight. Prior to the war long-tube sights were mounted through the windscreen, but improved sights were necessary as speeds increased. With the installation of bulletproof glass in late 1941 the tube sights disappeared in favor of an instrument panel reflector gun sight modified and improved throughout the war.

In the spring of 1937 the commander of aircraft in the Battle Force requested comments by the squadrons concerning experience gained and lessons learned on the administration, operations, and training pertaining to all aircraft within the command. Carrier commanding officers, carrier squadron commanders, and air group representatives responded in writing to specific questions and to other areas of concern. Jimmy was one of two respondents for VF-5B. All respondents were encouraged to be full and frank even with controversial opinions.[21] Some of the written responses in the 4 August 1937 compilation demonstrated considerable insight into future needs and policies while some opinions eventually proved wrong; however, all painted a portrait of contemporary thinking aboard carriers and in carrier squadrons.

Jimmy offered no comments to the six questions concerning administration, nor did he have any thoughts beyond those requested. For operations and training he had a lot to say, offering an opinion that more than one squadron attempting to do the same thing at the same place and at the same time was detrimental to all. As he saw it, an alternating schedule for squadrons would eliminate congestion at gunnery ranges and bombing targets. He then recommended that individual and squadron battle practice, both for fixed guns and bombs, be competitive only within the squadron because inter-squadron competition wasted time with umpiring, official rehearsals, record firing, and other administrative matters. A major advantage to these suggested changes would be continuous and routine squadron scheduling that should eliminate the protracted periods between gunnery practice since "a two month lay-off is very detrimental." In short, Jimmy advocated a more productive use of time that could produce a better pilot, not only as an individual but also for the squadron and group.[22]

For the questions concerning airplane characteristics and employment, Jimmy championed several ideas that were eventually addressed. While other respondents echoed some of his thoughts, neither he nor they knew what the others were writing. Jimmy noted the need for a monoplane design to provide better visibility.[23] He also stated unequivocally that all navy planes should be completely equipped for instrument flying,[24] and foresaw the need for strafing and low-angle attack by fighter-bomber planes "that in time of war" would be necessary against antiaircraft batteries and control parties at various locations on the ships.[25] Further, he advocated more guns for fighters "of great reliability," and—with other respondents—expanded on problems with the variance in speed between fighter and attack aircraft.[26] The first four recommendations were implemented before or during World War II, but the last continued to be a problem until 1945 and was then resolved only because fighters (F6F Hellcats and F4U Corsairs) were heavily utilized in attack roles.

Of course, not all of Jimmy's ideas, or those of the other respondents, proved viable. At the time of this formal introspection the U.S. Navy had only three aircraft carriers (*Langley* having been converted to a seaplane tender in late 1936) with two others scheduled for commissioning within a year. Consequently, Jimmy's suggestion that two carriers be assigned to the battle line and carry only scout planes to spot the battle line and fighters to protect it was no doubt influenced by the small number of U.S. Navy carriers. He did not foresee the eventual wisdom in the proposed carrier air group comprised of bombing, scouting, torpedo, and fighter squadrons mentioned in the list of questions. However, his thinking was well ahead of the commanding officer of Scouting Squadron Two-B (VS-2B) who stated: "Experienced fighting plane pilots in this squadron consider that there is no place on board a carrier for a pure fighting type of airplane. The carrier's potential power as a striking force is materially reduced by the presence on board of a fighting plane squadron."[27] When reading the comments of other respondents to this "characteristics and employment" question, it is apparent that the majority thinking was closer to VS-2B's commanding officer than to Jimmy's. In sum, at age thirty-one Jimmy's increasing experience and demonstrated competence had put him in position to have those in authority value his thinking. And as naval aviation continued to evolve through the late 1930s, it was evident that his ideas and vision of the future was much closer to reality than that of many others in the naval aviation community.[28]

On 22 October 1936 Jimmy had received orders revoking assignment to *Yorktown,* but on 17 March 1937 orders arrived directing him to NAS Norfolk and VF-8B, the "Shooting Stars." Two days after arriving at NAS Norfolk on 29 June 1937 VF-8B became VF-6 as a result of the 1 July 1937 change in the naval aeronautic organization. Fighting Squadron Six was assigned to *Yorktown's* twin sister, *Enterprise* (CV-6), which was being readied for commissioning on 12 May 1938. The most challenging days of Jimmy's career would come while operating from the carrier being built that would become the most decorated ship in World War II. However, he would have to wait until October 1942 before serving aboard "The Big E" as his tour of duty with VF-6 lasted only until 15 September 1937.

While VF-8B, which actually had been VF-1B, was awaiting its new 1 July VF-6 designation—the squadron number matching the hull number of *Enterprise*—Jimmy was busy changing his shoulder designation. Effective 30 June he was a full lieutenant, not an exalted rank in 1937 but a rank that meant much more then than it would during the war. In the two and a half months Jimmy was with VF-6, he split his flying hours between the Boeing F4B-4, which was being phased out, and the Grumman F2F-1. In July all his hours were recorded in Boeings (19.8 hours); in August and September all were in Grummans (37.7).[29] Training with VF-6 was as rigorous as it had been with VF-5B, the squadron particularly anxious to do well with the intersquadron competition with VF-5 that would go aboard *Yorktown.* A camera gun determined the outcome of the aerial matches during all Jimmy's days in fighters.[30]

In time Jimmy was not the only member of VF-6 during the summer of 1937 who would rise to flag rank. Lt. A. M. Jackson later earned three stars and Johnny Hyland earned four as did then-Ens. Thomas H. Moorer. Moorer also became chief of naval operations and chairman of the Joint Chiefs of Staff in the 1960s. Moorer no doubt wished he had stayed in fighters during the first months of the war when he was twice shot down while flying patrol planes. Another member of the VF-6 team who later had meaningful contact with Jimmy was an aviation cadet, Robin Lindsey, a pilot with artistic talent who designed the squadron's "Shooting Star" insignia. Later Jimmy also designed a squadron insignia, but when he and Lindsey joined company again there was little time to discuss their artistic inclinations.

In September 1937 Jimmy had orders transferring him out of fighters and out of the country. The several fitness reports for the fifteen-month period in fighters were outstanding, with only one grade as "low" as 3.7. Most were 3.8 or 3.9 with one 4.0. His ability, efficiency, and enthusiasm for aviation engineering drew special mention, as did his "E" for excellence in fixed guns. (This excellence was achieved by using a camera more often than bullets. Consequently, the problems of jamming were not fully appreciated until revealed by wartime conditions.) One category that evaluated presence of mind graded "the faculty of acting instinctively in a logical manner in difficult and unforeseen situations." Jimmy consistently received his highest marks for this category, the top grade reserved for those who were "exceptionally cool-headed . . . under all conditions." While receiving high marks and praise for his work, only one of his fitness reports through September 1937 verbalized his leadership capabilities (Brow, 1934) , and his evaluations in that category were not his highest. To this point in his career he had not been placed in a leadership role where his mettle could be fully tested. That soon changed, but documentation was overwhelming in his fitness reports that he was more than competent. Competence formed a solid foundation for future leadership as few, then or now, desire to follow the incompetent.

Cruiser Scouting Planes, First Leadership Role, and a Glimpse of War

Jimmy did not have to travel far on 20 September 1937 to his next assignment with the aviation unit of USS *Omaha* (CL-4) as the light cruiser was in the Norfolk Navy Yard undergoing overhaul and repairs. Having arrived from San Diego in June, Jimmy and his family remained in Norfolk until the cruiser was ready to steam to the Mediterranean where she would take up duty as flagship of the European Squadron. In the meantime Jimmy was assigned temporary duty with the fleet air detachment, and he immediately began flying the SOC-1 biplane as senior aviator of Squadron Forty-T attached to *Omaha*.

The Curtiss-built SOC-1 Seagull was fun to fly, but it was by no means the same as flying a fighter, whether Boeing or Grumman. Being launched from zero to seventy miles per hour on one of *Omaha*'s two sixty-five-foot catapults was always a thrill as well as a challenge—Jimmy recording each and every catapult shot in his log. The launch itself by the compressed air driven catapults was so explosive that Jimmy—like most other pilots—blacked out momentarily. But the officially listed top speed for the dependable two seat, in tandem, seaplane was only 160 mph (about 130 for cruising).[31] The six-hundred-horsepower Pratt and Whitney R-1340-18 engine did well to reach such a speed considering the drag created by the single large center float nearly as long as the plane itself. While scouting and observation for main battery gunfire were the basic functions of the plane, opportunity might occur for dropping up to 650 pounds of ordnance on surface vessels or submarines. For defense the Seagull mounted one fixed forward-firing .30-caliber Browning in the upper wing and one flexible mount in the rear cockpit. For the twenty-one months Jimmy was assigned to this duty all his flight hours were in the SOC-1.

Omaha was one of ten units of the *Omaha* class laid down during World War I but completed too late for any to see action. *Omaha*—commissioned 24 February 1923—and her sisters were built to function as fast surface scouts for the fleet and as raiders. Fitted with catapults in the 1920s, *Omaha*-class cruisers carried two scout planes and sufficient spare parts to constitute half of another. With their planes the basic scouting and raider functions of the cruisers were amplified, and the cruiser aircraft also served as main battery spotters. At the end of World War II the obsolete, long-serving *Omaha*-class cruisers—and the SOC aircraft that served aboard them—were stricken from active inventory.

Having been an engineering officer in several squadrons, Jimmy soon noticed one practice aboard *Omaha* and her sisters that required a change. Through his commanding officer, Capt. W. L. Lind, Jimmy suggested to the Bureau of Aeronautics that its influence be exerted with the Bureau of Construction and Repair to stop filtering aviation gasoline through chamois skins. Needed, he wrote, was a mechanical filter that not only excluded water and solids but also reduced a fire hazard. To further strengthen his proposal he noted that the use of chamois skins aboard ships' boats was not allowed.[32] The Bureau of Aeronautics was concerned about the $500 for each installation aboard *Omaha* cruisers, but Captain Lind was impressed by his senior aviation pilot's cogent argument.

On 23 February 1938 the shore-based temporary duty was over, and Jimmy was aboard *Omaha* on 24 February to prepare for sea duty. In late April the cruiser was under way to begin serving on European Station. Thinking he might return to Norfolk, Jimmy transferred his rental on Westmoreland Park to a friend (for $5.00 a month) and made arrangements for Dotty and youngest son, Ray Patrick, to board SS *City of Baltimore* on 15 April 1938 for a voyage to Le Havre, France. Four-year-old little Jim was left with his grandparents in Green Bay.

During the voyage to the Mediterranean Jimmy and the other officers aboard the cruiser discussed all the usual subjects, but the closer they got to Europe the more conversation turned to world events. Italy had attacked Ethiopia in 1935 and became party to the Rome-Berlin Axis in 1936. The Spanish Civil War—a dress rehearsal for World War II—had been under way since 1936, and Adolph Hitler was becoming more of a menace to Europe, having entered German speaking Austria on 11 March—just before *Omaha* left Norfolk. Consequently, showing the flag had significant meaning when the cruiser visited Gibraltar, Tangiers, Casablanca, and Algiers soon after arriving in the Mediterranean.

Home port while on European Station was Villefranche-sur-Mer, a French seaport, only a short distance to the Italian border. On 2 May Jimmy advised Captain Lind of the flying restrictions in the harbor. Local authorities permitted takeoffs and landings in the harbor, but the planes could not fly over land at any time. Further, they could not fly higher than the altitude of the headlands at the entrance to the harbor, must fly below the level of the headlands while proceeding to and from the sea, could not carry photographic equipment, and there was to be no bombing or gunnery practice. With southwestern neighbor Spain convulsed by civil war, southeastern neighbor Italy and eastern neighbor Germany in bellicose moods, the French were taking neutrality very serious. And the French were not alone with their concerns. On 14 June Jimmy responded to the executive officer's 13 June memo with a written report on how the aviation department would respond "at outbreak of war." His department would remove a 1,400-pound aircraft engine, 500 pounds of stowage boxes, and 2,000 pounds of excess structural parts. To clear the cruiser for action both SOC-1's, totaling 10,600-pounds, would be removed along with 21,000 pounds of fuel, 350 pounds of oil, and 3,000 pounds of structural spares and miscellaneous equipment.

The threat of war and the regulations imposed by local authorities were not the only considerations in reduced flight time. The cost of aviation gasoline was excessive,[33] and weather during the Mediterranean winter was not as warm as advertised. Even Dotty was disappointed with the weather, strongly preferring Florida, California, or Hawaii despite the obvious pleasure of mixing with the throngs of Europeans who flocked to the Riviera.[34] Throughout his thirteen months in the Mediterranean Jimmy recorded fewer hours per month in the Seagull scout plane than he had in fighters, averaging less than ten hours a month compared to over eighteen during his last year in fighters. As a result of these problems nearly 50 percent of the few hours in the air were "under the hood" in an effort to perfect blind flying ability.[35] The SOC-1 could stay in the air for a little more than five hours, but during his stay in the Mediterranean Jimmy flew only three flights matching his seaplane's endurance capability.

Flying from a cruiser was dangerous work, just as it was from a carrier, but a carrier did offer a solid deck. When Jimmy returned to *Omaha* after a flight, his first concern was to find the ship that sometimes was not where he expected it. Nearly always, he had to wait for the cruiser to make a sharp turn to knock down the top of the waves and create a slick in the lee of the ship. Landings were still a controlled crash, similar to landing on a carrier. The next step was to taxi in the open sea to catch the ship, taxi onto a sled, cut the engine, and engage a hook from the cruiser's crane onto a ring at the top of the aircraft's upper wing. The SOC would then be lifted aboard while the cruiser continued to steam at three to six knots. Getting back aboard was not always routine, especially during the Mediterranean winter of 1938–39. Strong winds created high waves causing Jimmy to lose sight of the ship, and there was always a possibility of slamming against the side of *Omaha* when approaching the sled. Danger was always a passenger with the back seat observer who had the responsibility of connecting the cable from the ship's crane to the ring on the upper wing. If the hook broke, or if an over-anxious crane operator hoisted the observer out of the plane, the American taxpayer lost a SOC and Jimmy would have to be fished out of the Mediterranean by a destroyer or ship's boat.[36]

Despite years of tension in Spain, open civil war did not begin until 1936. As it moved to a conclusion in the winter of 1939, Jimmy got his first glimpse of war. On 24 January *Omaha* steamed toward Barcelona, Spain, with orders to evacuate the American chargé d'affairs, the naval attaché, military attaché, and about thirty U.S. citizens. Arriving after dark on the evening of the twenty-fourth, Jimmy could see a British cruiser, a French cruiser, and three French destroyers on station for the same purpose. Before midnight thirteen Nationalist bombers attacked from thirteen thousand feet. It was not clear whether the bombs were meant for the Spanish Republican Army retreating up the coastal road from the city or to make a statement to the ships offshore, as only one of sixty bombs hit the road. The others struck the water, most about four hundred yards away, but a few splashed within fifty yards of the French destroyers. One of *Omaha*'s boats sent to shore to pick up the departing Americans was endangered, but fortunately the near misses were duds.[37] Watching the bombs near the ships, those that fell into Barcelona during another attack and the antiaircraft fire, Jimmy could not only see combat but feel it. Intellectually, he and others aboard *Omaha* knew a war involving the United States was somewhere in their future. Still, a portion of their minds refused to accept that possibility. Standing on *Omaha*'s bridge Jimmy felt excitement and exhilaration along with emotional distress as dire images of future conflict raced through his mind. While he could not see death in the dark night, he knew the illuminating bombs and machine-gun tracers were bringing eternal darkness to many. Only at such a moment can one be completely honest within oneself whether or not he can fully function under such conditions. On the night of 24–25 January 1939, Jimmy could answer that unasked question affirmatively.

Within days after the Barcelona evacuation, Jimmy and Dotty took leave for a visit to London and Paris. In London the weather was better than usual for late winter, and by coincidence the two American tourists arrived at Buckingham Palace just as the royal family was returning home. Jimmy was disappointed the trip could not have waited until spring, as he wanted to see the gardens in bloom and leaves on the trees lining the broad boulevards of Paris. Nonetheless, the trip was very enjoyable, in part because Jimmy knew well that war clouds were gathering over all of Europe.[38]

Upon return from their ten-day vacation, Jimmy and Dotty learned their next duty station was NAS Pensacola, Florida. Again, all of Jimmy's preferences had been passed over, but as soon as he read his 6 March orders, he knew the Pensacola assignment would put him in the air for many more hours than he had been able to fly during his present assignment. Dotty was just happy to know she would be warm again, emotionally with a reunited family and physically in the Florida sun. *Omaha* was to be relieved in July by *Trenton* (CL-11), one of her sister ships, but Jimmy was authorized to leave earlier. Dotty and Ray Patrick sailed on the SS *President Harrison* on 22 June, little Jim was collected in Green Bay, and the whole family was in Pensacola on 14 July.

When Dotty and Ray Patrick sailed from Europe, a middle-aged French widow, Jeanette Ebelmann, accompanied them. Jeanette's German husband had died before the Flatley's arrived in Europe, and Dotty employed her as a housekeeper and nursemaid. Jeanette had very little command of the English language, so Dotty had to learn French as fast as Jeanette learned English. In a short time the stout, affable widow endeared herself to Jimmy, Dotty, and Ray Patrick; and when orders came to return to the United States, the Flatley's could not return without her. Considered a member of the family, Jeanette remained with the Flatley's until after the war when she remarried.

Duty as *Omaha*'s senior aviation pilot had been rewarding in many ways for Jimmy, not the least of which was being in Europe during the waning days of peace. While not spending as much time in the air as he would have preferred, he knew within himself that the overall experience was beneficial for the continuing evolution of his development as a naval officer. His leadership experience aboard *Omaha* was modest but successful. His own assessment was mirrored by Captain Lind who wrote in Jimmy's 15 April 1938 fitness report that he was an "outstanding officer and excellent aviator . . . keenly interested in all branches of the naval profession in addition to his own specialty." Continuing, he wrote that Jimmy was "calm, even tempered and of sound judgment . . . conscientious, industrious . . . [and] maintains his unit in a splendid state of readiness at all times." In short, Lind viewed Jimmy as "a very promising officer."[39]

Back in the United States it was apparent to the Flatley family that economic conditions were better in 1939 than they had been in 1937. An improving economy was good news for everyone, and the navy was especially happy that 1938 legislation provided for a huge buildup in both ships and men. However, the cost for the end of the ten-year unemployment crisis was higher than most understood at the time. Great exertions and exercises in social legislation to the contrary, employment to build the instruments of impending war proved to be the most significant factor for the Great Depression's demise. Although a war-energized economy continued to improve economic conditions, many Americans who experienced the pain and deprivation of the 1930s never fully recovered emotionally.

3

Preparation for War

NAS Pensacola, War in Europe,
and the Impact on Naval Aviation

THE NAVY had maintained a presence in Pensacola since 1825 with the permanent naval air station dating from 1914. The city and station were familiar sights to Jimmy when he reported for duty on 4 August 1939 as it had been only eight years since he completed flight training at the northwest Florida "Cradle of Naval Aviation." Familiar too were the Saturday morning inspections in whites, swords, and the works. Still, he noticed a number of changes. The main entrance to the station had changed, and the old town of Warrington had been moved immediately across the bayou to the north, facilitating the station's expansion. The process began while Jimmy was there in 1930–31, but the movement of over three hundred buildings was not complete when he left. Still, the most pleasant sights to Jimmy since his days as a student aviator were several newly paved runways and much newer planes on the flight line and in the water. The training syllabus was essentially the same, his family residence in Quarters Q was adequate, the city of Pensacola offered amenities both Jimmy and Dotty appreciated; and all four Flatleys along with Jeanette looked forward to visiting Pensacola Beach and testing the fishing.

As it turned out, most of the fishing was done from the concrete piers and ramps near the hangars for the N3N-1 seaplanes. Dotty loved to fish and the two boys, then five and three, enjoyed going along. Little Jim, however, got a little too caught up in the catching on one occasion and fell into the water. Happily, an enlisted man saw the unintended immersion and pulled him out. This event was Dotty's most fearful single moment, but reminders of fear were ever present. Pensacola Bay was visible from the family's living quarters and the favorite fishing spots, but from these vantage points there seemed to be a never-ending parade of crash boats carrying the remains of Yellow Perils, the trainer biplanes used for student pilots, back to the beachfront. Nonetheless, this tour of duty had promise, or so it seemed in August 1939.

Less than two months after arriving at NAS Pensacola, the fears that accompanied Jimmy and Dotty from Europe materialized. Just before going aloft on 1 September 1939 for a two hour training flight with student aviators, Jimmy learned Adolph Hitler had hurled his Panzer divisions across the Polish border. Great Britain and France, after years of attempting to appease Hitler, declared war on 3 September, and for the second time in the still-young twentieth century, the United States became the arsenal of democracy.

In preparing for war the United States military faced two major challenges. The first was to produce ships, planes, guns, ordnance, and spare parts. Once produced, these instruments of war needed to be properly and swiftly distributed, not only to U.S. sailors, soldiers, and marines but also to the allies. Battleship construction had been suspended soon after World War I, but by the late 1930s the great powers and those aspiring to greatness were again building the mammoth floating symbols of international power. Jimmy was well aware of the construction schedules and benefits but he—like most everyone else in naval aviation—was far more interested in new aircraft carriers and carrier aircraft.

In September 1939 Jimmy and his fellow naval aviators could count only five aircraft carriers (*Lexington, Saratoga, Ranger, Yorktown* and *Enterprise*). A sixth, *Wasp*—an improved *Ranger*—was under construction (commissioned 25 April 1940). The 17 May 1938 Naval Expansion Act had authorized two additional carriers, USS *Hornet* (CV-8) and USS *Essex* (CV-9). *Hornet* was eventually commissioned 20 October 1941 but *Essex* not until 31 December 1942, a full year after the United States officially entered World War II. There were no escort carriers in the U.S. Navy in September 1939, nor were any under conversion or construction.

The situation with naval aircraft was not much better. On 1 July 1939 the navy had 2,098 planes with 1,316 of that total being combat types. On 10 October the chief of naval operations, Adm. Harold R. Stark, addressed the problem, "realizing that current developments in the international situation would necessitate an increase in fleet aircraft strength above normal standards of readiness."[1] Total numbers were known to be inadequate. However, neither Admiral Stark, Jimmy, nor others in naval aviation could appreciate the relative disparity until numbers announced during the summer 1940 Battle of Britain indicated the Germans had lost more planes in three months than the total inventory of the U.S. Navy.[2] Having just returned from Europe, Jimmy could share with other instructors his familiarity with monoplane development in Germany and Britain. Movie and still photography documenting the first weeks of the war quickly impressed naval aviators, and the absence of biplanes in the German blitzkrieg was particularly noted. The U.S. Army Air Corps had converted to monoplanes several years earlier (1935), and concern for naval air became a more popular subject for discussion in squadron meetings and over drinks at the end of the day. In September 1939 the best U.S. naval fighter was the Grumman F3F-3 biplane, great to fly in peacetime but of questionable performance against land-based monoplanes already serving in the new European war. Since late 1935 the navy had been working with Grumman and the Brewster Aeronautical Corporation, also based on Long Island, New York, to develop a new fighter. The Brewster XF2A-1 was a monoplane design from the beginning, whereas the Grumman XF4F-1 quickly evolved from a biplane to a monoplane in July 1936. In September 1939 production models of both planes were being fabricated, but none were ready for service.

With mixed emotions Jimmy spent his sixteen months in Pensacola watching the European war strongly influence the direction of naval aviation. On the one hand, he was pleased to see significant congressional appropriations for new carriers, new planes, and more personnel, but on the other were apprehensions concerning the future of countries he had just departed and how war would affect him and his family. With considerable interest, and a little envy, Jimmy learned that several acquaintances serving in the new PBY patrol planes were preparing flight plans to cover the Atlantic seaboard, to protect U.S. and foreign shipping from submarine attacks after President Roosevelt's September 1939 declaration of a limited national emergency. European democracies were allowed to transport domestic and military goods on a "cash and carry" basis in their own ships, and experience with German U-boats in World War I dictated a need to assure respect for America's nautical boundaries. Through the fall of 1939 and winter of 1940 the European war remained of relatively peripheral interest to Jimmy, but in the spring the naval personnel at Pensacola felt a much greater urgency in their training. April 1940 saw both Denmark and Norway capitulate to the Germans, and in May and June Nazi legions overwhelmed Holland, Belgium, and France. Europe very suddenly seemed much closer to Pensacola.

Europe also seemed much closer to Washington, D.C. Between June 1940 and 7 December 1941, Congress appropriated more money for military spending than it had for all of World War I. Particularly catching Jimmy's attention in the early summer of 1940 was the transfer of forty-three new Brewster F2A-1 Buffaloes to Finland. A total of eighty-one new Grumman F4F-3 Wildcats, originally ordered by the French, were transferred to Britain instead after the June collapse of France. When Jimmy left Pensacola in late 1940 only 11 new Brewster fighters (of an eventual 162) had been delivered to the U.S. Navy. And, less than two dozen new Grumman F4F-3 fighters had entered service.

The second challenge in preparing for war applied directly to Jimmy's new domain. To accommodate a greatly enlarged military force, new recruits had to be trained how to man ships, fly planes, operate guns, and maintain current inventory and all that would follow—including technology then unforeseen.

Training at Pensacola in 1939–40 was divided into five phases.

During this time a student could expect to fly about 350 hours over a period of nine to twelve months. Among the students were regular officers, aviation cadets (AvCads), and enlisted men (NAPs), the AvCads and NAPs having duties beyond those of the officers. AvCads devoted nonflying time and classes to officer training, and the NAPs seldom had opportunity to forget they were enlisted.

Forty percent of a student aviator's final grade was earned in Ground School. This classroom program ran concurrently with flight training, but was normally concluded before entering the advanced phases of flying. Subject areas in Ground School included aircraft engines, aircraft structure, navigation, tactics, gunnery, communications, photography, and aerology (atmospheric meteorology). The five phases of flight training comprised 60 percent of the student's evaluation; much the same as it was in 1931 when Jimmy completed training.[3] The first phase was Squadron One (VN-1D8), training in primary seaplanes that comprised 5 percent of the student's final grade. A student could expect several hours in a Naval Aircraft Factory N3N-1 biplane, a sturdy trainer that served as a seaplane when fitted with floats. Painted bright yellow on the wings as a warning to other planes and for high visibility if sea rescue was necessary, the two-man in-tandem plane was the introductory aircraft in 1939. In later -2 and -3 versions the Yellow Peril was used at Pensacola for training until 1961. Squadron Two (VN-2D8), primary land-planes, accounted for 20 percent of the final grade, with flying time in either the land version N3N or the look-alike Stearman NS trainer. Squadron Three (VN-3D8), observation land-planes, 10 percent of evaluation, placed students in intermediate training and into Vought O3U or SU Corsair observation scout planes, SBU-1 scout-bombers—all of the former were biplanes—and the North American NJ-1 or SNJ monoplane. Formation flying and navigation were emphasized in this phase as well as in Squadron Four (VN-4D8), advanced seaplanes, for 10 percent of the grade. Jimmy was pleased to see some of the large P2Ys similar to those he had flown in Hawaii transferred to Pensacola for pilot training along with the new Vought OS2U Kingfisher monoplane. He was especially gratified to be in position to impact aviators who could well appreciate the need for instructors with considerable fleet and squadron experience, having been ordered to Squadron Five (VN-5D8), advanced land-planes, the final 15 percent of a student's evaluation.

While the five phases remained in place through all of Jimmy's tour, significant changes in training were announced during his tenure reflecting the nation's response to the fighting in Europe and tensions in the Far East. The first matter addressed was expansion of the training program to procure more pilots. Less than a month after Hitler's invasion of Poland, the navy announced on 1 October that the training syllabus was being revised. The 465 ground-school hours were to be completed in eighteen weeks rather than thirty-three, and the overall training process was to be intensified for completion in six months rather than nine to twelve. Nine months later on 25 June 1940 the navy announced flight training was being expanded by assigning 150 candidates a month beginning 1 July, and was to be further expanded exactly one year later to 300 a month. In the year just prior to Jimmy's arrival at NAS Pensacola, 450 pilots had won their wings; and during his first full twelve months as an instructor another 708 successfully completed training. Projections for the following year called for over 3,000 (3,112 actual). While Jimmy and his fellow instructors contemplated how to absorb the new students, these announcements and number projections were particularly welcomed in the fleet. By the time the United States entered the war in December 1941, the pilot training program had expanded to 800 a month, and before the war ended as many as 2,500 were assigned.

For nearly all his Pensacola tour, Jimmy was directly involved training men to fly combat aircraft in addition to evaluating logistic and maintenance concerns. The 1 October 1939 revision to the syllabus affected Jimmy directly since the advanced program from that date separated student aviators into two groups: those assigned to patrol, utility, or observation aircraft and those assigned to combat types.[4] Seven months after he left Pensacola, the program became even more specialized when those selected for combat training were assigned to either fighters or to bomber-torpedo aircraft.

Upon reaching the final phase of training, a student aviator was taught special skills beginning with an intensive three-week course in instrument flying that included the Link blind-flying simulator and the

North American NJ and SNJ monoplanes. The fleet's first monoplane combat aircraft dating from 1937, the three-seat in-tandem Douglas TBD-1 Devastator, was flown in Squadron Five, as were the F4B-4 and F2F-1 biplane fighters. Jimmy's flight log quickly filled with hours, many monthly totals ranging from forty to sixty hours of flying. Nearly half his hours training students was recorded in the TBD and the other half in the F4B.

The TBD was easy to fly and was a very forgiving airplane. A major advancement in speed and technology when introduced to the fleet two years earlier, the sleek torpedo-bomber was obsolete before the United States entered World War II. So too was the F4B, but Jimmy's longtime favorite was the fighter most used in the final days of training student aviators in the late 1930s into 1940. The few hours a student and instructor dueled above the emerald green water and sugar white sands around Pensacola were all the individual combat hours a future fighter pilot experienced before going to the fleet. This, of course, placed somewhat of a burden on fighter squadrons, as it became the responsibility of squadron commanders and section leaders to continue training the neophyte until he could meet squadron proficiency standards. This practice was not adequately addressed until 28 July 1941 when the CNO directed establishment of "a continuing organization for training flight crews. The new policy was to . . . provide additional gunnery and tactical training . . . at Norfolk . . . and San Diego [so these] Advanced Carrier Training Groups . . . [could] indoctrinate newly designated Naval Aviators in the operation of current model carrier aircraft."[5]

Jimmy could not have known before the war that he would later be a part of the Advanced Carrier Training group at San Diego, nor could he have known how well his duties as an instructor in Squadron Five would translate into the development of student aviators. Instructor duty was—and is—teaching, and as years pass teachers have a tendency to forget the names and actions of their students. The only ones remembered well are those who were exceptional, either exceptionally good or exceptionally bad. One of several outstanding student aviators who received fighter instruction from Jimmy was later not only remembered but had an opportunity to do "graduate study" with his teacher. Jimmy first met Ens. Edward Henry "Butch" O'Hare in May 1940 when Butch was ready for individual combat training. In their Boeing F4Bs on 8 May each fought the other as well as several other opponents, but the tactical discussions on the ground and maneuvers in the air made that day and others to follow in the next two weeks memorable for both.[6] Jimmy was impressed with Butch's quick grasp of instructions, and Butch was impressed with Jimmy's experience and ability. Butch's grade for Squadron Five was his best for any of the training phases, and in Squadron Five he first demonstrated his later extraordinary aerial talents. Two years and two months later Butch repaid the tactical lessons learned from his former teacher with a new tactical lesson learned from a mutual friend.

A favorable educational experience Butch O'Hare and other student aviators carried away from their time with Jimmy Flatley was primarily based on Jimmy's ability to convey essential information in an effective and personable manner. In the words of Capt. Aubrey W. Fitch (later admiral), commandant at Pensacola, Jimmy was "a thoroughly capable officer, well rounded in aviation experience . . . [who] is vitally interested in aviation, studies his duties and executes them in a very efficient manner. He gets things done in a pleasant and quiet way."[7] Fitch also noted Jimmy's "pleasant personality, [and that he] creates a good impression."[8] The same attributes were noted later by Cdr. C. A. Nicholson, assembly and repair officer; and Fitch's successor, Capt. A. C. Read, who added comments regarding Jimmy's "courtesy . . . calm and sound judgment," and that he had "an excellent reputation among his associates."[9] From these official comments it may be deduced that Jimmy's "excellent reputation among his associates" was, in part, the result of the other attributes stated in his permanent records during his Pensacola stint.

Many experienced educators know that their own understanding of a discipline broadens when they teach. Jimmy's leadership experience at Pensacola was for the most part one-on-one, the best possible method for teaching. Such an experience, whether discussing tactics on the ground or executing them in the air, was very personal. Jimmy, and other officers, may or may not have understood all the ramifications of such an experience as it related to leadership of a group. If Jimmy had made the decision he would not have become an instructor at Pensacola. But the navy appreciated not only the benefits an experienced pilot like

Jimmy could bring to the training experience but also the value of the experience in further developing leadership qualities within the instructor. That not all officers acquired needed leadership qualities could not be blamed on the navy. The dynamics of personality are ever present and no matter how well intended the efforts of society, success in channeling behavior is never assured. In the end, an officer's conduct in training and in battle depended upon the degree of maturity and integrity developed within.[10]

Throughout 1940 the international situation continued to deteriorate, the Battle of Britain being one of very few bright lights of hope for democratic nations. The collapse of France and her neighbors in the spring propelled President Roosevelt and Congress to respond at an even more accelerated pace. While much of the new legislation was received with enthusiastic approval by navy personnel, appropriations and authorizations nonetheless signaled a justified state of alarm. Jimmy and other officers around him recognized that this legislation was not a long-sought redress of earlier requests for additional matériel and personnel but instead a response to looming peril.

As Paris braced for the arrival of German troops in June 1940, the 1938 Naval Expansion Act was revised to authorize more tonnage for aircraft carriers, an additional ten thousand planes, and the increase in naval aviation training noted above. A month later the Two-Ocean Navy Act was passed with additional carrier tonnage authorized and the number of planes increased to fifteen thousand. The first week in September the United States transferred fifty aging World War I destroyers to Britain in exchange for eight defensive bases, mostly in the Caribbean but stretching from Newfoundland to the northern coast of South America. Although the destroyers contributed to the Royal Navy's eventual success in the Battle of the Atlantic, the new bases eventually proved an equal value toward the same end. In September, Congress also passed the nation's first peacetime conscription law preparatory to drafting two million civilians for regular and reserve military service. While in no manner as momentous as the legislation passed during the year, a navy directive on 30 December to paint ship-based aircraft light gray erased any lingering hopes among naval aviators that the threat of war for the United States might pass.

NAS Jacksonville

With new carriers, planes, and personnel authorized in staggering numbers, it was apparent that the navy's infrastructure would have to expand, and rapidly. NAS Pensacola and the nearby subsidiary fields were enlarged in preparation for larger classes, but there was not enough space on the ground or in the air to handle all the men and planes scheduled for naval aviation. New training bases were needed, as had been foreseen in 1938 when the navy determined sixteen new air stations would be needed in case of war, and due to the favorable climate many were established in the South. In September Jimmy received orders to report to NAS Miami. Those orders were changed in October as the Bureau of Navigation requested the commandant (Read) at Pensacola to nominate ten officers for transfer to NAS Jacksonville to form a nucleus of instructors.

On 5 December 1940 Jimmy reported to Capt. Charles P. Mason, the commanding officer of the new installation, and his executive officer, Lt. Cdr. J. J. Clark. Again Jimmy had an assignment he didn't ask for, but he was in no way dissatisfied working for Captain Mason or Commander Clark. Despite Jimmy's being light years apart from Jocko in personality both were "all navy," both loved aviation, both had been fighter pilots; Clark knew he could depend on Jimmy—"my right-hand man"—and Jimmy was pleased that Jocko knew he could depend on him.[11] The new station had been commissioned only two weeks earlier and was still building. Clark had arrived only the day before, and there were no quarters on the station for Jimmy or his family. Then he and Clark discovered on their first day together that the required station regulations were nowhere near ready for the formal beginning of the station's training functions scheduled for 1 January 1941. Volunteering to help Jocko with this problem, Jimmy compiled, wrote, and edited the lengthy station regulations manual, "performing a colossal job in record time."[12] The manual covered everything from administration to aviation training, war plans to athletic programs, aviation assembly/repair to the issue of bicycles; and any question about the station activities that required an answer was to be entered in the manual. Captain Mason thought it could not be done, but no one was happier when Jocko and

Jimmy placed a finished copy on his desk on New Year's Eve. "Every page and every word was letter perfect, carefully proofread, without error. . . . A year later . . . these regulations were in full force with no modification.[13] Jimmy's reward was to be made station secretary and to have Captain Mason "strongly recommend" him for promotion.[14]

Both Jimmy and Jocko found Captain Mason an officer worthy of emulation. Mason was blessed with an incisive mind that rapidly absorbed details. After reviewing a problem, he stated what he wanted with quick and decisive orders. How to implement the orders were matters left to his subordinates. The system worked effectively because subordinates had a clear direction plus a vested interest. The vested interest was responsibility to get the job done. If it was done correctly, Captain Mason was generous with praise, and the wide latitude he gave to his subordinates facilitated a successful outcome. While Jimmy already knew the principles of this manner of leadership, Captain Mason's example was strong reinforcement of its value. Of course, there was the other side of the lesson. Jimmy learned from Jocko that the first executive officer to serve Captain Mason at Jacksonville did not take full advantage of the responsibility or latitude offered and was soon reassigned.[15]

While Jimmy was pleased to be a part of something new and significant, one word described the experience at Jacksonville: shortage! Jimmy and other officers did not expect a new station to have quarters for their families—no small consideration for Jimmy as his third son, Brian Anthony, was born 19 March 1941; but the shortages relative to training were frustrating. At Jacksonville Jimmy became increasingly involved in the engineering and logistics problems of a rapidly expanding navy. Jacksonville, like other new air stations, was not only training pilots but also aviation mechanics, radiomen, and ordnancemen. A pilot had no value if his plane could not fly, if no one knew how to load and care for the guns, bombs, and torpedoes, and if he could not effectively communicate before and during operations. But aviation mechanics, radiomen, and ordnancemen had little value if they had no tools or parts. Shortages occurred as a result of nonexistent stocks in addition to distribution problems. Early spring found the station's assembly and repair shop with six thousand spark plugs on hand that did not fit any of the aircraft on the station, but everyone realized these same plugs were no doubt needed elsewhere. To make matters worse, there was a major shortage of spark plugs for the engines that were in use at Jacksonville.[16]

After years of experience as an engineer as well as a pilot, Jimmy had a full appreciation for the fact new pilots and new planes required an infrastructure to keep them in the air. In this regard, Jimmy offered recommendations to the Bureau of Aeronautics that civilian representatives from major aircraft industries be assigned to naval air station assembly and repair shops. From Jimmy's point of view, this not only served the navy's interest but also that of industry as someone would be immediately available to ensure the correct use and maintenance of the company's product—as frequently occurred at Jacksonville when tachometers had to be returned to the factory for repair.[17]

Aircraft shortages were service-wide. On 1 July 1940 the navy had fewer planes than on the same date one year earlier including combat types (1,194 versus 2,098). The major reason was the transfer of planes to European nations, particularly new combat aircraft. More training hours for an expanding training program meant more hours on existing aircraft. When one crashed, the loss was doubly painful. Further, planes that did not crash were showing effects of the additional hours and were rapidly wearing out. Too often there were no spare engine or structural parts for the older planes. At Jacksonville, for reasons unknown to Jimmy or other pilots, the Stearman trainers were constantly ground looping to the right. Contributing factors could have been prevailing winds or problems with the newly paved runways; but regardless, nearly a dozen of these planes had broken lower-left wings. At one point early in the year three dozen aircraft of all types were grounded for lack of parts.[18]

One segment of Jimmy's duty at Jacksonville that suffered was flying time. For the ten months at Jacksonville from December 1940 into September 1941, Jimmy recorded only 121 hours compared to 583 hours through thirteen months in Pensacola. In April and May 1940 at Pensacola, he flew nearly the same number of hours (119) as in all his time at Jacksonville (121). During nine of thirteen months at Pensacola, he logged 25 hours or more, but only once during his Jacksonville tour did he top 25 hours in a month.

Not only were flying hours considerably fewer at Jacksonville, but the thrill of flying was also diminished. Instead of flying the nimble F4B fighter or even the TBD torpedo-bomber, Jimmy's Jacksonville assignment provided time mostly in utility transports. Only sixteen flying hours were logged in training flights emphasizing night flying, instrument flights, or testing; and many of these hours were recorded soon after arriving at the new station. Most of the remaining hours for the spring and summer of 1941 were administrative flights. The three aircraft in which Jimmy logged most of his hours were the SNJ, Grumman JRF Goose, and Beech JRB Expeditor. All three were monoplanes: the SNJ was a single-engine trainer often used as a two-man transport, while the JRF and JRB were twin-engine utility transports, the high-wing Grumman amphibian capable of accommodating ten—including crew—and the Beech, eight. Variations of the two utility transports were also used for instrument, gunnery, and aerial photography training. Although Jimmy had arrived at Jacksonville expecting to continue his instructor role, his value as an administrator placed him more often in the cabin flying from one meeting to another. Only once in this ten month period was he in the air for a "fighter pilot's joy ride." The Ryan NR-1, adopted by the U.S. Army Air Corps as the ST-3, was slow but highly maneuverable. Alone in the open cockpit of the two-man primary trainer, Jimmy ferried a new NR-1 from San Diego to Jacksonville from 21 through 26 August, a twenty-three-hour trip with several stops as well as several dives, loops, spins, barrel rolls, and snap rolls.

In early May, Jocko Clark received orders to become executive officer of *Yorktown*. There was only time for a quick goodbye, but both Jimmy and Jocko expected to see each other again. Things had gone well for both while contributing to the establishment of the new air station, and familiarity—especially in a successful relationship—would play a role in their next meeting.

Jimmy could not help but be pleased having been a part of the organizational period of the new air station. Being a new facility, there was much to do there; but there was a corollary satisfaction as accomplishments were highly visible and readily noted. When the CNO, Admiral Stark, visited on 5 June 1941, he was duly impressed with the progress of development and operations. Captain Mason, noting Jimmy's affable personality, tact, and courtesy with the CNO, his staff, and other dignitaries who visited the station, thought Jimmy well qualified for duty as a flag lieutenant or aide.[19] Although pleased with Captain Mason's complimentary observation, Jimmy quietly hoped no one would ever act on this particular thought.

On completing the preference section of his March 1941 fitness report, he listed his first choice as commanding officer of an AVP (small seaplane tender) to help broaden his naval aviation experience. But by summer the international situation was getting worse. War involving the United States was only a question of time, and if he was going to get shot at he did not want to be on a small seaplane tender or in a patrol plane. He wanted to be in something that would allow him to shoot back with at least even odds, and that desire brought him back to what he knew best—fighters. The one-on-one leadership experience at Pensacola, plus the broader administrative and engineering duty at Jacksonville, supplemented an expanding foundation for additional responsibility. Sooner than expected the sum of his leadership evolution and development would be put to the ultimate test.

4

Pearl Harbor

THROUGHOUT JIMMY'S duty at Jacksonville, a day did not pass when conversation at work or home did not touch on the war in Europe. At work, considerations of the war interrelated with the training mission. At home, Jeanette offered a more personal perspective, easily appreciated by Jimmy and Dotty having recently lived there themselves. On 11 March 1941 the Lend Lease Act was signed. On 21 May the *Robin Moor*, an unarmed American merchant ship, was lost to a U-boat in the South Atlantic, and on 27 May President Roosevelt proclaimed an unlimited national emergency. Surprise greeted the German invasion of the Soviet Union on 22 June, but attention quickly returned to the Atlantic on 4 September when the USS *Greer* (DD-145) was attacked (no damage) by a U-boat she was tracking.

Jimmy's attention was still on Europe and the Atlantic on 20 September when he left Jacksonville for his next assignment as executive officer of Fighting Squadron Two (VF-2) attached to *Lexington*. Reporting for duty with VF-2 in San Diego on 29 September, his preoccupation and familiarity with Europe—complemented by overwhelming media coverage of the European war relative to coverage of Asian problems—

was quickly diverted. Attention now was directed not only to the new responsibilities with VF-2, but also to threats of war with Japan. In San Diego and aboard *Lexington,* Europe was a concern, but Asia dominated thought and conversation.

Problems with Japan dated from just before Jimmy's birth. The United States had relieved Spain of her imperial burden as a result of the 1898 Spanish-American War and in so doing, took possession of the Philippines. Initially, this posed only a potential rivalry in the western Pacific, but succeeding events contributed to this foundation of contention between the future World War II antagonists. In August 1905 the Japanese were not at all pleased with the compromises President Theodore Roosevelt hammered out to help end the Russo-Japanese War. Leaving the deliberations at Portsmouth, New Hampshire, the Japanese felt they had given up too much already won in battle. Shortly afterward many West Coast residents demanded restrictions on nonwhite immigration, and the San Francisco school board announced it would not accept Oriental students. A lingering perception of Japan's inferiority was formalized with the five to five to three ratio (United States, Great Britain, Japan) agreed upon in the 1922 Washington Naval Treaty. But Japan had plans for expansion. In 1931 the Japanese moved into Manchuria, having previously obtained rights to the Marshall Islands, Carolines, Marianas, and other former Pacific holdings of Germany, as a result of the Treaty of Versailles, which ended World War I. Struggling with the effects of the Great Depression, the Western world could do little more than register verbal and written protests.

The Japanese response to diplomatic objections to their vision of a Greater East Asia Co-prosperity Sphere was withdrawal in 1936 from the League of Nations and from the Washington and London naval treaties. Soon after Japan signed the Anti-Comintern Pact with Germany in November 1936, the protracted conflict between China and Japan developed into open war in 1937. Hoping the presence of battleships would complement ever-stronger diplomatic overtures, President Roosevelt ordered the U.S. Fleet to base at Pearl Harbor in May 1940. This action—in conjunction with the July 1940 Export Control Act that prohibited export of petroleum products, scrap metals, and other items

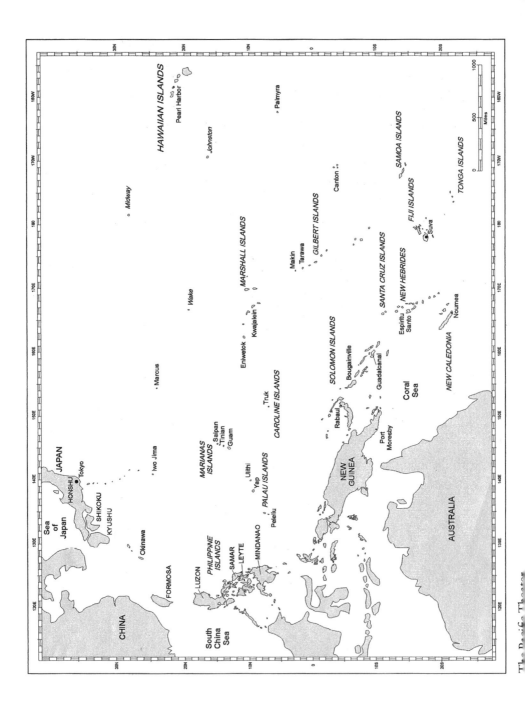

The Pacific Theater

outside the Americas and Great Britain, was interpreted in Japan as belligerency with a resultant rigidity of diplomatic stance. In June 1941 the United States froze German and Italian assets, and when the same action was taken against the Japanese on 25 July 1941, it effectively cut off nearly 90 percent of Japan's oil importation. This was essentially a declaration of war for Japan. While the drift toward the war in the Pacific was a protracted and complicated process that most certainly would have eventuated without the July embargo, the immediate deprivation of "black blood" and other strategic imports left the Land of the Rising Sun with only two choices: submission or war.

For a number of years, students at the Japanese Naval Academy had been assigned a theoretical problem how to plan an attack on Pearl Harbor. By the winter of 1941 the problem was still theoretical, but instead of Eta Jima midshipmen, selected personnel in the First Air Fleet of the Imperial Japanese Navy began studying the possibility of an attack on the Pacific Fleet. After the July embargo the study passed from the theoretical stage to a testing phase in war games and aerial exercises. By October operational planning began, a date was set, and on 5 November 1941 "Combined Fleet Top Secret Operation Order Number One" was released to those who would participate in the strike.

At Pearl Harbor and throughout the Pacific, naval commanders hoped for every day of peace that diplomacy could bring. Despite glowing publicity acclaiming the strength of the U.S. Navy in the fall of 1941 (*Life* magazines from the period are especially illuminating), those responsible for preparing the service for war knew the navy had only nine fighter squadrons to place aboard seven aircraft carriers (*Hornet* was commissioned on 20 October 1941).[1] The Marine Corps had four fighter squadrons. The new Grumman F4F Wildcat was in service with most of the carrier fighter squadrons but not Jimmy's VF-2. Fighting Squadron Six aboard *Enterprise* received Wildcats in May 1941 and was the only Pacific-based carrier with a full complement of the new fighter before the war. *Saratoga*'s VF-3, based at San Diego in the waning days of peace in the Pacific, had only fourteen Wildcats the first week of December 1941.

Fighting Squadron Two

Jimmy could not devote much mental energy to concerns about the Japanese as he had his hands full worrying about his family's move to California. He was familiarizing himself with a fighter not new to carrier aviation but new to him, and he was preparing for his most important leadership role to this point in his naval career. Dotty, like many navy wives, took charge of finding a house to rent and with Jeanette's assistance performed all the big and little chores necessary to transform it into a home. Wasting no time, Jimmy was aloft on his second day at San Diego in an F2A-3 Brewster Buffalo for a one-hour familiarization flight. *Lexington* was at Bremerton, Washington, for normal upkeep and not due back in San Diego until 11 October. On 14 October she was scheduled to steam to Pearl Harbor.

Jimmy was quite familiar with *Lexington*, having served aboard her earlier for lengthy periods. He was also familiar with VF-2, which had served alongside his old Fighting Squadron Five-B at San Diego and aboard CV-2. Fighting Squadron Two was the navy's highly regarded "enlisted man's" squadron. Competition to become a pilot from the enlisted ranks was fierce with only the best achieving a coveted place in VF-2. Once assigned to the squadron, pressure was ever present to prove worthiness, and throughout the squadron's existence the enlisted pilots demonstrated proficiency both respected and admired.

After Congress authorized the command structure in 1926, VF-2's enlisted pilots were always led by regular officers at the squadron, executive officer, and division levels. A squadron of eighteen planes was divided into three divisions under the squadron commander, the executive officer, and the flight officer. Each division was comprised of three sections. In a combat situation one division (a total of six planes) served as combat air patrol (CAP). Throughout World War II squadrons continued to be organized by squadron, divisions, and sections although numbers changed.[2] It had been known for a year that the fighter complement for squadrons serving aboard *Lexington*, *Saratoga*, *Yorktown*, and *Enterprise* would rise to twenty-seven upon completion of the contract deliveries of the Brewster F2A-3s and Grumman F4F-3s. The complement for *Ranger* and *Wasp* would remain eighteen.[3] Based on personnel estimates the target date for the increase was October 1941, but when Jimmy reported to *Lexington,* VF-2 was still operating only eighteen fighters.[4]

As his experience in fighters had been in biplanes, Jimmy took some good-natured ribbing from several pilots after his one-hour familiarization flight in the F2A-3. Some of the pilots were only too anxious to tell him how everyone from the squadron to the Bureau of Aeronautics fretted over the loss in efficiency the previous year when the squadron shifted from their Grumman F2F-1 biplanes to the new monoplane. The commander of Carrier Division One, Rear Adm. Aubrey Fitch, informed the Bureau of Aeronautics on 1 January 1941 that initial estimates indicated that the pilots of VF-2 would require one hundred hours to familiarize themselves with the Buffalo, particular problems being the much heavier weight and higher performance. From the beginning, pilots were also concerned with engineering and ordnance difficulties—all F2A-2s had been grounded in December 1940 due to engine failures after only a two-week period of limited operations. Compounding the general consternation was an acute shortage of .50-caliber ammunition that restricted actual gunnery training.[5] A year later not all the early problems had gone away, plus there were new problems with the more recent F2A-3 model. And now these problems were Jimmy's problems.

Jimmy had reached the highest plateau of his career to date as executive officer, but the promotion carried heavy responsibility. Many of the burdens were more quantitative than qualitative: there were more men to supervise, more papers to read, more reports to write. In many respects, no position is more difficult than that of an executive officer since every squadron member's problem became the problem of the XO. Ultimate responsibility for the squadron belonged to the commanding officer, but many of the CO's problems could be, and often were, delegated to an XO. Still, at age thirty-five, Jimmy, who wanted to be a leader, relished the opportunity. Jimmy appraised the challenge to Dotty: "If I am going to be a good squadron leader I must do everything better than anybody else."[6]

In addition to the flight division and section hierarchy, there was also a hierarchy on the ground. Department heads were appointed for engineering, material, navigation, communications, and flight, each department having an organizational structure and specific duties. Jimmy requested the department heads to carefully choose words for their general statements pertaining to respective responsibilities so that the documents could assist future members of the squadron. Considering the final product more important than the method used for its production, he encouraged consultation among the departments and squadrons.[7]

Logs, correspondence, inventories, maintenance forms, and records (especially serial numbers) always required particular attention aboard ship; and Jimmy's responsibility, like that of other XOs, was to ensure that all work was successfully completed. When not aboard ship, Jimmy also had to direct the crew in doing shoreside tasks: there were buildings and grounds to care for (even the return of coke bottles to empty racks), and whether aboard ship or ashore, the planes required extensive attention, right down to the placement of drip pans. As many items were in short supply, especially parachutes, everybody had to sign for everything. Daily schedules were always full; and when flight operations were heavy, always needed navigation, homing, radio, instruments, blinkers, Link trainer, and other training exercises were postponed.

In handling the complex responsibilities of being an XO, the keys to success were held by the XO himself. They could also be found in the leadership capabilities of the squadron commanding officer, and as a CO, Jimmy could not have found a better man to work for than Cdr. Paul H. Ramsey.

Jimmy and his commanding officer, an Ohio native, had never served together though each had similar career assignments. A 1927 Naval Academy graduate, the tall athletic Ramsey had assumed command of VF-2 in May 1941. Earlier he had served in Fighter Squadrons Three and Six aboard *Lexington* and *Saratoga,* respectively. Competent as a pilot and administrator, Ramsey possessed a personality that enabled him to give orders and instructions in a manner that left an impression he was doing others a favor by allowing them to accomplish his directives.[8] "He's a d— good leader and an excellent flyer," Jimmy wrote to Dotty soon after joining the squadron, adding shortly thereafter, "what I think of Ramsey keeps mounting every day . . . [and] he has the courage of his convictions." Ramsey rose to the rank of vice admiral in 1963, indicating that others in addition to Jimmy obviously thought, "He's splendid."[9]

The busy schedule of daily duties ashore was directed to the ultimate purpose of flying. Rather than being a joy for pilots to fly, the F2A-3 Buffalo required great exertion. The earlier F2A-1 (most transferred to Finland) and F2A-2 models provided better performance than the F2A-3. The latter had heavier self-sealing fuel tanks. There were forty gallons in the fuselage tank and two twenty-gallon tanks in the leading wing edge. The main wing tanks were unprotected for the remaining eighty gallons—and there was protective armor for the pilot. The value of both became apparent early in the European war. Whether the additional weight could have been offset by a more powerful engine than the Wright twelve-hundred horsepower R-1820-40 was a moot point since the stubby F2A-3's airframe design was restrictive. Further, the additional weight often contributed to landing gear failure and blown tires.[10]

Engine problems in the Buffalo required special attention. Problems causing engine failure in the first planes delivered to the squadron had been identified, but some could only be controlled rather than fixed. For instance, a pilot had to remember that a manifold pressure greater than twenty-four inches up to two thousand feet with fifteen hundred revolutions per minute would take too much power and could damage the engine. Cylinder head temperature had to be constantly monitored (stay below 200 degrees Celsius), and propeller control had to be altered before landing or going into a dive. Further, a pilot could not forget to use outside air when at full throttle, taking off, or landing; but he must use protected air (inside air, similar to reciprocating air on an automobile air conditioner) whenever flying in fog, clouds, rain, or whenever the dew point and the temperature were within five degrees of each other. If an F2A-3 carburetor iced up, it could not be cleared and a forced landing resulted.[11]

Approaching aerial combat, the pilot had to address all the mechanical concerns in addition to charging the four .50-caliber guns (two in the fuselage, two in the wings), releasing carbon dioxide into the unprotected main wing tanks, and ensuring that fuel pressure did not rise too high. The pilot had to complete the mental tasks simultaneously with squadron, division, and section tactics while he was observing the approach and tactics of the enemy. Obviously, there was no time for any extraneous thoughts, including patriotism. Fear was a death sentence.

Countdown to Pearl

In September the Flatley family moved into a small rental on G Avenue in Coronado, near the air station, and Jimmy stayed with them for the first two weeks VF-2 was ashore. After a second familiarization flight on 1 October, Jimmy took his place as leader of the second division and recorded nearly fourteen hours in the F2A-3. During those first two weeks the squadron concentrated on night tactics and field carrier-landing practice (FCLP). But just as the family was getting settled, *Lexington* and VF-2 sailed for Hawaii on 14 October as scheduled. Jimmy immediately thought he had made a mistake moving to San Diego rather than Hawaii.[12] Dotty and the family remained in their Coronado rental.

Jimmy was a prolific letter writer and during the following months, wrote detailed letters to Dotty about the 14 to 22 October trip to Hawaii and *Lexington*'s activities in Hawaiian waters. At sea on 14 October Jimmy wrote Dotty, "I awoke today with a very heavy heart. Leaving you last night to walk out of our family life, so wonderful to us both, was the hardest thing I've ever done." Knowing *Lexington* would be in Hawaiian waters for nearly six months and that they would be separated until 1 April 1942, he wrote from *Lexington* on the twenty-second, "Don't ever lose hope dear heart, you can't tell when we might pop up." In nine years of marriage neither love nor passion had diminished. In a constant stream of letters the dominant theme was perhaps best expressed in a 23 October letter: "Sweetheart, another day without you. Life is very bitter."

Jimmy and Dotty attempted to make plans for her to come to Hawaii for a two-week visit around Christmas, the three "rascals" remaining in Coronado with Jeanette. Ramsey was also attempting to arrange for his wife to visit. A first concern for both Jimmy and Paul was to find two places for their wives to rent for their visits, as the time of their visits probably would not coincide. Separation, an inherent problem in navy marriages, contributed to a number of family problems. Emotional separation topped the list, followed by the financial problems that occurred when one partner received bills while the other had the checkbook, so it was not a complete surprise that soon after Jimmy arrived in Hawaii, Dotty informed him that yet another navy couple close to them was splitting up. Jimmy responded he was sorry to hear the news and wrote, "As far as I know the husbands out here tread the straight and narrow. I suppose the enforced separation will result in lots of divorces. Almost daily one of the men asked for a transfer because his wife is going to leave him if he don't [*sic*] get back."[13]

Finding a rental house in and around Honolulu and Pearl Harbor was almost impossible in the fall of 1941. "So far no one on this ship has found a house," Jimmy wrote in an October letter, and after investigating further he later wrote Dotty to tell her "it would be financial suicide to have a home out here." Through a friend, Lt. Lance E. "Lem" Massey (USNA 1930) who had made the voyage to Hawaii aboard *Lexington* en route to his next assignment on *Enterprise,* Jimmy learned a house was being vacated and would rent for $100 a month.[14] That was big money for an officer making $230 a month plus $110 for flight pay. Hopefully, something could be found for $75 to $80 a month. And Jimmy fully expected to be on the November promotion list; the increase in pay for a lieutenant commander being most welcome. In the meantime, a single phone call ($37.60) and many letters ("all the 3 cents variety but each one worth a million dollars") had to suffice.[15]

Following *Lexington's* departure for Pearl Harbor on 14 October, Jimmy had settled into a single stateroom, a privilege signaling his rise to a leadership position. On the fifteenth he was piloting his aircraft above the Pacific to test a radio innovation and refresh his navigation. Jimmy led his division from sight of the carrier a distance of 125 miles and back, repeating the flight six times without incident and impressing his pilots with his navigating skill. But real respect came when he was able to "attack" *Lexington* before Ramsey's division could intercept— and then successfully "defend" the carrier with his and Ramsey's positions reversed.[16]

Flying mornings and afternoons during the cruise to Hawaii, the squadron made good use of the time, emphasizing tactics and aerial gunnery. But there was also time for relaxation. After the evening meal, a movie was shown on the hangar deck, "which helps a whole lot," and one evening, the seventeenth, Jimmy and a small group of pilots joined the carrier's commanding officer, Capt. (later admiral) Frederick C. "Ted" Sherman, for dinner. Sherman "likes to hold the floor and is very opinionated," Jimmy wrote to Dotty, but "he's a good captain."[17] By 1943, Jimmy and Ted Sherman had become close professional colleagues; then after the war and Sherman's 1947 retirement, the two became good personal friends. Upon Sherman's death in 1957 his widow forwarded her late husband's baseball-type cap, which he had worn during many months in combat, to Jimmy as a present.

On Sunday 19 October *Lexington* returned to Pearl Harbor, but on the twenty-third the carrier and squadron were back at sea for another week. The last day and night in port Jimmy had the duty as watch officer, "not much to it . . . just be aboard to represent the squadrons." Going back to sea was welcome, however, because

> the paperwork is eliminated. . . . In port it piles up very high . . . about 50 admirals out here and they all write at least a blast a day. . . . From the looks of our operating schedule none of us will have any time for anything except work . . . its tough and I'm not fooling . . . [but] I'm very much pleased with the ship as a whole. I believe (Ramsey and I) will have the best fighting squadron in the fleet. Fighters have taken on tremendous importance in naval operations. Naturally our performance is closely watched and I am sure we will measure up.[18]

Rain interrupted flying operations on more than one occasion between 23 October and 1 November when *Lexington* again returned to Pearl. Lost flying time was converted into navigation problems and conferences on future exercises. Saturday 25 October, however, was a particularly frustrating day. "A hectic day: nothing went right . . . up at 0430 [and] took [to] the air at 1330. In between times we just sat around in a daze." But Jimmy also reported, "VF-2 is doing a very nice job of flying on and off the carrier . . . I think that in a month or two no one will be able to touch us.[19]

At the same time Jimmy was having his frustrating day of 25 October—six large aircraft carriers, two battleships, two heavy cruisers, one light cruiser, eleven destroyers, and eighteen tankers and supply ships were assembling in Japan for a dress rehearsal for the Hawaii operation. Two weeks later the armada began moving toward Hitokappu Bay off Etorofu Island in the Kuriles.

Although *Lexington* stayed at sea for a week, the pilots often returned to Pearl for lunch and fuel before continuing their daily exercises. For a fighter pilot Jimmy took special delight in bombing exercises: "It's really a thrill to come zipping down in a dive at 400 mph." Diving on the old battleship *Utah*, which served as a target ship, Jimmy got two hits with his four practice bombs: Ramsey went four for four.[20] Doctrine was very explicit as to the defense function of the fighter, and fighters of VF-2 had a standing order in case of war not to even attempt a strafing run on a ship unless specifically ordered to do so.[21]

On 28 October Jimmy wrote Dotty, "Our planes are really the stuff," but less than a month later he sang a different tune. "Darling, am I mad! After all our very serious work on the landing gear, Paul went out with 12 planes for night carrier landings and only came back with nine. One hit the barrier . . . which is a crash landing and the other two blew tires. All three of the missing planes were piloted by our officers."[22]

On 22 November, the day Dotty received Jimmy's letter expressing his concerns about VF-2's planes and downed pilots, the last of six Japanese carriers arrived in Hitokappu Bay in preparation for their sortie to Hawaii if a diplomatic solution was not achieved by 29 November.

On Thursday 20 November *Lexington* left Pearl for sea. Jimmy wrote, "We stay aboard for several days, a fleet exercise or something," but the ship was back in time for Jimmy and the crew to listen to the Army-Navy game on Saturday the twenty-ninth.[23] Jimmy noticed that *Enterprise,* the only other carrier then operating out of Pearl, was gone. But he did not know her mission was to carry a dozen Marine Corps fighters of VMF-211 to Wake Island, nor did he know Vice Adm. William F. Halsey had issued Battle Order Number One to the crew aboard "The Big E."

Two days earlier six Japanese carriers—*Akagi, Kaga, Hiryu, Soryu, Shokaku,* and *Zuikaku*—had steamed from their Hitokappu Bay rendezvous into the open sea. Aboard the carriers were 135 dive-bombers, 140 torpedo bombers, and 81 fighters.

Although Halsey anticipated possible combat with the Japanese,

Jimmy and other personnel attached to *Lexington* were concerned but not ready for hostilities. None of Jimmy's many and lengthy letters to his wife mentioned anything about Japan until 4 November when he wrote, "The Jap situation seems to get no better but I don't think they've got the guts to fight us . . . they couldn't win." While considering Dotty's travel plans to Hawaii, he wrote on the eighth, "Should know in a week about our little yellow friends in Japan," and after Dotty set a tentative date for the first week in January he responded, "Of course it all hinges on the Jap crisis. The little yellow devils. We will wipe them up so fast they won't know what hit them." But in his next letter on the eighteenth, he was more objective, "I still want you to plan to come barring war with Japan." On Sunday 30 November he was even more objective, writing, "Things look pretty grim this morning. However, I think the Japs will back down. Certainly hope so."

On that same Sunday, the Pearl Harbor Striking Force was over halfway to their destination. Although the order to execute the attack was not received until 2 December ("Climb Mt. Niitaka"), the force proceeded with stealth through rough seas to a point eight hundred miles north of Oahu where the ships were to refuel. Turning south the carriers would race through a late autumn night to within two hundred miles of Oahu, the carrier planes launching just before the first glow of 7 December's daylight.

On Wednesday 4 December Jimmy wrote Dotty to tell her he was looking forward to playing golf on Friday, bad weather was delaying Clipper flights, *Saratoga* was expected in Pearl on Friday the twelfth, and the Matson liner *Lurline* had arrived that day. *Lurline* just might be the ship that would bring her to Hawaii on the new target date of 31 January 1942, a medical procedure delaying her earlier arrival. Personal news written he continued with his concerns of war. "I don't think the Japs can afford to go to war with us. We have everything they need if they will play ball. Just so we get to stay in the Pacific. They [Atlantic Fleet] are already at war in the Atlantic. They say it's really grim over there." The next day Jimmy's Friday golf game was postponed as he wrote, "We are sitting here waiting for word to take off for the carrier . . . I hope the Jap situation clears up today . . . this is the day Japan replies."

Aboard *Lexington,* Jimmy stood on the flight deck and examined the eight Vought SB2U-3 Vindicator scout bombers of Marine Scouting Squadron 231 (VMSB-231) the carrier was transporting toward Midway Island. *Lexington* had sailed from Hawaii with Task Force Twelve on Thursday the fifth. But despite the circumstance, Jimmy was not overly apprehensive. He did not stand on the flight deck thinking he might not return or that things would be any different when he did. For all his written comments from 4 November through 5 December concerning Japan, one sentence in the letter to his wife on 5 December revealed his true perception of the near future: "Get your operation after 1 January and then make reservations."

War

Lexington was two days outbound from Pearl Harbor when Japanese planes began their infamous attack on 7 December. As unwarned men died, moored battleships sank, and parked planes burned, *Lexington* received word to abort her voyage to Midway Island, retain the Marine planes on board, and search for the enemy. After having been aloft for 2.7 hours on combat air patrol above his floating home, Jimmy returned aboard the carrier that day too tired and preoccupied to write Dotty. The following day, however, he poured out his thoughts and feelings in a letter, part of which follows.

> At Sea, Dec. 8, 1941
>
> My dearest Sweetheart,
> You have been my one and only thought since word of the war reached me yesterday a.m. Poor darling, all by yourself without any information except rumors. And we heard over our radios that CBS had announced the *Lexington* as lost. Well we aren't lost. We just aren't there but we will be, and I hope the Japs haven't gotten away before we get a crack at them. . . . Right now I have a feeling that the Lex will come through this thing with flying colors, but we're bound to lose a few pilots. . . . You can rest assured that they will not have gotten me before I get 3 or 4 of them. . . . I've asked my guardian angel to keep a sharp lookout astern at all times.

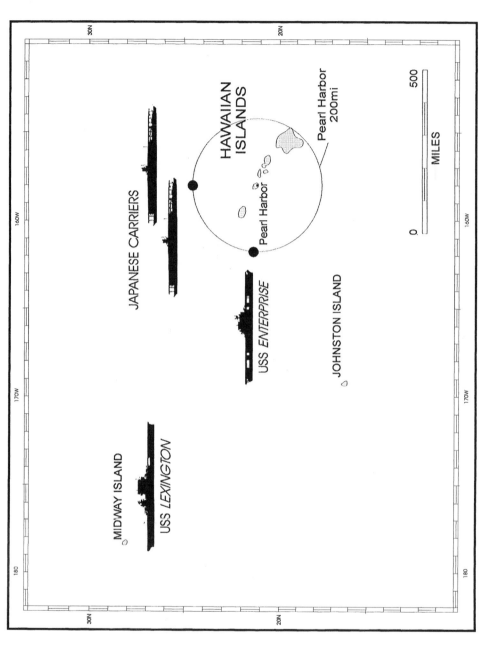

Carrier Locations, 7 December 1941

Letters containing similar information were not possible in the future as wartime censorship was soon in place. Even all previous one-letter signals used by carrier planes to signal each other were changed on 24 December.

On 8 December Jimmy was on combat air patrol for 6.7 hours. *Lexington* and *Enterprise* were looking for the enemy carriers, but both were looking south of the carriers' retreat. What little information there was indicating the true direction the Japanese carriers had taken was overwhelmed by the long-held belief that any such attack would have to come from the enemy-held Marshall Islands to the southwest. It was also believed the northern route actually used would have presented too many logistical and weather problems. However, the search in the wrong direction for the Japanese was a blessing of the first magnitude: had the two U.S. carriers found the Japanese, undoubtedly the Japanese would have sunk the Americans. Only 29 of the 360 enemy planes were lost to all causes in the Pearl Harbor operation, which later appraisals from both sides confirmed. Several *Enterprise* planes had flown into the fight above Pearl and some were lost. Aboard *Lexington* there were deck problems that would have presented a challenge even in peacetime. With only two relatively small, slow elevators—thirty-four seconds one way compared to thirteen seconds on later *Essex*-class carriers—on *Lexington* (and her sister ship *Saratoga*), planes scheduled for operations usually were not stowed in the hangar to save time.[24] Canvas covers were placed over the planes to afford some corrosion protection from the salt air while heavy planks were inserted into the flight deck forward as a windbreak. Battens were placed to secure controls and prevent damage to planes when the wind shifted, and lines secured the aircraft to eyebolts in the deck. And the presence of eighteen additional planes, although welcome for the added firepower, presented an even greater challenge than the usual placement and movement of aircraft for launching and landing operations. It was little wonder, then, that some launches on 7 December were made over the stern.

Had all the deck problems been overcome on *Lexington* and had *Lexington* and *Enterprise* found the Japanese carriers, both might well have been lost. Not only were the two U.S. carriers outnumbered better than two to one in planes, the qualitative differences of the aircraft were not then known. Six months later at Midway a squadron of Brewster F2As encountered the Japanese Mitsubishi A6M2 Zero and was annihilated. So too were the obsolete SB2U Vindicator's and the TBD Devastators. The only Wildcats available and operational on the two carriers on 7–8 December were the fourteen on *Enterprise,* and these could not have defended their own carrier much less have protected a strike group, *Lexington,* or the cruisers and destroyers steaming with the respective carriers.[25]

The VF-2 operating procedures written by Ramsey and practiced by the squadron offer some insight as to what probably would have happened had the F2A-3s met Japanese planes in combat immediately after Pearl Harbor. The squadron's combat air patrol doctrine was to "destroy enemy aircraft . . . our greatest value is in preventing attacks from reaching our ship." Such defense required VF-2's fighters to first attack heavy planes as fighters could do relatively little damage to a capital ship. Provision was made in the doctrine for "scram" takeoffs (in which first pilots to the flight deck get into whatever fighters are ready, launch, and take command until division and section leaders are aloft). Using the sun to obscure the enemy's vision, pilots were to limit ammunition in firing passes and to stay with section leaders. But it was expected that after each firing run, no matter from what direction it had begun, the sections would reform *out ahead of the enemy* and then attack again. One can only imagine the shock Paul Ramsey, Jimmy Flatley, and all other VF-2 pilots would have felt when discovering the Japanese heavy planes were nearly as fast as their own fighters. Two months later the commanding officer of VF-6, Lt. Cdr. Wade McClusky, had exactly this experience during the first raid on the Marshall Islands when his Wildcat could not catch up to enemy bombers. United States Navy fighter squadron experience against other squadrons and U.S. Army Air Force planes had been good practice, but it was not good enough to defeat the better-than-expected Japanese. Doctrine and tactics would have to change.

Numerous false alarms and sightings punctuated searches for the enemy in the first week after the assault on Pearl, and on 13 December *Lexington* returned to the wounded base. Despite ongoing serious problems with landing struts on the Brewsters, Jimmy and the other pilots of VF-2 flew onto Ford Island with the added weight of two 100-pound bombs. The view of the harbor and its smell were equally sickening, and instead of treasuring the time ashore the pilots were only too happy to return to sea on the fourteenth as part of new Task Force Eleven.[26] Task Force Eleven, comprised of *Lexington,* three heavy cruisers, an oiler, and nine destroyers headed for Jaluit Island in the Marshalls for a diversionary raid to draw attention from the Wake Island relief force (Task Force Fourteen). Wake Island was putting up fierce and effective resistance against a Japanese invasion force, but when two enemy carriers (*Hiryu* and *Soryu*) left the other Pearl Harbor raiders to join that fight, the balance tipped. Wake fell just before Christmas, leaving no purpose worthy of the risk for the U.S. task forces. In a spirit of the crews' dejection, *Lexington* and all other American ships reversed course for Pearl.

For Jimmy's remaining days with VF-2 there were more false alarms of submarines, more problems with the F2A-3s, and more groping at sea for an elusive enemy. But the VF-2 roster of pilots of which Jimmy was executive officer was destined never to find or fight the enemy.

On 19 December the squadron posed for pictures with twenty-one of twenty-two pilots present. It was just as well that none could see the future, as six of the twenty-two were dead in less than nine months and a seventh, four months later. But those pictured also accounted for thirty-five enemy planes by war's end. The pilots of Fighting Squadron Two proved to be as good as everyone thought they would be.

New Rank, New Fighter, and New Orders

On 2 January 1942 Jimmy's promotion to lieutenant commander became official along with promotions announced for many others on the same date.[27] The new gold leaf insignia was welcome, as was a new fighter, the Grumman F4F-3A Wildcat. Although neither VF-3 nor VF-6 was at full strength, VF-2 began trading in their Brewsters on 26 January for the Wildcats. All of Jimmy's 32.5 hours in January were in the F2A-3, his familiarization flight in the Wildcat lasting one hour on 1 February.

Jimmy was pleased to be transferring to the Wildcat, but the delay in acquiring enough of them to equip the full squadron required time, as did familiarization and training. In the meantime, VF-3 replaced VF-2 aboard *Lexington.* Fighting Squadron Three was available because a Japanese submarine had placed a torpedo into the port side of *Saratoga* on 11 January 1942. Although refitted only four months previous, the damage required *Saratoga*'s return to Bremerton for full repairs and modernization. Sorely missed for over four months, the big carrier was unavailable in May for the Battle of the Coral Sea and returned too late for combat in the Battle of Midway in June.

While *Lexington,* with VF-3 aboard, steamed off to the southwest Pacific and combat, VF-2 got acquainted with their new mounts. The marines of VMF-111 formerly flew most of the Wildcats transferred to VF-2 and of the first eleven, ten were F4F-3As that were not quite equal to the overall performance of the F4F-3. The other Wildcat was the sole experimental XF4F-4, different by virtue of its folding wings that allowed many more fighters to be stowed in carrier hangar bays.[28] Jimmy recorded his first hours in an F4F-3A, but then latched onto the XF4F-4. Most Wildcats then scheduled for the fleet were F4F-4s, and Jimmy correctly determined this was the type of aircraft he would most likely have to take into future combat.

When *Saratoga* departed Pearl for Bremerton on 9 February, Jimmy plus two officers and seven NAPs flew aboard in their Wildcats to help the scout bombers of VS-3 and four destroyers defend the carrier. He just missed making the fifty-nine thousandth landing aboard, but he nonetheless enjoyed his share of Chief Gordon Firebaugh's cake, baked for the occasion, as Jimmy smiled broadly for pictures snapped during the small ceremony. Happily, the voyage proved uneventful, and on the fifteenth, Jimmy and the other pilots of the VF-2 Detachment flew to NAS Seattle before flying on down the West Coast to NAS Alameda and finally to NAS San Diego. There the detachment assumed temporary duty with the Advanced Carrier Training Group from 16 February until May when *Saratoga* would need them to cover her return to Hawaii. Before that scenario played out, however, Jimmy had new orders and passed command of the detachment over to Lt. Louis H. Bauer on 27 March.

Although Jimmy had only a few weeks in San Diego, it was a most pleasant bonus. The move to San Diego from Jacksonville had not been a mistake after all. Every hour spent with the family was treasured, and for once, Jimmy had some success in leaving the mental aspects of his job on the air station. Beginning with his 1933 marriage, Jimmy had attempted not to burden Dotty with the difficulties of his duty. He had always brought thoughts of his duties home with him, and he shared many of them with his wife at appropriate moments. But in late February and all of March 1942 his life at home was filled with football, baseball, and wrestling with the three rascals—plus conversations with Dotty on anything but the war.

End of the Apprentice Period

Personal Development

Just as a human being crawls before learning how to walk, Jimmy Flatley had to learn how to become a leader. Toward the end of his career he wrote that leaders were not born.[29] His apprenticeship to become a leader began informally in the home as the oldest of six siblings. This process of learning was more fun than challenge as he enjoyed playing with, protecting, and teaching three sisters and two brothers how to walk, talk, play, hold a fork, button or tie their shoes, and every other endeavor youngsters needed or desired to learn. Rewards for being a good brother were the result of his intrinsic interest although parental appreciation included some extrinsic as well as intrinsic laurels. Jimmy attended parochial schools, where expectations were proclaimed daily and failure to comply brought swift, harsh, and consistent punishment. At home and at school, Jimmy's innate attributes merged with his formal train-ing, all helping to develop his personality. Later at the Naval Academy, where the essence of Jimmy's experience was to develop leadership, he began to learn how to lead others by meeting criteria in a highly struc-tured program that allowed for graduated responsibility.

In learning to be a leader Jimmy, like so many others, first had to know his own direction, but the path he walked from adolescence to age twenty-six was neither straight nor fully understood. His indulgence in and exuberance for some of life's forbidden fruits can be attributed in part to fears generated during his protracted confinement with the hip injury. The confluence of several personal problems in 1932 impacted on his nascent naval career, and the influence of mentors during that difficult time played no small role in Jimmy's transition from protracted adolescence to adulthood. Before a problem can be addressed it must first be verbalized, and Jimmy's priests and squadron commander, Lt. Cdr. W. M. "Dutch" Dillon, helped define the young ensign's problems quite clearly. While Jimmy's priests were perhaps more eloquent, Dillon's written words on Jimmy's permanent personnel records cut through his juvenile fog and fantasy. His direction was further stabilized at age twenty-six by his marriage to Dotty, who in her own way qualified as a mentor as well as a life partner. His being leader of the family never kept him from seeking her counsel.

From late 1932 Jimmy began to display a consistent demonstration of purpose in his life. This sense of purpose provided the foundation for future leadership success. Through the teachings of the church, particularly Daniel 1:8 ("he purposed in his heart"), the seed of understanding purpose was planted and then watered by family words and actions. Jimmy's mother was especially devout, and daily guidance for the lessons of life was often accompanied with scriptural reference. As will be seen later, many of those who served with Jimmy recall his paternal approach in training and combat, in addition to a similar attitude in less demanding social situations.

Jimmy's inner sense of purpose was service to his church, country, navy, family, and friends, which were not merely additions to his life, or parts of his life. These *were* his life—his self-perception, goals, status (position in society with certain rights and responsibilities), and roles (expected behavior) having merged. His effective leadership later on was facilitated by his consistent devotion to the entities that comprised the whole of his life. His consistently living what he believed and said facilitated the respect others had for him as a leader. Greek philosophers who advocated the pursuit of excellence rather than happiness would have been pleased with Jimmy, but in pursuing excellence within himself and encouraging others to excel, he found happiness.

Jimmy's sense of purpose enabled him to never leave the second stage of the institutional cycle, and this in turn contributed to his effective leadership. This theoretical concept contends that institutions (family, religion, government, economy, education) and the people directly associated with them may travel through five stages. The incipient stage is characterized by great enthusiasm. The second stage is efficiency, wherein enthusiasm merges with experience to create maximum productivity. The third stage, formalism, begins a downward trend as one goes through all the correct motions although enthusiasm has considerably waned. The fourth state is disorganization; and the fifth, reorganization—often in a new setting—is a hope of rekindling enthusiasm and a new efficiency. Jimmy remained in the second stage of this theoretical cycle due to the intrinsic nature of his status and role. Throughout his adult life and career there were always family, friends, and sailors in need. With needs always present, and gratification from addressing those needs a daily process, no reason arose for him to move into formalism or subsequent stages.

Watching his first combat from *Omaha* off Barcelona in 1939, Jimmy knew he could perform in combat if that challenge were ever placed before him. Fighting in a war was not incompatible with the sense of purpose that directed his life. Letters to his wife and parents document he was not a war lover. And more fortunate than many of his generation, the effects of the Depression on Jimmy seemed to have had no long-term negative effect. By December 1941 Jimmy's personal development had reached the plateau where it remained for the rest of his life.

Professional Development

Jimmy learned many lessons during his apprenticeship years that were vitally important to professional development before he had to face the crucible of war. While some or parts of these lessons could have been appreciated without having a well-defined sense of purpose, their full understanding and utilization may not have found the same degree of expression in effective leadership.

First, Jimmy learned the difference between compassion and empathy. These words are occasionally used interchangeably but are vastly different in understanding human nature and its impact on leadership. Jimmy quite often demonstrated compassion, a sympathetic expression, but empathy—an understanding so intimate that the feelings of another were almost fully comprehended—was almost exclusively reserved for his family. Like many others he understood that empathy was dangerous in military relationships as the very nature of the concept could cloud judgment at critical moments. One example was related in a 19 November 1941 letter to Dotty in which Jimmy noted his dissatisfaction with two pilots. One, a former aviation cadet, had three years experience flying dive-bombers with Bombing Two, but Jimmy did not believe he had the makings of a fighter pilot. Regrettably, Jimmy's concerns proved correct when on 25 May 1942, the former bomber pilot failed to pull out of a practice dive in time and died in the crash. The second pilot survived the war but scored no aerial victories. While assigned to VF-2, Jimmy was more successful in convincing Ramsey to remove other pilots from the squadron. Both Jimmy and Ramsey understood there was no compassion in allowing a pilot without sufficient talent to risk his own life.

Dotty Flatley and several of the pilots who flew with Jimmy have stated separately that for all his eagerness to help other pilots, once he determined they did not measure up, whether for lack of courage, intelligence, or industry, an attempt was quickly made to transfer that pilot.[30] Butch O'Hare once told one of his best pilots, Ens. A. Willie Callan, that if he didn't follow orders in the air he would find someone that could.[31] Callan learned that lesson fast, and went on to success not only with Butch but also for a career. And Jimmie Thach was quite clear on this issue stating, "Any pilot who is not suited . . . is not a zero quantity in a battle, he's a minus . . . a hazard . . . He does more harm than good."[32] Other examples of this lesson are presented later, one especially significant as it involved Jimmy not allowing a particularly talented pilot to fly.

A second lesson was closely associated with the first. One had to know his job and Capt. W. L. Lind's statement that Jimmy was "keenly interested in all branches of the naval profession in addition to his own specialty" speaks volumes to competency—in addition to identifying a necessary component for success in the navy.[33] And, one had to know his job not just to succeed but to live. Jimmy's fitness reports reveal consistent growth both in learning to fly and performing as an engineer who could know, maintain, and improve his assigned aircraft. Further,

Jimmy's learning process was enhanced by duty as an instructor. In teaching, one's understanding expands and deepens as a result of "learning twice." But a teacher—even one quite knowledgeable—is not necessarily a mentor. One of the most brilliant minds in naval aviation during the 1930s and World War II was Capt. Miles R. Browning, whose ideas, strategy, and advice to Rear Adm. Raymond Spruance during the Battle of Midway played a major role in that victory. However, Browning's exceptional insights into naval aviation matters did not always transfer to interpersonal relations. Several unfortunate incidents cost him promotion to flag rank, but as important were the lost opportunities for him to share his extensive aviation knowledge. Renowned Naval Academy Prof. E. B. Potter wrote in his book on Admiral Halsey that Browning "knew his business, the pilots agree, but his aloof and condescending manner prejudiced them against his opinions and advice."[34]

A third lesson was learning when to "let go" and when to "grab hold." For the most part, both personally and professionally, Jimmy could let go and transform mistakes and misfortunes into leadership tools. While keeping the emotional distress of mistakes out of his mind, such as crashing due to running out of fuel and trying to land without lowering the landing gear, he did not forget the events themselves. When evaluating other pilots, especially in training at Pensacola and Jacksonville, his own mistakes helped him maintain equilibrium when grading and assessing students' potential value to naval aviation. In short, he understood he might have to lose some of the little battles in life in order to win his own personal and professional war.

Jimmy learned a practical lesson in taking hold of opportunities. Flying the big patrol boats was not a highly desired choice of duty, but he made the most of the experience both in the air and as engineering officer. While they were certainly not unusual, Jimmy recognized that some superiors, like Jocko Clark, had a promising future in the navy. Never interested in becoming a barnacle on the ship of success, he was interested in opportunities that provided challenge, fulfillment of career goals, and if that also led to promotion, then so be it. And, having had an opportunity to offer comments as a squadron representative while a fighter pilot with VF-5B in 1937, Jimmy learned there was little difference between opportunity and responsibility. As time moved forward, it appears that the two concepts became one in Jimmy's thinking and actions.

A fourth lesson was absorbing the traits of his mentors. Jimmy adopted some of their practices but seems to have understood that the mannerisms of others did not always fit his own personality. From priests he learned that honesty paid a dividend beyond scriptural compliance. Honesty translated into credibility and throughout his career, "you could take what Jimmy said to the bank."[35] From Commander Dillon, Jimmy learned balance in weighing performance against potential. From Captain Mason and Commander Lind he gained appreciation for the specific and detailed mention of commendable accomplishments and generous praise—when deserved—in performance reports. Efficiency and enthusiasm were Jocko Clark's legacy to Jimmy, while Commander Paul Ramsey's organizational skill and special manner in relating to subordinates made a significant impression.

Although these experiences were not necessarily lessons, by the end of his apprentice period Jimmy had developed some patterns of thinking and action that provide insight into his personality. On the eve of World War II, Jimmy was more a realist than optimist. Although he actively sought betterment in all phases of his life and career, for the most part he saw things as they were and attempted to move ahead from that point. And while it is not fair to say he was ahead of his time, he was forward looking and had a much better perspective of how small actions and events fit into the larger picture.[36] When discussing tactics he was especially good at relating how the conduct of individuals, sections, divisions, and air groups affected overall battle success or failure. Moreover, he carried his example on to consequences for the nation, the world, and, ultimately, one's soul. Connectivity and a frame of reference were favorite subjects both for the topic at hand and as a teaching method. By relating how individuals had a vested interest in the broader scheme, Jimmy kept his listeners alert and interested. Consciously or unconsciously, he was sharing a method of teaching they could adopt.

Many of the outstanding leaders during World War II emerged or evolved into leadership roles as the demands of war challenged them. The first year of World War II proved to be naval aviation's greatest combat challenge. Confronted by an enemy with considerable combat experience and superior carrier aircraft, United States Navy carrier squadrons entered the first months of the war relatively unprepared. Carrier squadrons had no combat experience, experienced insufficient training in many squadrons, flew several types of obsolete aircraft, had too few planes of all types, and flew tactics untried in combat. As worrisome was the leadership capability of those men at the air group and squadron levels who were untested in combat. After Pearl Harbor time and commitment addressed the problems of training and matériel, but concerns pertaining to combat leadership and the development and implementation of aerial combat tactics rested on the shoulders of a small group of middle-grade aviators. Despite efforts to the contrary, some of these men failed both in leadership and effective development of tactics. In more than one battle these failures resulted in tragedy.

This was the situation and setting in early 1942. For Jimmy Flatley and other naval officers near his career level, the period of apprenticeship was over. Life or death, victory or defeat depended upon personal and professional foundations developed and lessons learned. Of necessity, the apprentice had to become a masterful leader.

5

Battle of the Coral Sea

ON 23 MARCH 1942 orders issued from the Bureau of Navigation began making their way to Jimmy. On the twenty-fifth he knew he was to report to Fighting Squadron Forty-two (VF-42) as commanding officer. The excitement of having his own squadron mitigated the pain of leaving his family, and very quickly the demands of his new assignment permeated his thoughts. Getting to VF-42 was not going to be easy: the squadron was somewhere in the Pacific, but in late March he did not know exactly where. Making matters worse, finding transportation to Pearl Harbor was now a lot more difficult than it had been in peacetime. Just getting there was a challenge, and on 4 April Jimmy had to request authorization from the Bureau of Navigation to travel by air as surface delays were keeping him from reporting to his assignment.[1]

Arriving at Pearl on 11 April after a seventeen-and-a-half-hour flight on a large four-engine PB2Y Coronado flying boat, Jimmy was assigned temporary duty with Fighting Squadron Three. In early April Paul Ramsey's VF-2 had borrowed many pilots from VF-3, leaving Fighting Three's shorthanded commanding officer, Lt. Cdr. John S. "Jimmie" Thach (USNA 1927), charged with aerial gunnery training for new pilots arriving at Pearl. Most pilots reported directly to Thach from the Advanced

Carrier Training Group in San Diego, adequately trained for carrier landings and familiar with the Wildcat, but they could not shoot.[2] Having already engaged Japanese planes off Rabaul and over Lae and Salamaua, Thach had practical experience to share. Jimmy Flatley could shoot and had registered gunnery hours in February and March, but he welcomed the additional hours from 15–18 April with VF-3. Just as important as the gunnery practice, however, was the time the two spent together on the ground, talking fighters and tactics.

In this time Jimmie Thach and Jimmy Flatley stayed up late at night discussing the number of fighters that should comprise a section and division, and the merits of a weave tactic. The essence and results of these discussions are presented later. However, another experience during this period recalled by Thach clearly describes how unprepared the United States was for war in early 1942, and demonstrates that army and navy pilots were not always at each others' throats. The army had responsibility for the defense of Hawaii, but their P-39 Airacobra fighter squadrons never had any experience firing at towed sleeves. Knowing the deficiencies of firing only at ground targets, P-39 pilots asked to learn the navy process. Having no tow planes of their own for such practice—and no cameras for IBP—Thach accommodated the army pilots by providing time for them to participate as he put navy pilots through aerial gunnery training. The army pilots flew all the maneuvers except the overhead approach, for which they claimed their streamlined P-39 was too fast. Volunteering to test their fears, Jimmy Flatley was checked out in the army fighter. Shortly after he was in the air making perfect overhead attacks, much to the delight of the army pilots.[3]

During those few days together in mid-April 1942, neither Jimmy Flatley nor Jimmie Thach could have known how significant their discussions were or the momentous impact they were making on naval aviation. Although Butch O'Hare (Flatley's former student and Thach's former squadron mate) was then and now acknowledged for a heroic action off Bougainville on 20 February 1942, by the end of 1942 the two "Jim's" were recognized—then as now—as naval aviation's pre-eminent tactical innovators and fighter squadron commanders. Butch's opportunity to lead a fighter squadron into battle was limited, and very early as an air group commander he was killed during another heroic action on

26 November 1943 during a night interception of Japanese planes, the first one from a carrier. Still, he garnered a special place in the lives and tactical contributions of both Jimmy Flatley and Jimmie Thach. It was also somewhat ironic that the two Jim's were first sharing their wartime tactical thoughts during the week Butch was en route to Washington to receive the Medal of Honor.

One Squadron Commander Too Many

On 20 April Jimmy boarded another PB2Y for a three-day flight to Tongatabu in the Tonga Islands—about two thousand miles east of Australia—via Palmyra, Canton, and Suva. Reporting aboard *Yorktown* on the twenty-fourth, he learned his new squadron was completing the arduous process of replacing self-sealing fuel tanks. The chemistry between the original tanks and gasoline did not work, and as the liners disintegrated, filters clogged and engines quit. Although pleased to know this serious problem was apparently being resolved, he was not pleased to learn there had been a breakdown in communication and that a fellow '29 classmate, Lt. Cdr. Charles R. Fenton, who was serving on board *Yorktown,* had already been named commanding officer of VF-42. According to the Bureau of Navigation Jimmy was the new commanding officer of VF-42, and Fenton was to assume another command. But this information was not known aboard *Yorktown* as the 17 February orders for Fenton had been routed to the Atlantic-based *Ranger,* which had two fighter squadrons assigned to her—VF-41 and VF-42 (both carrying *Ranger*'s 4 hull number, the figures 1 and 2 added to differentiate between the two squadrons). Fighting Squadron Forty-two went aboard *Yorktown* for temporary duty in the late spring of 1941 while VF-5, *Yorktown*'s own fighter squadron was transferring from F3F biplanes to the F4F Wildcat. Upon the outbreak of war *Yorktown* was quickly ordered to the Pacific and VF-42 went with her. Without knowing the intentions of the Bureau of Navigation, Lt. Cdr. Oscar Pederson—the newly appointed air group commander (CAG) aboard CV-5, had recommended his old executive officer, Fenton, for promotion, and the carrier's commanding officer, Capt. Elliott Buckmaster, approved.

The most often quoted source for the resolution of this matter has been Stanley Johnston's 1943 book, *The Grim Reapers*. Written during the war and intended for a public very much in need of a morale boost, Johnston's version is essentially correct in essence, but the tone and details—particularly Jimmy's dialogue—invite reconsideration. But in fairness to Johnston (who was a correspondent employed by the *Chicago Tribune*), one must understand that he was aboard *Lexington* rather than *Yorktown* during that period and did not begin to get the story until he and Jimmy met on the voyage to San Diego over three weeks later. Also, Johnston wrote in his 1942 *Queen of the Flattops* that he himself did not know whether or not his dispatches were getting to his publisher, nor to what degree censors at Pearl Harbor edited his work.[4] Indeed, Jimmy was disappointed with the mix-up, and the justifiably perturbed officers aboard *Yorktown* had a problem requiring resolution. But they also had a war to fight, and on 27 April *Yorktown* steamed away from Tongatabu heading westward toward the Coral Sea. *Yorktown*'s officers and Jimmy knew combat was more than probable, all knew the value of an experienced fighter pilot, and Jimmy was especially desirous not to miss a combat opportunity. Missing from Johnston's version of events, however, was Jimmy's apparent direct influence in obtaining orders that allowed him to stay with VF-42 long enough to see battle and find another fighter squadron to command.

Fenton's earlier orders were canceled, and the Bureau of Navigation on 28 April approved his assignment as commanding officer of VF-42. Jimmy's orders were modified on 29 April by a short message that included the phrase "report . . . duty involving flying as CO Fightron Ten." The more formal orders prepared later read, "Report to the Commanding Officer, Fighting Squadron Forty-two for temporary duty involving flying and when directed in May, proceed and report to Commander, Carrier Replacement [Air] Group Ten for duty involving flying as Commanding Officer, Fighting Squadron Ten." The language of the orders was no surprise to Jimmy as a handwritten memo in his extant files dated 27 April 1942 indicates he helped write the draft. Having been in San Diego only two weeks previous he knew that Carrier Replacement Air Group Ten was about to be formed (established 16 April 1942), and he certainly did not object to returning to his own backyard to help form it. Further, the relatively imprecise phrase in his formal orders "when directed in May," also included in the 29 April message, was no afterthought. On 27 April no one aboard *Yorktown*—then under radio silence—knew exactly when they would contact the enemy, but the contact was expected sooner than later, and the ambiguous language Jimmy wrote into the draft provided leeway for him to stay aboard long enough to see action. This scenario finds some further validation in Jimmy's reporting orders on 3 June 1942 wherein Air Group Ten's CO, Cdr. Richard K. Gaines, wrote, "You will assume *temporary* command as senior officer of Fighting Squadron TEN." The Air Group Ten commanding officer may or may not have known Jimmy's role in obtaining the VF-10 assignment, but Gaines knew it wasn't his idea. However, the incident never became an issue as Gaines quickly appreciated what Jimmy brought to his new air group. In sum, Jimmy's role with VF-42 was quickly resolved, and before his first flight (two hours of tactics and gunnery) from *Yorktown* on 2 May, his status as executive officer of VF-42 was happily accepted by all.

Into the Coral Sea

With *Yorktown* in Task Force Seventeen were three heavy cruisers, six destroyers, and the oiler *Neosho*. Steaming toward the same area was Task Force Eleven with two heavy cruisers and seven destroyers escorting the *Lexington*. Once the two carrier task forces joined, command was to be exercised by Rear Adm. Frank Jack Fletcher with his two-star flag in *Yorktown*. Had the plan materialized as desired by Adm. Chester W. Nimitz, commander in chief of the Pacific Fleet (CinCPac), Task Force Sixteen, comprised of *Enterprise* and *Hornet*, also would have joined with overall command passing to Vice Adm. William F. Halsey. In late April "The Big E" and *Hornet*, with their attendant cruisers and destroyers were returning to Pearl from their launch on the eighteenth of Col. Jimmy Doolittle's B-25s to bomb Tokyo and other cities. The raid hurt Japanese pride much more than the minimal physical damage and provided a major boost to American morale. But the raid delayed TF 16's arrival in the Coral Sea, and when enemy movement in the

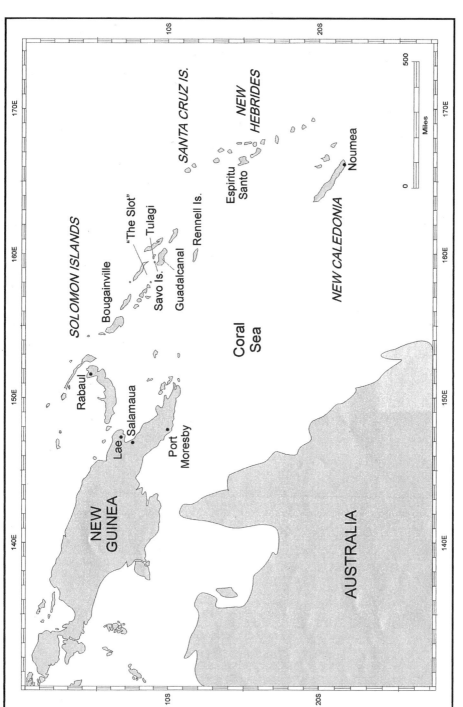

Coral Sea and the Solomon Islands

Solomon Islands was spotted on 3 May, it was apparent battle would begin before Halsey's carriers arrived.

Naval intelligence knew the enemy intended to move toward Port Moresby, located on the southeastern coast of New Guinea, and into the Solomons situated immediately to the east. Japanese possession of Port Moresby presented a direct threat to Australia's logistics and communication lifelines. Now after a series of defeats and lost territory in the first six months of war, the United States Navy was in position to effectively challenge the heretofore uninterrupted Japanese advance. Aboard *Yorktown* on 3 May Fletcher and his staff correctly determined their planes could catch enemy ships unloading in Tulagi harbor on the morning of the fourth. Next morning a strike of forty SBDs and TBDs lifted off *Yorktown* and attacked. Although later analysis proved the several attacks on the fourth against enemy ships not to be as successful as first thought, occupation of Tulagi was nonetheless disrupted.

While strike groups descended on targets near the small island just off the north coast of Guadalcanal, Jimmy twice led his division on combat air patrol above CV-5 for a total of 5.6 hours. At the end of the day he recorded in his flight log that the "*Yorktown* Air Group attack[ed] Tulagi . . . [and] sank 3 CL [light cruisers], 3 DD [destroyers], 3 AK [transports and] 1 CA [heavy cruiser]." However, cruisers did not accompany the Tulagi invasion force and actual losses consisted of one destroyer, a minelayer, and two small minelayers. Greatly inhibiting the success of the SBDs on 4 May, and soon after, was fogging of the through-the-windshield gun sights as the dive bombers passed from the cooler air at high altitude into the warmer, more humid air.[5] Although Jimmy's first log entry for the fourth was overly optimistic, his second entry proved correct. Unopposed by aerial opposition during the morning, enemy observation planes challenged the carrier's strike planes early that afternoon. SBDs downed two of their attackers, but when word reached *Yorktown* that the strike planes were being attacked, four fighters were hastily ordered to intercept. Jimmy's log credits the fighters with three kills.

On 5 May *Lexington* and her escorts joined *Yorktown*, the combined strength then designated Task Force Seventeen. Admiral Fletcher retained overall command; Rear Adm. Aubrey W. Fitch—a naval aviator; Fletcher was not—assumed responsibility for both carriers; the cruisers and destroyers were divided between Rear Adm. Thomas C. Kinkaid and the Royal Navy's Rear Adm. John G. Crace. Alerted to the presence of American carriers by the previous day's raid on Tulagi, the Japanese striking force, built around the fleet carriers *Shokaku* and *Zuikaku,* began a search for Task Force Seventeen. On the fifth there was only one direct contact by a Kawanishi Type 97 flying boat that did not have time to send a report to any Japanese force. Just as the two American carriers reached their appointed rendezvous, the enemy patrol craft was detected and quickly shot down. Stanley Johnston devoted two pages in both *Queen of the Flattops* and *Grim Reapers* vividly describing how Jimmy Flatley downed this plane. However, Jimmy was not in the air when VF-42's Lt. Vincent F. McCormack, Ens. Walter A. Haas, and Lt.(jg) Arthur J. Brassfield flamed the four-engine plane in less than thirty seconds. Later in the day, though, Jimmy was on combat air patrol for two hours.

The following day both sides expected their planes to make visual contact, but didn't. They were close, and there was little doubt as darkness closed the sixth of May that the seventh would bring the expected battle. On the evening of the sixth, Jimmy retired to his stateroom to write two letters. One was addressed to his wife and children, the other to his parents. Both envelopes were sealed and were not to be opened until his death. Stashed away and forgotten after the war, they were opened many years later. The wording and tone were identical to that of his first letter at the outbreak of war, except that he asked his Protestant wife to raise their children as Catholic, and that he now expected to get six enemy planes before they got him. Jimmy's mood was somewhat melancholy not only because he and everybody else expected the first carrier-versus-carrier battle the next day, but also due to concern that organized resistance to the Japanese invasion of the Philippines might soon cease (it did that same day). After writing the two letters, and too tired to worry further, he dropped off to sleep. The catharsis of writing letters helped as he slept surprising well. Indeed, he needed all his strength the following day.

The Battle of 7 May 1942

Neither antagonist had to wait very long on the morning of 7 May for visual sightings of the other. Ironically, the sighting reports for both sides were inaccurate, but the advantage went to Task Force Seventeen. After locating what was believed to be a carrier and a cruiser, seventy-eight Japanese planes lifted off *Shokaku* and *Zuikaku*. Heading south of their carriers the Japanese pilots found the oiler *Neosho* and destroyer *Sims* (DD-409) instead of the carrier and cruiser they expected. Nonetheless, they attacked and sank *Sims* and left the lightly armed *Neosho* mortally wounded. While this action transpired, planes flew northwest from *Yorktown* and *Lexington* expecting to find *Shokaku* and *Zuikaku*. Instead they found the enemy invasion covering force that included the light carrier *Shoho,* her eighteen planes, four heavy cruisers, and a destroyer.

The ninety-three planes from Task Force Seventeen consisted of twenty-eight SBDs, twelve TBDs, and ten Wildcats from *Lexington* plus twenty-five SBDs, ten TBDs, and eight Wildcats from *Yorktown*. Bombs were fused for one one-hundredth-second delay (to inflict maximum damage to a flight deck) and torpedoes were set for a depth of ten feet.[6] Jimmy led the eight Wildcats from *Yorktown,* three of which were to follow him in defense of the slow TBDs, with the others joining Vince McCormack to escort the SBDs then climbing to eighteen thousand feet. Last to leave the carrier were the fighters, and as Jimmy looked over his shoulder soon after departure, he counted four Wildcats in addition to his own. Jimmy expected to see his assigned wingman, Ens. John D. Baker, and his second section comprised of Lt. (jg) Brainard T. Macomber and Ens. Edgar R. Bassett. All were in place. But he did not expect to see Ensign Haas, McCormack's wingman, who had mistakenly joined Flatley's division. Vince McCormack flew on toward the enemy minus his own wingman. This, as it turned out, was only the first of many miscues in the two-day air battle.

Approaching the enemy Jimmy, like some of the other fighter pilots with him, could not help but ponder his fate. Confidence was based on knowledge, training, and experience. But this was the first battle of its kind, enemy tactics and aircraft capabilities were not fully known, and certainly Jimmy was concerned about his total absence of training with this squadron. It was ironic, he thought, that his former squadron aboard *Lexington* and its commanding officer, Paul Ramsey, were making a similar flight. He knew what Paul would do in combat, and he suspected that Ramsey was probably having the same thoughts and wishing Jimmy were still assigned to VF-2. Soon after, Jimmy overtook the ten Devastator torpedo-bombers he was assigned to protect, and his thoughts turned to the prewar doctrine for escorting strike planes. That doctrine called for fighter aircraft to keep their strike group in sight, leave them only long enough to dispose of an enemy fighter, and then resume close escort. This was how it was supposed to work, but theory would last only as long as it took to fly 175 miles. One way or the other, theoretical questions were about to be answered . . . if only he could live through his first real combat.

In the action report he wrote for the seventh, Jimmy described the fighter escort tactics employed in protecting the low-flying torpedo planes.

[The] TBDs left own [*Yorktown*] carrier about 20 minutes before VF [fighter] escort was launched. VF overtook about half way to the objective which was about 175 miles distance. This procedure conserved fuel for the VF. To assist in locating own TBDs down low, an Aldis lamp was used by torpedo planes as we caught up with them. During the run to the objective the VF stayed about 6,000 feet above and up sun. This put us between our TBDs and the most likely direction from which an attack might develop. At the same time it allowed us to see them much more easily. Normally if the group being escorted is at any appreciable altitude above the water, I prefer to fly about 2,000 feet above and abreast of them and down sun. From such a position it is much easier to observe the sun lane and the VF are in position to dive between the planes being protected and incoming enemy fighters. When up sun there is great danger of the enemy diving past the VF before they can counter.

After the objective came in sight the escort fighter leader [Jimmy] informed the low flying VT of the enemy disposition, bearing, course and speed.

Expecting an attack from above, the escort VF increased altitude to 10,000 [feet] remaining up sun so that they could clearly see their own VT.

In clear skies with unlimited visibility from ten thousand feet, Jimmy could see *Shoho* fifteen miles distant. He thought there was no damage to the carrier or to the destroyer and four heavy cruisers protecting her. But at least two bombs and five torpedoes from *Lexington's* SBDs and TBDs had seriously wounded *Shoho*, her earlier circular defensive course no longer possible due to steering damage. Drawing nearer, Jimmy could see smoke rising from the carrier. Now an easy target, SBDs from *Yorktown* descended and recorded additional hits on the stricken ship. Finally, time came for the attack by the ten Devastators of *Yorktown's* VT-5 led by Lt. Cdr. Joe Taylor. Jimmy's action report reads:

> Our VT was below 1,000 feet and I coached them in from my position above. The *Yorktown* dive-bombing attack commenced about 1200 [noon] and scored at least 6 direct hits. The carrier was burning badly when [the] first torpedo was dropped about 1210. I made an effort to divert a part of our torpedo planes to another target but they were already in their approach.

Shoho was already finished when VT-5's torpedoes ripped into her. Explosions now were occurring so fast it could not be determined whether they were being caused by VT-5's torpedoes or secondary explosions set off by earlier bombs and torpedoes. Less than twenty minutes after the first hit, the 11,262-ton former submarine support ship went under. Only two hundred of her eight hundred officers and men survived, and all her planes were lost. However, at least six of her fighters contested the attack and Jimmy got a real good look at them, two in particular. His action report continues:

> Up to this time no enemy planes were observed. Shortly thereafter our VT was attacked by four Jap type 96 fighters. We dove to their defense. . . . Attacks employed were overhead and astern approaches. The leader [Jimmy] of own VF shot down the first plane attacked [TBD] by diving in at an angle of 60 degrees and using splashes on the water as an aid in aiming. Enemy VF was not over 100 feet above [the] water. The leader recovered above. Following VF [Baker, Haas, Macomber,

Bassett] . . . employed similar first approaches but flattened out and stayed close to the water. This procedure was in error although the results were excellent. It was in error because the enemy fighters are infinitely more maneuverable than our own F4F.

Jimmy continued this section of his report emphasizing what should have happened and what tactics should be used in the future.

The most effective attack against a more maneuverable fighter is to obtain altitude advantage, dive in, attack, pull up using speed gained in dive to maintain altitude advantage. The old dogfight of chasing tails is not satisfactory and must not be employed when opposing the Jap VF planes. On this occasion the enemy fighters resorted to steep wing-overs, rolls and loops at low altitude. They are extremely clever aerobats [*sic*] and apparently have found some way to overcome the effects of "blacking out." However, their planes can climb away from our own and it is thought that they will soon get the news. In the engagement the leader [Jimmy] tried to overtake a Jap VF that was running for it. He climbed rapidly away without any difficulty.

The air action Jimmy fought in and later described in his required action report lasted about two minutes. Somewhat surprised to find the enemy fighters at low altitude, Jimmy's section had made the adjustment quickly in a steep spiral and prevented any damage to Taylor's TBDs. Prevention of damage alone made the mission a success, and the downing of three enemy fighters made it even better. Easing back his stick quickly but smoothly, Jimmy zoomed upward while his target fell into the transparent blue-green Coral Sea. Having bottomed out at five hundred feet, he did not immediately look for his wingman, but before he resumed level flight he knew he was alone. That couldn't be helped so he scanned the sky for another challenger. Looking down he saw another fighter with a red ball insignia on each wing. Although his first opponent most likely did not see him before they engaged, this one spotted Jimmy diving to attack. Despite the high speed gained in the F4F's dive, he could not overtake the faster enemy fighter and quickly gave up the chase.

Later analysis confirmed that Jimmy had shot down a Type 96 fighter and the plane that he could not catch was a Zero. For those who had not seen it, the long canopy of the Zero made it appear to be a slower strike aircraft. Also confirmed were two enemy fighters shot down by "the lost wingman" Walt Haas, one of those two being the first Zero to be downed by a navy or marine pilot.[7] None of the *Yorktown* fighters or torpedo planes were lost on 7 May, but one SBD failed to return to the carrier: happily, the crew was rescued. Back on *Yorktown* after the 2.7-hour flight and fight, Jimmy made his oral report to the air officer, intelligence officer, and other staff; then lit up a cigarette, grabbed a soda, and briefly went to his stateroom to make a few notes. In his log book he wrote, "Accompanied VT-5 in attack on enemy CV *Ryukho* [*sic*] CV sunk. Own VF shot down 3 VF. I shot down my first enemy fighter." Jimmy's first battle was over and despite some mistakes it had turned out good. But, it was early afternoon and there were still two enemy fleet carriers in the area. Further, there was no indication the Port Moresby Invasion Force had reversed course. It had been a long day and it wasn't over. Notes and log book back in their place, Jimmy crushed another cigarette into an ashtray and headed back to the ready room.

From midafternoon to just before dark, it seemed to Jimmy that the 2.7 hours in the air that morning would be it for the day. Weather around the task force was not at all good, and some voiced the hopeful opinion that poor visibility, intermittent showers, and approaching night would preclude any further air operations. But radar contacts just before 1800 hours sent Jimmy and other VF-42 pilots running from the ready room to their planes. It was not unusual to see someone in the cockpit of a fighter just before takeoff, but when Jimmy climbed onto the wing of his F4F-3, the face in the cockpit belonged not to a mechanic preparing the plane for takeoff but to Lt. (jg) E. Scott McCuskey, who had been grounded for losing two Wildcats on the fourth. McCuskey literally begged for a plane but Jimmy reminded Scott that orders were orders, and Scott obediently climbed out of the cockpit.

At 1800 hours Jimmy was aloft with six other Wildcats taking their places beside and behind him. Flying wing for Jimmy was John Baker (again) plus Ens. Harry Gibbs while Macomber and Bassett formed a section and Lt. (jg) William Woollen and Ens. Leslie L. B. Knox formed a third section. The fighter director officer (FDO) vectored all seven planes in the direction of an incoming strike of twenty-seven bombers and torpedo planes from *Shokaku* and *Zuikaku*. Paul Ramsey and three of his VF-2 Wildcats had already intercepted the enemy planes flying under the overcast sky and mistakenly identified them as fighters. That, however, was the only mistake Ramsey made. Diving in from above, he caught the torpedo planes by surprise and shot down two in one pass. Low on fuel, Ramsey then radioed Jimmy, who was fast approaching, for an assist. Flying at two thousand feet through broken clouds, Jimmy and his two wingmen flew over the enemy planes heading in the opposite direction. Not getting a good view, Jimmy asked Paul what type of planes to expect. "Fighters!" came the wrong answer. However, Ensign Knox, flying behind Jimmy, got a better look and immediately executed a wingover to pursue. Woollen followed and shortly Knox downed two of the enemy. Just as Knox and Woollen turned to chase their prey, Jimmy spotted Type 99 carrier bombers and he and the others took up the chase. The lead plane got bursts at the targets and one fell, but the pursuit ended quickly as the planes entered the low clouds. Without a target and the dusk growing ever darker, Jimmy decided to head back to *Yorktown.*

The sharp battle had lasted only about twelve minutes, but Jimmy was in the air for another hour and a half. Getting back aboard proved to be anything but easy. Assigning John Baker to use his homing device to lead the section back to the carrier, Jimmy kept his radio on the fighter frequency in case he was directed to make another interception. Only slivers of daylight remained about 1830 as Jimmy arrived back over the task force, and as darkness settled over the carriers, so did confusion. Not everyone in the air had extensive experience in night landings, which were not easy even in peacetime. Several planes nearly collided as more than one attempted to land at the same time. Then to make matters worse, several of the Japanese planes that had intended to bomb or torpedo the American carriers arrived overhead. Thinking the carriers might be their own, the enemy pilots began to flash signals. Since their identity was not positive, and because Jimmy and several other VF-42 planes were still aloft, no order was given to open fire. Taking a wave-off, Macomber in his pullout flew close enough to three of the enemy planes to know they weren't friendly, and he opened fire. This apparently confirmed the presence of enemy planes. For gunners on the heavy cruiser *Minneapolis* (CA-36) and several other escorting ships, temptation to shoot could not be overcome. Now friendly planes still in the air were in even greater danger. Even some *Yorktown* gunners joined the fray, damaging one returning fighter. After some thirty minutes a semblance of order was restored, and just before 2000 everyone who was returning was back aboard. Regretfully, two of the seven who lifted off *Yorktown* with Jimmy two hours earlier did not return.

It is not known for sure what happened to Leslie Knox other than he shot down two planes and was last seen chasing a foe into a cloud. The exact final moments of John Baker's life are not known either, but Jimmy and others aboard *Yorktown* wished they did not know as much as they did about the events immediately before his loss. Having used his homing equipment to guide Jimmy and his division within sight of their carrier, John Baker had to pull away with the others when the ships opened fire on them and the Japanese intruders. When the shooting stopped both *Lexington* and *Yorktown* could hear Baker, but apparently his radio was set only to send and not receive. He was too close for his homing device to work, and the carriers could not turn on their lights since the Japanese planes were still thought to be close. None aboard *Yorktown* could have known that the enemy planes had already dropped their ordnance even before their accidental overflights. At length, directions were radioed to Baker in the hope he could fly to the nearest land, but . . .

To lose his wingman under any circumstances was bad enough. To lose him in the manner he was lost was all but unbearable for Jimmy. He knew the last face John Baker ever saw was his.

Later, equally bad news arrived from *Lexington*. Another Baker, this one Lt. (jg) Paul Baker, was missing. Paul shot down one of the incoming enemy torpedo planes just as Jimmy got into the fight, but he either collided with his target or was too close when it exploded. Paul Baker, who had two other kills to his credit that morning, was an enlisted pilot in VF-2 who had earned his wings in 1935 and upon the recommendation of Paul Ramsey (with Jimmy's full approval and verbal support) was promoted to lieutenant (junior grade) in late March 1942. A few weeks later, Jimmy sorted through some papers at his home in Coronado looking for a letter Paul Baker had sent him in early March. Then both were still in VF-2: Jimmy was with the VF-2 Detachment in

San Diego while Paul remained with Ramsey in Hawaii. Paul Baker was a man of considerable depth who sought and found the words to convey his inner thoughts. Some phrases in his letter caused Jimmy to pause: "Now that the disappointment about not getting to go home with you has worn off . . . I felt very guilty about some of the things I said when you first informed me that I was to be left here . . . but I am sure you didn't take offense." Even though most of the remainder of the letter was news that was now old news, Jimmy read it all remembering that its last paragraph worded the essence of their relationship: "we all hope that you can come back to us."

The Battle of 8 May 1942

Long before the first light of 8 May, Admiral Fletcher knew he would have to fight two big enemy carriers before he had any opportunity to attack the convoy heading for Port Moresby. And there was no doubt in the minds of the Japanese carrier brain trust during the early morning hours that they would soon have an opportunity to avenge the loss of *Shoho*. Although they did not know it during the night, the Japanese —then approximately two hundred miles northeast of Task Force Seventeen—would have the weather on their side for the battle. Thick clouds and poor visibility surrounded their ships while the carriers and escorting ships of Task Force Seventeen steamed under relatively clear skies. But for Jimmy and some TF-17 pilots, the light overcast and a few scattered clouds in the morning sky would create some problems.

Soon after daybreak, search planes from both sides located their opponents, and by 0930 bombers, torpedo planes, and escorting fighters were flying toward their targets. Although unaware of the other's thinking and directives, both carrier groups turned to steam toward each other to shorten the return flights for their aircraft. Before the enemy was sighted, Jimmy led three other Wildcats into a clear sky shortly before 0800. Supplementing this combat air patrol division from *Yorktown* were eight SBDs (plus fifteen more from *Lexington*) for defense against torpedo planes. Given the small complement of fighters available, there was little choice but to press some of the Dauntless dive-bombers into this service. Flying wing for Jimmy was Lt. (jg) Richard G. Crommelin while Brainard Macomber led the second section with Edgar Bassett on his wing. Within sight was Jimmy's friend Paul Ramsey leading a division of Wildcats off the *Lexington* for combat air patrol. Jimmy, Paul, and the other six fighter pilots climbed above their respective carriers to ten thousand feet, observing radio silence throughout their circular, protective flight.[8]

Exactly how many attacking planes might arrive over *Yorktown* and *Lexington* was not known, but the math was not overly difficult. Jimmy knew the two American carriers could send as many as 102 bombers and torpedo planes at the enemy if all were operational. Even allowing for those lost the previous day and the SBDs being employed for torpedo-plane defense, they could still count on a strike of about seventy (the actual number was seventy-five). Therefore, at least as many enemy strike planes could be expected to hit Task Force Seventeen (the actual number was sixty-nine). Jimmy knew the seventeen fighters available to cover the two carriers were not enough to handle the threat, but that's all that were available. Another fifteen F4F's were employed as escorts for the sixty SBDs and TBDs flying to attack Japan's two newest carriers. More than once the thought crossed Jimmy's mind that the twenty-three SBDs complementing the fighters for combat air patrol could better contribute in the attack role for which they were designed.

The previous day *Lexington*'s Scouting Two, Bombing Two, and Torpedo Two attacked *Shoho* about fifteen minutes before *Yorktown*'s Scouting Five, Bombing Five, and Torpedo Five. On the eighth *Yorktown* squadrons arrived over the enemy forty minutes prior to those from *Lexington*. Whereas on the seventh they had basically provided the coup de grace for the small *Shoho,* this day *Yorktown* squadrons recorded the first and most telling blows. *Zuikaku* was hidden from view for most of the battle and was not attacked; but Bombing Five scored two 1,000-pound bomb hits on *Shokaku,* one forward and one behind the starboard island structure. The two bombs terminated flight operations for the Pearl Harbor veteran. Less than an hour later a third 1,000-pound bomb dropped by *Lexington*'s VS-2 landed near the wreckage created by the second bomb. Given the fogging problems for windscreens and bomb sights as the SBDs descended from cool air into warm humid air, it is perhaps surprising any hits were registered. No torpedoes launched by either VT-2 or VT-5 found their mark although several hits were claimed, as TBD pilots believed bomb near misses to be the result of their weapons.

Jimmy learned the details of the attack on *Shokaku* later on the eighth, as combat air patrol was his mission for the entire day. His first 2.4 hours in the air (previously noted) were uneventful, but his second flight of 1.3 hours was filled with action and, once again, frustration. Landing about 1015, Jimmy, Richard Crommelin, Brainard Macomber, and Edgar Bassett had less than an hour to rest, smoke, eat, drink, and ensure their planes were serviced and ready to fly again. The relief combat air patrol division led by Vince McCormack was airborne before Jimmy's group landed. After several false alarms the radar screens on both carriers picked up the anticipated enemy counterstrike just before 1100. McCormack's division and another from *Lexington* (eight Wildcats total) were directed by the FDO to remain over the two carriers. Jimmy's division of four F4Fs and Ramsey's division of five F4Fs was launched to intercept the enemy before they could reach the carriers. In making the intercept Ramsey led his division to gain altitude as quickly as possible ("Buster!"). Jimmy's division was also told to "Buster!"

In his 8 May action report Jimmy detailed the first minutes of his second flight of the day.

> Prior to leaving the ship, I was informed that an attack was expected. I was given no other information. As soon as I took to the air, the FDO aboard the USS *Lexington* directed me to proceed to a point 10 miles distant from the carrier and to circle there at 2,000 feet. I naturally thought that the radar screen showed enemy planes approaching at low altitude possibly torpedo planes, so I was alert for their appearance. I waited a few minutes and when nothing happened I asked for information. I was then directed to climb and intercept an attack approaching above 10,000 feet. The order was late and by the time I broke through the scattered clouds at 6,000 feet, the torpedo and dive-bombing attack on [our] own fleet was well developed. I headed for [our] own forces and when about 5 miles from [the] center of our disposition, I saw Jap fighters attacking some of our planes which I took to be SBDs who were acting as an anti-torpedo plane patrol. I went to their assistance.

In the course of the ensuing engagement, I shot down one Jap "Zero" fighter. . . .

In tone Jimmy's report presented a macro view of the action whereas his wingman's report for the same action was a micro view. This is not surprising given their difference in rank, age, and experience. The report written by Richard Crommelin adds pertinent details.

Shortly after starting the climb, the leader [Jimmy] requested instructions and was told to return and defend the ships. At this time bomb and/or torpedo splashes around the ships, plus heavy antiaircraft fire indicated that the enemy's attack was already well developed. We continued the climb at full power and headed toward the ships. Upon reaching about nine thousand feet, the division leader [Jimmy] started a full power shallow dive and at about six thousand feet opened fire on a Zero, which was crossing us at about 90 degrees. It was relatively simple for me to get my sights on this same plane, which I did, and opened for approximately a 2-second burst—this distraction, however, caused me to lose my leader, who apparently steepened his dive after firing and went out of sight below and behind me.

Crommelin's quick "distraction" had indeed separated him from Jimmy but not from enemy fighters. Involved in furious combat, Crommelin indicated how difficult it was to assess time during an aerial battle by writing in his action report the phrase "during the ensuing few minutes or seconds." Richard made no claim for the Zero Jimmy attacked and claimed, but while acknowledging he did not see any planes he fired on hit the water, he did claim two kills and damage to two others. He made it back to *Yorktown* but not in his Wildcat. During the melee, an oil line was shot or carried away, his engine froze, and he made "a fairly smooth water landing."

Of course, it did not take Jimmy but a second or two to realize he had not only lost Crommelin but also Macomber and Bassett.

My other three planes not being in sight, I circled [our] own force looking for enemy aircraft. Finding none, I returned to the scene of my first action and found three type Zero fighters milling around. I attacked again and definitely winged one. However, I was badly outnumbered and broke off the engagement. I returned to my carrier, landed, re-serviced and took to the air with 4 planes for combat patrol duty. We saw no more of the Japs that day.

Like his wingman, Jimmy too lost track of time while in the air, but upon landing back aboard *Yorktown* after the interception, he determined the time to have been 1.3 hours. It felt like 13. Quickly back in the air for another three-hour combat air patrol, he touched down for the last time that day at 1530.

Postwar analysis of Japanese records indicates that none of the Zeros Jimmy and Richard Crommelin engaged were shot down on 8 May although three of the nimble fighters were so badly damaged they had to be jettisoned upon return to *Zuikaku*.[9] But, it did not take postwar analysis for anyone aboard *Yorktown* to know that the battle was a tactical loss. *Shokaku* was badly damaged, and damaged sufficiently to cause her to miss the crucial Battle of Midway one month later. *Zuikaku* was undamaged, but significant aircrew losses kept her from sailing toward Midway. *Lexington,* however, never sailed again to battle or port. Despite the best efforts of Jimmy, Richard Crommelin, Paul Ramsey, and the other fighter pilots of VF-2 and VF-42, the big carrier had taken two torpedoes and two bomb hits during the late morning attack. By early afternoon her fires were out, and although down slightly by the bow, she was steaming at twenty-four knots and appeared able to steam away for repairs and fight again. However, aviation fuel vapor permeated the ship forward, and at 1247 a spark or heat from a generator touched off the first in a series of violent explosions that left the carrier aflame. At 1707 the crew was ordered off and after Captain Sherman and his department heads went over the side, the destroyer USS *Phelps* (DD-360) loosed five torpedoes into the blazing hulk. At 1952 waves closed over the carrier that thousands of sailors, Jimmy, and many other naval aviators had once called home.

Yorktown fared better than *Lexington,* but she did not emerge unscathed. One bomb penetrated the flight deck just forward of the number two elevator near the island and continued downward before exploding on the fourth deck. The blast destroyed an aviation storeroom and killed or seriously wounded sixty-six men, but it only impaired flight operations for a few minutes. Several near misses, however, damaged the hull, one opening a fuel oil bunker. Speed was reduced to twenty-five knots shortly after the attack, but effective damage control soon had the carrier steaming at thirty knots. Although in no danger of sinking and able to continue fighting if necessary, it was obvious she would soon have to find a dry dock for repairs.

For the first two days after *Lexington* was lost, Jimmy and the remainder of VF-42 and VF-2 were occupied with thoughts of further combat as *Yorktown* and the other ships of Task Force Seventeen sped southwest into the Coral Sea. Admiral Fletcher, Jimmy, and all others in the Allied force did not then know their efforts had won a strategic victory or that the enemy had serious problems of their own. The Japanese postponed the Port Moresby invasion, and *Zuikaku,* though undamaged, had less than two dozen strike planes operational. These factors, in combination with a need for fuel and severe damage to the already departed *Shokaku,* dictated that the remaining strike-force ships also retire from the battle. When combat was no longer believed imminent, Jimmy turned his thoughts back to the problems of the week's battle.

Fighter Squadron Lessons of the Coral Sea Combat

Jimmy's action report for 7 May and the separate 8 May report reveal not only tactical thoughts but also his frame of mind while recording them. The battle on the seventh left VF-42 feeling pretty good about their overall performance although the loss of fellow pilots, exhaustion, and the knowledge they would fight again the next day precluded any celebratory spirit. After providing all the essential details of the day's aerial battle, Jimmy went a step further and ended his report with "Hints To Navy VF Pilots." The signed copy of that action report included eight such hints although his draft actually numbered nine items, plus an unnumbered repeat of the fourth item in the list for emphasis. The first eight hints are presented exactly as Jimmy wrote them except for minor punctuation and spelling changes. Comments by the author of this book are in square brackets.

(1) Gain plenty of altitude before contact with enemy fighters. You can lose it fast but you can't gain it fast enough when up against enemy VF. [Obviously, Jimmy's two successful diving attacks inspired this hint, particularly the first attack when he quickly descended and ambushed the Type 96 fighter. Also, he well remembered the Zero he tried to overtake that "climbed rapidly away without any difficulty."]

(2) Use hit and run attacks diving in and pulling out and up. If your target maneuvers out of your sights during your approach, pull out and let one of the following planes get him. If you attempt to twist and turn you will end up at his level or below and will be unable to regain an altitude advantage. Following planes employ same tactics until you have destroyed the enemy one by one. Two planes are sufficient to carry out this type of attack. If you have others with you, leave them overhead on guard.

(3) If you get in a tough spot, dive away, maneuver violently [and] find a cloud.

(4) Stay together. The Japs air discipline is excellent, and if you get separated you will have at least three of them on you at once. [Having lost his designated wingman, "volunteer" wingman, and second section during the very first combat maneuver, one might have expected to see this hint presented earlier. Its significance, however, was emphasized at the bottom of the original draft, Jimmy writing "The lesson that impressed itself most on the fighter pilots was 'Do not become separated from your formation.'"]

(5) You have the better plane if you handle it properly, and in spite of their advantage of maneuverability you can and should shoot them down with few losses to yourselves. The reason for this is your greater firepower and more skillful gunnery.

(6) Don't get excited and rush in. Take your time and make the first attack effective.

(7) Watch out for "ruser" [ruses]. Japs have a method of creating smoke from their exhaust that doesn't mean a thing. Set them on fire before you take your guns off of them. They also have a method of releasing a gasoline cloud from their belly tanks.

[Jimmy may have assigned too much credit to the enemy regarding "a gasoline cloud."]

(8) Never hesitate to dive in. The hail of bullets around their cockpit will divert and confuse them and will definitely cause them to break off what they are doing and take avoiding action.

Appearing only on the draft of the 7 May action report was a worthy comment probably deleted from the signed version as Jimmy realized it was more a statement of need and fact rather than a hint. The deleted item read:

(9) We must have more VF on our carriers. A minimum of 27 and preferably 36 would not be too many. The F4F-3 airplane properly handled can beat the enemy carrier based fighters encountered so far. This includes Type Zero.

Immediately following this comment, Jimmy then listed what were believed to be the aircraft and personnel losses for 7 May. His assessment for "own" losses was simply that reported for Task Force Seventeen, but not unexpectedly the assessment for damage to the enemy (twenty-two fighters) was considerably overestimated. In keeping with the overall somber mood after the following day's battle, Jimmy offered no statistics for either side.

The tone of Jimmy's 8 May report barely disguises his emotions. The report is very matter of fact, and his disappointment is apparent regarding loss of *Lexington* and having his wingman and division not stay with him again (and again on the very first combat maneuver). While between the lines one deduces his emotional disappointment, no such process is necessary to discern his disgust concerning fighter direction for the eighth. His report reads:

With our carrier expecting an attack, one half of available VF were sent as escorts with [our] own attack group. This left only about 16 to protect two carriers. It is estimated that enemy escorting VF numbered about 30. It was a grievous mistake to divide our pitifully few fighters.

The few fighters that we did have were handled very poorly. The original radar contact was made with the enemy 68 miles distant.

Instead of sending all fighters out to intercept at a maximum distance, they were divided into at least four groups, and were dispersed at various altitudes and distances. As far as is known, no fighter group intercepted the enemy aircraft before they started their attack.

Jimmy's observations were correct, and even though he knew and understood most of the mitigating factors contributing to the poor fighter direction, he knew there was value in unequivocally stating the disappointing results. All relevant commands in the Pacific and bureaus in Washington needed to have the facts, cold and hard as they were. Even though *Yorktown* had been in commission for little more than four years, no thought had been given during her design regarding space in the island structure or the gallery deck immediately beneath the island either for radar or fighter direction. Radar, still in its infancy but maturing rapidly, began appearing on carriers three years after *Yorktown*'s commissioning in 1937. By 1943 *Essex*-class carriers entered the fleet with a combat information center (CIC) that accommodated both radar and fighter direction. On *Essex* and her sister ships, the CIC was located on the gallery deck immediately under the island, but on *Yorktown*'s sister ship, *Enterprise* (Jimmy's next carrier), a compartment was altered within the island during an overhaul in late 1943.

An adequate compartment, however, was only the beginning of a solution. Radar equipment had to improve, and throughout the war there was a steady improvement in quality. Although the early CXAM radar could detect aircraft up to eighty miles, it was not precise indicating altitude. This lack of precision in the radar contributed to Jimmy's inability to find the strike group on the eighth as he was flying at two thousand feet and mostly looking down while the enemy passed over him at four thousand feet above the scattered clouds. Additionally, the IFF (identification friend or foe) gear was not installed in all friendly fighters, therefore, the FDO could not always determine whether the radar blips were friend or foe. All things considered, the FDOs on both *Lexington* and *Yorktown* did as good a job as could have been expected given all the shortages and inadequacies of the technology available. Indeed, both Lt. Frank F. "Red" Gill aboard *Lexington* and Lt. Cdr. Oscar Pederson aboard *Yorktown* were seasoned naval aviators, and the

Battle of the Coral Sea was not their first combat experience. Still, fighter direction had to be improved, and fast!

Nothing could be done for *Lexington*, Paul Baker, John Baker, Les Knox, or any other lost comrades; and even before Jimmy arrived in San Diego, he had driven those thoughts into a deep recess in his memory where matters too painful to dwell upon are held in abeyance. Nor was there any reason to dwell on wingmen who did not stay with their leader. Jimmy could understand how his wingmen became separated as he and they never trained together. But what really bothered him were the many separations by the other pilots during the two-day battle. How could they stay together in combat if they had difficulty even forming up immediately after launch? Still, Jimmy's concerns centered on discipline and training. It had to because Haas, Crommelin, Macomber, Bassett, and the other pilots of VF-42 as well as those in VF-2 had demonstrated an abundance of courage and fighting ability.

In some respects the greatest lesson Jimmy Flatley carried away from the Battle of the Coral Sea was understanding the critical need for solid leadership—he sensed a vacuum of leadership in some aspects of the strikes against the enemy ships, aerial discipline, and target coordination —a target coordinator was needed to manage the strikes. Unlike courage, leadership and discipline could be taught. And more mistakes in battle would eventually result in target coordinators being assigned to keep mistakes from happening.

6

"The Navy Fighter" and Fighting Squadron Ten

ON 15 MAY 1942 Jimmy left *Yorktown* at Tongatabu to board the ninety-four-hundred-ton transport *Barnett* (AP-11 built in England as a passenger steamer). Along with another transport, *George F. Elliott* (AP-13) and the heavy cruiser *Chester* (CA-27) as escort, *Barnett* would carry him and *Lexington* survivors to San Diego. The voyage provided time and a relative degree of serenity for Jimmy to sort through his recent experience and commit some ideas to paper. The Battle of the Coral Sea was behind him, but he knew he could not take his new Fighting Ten into battle and hope to survive and win with another performance like that of 7–8 May. Japanese air discipline had been very good in the Coral Sea, and, no doubt, it would be as good or better when he met them again. Except for several conversations with correspondent Stanley Johnston—who now knew first hand what it was like to abandon ship —Jimmy devoted his time to reflecting on the several air engagements fought on 7–8 May. Aboard *Yorktown* late on the eighth and through the ninth, the attitude among many of the aviators had been mixed. The sinking of *Shoho* helped but did not compensate for the loss of *Lexington*. Some fretted over the now known capability of the Zero and the relative inferiority of the Wildcat in climb and maneuverability.

However, discussions pertaining to the Zero were balanced against the claims for enemy fighters downed over the two-day battle. Even though the claims were exaggerated (on both sides), it was nonetheless quite significant that some—not all—of the U.S. carrier pilots truly believed they had defeated and could defeat enemy fighters. The perception of confidence at that time was the key, and upon that keystone Jimmy would build his squadron.

Upon reporting to Air Group Ten at NAS San Diego on 3 June 1942, Jimmy arranged his Coral Sea action reports and notes made while aboard the *Barnett*. It would be July before "Combat Doctrine: Fighting Squadron Ten" was complete, but that was not a problem since during the first week of his new command he had only himself, six pilots, and five planes.[1] As one of the two newly authorized carrier replacement air groups, Air Group Ten was not yet fully staffed or equipped; but pilots and planes would soon arrive, and by the time the personnel and matériel components were in place, Jimmy's latest "book" would be ready. Basically arranged like the Jacksonville station manual that he had written eighteen months earlier, "Combat Doctrine" was considerably shorter (fifty-three pages including diagrams) and much different in tone. In a cover statement Jimmy wrote, "This compilation of combat data for fighter aircraft is the only available information, at this time, concerning combat doctrine under actual war conditions." Continuing, he noted that "it is not a complete bible."

If not a bible it was a fighter pilot's Sermon on the Mount. Jimmy began the unofficial manual in parable style comparing fighter pilots to a football team, and made the point that individualism had no place on a team. Only a team effort was acceptable, and every pilot must be a "potential quarterback." Jimmy explained that "the quarterbacks are the flight leaders. In our games with opponents, we play for keeps, and if a flight leader is knocked out, the next man in line must be able to take over and execute the plays" (pages 1–2). Concluding his introductory comments, Jimmy discussed five attributes (leadership, morale, indoctrination, material readiness, and pilot efficiency) necessary to ensure the success of a fighting squadron (pages 3–6). The main body of his manual dealt with squadron doctrine specifics on everything from training to formation flying to fighter director orders. All this was necessary, but the heart of the manual centered on Jimmy's discussion of the methods of attack against enemy aircraft. The methods emphasized advantages and disadvantages of overhead, side, opposite, and astern approaches; when to shoot ("target in the bubble"), when not to shoot ("not over 250 yards, and not if you have to leave your wingman"), and how long to shoot ("usually not over three seconds"). Frequent problems known to fighter pilots were addressed (ammunition expenditure, radio failure, and fuel supply) as well as potential advantages (altitude advantage and sun/cloud cover) (pages 7–39). Following were twelve pages of hand-drawn diagrams depicting aerial tactics. No better assessment of its value can be offered than that of former South Dakota governor and Medal of Honor recipient, Joe Foss. En route to Guadalcanal on a transport in September 1942, the young Marine fighter pilot later recalled that, " We talked aerial fighter tactics by the hour after boning up on Lt. Commander Jimmy Flatley's Fighter Doctrine [*sic*], an information-packed little manual."[2] During the Guadalcanal campaign, Captain Foss shot down twenty-six enemy planes and had several opportunities to discuss tactics and Jimmy's "Combat Doctrine" while both were on the contested island in late 1942.[3]

"The Navy Fighter"

Nowhere in the lengthy "Combat Doctrine" was there any mention of the Wildcat, the fixed-wing, four-gun F4F-3 or the heavier, folding-wing, six-gun F4F-4. Nor was the Zero discussed. Fighters for both sides were referred to only in generic terms. However, toward the middle of June 1942, Jimmy felt compelled to defer work on the squadron manual to write another epistle. Intelligence reports criticizing the F4F-4—before and after Midway—were being circulated. Particularly influential comments were offered by Midway participants including fighter squadron commanders Lt. James S. Gray Jr. (VF-6 on *Enterprise*), and Lt. Cdr. Jimmie Thach (VF-3 on *Yorktown*). Equally important were the thoughts of two other heroes of the decisive early June battle. In a 13 June confidential memo prepared for Rear Adm. Raymond A. Spruance, his chief aviation adviser, Capt. Miles R. Browning, wrote that the F4F-4 "performance [was] greatly inferior to Jap 'zero' VF . . . [and] range and endurance totally inadequate." Spruance agreed.

None of the pilots who fought at Midway had returned to San Diego by 25 June when Jimmy's nine-page letter, "The Navy Fighter" was forwarded to the commander of carriers in the Pacific Fleet, but scuttlebutt has always traveled faster than men. Copies of "The Navy Fighter" were then forwarded to the Bureau of Aeronautics, the navy's commander in chief (Admiral King) and the commander in chief of the Pacific Fleet (Admiral Nimitz). The problem was even more serious than Jimmy suspected. On 21 June 1942 Admiral Nimitz, who was cognizant of all the Midway participants' reports on the F4F-4, forwarded a secret message to Admiral King regarding the relative inferiority of the Wildcat to the Japanese Zero. In the message Nimitz asked King to consider providing "[Army] P-40 planes or comparable type for all Marine fighting squadrons . . . [and] if P-40 or comparable type can be modified for aircraft carrier operations, provide these planes for carrier fighting squadrons." In the same message Nimitz also requested steps to lighten the F4F-4 and "increase ammunition capacity even at [the] cost of reduction in [the] number of guns."[4] This was an indictment of the first magnitude for the navy's F4F-4 Wildcat fighter. The last thing Jimmy needed at that time was the burden of controversy added to the inherent challenges concomitant with forming what would be the first carrier replacement fighting squadron to see combat.

The general public would not know until 26 September 1942 that *Yorktown* had been lost during the 4–6 June Battle of Midway, although Jimmy knew before the end of that month that his most recent carrier home was gone. The public did know a great victory had been won, and that four of the six Japanese Pearl Harbor carrier raiders—*Akagi, Kaga, Soryu,* and *Hiryu*—had been sunk. However, at the Battle of Midway there simply had not been enough fighters to adequately protect the strike groups—the torpedo squadrons incurring horrendous losses—or to defend the carriers. As a fighter squadron commanding officer who knew combat was not far distant, Jimmy had to address the acerbic comments offered on the performance of the F4F-4 Wildcat. The group Jimmy primarily wished to influence was Fighting Squadron Ten. Unless his new charges could maintain focus and develop confidence, they were defeated before leaving San Diego. Given the recent, frequent, and large numbers of pilots transferred from one squadron to another, Jimmy did not know for sure from where all his pilots would come. Consequently, he decided to forward his message to those who had the authority, if they so chose, to ensure all fighter pilots saw it.

Although Jimmy flew only the F4F-3 Wildcat during the Battle of the Coral Sea, he was no stranger to the F4F-4. Significantly, however, the experimental XF4F-4 was equipped with four guns, not the six mounted in the F4F-4s at Midway. While still with VF-2 he had flown the sole XF4F-4 a total of 21.2 hours in February and March, plus another 2.0 hours in two other F4F-4s. During his first month with VF-10 (June), he recorded another 13.8 hours in F4F-4s for testing, gunnery, and tactics flights. In March he and Dotty had entertained Lt. Cdr. Dale Harris one evening at the Flatley home. Harris, assigned to the Planning Division of the Bureau of Aeronautics, got a lengthy after dinner dissertation from Jimmy on the problems with the F4F-4.[5] It was heavier than the F4F-3, and did not have as good a rate of climb as the earlier Wildcat. Not having faced enemy fighters at that time (March 1942), a comparison between any Wildcat variant and the Japanese Zero was not possible, particularly relating to maneuverability and speed. Still, Harris left the Flatley home aware that Jimmy was not overly impressed with Grumman's latest model. But after facing enemy fighters in the Coral Sea, Jimmy knew that it made no difference whether his pilots flew the -3 or -4 Wildcats: both were inferior to the Zero one on one. The answer was simple: fight as a team, and don't dogfight with the Zero.

Butch O'Hare was the first fighter pilot to have a stage or platform as a result of his February 1942 heroic battle against enemy bombers, but he had not yet fought the vaunted Zero. And speaking, writing, or leading a crusade was not his forte. "The Navy Fighter" was the platform upon which Jimmy stepped forward to address the crisis of confidence in the Wildcat fighter. His goal, described at length in "The Navy Fighter," was to persuade and convince those fighter pilots then in the Pacific, and those in training, that their fighter, when properly used, was not only the equal to the best the Japanese could offer, it was superior. The last line of his manuscript captured its essence: "Let's take stock of ourselves and get down to work and quit griping about our planes."

It is apparent in "The Navy Fighter" that Jimmy did not have complete information or details from the recent Battle of Midway. Indeed, there were a few pilots, like Coral Sea veterans Lts. (jg) William N. "Bill" Leonard, Scott McCuskey, John Adams, Richard Crommelin and a few others who had seen the Zero more than once. But, aside from this, the epistle was on track.

Although Jimmy hoped his letter would be well received by his VF-10 pilots more than any other person or group, he was pleased to learn from more than one within the Bureau of Aeronautics that the letter was apparently having impact. From Commander Harris he learned it "received most favorable comment."[6] And from the Engineering Department of the Bureau, Cdr. J. B. Pearson wrote, "Your letter . . . coming as it did after severe indictments of our fighters by the Fleet . . . has tended to restore our faith in the good sense of at least a part of our operating personnel." Pearson added, "I have heard nothing but the highest praise for all of the remarks that you have made. . . . This praise has come from the Bureau of Aeronautics, as well as Cominch [sic] personnel." Highest praise, however, came from Frank Knox, the secretary of the navy. On 29 July 1942 Knox wrote Jimmy the following letter.

> My dear Commander:
> I have just found time to read your discussion of the Navy fighter contained in a bulletin sent out to the men of the Fleet and discussing the comparative merits of the F4F-4 and the "Zero" fighters.
> I cannot refrain from expressing my very great admiration for this entire communication and the spirit in which it is written. This is especially true of the latter portion of your communication. That is the kind of spirit that wins wars. What we must do in this war, if we are going to win, is not to wait until we have everything exactly as we want it, but rather to do the best with what we have and rely upon those at home to get better equipment to our fighting squadrons just as fast as it is humanly possible to do so.
> My warm congratulations and felicitations!

It was a long time before Jimmy learned about the essence of the classified message between Nimitz and King. As that information became known, he also had a better appreciation of why Secretary Knox was so pleased with Jimmy's lengthy letter. Although many agreed with the intent and spirit of "The Navy Fighter," some could not immediately join in the hosannas. While Jimmy's document put the F4F-4 fighter in proper perspective, his constant references to the six-plane formation (division) raised the eyebrows of Capt. J. M. Shoemaker in the administration office of the commander of carriers in the Pacific Fleet. On 15 July 1942 he submitted "The Navy Fighter" to Jimmie Thach, "the most experienced fighter pilot in this area, for comment." Further, Shoemaker proposed the essence of "The Navy Fighter," as revised by Thach, be included in a revision of chapter 3, part 2, "United States Fleet 74 Revised" (USF-74), the "book" on carrier squadron operation, and then be "promulgated to the Service."

Jimmie Thach opened his undated four-page response acknowledging "The Navy Fighter" as "an excellent approach to a subject, which in the past has been given too little attention by those responsible for the overall training of carrier-based pilots." He further acknowledged Jimmy Flatley's document noting that "it is possible by increasing each squadron to thirty-six (36) fighters and by exploiting to the fullest extent the personnel and material *now on hand* [by this Thach meant the F4F-4] to successfully attack enemy carriers and to effect complete annihilation of an enemy carrier attack group before their arrival at the point of dropping torpedoes or bombs." Thach completed his opening comments noting "that an aircraft carrier under attack by enemy dive-bombers and torpedo planes can escape damage only so long as her fighter squadron is adequate in number and performance."

The remainder of Thach's letter concerned the advantages of the four-plane division ("flight" in the original) of two sections as opposed to Flatley's favored six-plane division.[7] At Midway, Thach had successfully used the "mutual-support" beam defense, shooting down three Zeros, and he and his wingman used the tactic to defend themselves against a much larger force for nearly twenty minutes—a very long time in aerial combat. Alluding to this experience, Thach argued, "For mutual support and counterattack two sections can keep track of each other continually, but a pilot cannot keep two other sections plus enemy aircraft in sight when he is under heavy attack." With carrier fighter squadrons about to jump up to thirty-six, Thach advocated an organization of three four-plane divisions. A squadron of thirty-six should allow twelve planes to accompany an attack group (stacked to protect above and below), twelve for combat air patrol, and twelve on deck to be launched as additional CAP when an attack was imminent. In concluding his letter, Thach, as he had done just before his pilots flew at Midway, wrote that to defend their carrier, pilots out of ammunition should use ramming tactics, which "if properly executed [it] can be done with relative safety."[8] In his comments about ramming tactics, one of the navy's most experienced and influential fighter squadron commanders reveals an almost desperate tone concerning carrier defense in July 1942.

For nearly all of July, Jimmie Thach was in San Diego on leave before traveling to his next assignment, which turned out to be a two-year tour with the Operational Training Command at NAS Jacksonville. One of the first visits for Commander Thach and his wife, Madeline, was to the Flatley home for dinner. (The Flatleys were in the process of buying the Coronado house they had been renting.) Just as they had before the war, the men and women separated before dinner, and conversation during dinner was centered on children and personal matters. Still, some sad matters could not help but make their way into the discussion before and after the children left the room. Thach had briefly witnessed the last few seconds of Lem Massey's life at Midway, and Jimmy Flatley related how he and Lem sailed together out to Pearl ten months earlier. Memories of other mutual friends and squadron mates were shared. Edgar Bassett, who had performed so well at Coral Sea, did not survive Midway. Both men raised a glass to Massey, Bassett, and all the others so recently lost. The natural desire to discuss tactics, "The Navy Fighter," and Thach's response was briefly held in abeyance. Filling that evening was the spoken and unspoken joy of good food, good fellowship, and remembrance of good friends.[9]

Even though the two naval officers were very good friends, their friendship was not based on any understanding that they would always agree with each other. Professional differences did not transfer to their personal relations, and indeed, their differences of opinion seemed to have drawn them closer during the war. Thach carried pocket-sized notebooks with black covers in which he recorded significant tactical thoughts —with notations to inform Jimmy Flatley and others concerning certain ideas—and mundane notes (such as laundry lists) side by side.[10]

Jimmy Flatley often noted Thach's comments to him during the San Diego visit and afterwards. [11] And when each was serving as an operations officer with one of the two fleets pounding the Japanese in 1944 and 1945, there was a stream of communication between them. Although their interests and career assignments during World War II were very similar, their personalities were less so. The following anecdote from Capt. Stanley W. "Swede" Vejtasa (retold below) illustrates one of the differences.

While at North Island in June and July 1942, Jimmy Flatley's VF-10 pilots when flying practice sorties, delighted in jumping other fighters or any group of planes in the training areas. This was a profitable experience, even for the planes suddenly coming under attack. However, Thach did not think this was such a good idea. Fighting Ten pilots quickly passed the word when Thach came striding across the hangar floor, as they knew he was headed for Flatley's office to vociferously complain "about those wild and dangerous pilots of VF-10." Flatley would sit quietly and listen intently, interrupting only to offer Thach a cigarette. "Light?" he would say casually. After a few long draws on their Camels, Thach would continue his protests, although now with less ardor. Cigarettes finished, Flatley would then note it was lunchtime and perhaps they might retire to the North Island Officers Club to discuss some innovation he had in mind that might be worthy of experimentation. Vejtasa recalled that this tactful approach always worked as Thach never passed up an opportunity to discuss tactics. And Jimmy Flatley was always generous with the cigarettes, coffee, or bourbon whether at home, in the office, or at the O club. Forgotten, at least for the time being, was the matter of "those wild VF-10 pilots." Later, Flatley related the complaint to his men, counseling them "to use good judgment and not overdo it. Always accompanying the admonition was a wry smile."[12]

Success and recognized leadership accrued to only a few navy fighter squadron commanders from late 1941 through mid-1943, Flatley, Thach, and O'Hare ranking at the top despite their junior rank. The innovative and leadership success of the three was no accident. As noted, Thach and O'Hare served together in VF-3 for much of the two years prior to the war and the first several months after the day of infamy. Thach and Flatley did not complete flight school together as has sometimes been reported, but their commitment to excellence brought them together to discuss their mutual labor of love. What could be considered an accident is that shortly before the war, Flatley and Thach had reached the place in their careers that put them in position to assume air group or squadron leadership assignments. The lives of the three naval aviation innovators were interrelated, and those relationships directly influenced the conduct of carrier fighter tactics from the desperate first months of the war to its end. Still, the major tactical contribution attributed to their interaction was not immediate. When Thach left San Diego in late July for his new assignment in Florida, he had not converted Jimmy Flatley to the full value of mutual-support beam defense and the four-plane division. Thach had thoroughly made his tactical argument, but another month passed before his disciple, Butch O'Hare, completed the transformation.

Finally, it must be remembered that the continuing dialogue between Jimmy Flatley and Jimmie Thach began while the two were in Hawaii in mid-April 1942. Thach remembered that their "many discussions night and day, sometimes late in the night, [were] about what was the best thing to do. Neither one of us knew it for sure. He [Flatley] said, 'I think the four-plane division is good, but I think we shouldn't all try the same thing. Why don't I try six planes in a formation, and you go ahead and try the four, and we'll see which one makes out the best.'"[13]

Building Fighting Squadron Ten

Fighting Squadron Ten's roster of officers listed only thirteen pilots after Jimmy's first month, but by the end of July a full complement was in place. While the personnel problem was being resolved, the problem of obtaining sufficient F4F-4 Wildcats went unresolved until the squadron arrived in Hawaii in mid-August. Still, the time at North Island (NAS San Diego) was put to good use.

As none of the other Air Group Ten squadron commanders or the group commander had ever been in combat, Jimmy was soon recognized as the "head coach."[14] The group commander, Cdr. Richard Gaines, (USNA 1925) "was a nice guy, but less than forceful."[15] Like many other officers in similar leadership positions in 1942, Gaines had been more an administrator than pilot in recent years. Just before the war began and in the early months following, many such officers returned to the cockpit to find themselves unfamiliar with newer aircraft, ordnance, and tactics. To Commander Gaines's credit, he recognized his limitations and gave considerable latitude to his squadron commanders, especially Jimmy. Despite their lack of combat experience, the three other squadron commanders in Air Group Ten—Lt. Cdr. James A. Thomas (VB-10); Lt. Cdr. James R. "Bucky" Lee (VS-10); and academy classmate Lt. Cdr. John A. Collett (VT-10)—were highly competent "and did the best they could to prepare us for war."[16]

As the de facto air group commander (CAG), Jimmy "was intensely interested in the characteristics and capabilities of all the aircraft, and frequently chatted at length with junior pilots regarding their thoughts on tactics and the best utilization of a plane's capabilities. Although primarily a fighter pilot, he always looked at the big picture of air group operations and multigroup attacks. He thought about formation, base squadrons, speed, defensive tactics, offensive tactics, and coordinated attacks."[17] Rear Adm. (then a lieutenant junior grade with VS-10) Martin D. "Red" Carmody recalled:

> He had a warm personality and impressed all of us with his dedication to win in the combat arena. He was a tireless instructor and spent much time with each of our three squadrons providing all the lore and experience he had acquired in his engagements with the Japanese. He repeatedly emphasized to our dive-bomber and torpedo pilots the importance of flying a tight formation and to avoid lagging behind. Perhaps that is when the expression "when you lag you lose" was coined. He made it crystal clear why it was so important to join up after an attack so the few fighters we had could provide us cover against the Zeros.
>
> His tutorials provided all of us with an insight as to what we could expect in the realities of combat. He constantly preached the importance of being aggressive and made each of us feel like key players. I'm certain, speaking for myself, that those briefing sessions helped to build our confidence and to dispel fear of the unknown.[18]

While Jimmy was pleased to share his experience with the officers of Scouting Ten, Bombing Ten, and Torpedo Ten, his primary responsibility resided with Fighting Ten. For the first month he could look only to Lt. Swede Vejtasa and Lt. Frederick "Fritz" Faulkner for leadership assistance. Both had seen combat with Scouting Five in the Coral Sea flying SBDs on bombing strikes and with the supplementary combat air patrol. Swede had downed one enemy plane at Coral Sea with his SBD, and was greatly comforted to know that the next time he faced the enemy he would be in a Wildcat. For the first two months of Fighting Ten's existence, he served as executive officer, and with Faulkner, they worked to indoctrinate the squadron's new arrivals, most of whom reported directly from flight training.

The daily schedule while at North Island was consistent. "Skipper Flatley was a master of delegating responsibility," and although there were morning meetings, everyone knew their duties and worked using their best judgment to accomplish assigned tasks. The war caused a sense of urgency, but Jimmy, being a family man himself, urged the pilots to enjoy a degree of social life, and encouraged the married men to spend as much time as possible with their families. As a result of this approach, much more was accomplished in a short time than most expected.[19]

Not overlooked in the early days of Fighting Ten was Jimmy's interest in establishing a team spirit, and how better to accomplish this than to have a unique identity. This had been no small matter with his earlier squadrons, and even though VF-5B had a good reputation, Jimmy was particularly impressed with the reputation and spirit of VF-2. In addition to the usual squadron insignia, VF-2 carried the nickname "Fighting Chiefs," and had a particularly unique motto, "Adorimini," meaning "Up and at 'em." For Fighting Squadron Ten, Jimmy wanted something equally distinctive. While aboard *Barnett,* he came up with a nickname of "Grim Reapers," and ran it by Stanley Johnston, who approved. Feeding off the thoughts of each other, the motto "Mow 'em Down" was born along with a concept for an insignia. A young enlisted man from *Lexington* with artistic talent, Jimmy Wilkes, was asked to improve Johnston's sketch of a skeleton armed with a scythe. Wilkes's final version, completed after arrival in San Diego, depicted the head of the skeleton wearing goggles trailed by its skeleton body like a comet. From the bony shoulders sprouted embryonic wings, and in its hands was a blood-dripping scythe, and the death head zoomed downward at a 45-degree angle to attack. The new VF-10 squadron commander originally placed the six-by-eight-foot banner on the wall behind his desk, even though he was convinced Wilkes had used him as a model for the skeleton. Enthusiastically received by the original squadron, when they went aboard *Enterprise* the banner went with them.[20] Later in the war when the squadron was assigned to *Intrepid* (CV-11), the banner followed. By then it carried a number of Japanese flags, one for each enemy plane shot down by VF-10. But for the two months the squadron was in San Diego (June and July 1942), Wilkes continued to offer his talent with a series of drawings depicting the skeleton ("Ole Moe") inflicting all kinds of grief upon one or more Japanese. Even the invitation for the squadron's commissioning party featured a Wilkes original.

The squadron nickname and banner were outward signs of what Jimmy hoped to internalize within his pilots. Not one to trust letting another read between the lines to figure out what he wanted, Jimmy was quite outspoken. In every meeting he emphasized that the pilots must know each other, take care of each other, and be helpful in every way possible.[21]

Of course, training in the air was the main order of day. The shortage of planes meant that all hours had to productive, especially since the F4F-4 was new to most. Still, Jimmy recorded nearly all his 45.7 hours for July in the F4F-4. Despite a well-organized schedule, he nearly always gathered the pilots for post-flight analysis. Although Jimmy strongly advocated the cool, aggressive, slashing type of attack with the axiom to never give the enemy an advantage and to keep moving, he still discussed details and asked for input on how tactics and training could be improved. This probing interest and open communication instilled remarkable confidence, for veterans and rookies alike.[22]

With two-thirds of his new squadron rookies, the nickname, insignia, and banner had special meaning. Theirs was a most dangerous occupation, a killing profession in which it was understood that quality of life had to be more important than concerns for longevity. Hard work and realistic training translated into survival. And while work and training demanded 100 percent of their attention, time was also given to leisure. Just prior to VF-10's departure for Hawaii, a commissioning party was planned for 31 July, with Jimmy providing as many ideas as the other pilots appointed to an ad hoc committee. Larry Crosby, a brother of Bing and Bob, was invited along with Bing and a number of

Hollywood starlets. Flying from Los Angeles, the guests arrived at North Island, and while en route by car to Point Loma, the planes of VF-10 "entertained" them with a mock attack. The attack and later party were equal in success and merriment.[23]

The Grim Reapers in Hawaii

On 8 August the Grim Reapers left California for Hawaii, and by 24 August the squadron had drawn enough F4F-4 Wildcats to resume training, although by 2 September the squadron had only eighteen of the twenty-seven planes they were then allowed.[24] A training accident took the life of Ens. R. L. Von Lehe, and another accident left injuries serious enough to require a replacement pilot. Still, by late September a roster of pilots who would fly under the Grim Reaper banner of Fighting Ten was in place. Lt. T. E. "Bobby" Edwards (USNA 1937) had relieved Vejtasa as executive officer in July, Lt. Stanley E. Ruehlow (USNA 1935) relieved Edwards in September, and just before going into combat in October, Lt. Commander W. R. "Killer" Kane (USNA 1933) assumed the XO post. Even with the addition of several experienced pilots, the two-thirds ratio of rookies to veterans held. Another veteran of note who came late (on leave until late July) was Lt. (jg) John A. Leppla, who had been credited with four planes while flying an SBD with Scouting Two at Coral Sea (post war analysis confirmed one). Like Vejtasa and Faulkner, there was no F4F-4 controversy in Leppla's mind. While only two (Jimmy and Swede Vejtasa) of the thirty-eight pilots with Fighting Ten in mid-October 1942 would achieve "ace" status (five kills) prior to the end of the year, twelve—including seven rookies—were so recognized by the end of the war by the American Aces Association.[25]

With personnel in place and F4F-4 Wildcats assigned to the pilots, the new squadron began to round into shape from late August into early October. The lack of experienced fighter pilots caused no undue stress on Jimmy. Combat losses and a need for the remaining fighter pilots to lead and train new pilots simply meant they were not available to VF-10. The twenty-two young ensigns who had demonstrated potential and made the squadron roster received considerable attention from

Jimmy. Most of the combat veterans were ex–dive-bomber pilots whose only fighter experience had been to use their SBDs as supplemental fighters at Coral Sea. Still, Jimmy felt he had the right men to train the rookies as the combat veterans were tough-minded, experienced, and "had no preconceived ideas or faults which needed to be erased."[26] Obviously, Jimmy was still thinking about the several discipline lapses demonstrated by the pilots of VF-42 at Coral Sea. That squadron had exceptional individual talent, but had not fought as a team to the degree expected.

The five "right men" were Vejtasa and Faulkner, formerly of *Yorktown*'s Scouting Five; Leppla and Edwards, formerly of *Lexington*'s Scouting Two; and Lt. Albert D. "Dave" Pollock Jr., formerly with *Lexington*'s air department. Lt. John C. Eckhardt Jr. (USNA 1938), Lt. Leroy E. Harris (USNA 1939), Lt. Frank Donald Miller (USNA 1939), and Lt. Macgregor Kilpatrick (USNA 1939) did not have combat experience, but at least they had a little more flying time and age (average twenty-six) over the mostly twenty-two-year old ensigns. Actually, Vejtasa and Faulkner were assigned to VF-10 before Jimmy: Swede's orders dated from 17 February 1942. Aboard *Yorktown* just before the Coral Sea battle, Vejtasa and Faulkner were about to cross via hi-line from the carrier to the oiler *Neosho* for a ride east with the eventual destination San Diego and VF-10. One bag of gear had already gone over to the oiler when Cdr. Murr Arnold, *Yorktown*'s air officer, appeared and said, "We are expecting some action real soon and we will need all the experience we can muster. . . . We want to keep you pilots aboard." Both pilots were delighted with this—what was for them—great news, and it became even greater shortly afterward when the news arrived that *Neosho* had been attacked and was sinking.[27]

Jimmy knew that the twenty-eight-year-old Vejtasa, a six-foot-two-inch Montana native of Scandinavian descent, had made a study of fighter tactics and individual combat while in Scouting Five. Too, he had flown many flights with Lt. Cdr. William O. "Bill" Burch who was an expert in countering attacks and utilizing less powerful and maneuverable aircraft. Jimmy encouraged Swede to share that knowledge and experience not only with VF-10 but also with the other squadrons of Air Group Ten. By the time Jimmy and Swede parted six months and several furious air battles later, Jimmy considered Swede to be "the great-est of the fighter pilots."[28] Engineering Officer Fritz Faulkner likewise was recognized as an expert, his expertise being aircraft maintenance and engine performance. Jimmy, always interested in aircraft engineer-ing, was pleased to find that Fritz could teach others how to maintain maximum fuel consumption, plus he was outstanding in helping train new mechanics and plane captains.[29]

Material Officer John Leppla, like Vejtasa, had proven courageous and tenacious in battle. A veteran of the Lae and Salamuna raids and Coral Sea, the always cheerful Mediterranean descendant from rural Ohio much preferred the F4F-4 to the SBD, but flew both planes as if they were tanks—an extension of his combat tenacity. "Destined for greatness,"[30] John was a friend to everyone in the squadron, and despite his modest rank the twenty-six-year-old bachelor "became an example whom we all tried to emulate."[31] Although not as charismatic as Leppla, twenty-seven-year-old Bobby Edwards (assistant executive officer) and Dave Pollock (operations officer), also twenty-seven, were good leaders both in the air and on the ground.

Of course, thirty-one-year-old Lt. Cdr. "Killer" Kane and thirty-year-old Lt. Stan Ruehlow were "right men" and experienced fighter pilots, but both reported very late in VF-10's formation and training period. Kane later became commanding officer of VF-10 and then commanding officer of Air Group Ten along with earning ace status. Ruehlow flew with VF-8 during the Battle of Midway, but was one of the pilots mistakenly led away from the battle, which resulted in five traumatic days in a life raft. Like Kane, he soon proved his worth in combat.

Throughout the Hawaiian period (20 August–16 October), training emphasis in the air centered on gunnery and squadron/group tactics. The ultimate purpose of any fighter was to put as many bullets as pos-sible into a target. Without this capability the fighter had no worth. Of Jimmy's 72.7 hours in this seven-week period, nearly one-third (22.7) were devoted to gunnery. Indeed, the most worrisome feature of the F4F-4 was its relative paucity of firing time: therefore, accuracy became even more critical. Jimmie Thach had written the Bureau of Aeronautics on 28 May to declare the six-guns of the -4 to be unsatisfactory as the additional two guns reduced firing time to about twenty-four seconds, down from about forty seconds (240 rounds versus 450). This was the one attribute of the -4 Jimmy Flatley chose not to defend except to recommend holding two guns in reserve. Even though he had strong arguments to overcome the other perceived deficiencies of the planes, Flatley, like Thach and every other fighter pilot, wanted more firing time. Swede Vejtasa recalls Flatley's intense interest in the subject:

> The Skipper took great interest in the guns in the F4F-4 and in conference with other pilots, discussed such things as bore-sighting and plans utilizing two, four or all six guns at a time. We had access to several competent engineers who could figure bullet concentration, depth of bullet fields and arrive at good scientific solutions to such questions. Then an added question was what the load should be using tracer, ball and any other rounds available. All of these things were made part of squadron doctrine during the training period.[32]

The second third of Jimmy's (22.8) and the squadron's flying hours was devoted to tactics,[33] most hours to squadron tactics with group tactics emphasized just prior to sailing for combat. In Hawaii training became progressively intense, and as Fighting Ten began tactical training to escort and defend the scouting, bombing, and torpedo squadrons—mental intensity surpassed the physical. This was a difficult operation, and Jimmy worked overtime on this phase with several innovations and testing of positions and defensive maneuvers. His continual experimentation and method of involving the thinking of the other squadron COs and their pilots resulted not only in "excellent rapport" but also "a fine brotherhood developed."[34] After trying and testing his six-plane division in these training exercises, he began to experience some of the problems Thach expressed to him personally and in his written response to "The Navy Fighter." And Thach's protégé, Butch O'Hare (then CO of VF-3 on Maui), was in near daily contact with Flatley to continue to challenge the six-plane division.

Between the two officers, Jimmie Thach was the more confrontational—in part because he was senior to Jimmy Flatley—but Butch was no less firm. And Butch was renowned for saying much with as few words as possible. The most convincing evidence, however, was in the air, and toward the end of September, Jimmy Flatley could see that the ultimate objectives of his fighter squadron could be best served with the four-plane division of two sections and Thach's mutual-support beam defense. One of the several factors that influenced Flatley's decision was his engineering interest. O'Hare related to Flatley how in the initial experiment of the beam defense, Thach had modified the controls on the planes in his division while allowing Butch's division to retain full power. That thought dovetailed with Fritz Faulkner's practice of optimum fuel consumption, no small matter as Flatley retained seventeen-hundred revolutions per minute (cruise setting) in battle while others often went to twenty-two hundred.[35]

In short, the four-plane, mutual-support beam defense began to show advantages in Jimmy Flatley's mind on several levels. Without fanfare, the change was made, the squadron doctrine modified, and the transition accomplished. As Swede recalls, "It took little practice to note the many advantages."[36] Jimmie Thach, who already knew the maneuver was offensive as well as defensive, later recalled that Jimmy Flatley communicated to him that "the four-plane division is the only thing that will work, and I am calling it the Thach Weave. . . . The two extra (planes) get lost." Further, "the weave was the only way for Navy fighters to fight against superior enemy fighters."[37] And Butch O'Hare, the navy's first World War II ace who had received his fighter training at Pensacola in May 1940 with Jimmy Flatley as his instructor, had repaid a favor. Dividends accrued to Jimmy, his squadron, and in short time, all of naval aviation.

IN ADDITION to having a common interest in flying and squadron leadership responsibilities, Jimmy Flatley and Butch O'Hare had another interest in common, Countess Alexandra Von Tempsky Zabriskie ("Alexa," or "Lex," to those who knew her best) and Erehwon (nowhere spelled backwards) Ranch. With nephew Gordon Von Tempsky flying with the U.S. Army Air Force, Alexa and all the family felt a special closeness with aviators. And like others who lived in the islands, it was understood that all that stood between them and their livelihoods were servicemen. Divorced and childless, Alexa was forty-nine in the summer of 1942 when Jimmy, Butch, and their men first met her. A skilled artist, she was an accomplished conversationalist, and more significantly, a sympathetic listener. For Butch, Alexa became a surrogate mother,[38] for Jimmy a surrogate sister, and "a very emotional subject" for others who remember "a superb lady."[39] The countess was on a first name basis with Fleet Adm. Chester Nimitz, and after the war the admiral presented her with a signed photograph of the Japanese surrender, noting that she "as much as anyone present at this ceremony [was] responsible for making possible this picture.[40]

The estate where Jimmy, Butch, and hundreds of others came to visit, picnic, party, share conversation over dinner, play cards, ride horses, and hunt, was located 3,500 feet up on the slopes of Haleakala, a 10,025 foot extinct volcano. The beautiful verdant grounds were complemented by a spectacular view of the valley and ocean. More beautiful than anything else, however, was the emotional tranquillity. Birds sang, and they were heard. Vespers were ever present, and they were felt. Pilots talked about everything except planes; and relationships, at least for a brief moment, became empathetic rather than categorical. From here, the war was very far away, if indeed it still existed. Jimmy later told Stanley Johnston that Alexa "was a one-woman USO, and more."[41] The portrait of Jimmy she painted to surprise Dotty for Christmas 1942 (Dotty's favorite image of her husband) still exists although it was damaged when Dotty's home burned in 1958. But, like all such moments in time, the visits to the Von Tempsky estate ended all too soon. At the farewell party, gifts were exchanged between Alexa and Fighting Ten, and promises were made to correspond and to return. Letters came and went, but some could not control destiny to fulfill the promise of a return visit.

On 30 September Jimmy stood at attention on *Enterprise*'s flight deck while Admiral Halsey pinned the Navy Cross on his summer white uniform, for the heroism and courage he had demonstrated in the Battle of the Coral Sea. The formal occasion was in many ways a signal that the particularly memorable formation and training period for the new air group was closing. The reality of the world's troubles again came more into focus as in early October the air group concentrated on field carrier landings before attempting both day and night landings on their carrier. On 15 October *Enterprise,* then one of only two fleet carriers operational in the Pacific, was being made ready for sea, and Air Group Ten was completing final details prior to flying aboard. Material Officer John Leppla was not quite ready. Shortly before midnight, he grabbed his newly arrived assistant just transferred from O'Hare's VF-3, Ens. Edward L. "Whitey" Feightner, and instructed him to "C'mon! We are short on some starters and we're shoving off to war at 0630 tomorrow morning." Jumping into a pickup with some enlisted men, the group drove over to the compound where spare aircraft were parked, and Leppla walked up to the marine sentry and pulled his pistol. While Whitey and the others watched in disbelief, Leppla gently spoke to the marine: "Now son, hand me your rifle and go over there and sit down and just be quiet. I am Lt. John Leppla and we have a little work to do here." With that, the small band of sailors went into the compound and took off the starters that were needed, threw them in the back of the truck, and came back out. After driving about twenty feet away, Leppla laid the sentry's rifle down and said, "Okay son, you can come and get your weapon, and I suggest you forget we were here." Turning to Whitey, Leppla said, "The skipper doesn't need to know about this. We're going off to war and we're the people who are going to need these, and there just wasn't time to argue about it. If they want me, they'll have to come after us in the Solomons. We've got work to do."[42]

7

The Grim Reapers and
the Battle of Santa Cruz

WHILE JIMMY was at San Diego from June through July 1942 and in Hawaii August through early October, the Pacific war remained in high gear. The momentous Battle of Midway had not turned the tide of war, but it seriously retarded the Japanese tide from its eastern flow. Nonetheless, the Japanese had moved far to the south and southwest through the Philippines and South China Sea. While the drive to Port Moresby on the southeastern coast of New Guinea had been aborted, the enemy still had major strongholds off the northeastern coast of that large island, particularly at Rabaul. From Rabaul, Imperial Japanese forces could support strategically located bases further southeast down the Solomons. If firmly ensconced in the southern Solomon Islands, they could pose a serious threat to the lines of communication and logistics between the United States and Australia.

In the upper chain of the Solomons, the Japanese continued establishing bases on Bougainville while in the lower Solomons they had the small base at Tulagi over which Swede Vejtasa, Fritz Faulkner, and other SBD pilots had such a difficult time on 4 May with their fogged sights. From their large bases at Rabaul and on Bougainville or the small seaplane base at Tulagi, the Japanese could not command either the sea or air lanes to and from Australia. However, from the large new base they began building in June on Guadalcanal across the sound from Tulagi, they might. Further, a major air base on Guadalcanal was a direct threat to allied bases recently established to the southeast in the New Hebrides and New Caledonia. And, although Guadalcanal was not part of the prewar "Orange" plan for the conduct of potential war with Japan, in February 1942 a decision had been made to occupy Tulagi and move up the Solomon chain to take or neutralize Rabaul and secure New Guinea. Consequently, there was no time to expend indulging in protracted celebrations for the success at Midway. On 7 August while Jimmy and Air Group Ten were preparing to sail from San Diego to Hawaii, a large U.S. naval force landed troops on Guadalcanal and Tulagi.

Supported by three carriers, *Enterprise, Saratoga,* and *Wasp,* the first hours of the Guadalcanal operation went relatively well. The transport *George F. Elliott,* which had steamed with *Barnett* carrying Jimmy and many *Lexington* survivors from the Coral Sea, was one of the two ships lost early on the eighth in the invasion. Arriving undetected, the attack force encountered little resistance on Guadalcanal, and many of the two thousand enemy troops (mostly labor) building the new airfield declined a fight in favor of flight into the nearby forest. A smaller enemy force on Tulagi delayed Allied control of that small island until the afternoon of the eighth. That evening, however, an enemy force of five heavy cruisers, two light cruisers, and one destroyer surprised the Allies off nearby Savo Island just after midnight and sank three U.S. Navy heavy cruisers (USS *Astoria,* CA-34; USS *Quincy,* CA-39; and USS *Vincennes,* CA-44) and one Australian cruiser (HMAS *Canberra*). As the carriers had withdrawn from the immediate area, the transports were compelled to leave on the ninth, leaving the marines short on supplies. There followed a progressively more intense effort by both sides to pour men and matériel onto the island. Indeed, the battle for Guadalcanal could determine the tide of the Pacific war as both sides were meeting for the first time on fairly equal terms.

Soon after the Allied landings on Guadalcanal, the Japanese Combined Fleet, including the two surviving Pearl Harbor raiders and Coral Sea veterans, *Shokaku* and *Zuikaku,* plus the smaller carrier *Ryujo,* steamed south from Truk. The objective was to sweep aside the American carriers, neutralize the still incomplete airfield on Guadalcanal—named for an aviator, Maj. Lofton R. Henderson, USMC, lost at Midway—and cover the landing of troops. This accomplished, the Japanese would then not only have command of the air, but also the ocean approaches to Guadalcanal. Without adequate land bases near enough to conduct effective combat operations, the Allies would have no choice but to withdraw. Without command of the air there could be no command of the sea, and hence, no command of the land.

On 24 August (the same day Jimmy's VF-10 began training flights in Hawaii), planes from the three Japanese carriers joined battle with those from *Enterprise* and *Saratoga* in the third major carrier-versus-carrier battle of the war. During the Battle of the Eastern Solomons, the Japanese lost *Ryujo* to *Saratoga*'s air group, while *Shokaku* and *Zuikaku* escaped damage. Planes from "Sho" and "Zui" did not attack "Sara," but did strike "The Big E." The air group aboard *Enterprise* had fatally damaged *Akagi* and *Kaga* at Midway on the 4 June morning strike, and a composite group of SBDs launched from *Enterprise* sank *Hiryu* that same afternoon. But on 24 August *Enterprise* was on the receiving end, taking three bombs that killed seventy-four. Major damage to the carrier included a destroyed 5-inch gun group starboard aft, a flight deck holed in three places, a damaged elevator, warped hangar deck aft, several shattered compartments, and holes in the hull on the starboard side aft above and below the waterline. Tactically (one enemy light carrier sunk) and strategically (Japanese task force unable to land all troops or destroy Henderson Field), the Battle of the Eastern Solomons was an American victory. But *Enterprise* required major repairs and returned to Pearl Harbor and a dry dock on 10 September, while Air Group Ten prepared to go aboard her for the carrier's next battle. Even during the ceremony on 30 September, when Jimmy received his Navy Cross on "The Big E's" flight deck, repair and maintenance work continued below.

Although "The Big E" was away from the waters around Guadalcanal for only seven weeks, the tactical situation darkened considerably in that time. On 31 August *Saratoga* took her second submarine torpedo of the year and had to return to Pearl for repairs. Then on 15 September, three torpedoes launched by I-19 struck *Wasp,* which missed the Eastern Solomons battle while refueling. In what proved to be the most successful single launch by a Japanese submarine during the Pacific war, *Wasp* was sunk, the new battleship *North Carolina* (BB-55) was damaged, and the destroyer *O'Brien* (DD-415) was fatally damaged. *Hornet, Enterprise*'s only surviving sister ship, arrived on 29 August, and there was no question on either side that another thrust toward Henderson Field was imminent. At Pearl on 16 September, Admiral Nimitz directed a large sign to be placed beside *Enterprise* ("Number One Ship" Get this Job Done!), unnecessarily reminding shipyard workers and crew alike that the big carrier was needed back in the Solomons. And for the first time since she was commissioned in May 1938, her own air group would not be aboard. The air group had left a memorable legacy: extending from the attack on Pearl Harbor to the early raids on Wake Island, Marcus Island, and the Marshalls; to the escort of Doolittle's B-25s for the raid on Tokyo; to the great success at Midway and the successful Battle of the Eastern Solomons. But the group's casualties had been as great as their victories, and time was needed to heal and reorganize.

Air Group Ten (still officially Carrier Replacement Air Group Ten, CRAG-10) was not distracted by the challenge of equaling the record of the original *Enterprise* air group. Those considerations were for another time, and with the prospect of early combat, mental energy was directed to that which was to come rather than that which had passed. Indeed, Jimmy's Grim Reapers banner was not the only painted canvas carried on board the *Enterprise*. Commander Collett's torpedo squadron (VT-10) had adopted an insignia depicting a buzzard flying a mop, and declared themselves "The Moppers" of "The Buzzard Brigade."

After a carrier qualification voyage on 10–11 October, the repaired carrier departed Pearl on the sixteenth headed southwest. While the new air group flew training and patrol missions, gun crews on the carrier trained, elevated, and fired their weapons at target sleeves. During the week and a half voyage, air group leaders incessantly continued tactical discussions; the tone of their deliberations growing more solemn as the big carrier neared the Solomons. Although proud of their original air group, the *Enterprise* crew was not overly concerned about the change. Indeed, many enlisted aviation specialists formerly assigned to the air group were now assigned as ship's company. Moreover, the crew of the *Enterprise* had seen the enemy up close, and those earlier experiences —especially the damage resulting from the Battle of the Eastern Solomons in August—remained particularly fresh. Additionally, among the ship's company the new air group had to share scuttlebutt time with the new 40-mm guns now mounted in place of the 1.1's. Before Eastern Solomons, Cdr. John G. Crommelin Jr., air officer during the 24 August air attack (and later executive officer), had expressed the view that all antiaircraft guns on a carrier were a detriment to air operations. Now, he advocated placement of antiaircraft barrels in every available location.[1]

Santa Cruz Preliminaries

Having already been in combat, Jimmy knew his first function was to instill confidence within his pilots. While he counseled with all, especially the two dozen rookies, he also encouraged Vejtasa, Edwards, Leppla, Faulkner, and Howard S. Packard, an aviation pilot first class, not only to share their combat experiences but to do so in their own manner. This entreaty to the combat veterans required only one statement for direction and understanding. But, unlike Butch O'Hare, who spoke once and only once on a similar topic, Jimmy repeated his exhortations. His small cadre of experienced pilots never took the repeats to be anything more than cheerleading as they fully understood they had Jimmy's full confidence. Although Jimmy and Butch had markedly different personalities and mannerisms, both were equally effective in their leadership communication.

And even though experience could not be communicated, specifics of combat situations could be addressed. Always demonstrating an optimistic spirit and unrelenting drive, Jimmy did not let any moment go by that could be employed in some aspect of training for a battle only days away. A normal day during the voyage began well before dawn with breakfast finished and flight quarters called by 0430. By 0530 planes were in the air for patrol and training. Lunch servings began at 1030, flights continued throughout the afternoon, and from 1615 until about 1800 supper was served. A ship was always darkened at sunset, but if a pilot was asleep by 2000, he was lucky. Any veteran of carrier operations during World War II remembers that nothing other than female companionship was missed more than sleep.

Less than a week out of Pearl, *Enterprise* had a new commanding officer, Capt. Osborne B. Hardison. John Crommelin was not overly enthusiastic with the change announced on the twenty-first, but Hardison, like Capt. A. C. Davis before him, had the good sense to leave the air department to Crommelin.[2] Before the day was over Crommelin was also distressed to learn that his fighter squadron commander had a broken foot. On the afternoon of the twenty-first, Jimmy and other members of the squadron were exercising on the flight deck. Carrier decks were never intended to be athletic fields, but they were constantly used for everything from impromptu football games to well-planned track meets. Basketball games and boxing matches were held on the hangar deck, even though it was sometimes difficult to tell which was which. Always anxious to enjoy any activity involving a ball, Jimmy was participating in a game of "Bull in the Ring" wherein the man inside the circle (the bull) attempted to touch the ball as it was passed along or across the circle. A touch released the bull, but the fun ended when two human-sized bulls, Ens. William K. Blair, Ens. Roy M. "Butch" Voris, and the ball arrived at the same spot at the same time. The spot was the top of Jimmy's right foot. Blair and Voris were each nearly a hundred pounds heavier than Jimmy, Voris also being nearly a foot taller. All things considered, Jimmy was fortunate to have only a broken bone on the top of his right foot. Still, feet were as important as hands while flying a Wildcat, so he and several other Reapers devised a plan to put a strap on the top of the rudder pedal to allow him to brake with one foot on carrier landings.[3] For the aircraft to turn in the air, both feet would have to be used; but these were motions that should not overly stress the top of Jimmy's right foot. Practicing prudence, he decided not to fly again until it was required for combat.

Jimmy had little time to think about his broken foot and the necessary adaptations to facilitate flying. He still had to think about everyone else, and information filtering down to the squadron indicated combat could be joined at any time. On the twenty-second, intelligence provided indications of a major enemy ground, air, and sea thrust on Guadalcanal. While details were not known, nearly everyone could surmise that Japanese troops were continuing their attempt to overrun Henderson Field. Further, it was expected that additional troops would be landed on the northern coast of Guadalcanal—east, west, or both—near the airfield, and that surface units and carriers would likely support the ground forces. On the twenty-third there were several sightings of Japanese naval vessels north of the Santa Cruz Islands to the east of Guadalcanal. On the twenty-fourth Task Force Sixteen, led by *Enterprise* and the new battleship *South Dakota* (BB-57), met Task Force Seventeen with *Hornet* —commanded by Jimmy's former boss at Jacksonville, Capt. Charles Mason—and her escorts. Combined, the two became Task Force Sixty-one under the command of Rear Adm. Thomas Kinkaid aboard *Enterprise*.

With combat operations imminent, Jimmy made one final attempt to pass the best he had to offer to the pilots of his squadron. Tactical instruction and technical advice already imparted would have to suffice. Confidence now existed—or didn't—based on respective internal evaluation of lessons learned minus the inevitable concern for the lack of desired experienced. Knowing that this week in late October would be the last for one or more of his officers, Jimmy felt compelled to offer food for their souls.

> I began to worry about the boys spiritually. Many were very young. Although strong in mind and body, they were just between ages. They were no longer boys, of course, but it would be several years before they reached maturity.
>
> Being a practicing Christian myself, I wanted to complete my job. The ship's Chaplain was there, naturally, to give these young men comfort if they should approach him. But I wanted to do something more for them if I could.[4]

Although there was no question in his mind that this was something he needed and wanted to do, it was no easy task. Expressing spiritual concerns to a group of men trained to kill required a deft touch, and after considerable thought and prayer, Jimmy decided the best manner to express himself was through the written word rather than his usual oral approach. On the evening of the twenty-fourth, Jimmy wrote a memorandum addressed to "The Reapers." The subject, "Your daily prayers." The memorandum was accompanied by "a few simple prayers common to all Christian religions and found in the Bible." It was, and is, apparent the memo was written by an officer, a patriot, a sinner, a "man's man," and a genuinely compassionate human being. Recalling Jimmy and the memo years later, Rear Adm. Whitey Feightner stated, "The group respected Jimmy, and his religious thoughts were well received. The Reapers took it in the form it was offered. It was just part of him."[5] Cdr. Hal L. Buell, who had been on *Yorktown* with Jimmy during the Battle of the Coral Sea and was with VB-10 at Santa Cruz, also remembered the memorandum. Although addressed to "The Reapers," copies made their way to the other squadrons of the air group. "Jimmy was religious without being obnoxious and made you proud to be a Christian," recalled Buell. "Jimmy knew this [Santa Cruz] was going to be a tough one, and said 'let's see if we can't get a little help.' It was a sincere approach, not holier than thou or evangelistic. As his personal life lived up the ideal, his religion had an impact. A superficial sell would not have sold."[6]

Before dawn on the twenty-fifth, Jimmy and all of Air Group Ten were making final checks on their planes and plotting boards. *Enterprise* had the duty on the twenty-fifth and was therefore responsible for combat air patrol. While AG-10 had the flying duties, *Enterprise* also had the radar and fighter direction responsibility. Unhappily, there was a spectacular loss when Bill Blair attempted to land after his propeller froze at a pitch that allowed only a high-speed, relatively uncontrolled landing. Blair's barrier-hopping crash destroyed not only his own plane, but also three SBDs. At least Jimmy's young foot-stomping ensign was spared serious injury.

Hornet, steaming five to ten miles away, was by no means inactive. She had her squadrons (VF-72, VB-8, VS-8, and VT-6) ready for a strike if AG-10 planes discovered enemy targets. Around noon, the first of several land-based aircraft located Japanese carriers about 350 miles west of the two American carriers and some 150 miles north of Henderson

Field. Such a concentration of Japanese carriers so near Henderson was confirmation of the enemy's major effort to gain control of Guadalcanal.

Although the Japanese position was known, the enemy carriers were still about 150 miles too distant to justify launching a full strike. However, if the enemy remained on the same course, there would be time to strike before the end of the day. Not helping matters for Kinkaid, however, was the need for his force to turn away from the enemy into the prevailing easterly winds over his carriers' decks for launch. Although *Hornet* was prepared for such a discovery, a strike group with a Reaper escort rose from *Enterprise,* off to find and hit the enemy. But the Japanese did not remain on course, and by the time the AG-10 flyers ended their protracted search, all knew they could not be back over "The Big E" before dark. One Reaper, twenty-six-year-old Wichita native Lt. Don Miller, was the first of several to run out of fuel on the return trip. After a farewell wave to his wingman, the newlywed gunnery officer who loved diving and architecture dropped out of formation and was never seen again. Before the flight deck closed that night, the air group had lost a dozen planes to all causes.

The twenty-fifth had been an inauspicious beginning to the Battle of Santa Cruz for TF 61, and especially for Air Group Ten. A midnight attack utilizing the light of a full moon was contemplated by Kinkaid, championed by Jimmy, and the *Hornet* was ready to launch. But after everyone had been kept up later than desired, a decision was made to wait for the next day to engage.

Escort for a Strike Mission

When Jimmy awoke in the dark early hours of 26 October, he knew combat was a certainty for that day. And for the first time in nine days he would fly again, broken foot and nonregulation cockpit modifications notwithstanding. Not exactly known was which enemy carriers and air groups he might encounter. Except for an engine room fire aboard *Hiyo* on the twenty-first, Jimmy and TF 61 would have faced five enemy carriers. But while *Hiyo* steamed west, Adm. Chuchi Nagumo's Striking

Force with Japan's two best carriers, *Shokaku* and *Zuikaku,* plus the light carrier *Zuiho,* prepared to attack the American force. A fourth Japanese carrier, the *Junyo,* a twenty-four-thousand-ton converted merchant ship steaming with a second large force, would also engage. *Zuiho* and *Junyo* were not as big or fast as "Sho" and "Zui," but the nature of the day's battle made those considerations moot. Nagumo, winner at Pearl Harbor and loser at Midway, had nearly 150 aircraft aboard the three carriers of his strike force and just less than fifty aboard *Junyo*. *Enterprise* and *Hornet* could counter with about 125 operational planes.

Unlike Jimmy's Coral Sea experience, there was no long wait to ensure the enemy's location at Santa Cruz on the twenty-sixth. Both large Japanese forces were discovered before 0800 when Jimmy was in his Wildcat to lead Reaper One (Flatley, Ens. Russell L. Reiserer, Ens. Roland R. "Cliff" Witte, and Ens. Edward B. Coalson) as escort for a strike group of nine TBF Avengers and three SBDs. Jack Collett would lead the small strike group, while Commander Gaines—carrying no ordnance in his TBF—flew only as strike evaluator, a policy mandate not of his making. Also escorting the twelve strike planes was Reaper Six with John Leppla leading ensigns Albert E. Mead, Willis B. Reding, and Raleigh E. "Dusty" Rhodes. All eight VF-10 Wildcats carried one wing-fitted, fifty-eight-gallon auxiliary fuel tank, an addition to the F4F-4 variant aboard *Enterprise* appreciated by all pilots.

The original plan had been for the *Enterprise* strike group to join with the *Hornet* group, but just as Jimmy was about to launch, he read a hastily painted sign that read "Proceed without *Hornet.*" The last second change of plans was disconcerting. Evidently someone on the bridge knew something he didn't. Still, this did not set well with him. As the *Hornet* planes turned and flew northwest toward the enemy, the twenty planes of AG-10 launched into the southeast breeze before also turning onto a northwest heading. Although the location of the two Japanese forces was known to TF 61, the Japanese also knew the location of the task force. Shortly after 0700, aircraft from Nagumo's three carriers began lifting off their decks heading southeast.

Only thirty minutes and approximately seventy miles into their flight, the AG-10 formation was in trouble. Following behind the *Hornet* strike, led by Lt. Cdr. William J. "Gus" Widhelm (USNA 1932), none of

Jimmy's pilots—or any of the TBF or SBD crews—heard radio transmissions from the VF-72 escort that VF-72 had spotted Japanese planes flying in the opposite direction. Only by gliding in wide turns at 140 knots could Reaper One and Reaper Six—with a division on each side of the bombers—remain with the slower strike planes that were still gaining altitude. However, on an outbound leg of the turns, the fighters briefly lost sight of their charges. Flying one thousand feet above the strike planes, Jimmy, John Leppla, and their six rookies did not realize the presence of nine enemy fighters from *Zuiho* until shells arced through the strike group, then nearing seven thousand feet. Instantly, Jimmy's academy classmate Jack Collett in the lead TBF was hit. Before the burning Avenger began its final plunge, Collett was seen to emerge and jump. But the "Buzzard Brigade" squadron leader was never seen again. Moments later, a second Avenger exploded, and then a third dropped out of formation. Later, a fourth was too badly damaged to continue the mission.

By the time the third Avenger was hit, Leppla—who, while turning back toward the strike planes, had just realized he was fighting with only one of his six guns functioning—had ordered his charges to drop their auxiliary tanks and follow him into the fray. If things were not already bad enough, now everything began to go wrong. Reding's auxiliary fuel tank dropped, but his fuel line lost its prime and down he went. Rhodes's tank refused to drop, and the fifty-eight-gallon potential torch went with him as he descended behind his wingman, Reding. Mead's tank narrowly missed the two troubled Wildcats, and all four F4F-4s of Reaper Six were fighting without a critically needed altitude advantage. While Leppla and Mead chased what they thought were the last of *Zuiho*'s Zeros that struck VT-10, others from above quickly zoomed in behind.

Alternately swinging his head up and to the right in search of other attackers, Jimmy could allow only quick glances at the heart-rending scene to his front and left. That trauma began to disappear over his left shoulder as Reaper One and the then nine remnants of the strike group continued straight ahead. But before the full impact of the disaster could be contemplated, Jimmy saw one of the Zeros maneuvering for another attack on the Avengers. Ordering his Reapers to drop tanks, he turned toward the sleek enemy fighter. In succession, the four Wildcats fired deflection shots. Anticipating that his target would climb away from Reaper One, Jimmy also poured on the power to climb but not directly behind the enemy. At the end of the maneuver, Reaper One was above their prey and behind it, a fighter pilot's dream. With deafening noise drowning out all but the pilots' concentration on the distant object now running away from them, four sticks slid gently forward, then eased back, slowing only when their target was a "plus sign" seemingly near the bottom of their props but centered in their gun sights. Right thumbs caressed the firing button, and after Jimmy gently pressed his, three others—in turn—pressed down hard, seemingly to ensure that their bullets be propelled more vigorously toward the target. Smoke emerged, but the enemy plane flew on. Soon, however, projectiles from one or more of the Reapers apparently found the Zero's pilot in addition to the engine as the target continued straight ahead.

The four Wildcats attacked again, swooping down after gaining altitude with all firing buttons pressed. Emotions absent, the four Reapers applied full technical focus toward erasing the target. Moments later the Zero smashed into the ocean.

With the one visible Japanese fighter now destroyed, Jimmy had to make an instant judgment whether to fly 180 degrees away from the remaining strike planes to find and help Leppla's Reaper Six or continue to defend the TBFs and SBDs. There was no time to give his heart a vote. Understanding his mission and duty, he immediately led Reaper One back to a position above the remaining eight strike aircraft.

Emotion may have been absent while Reaper One guns dispatched the Zero, but Jimmy was getting hot under the collar even though the strike group and escorts were nearing the cold air at ten thousand feet. Now some ten minutes after the engagement with the Zeros, the status of Reaper Six was unknown. But from what Jimmy had last seen, and what he had not heard over the radio, it couldn't be good. Spotting a second *Hornet* strike group, he recommended to Gaines that the remnants of the *Enterprise* strike join up to facilitate protection. "No," Gaines answered, the recommendation rejected. Rapidly becoming convinced that no one on the bridge of the carrier, or now in the air, seemed to grasp lessons the war was teaching, Jimmy cooled when he heard Widhelm's report of a carrier sighting. Just before 0930 enemy ships were sighted; but AG-10's bad luck held, and the SBDs and TBFs separated, Reaper One remaining with the TBFs. Once over the ships, no carriers were sighted, and due to their necessary early release of the auxiliary tank, Jimmy was forced to acknowledge his division did not have sufficient fuel for a continuing carrier search. At that point, the four Avengers with ordnance descended to attack the cruiser *Suzuya*, but none of their torpedoes found the swift target. Diving on the same cruiser, Reaper One strafed, attempting to divert antiaircraft fire and reduce the number of men beside and behind the guns. The unseen three SBDs had a little better luck as one of their bombs exploded near the cruiser *Chikuma*, opening the hull. Ordnance gone and fuel gauges reading less than half, the TBFs and Reaper One turned onto a southeast heading, this time to search for their own carrier. Still unseen by the Reapers or TBF crews, the three SBDs also began the long journey back.

The Reapers Defend Enterprise and Hornet

In the nearly three and a half hours Jimmy was on his mission, events were just as busy, dramatic, traumatic, and confused over the two separate United States Navy carrier formations comprising Task Force Sixty-one. The *Zuiho* fighters that had ambushed Jimmy were themselves escorts for strike groups from *Shokaku* and *Zuikaku* The fighter director officer aboard *Enterprise,* Cdr. John H. Griffin, was as experienced as any officer encamped in radar plot attempting to interpret radar returns and radio reports. On this day Griffin had the combat air patrol responsibility not only for *Enterprise* but also for *Hornet*. Even before the CXAM radar on *Enterprise* malfunctioned during the imminent attack, it did not reveal the approach of the enemy's first strike in time for Griffin to direct the CAP to gain altitude. As the Japanese approached between seventeen thousand and twenty-one thousand feet, the *Hornet* VF-72 CAP and the Reapers aloft were patrolling near ten thousand feet. Broken clouds also obscured the enemy, and as their dive-bombers descended on *Hornet,* course changes and relative bearings did not help clarify instructions from the FDO to the defending fighters. Just after 0900 *Hornet* took three bombs and two torpedoes. Bomb damage was serious, but the more significant damage resulted from torpedo hits amidships on the starboard side, which flooded two fire rooms and an engine room. Power gone, the newest American carrier—in commission for only a year—glided to a halt, listing to starboard.

Despite being too low and out of position, and finding the enemy aircraft only after they began their attack runs, Swede Vejtasa caught a dive-bomber heading for *Hornet*. Shortly afterward, other Reapers began to score. Dave Pollock and Stan Ruehlow downed dive-bombers while Ens. Don Gordon picked off a torpedo plane and Lt. (jg) James D. Billo accounted for an escorting Zero. As the first group of enemy planes disappeared, the now widely dispersed Reapers awaited altitude and directional orders from Griffin. However, less than a dozen Reapers were in the air when a second strike appeared on radar just before 1000. Despite being under a rainsquall, the second strike found *Enterprise* while she was taking aboard nearly three dozen of her own planes plus the now homeless *Hornet* aircraft. Despite functioning radar, Griffin was especially vexed in determining altitude and which planes were friend or foe. Again, most of the few Reapers in the air were too low, and only Whitey Feightner flamed a dive-bomber before this attack began. At 1017 one bomb hit *Enterprise* well forward on the flight deck, followed by a second a minute later.

Low on fuel and ammunition, the Reapers still available to fight had their greatest challenge ahead in the next thirty minutes. As the surviving *Shokaku* dive-bombers departed, over a dozen planes from *Zuikaku* moved into position to launch their torpedoes at *Enterprise*. Built to the same plan, both *Enterprise* and *Hornet* possessed the same design flaw that accounted for the loss of their third sister, *Yorktown*. All three ships were constructed without alternating engine and fire rooms. A well-placed torpedo amidships could stop any one of the three, as they had in June to *Yorktown* and again on this day to *Hornet*. At this critical moment, Griffin had most of the information required to provide needed directives, and for the first time on the twenty-sixth several Reapers had altitude. Swede Vejtasa and Lt. Leroy Harris quickly downed one enemy aircraft, and then Swede proceeded to shoot up three others, possibly downing one. These aerial victories, the disruptive effect of other Reaper attacks, effective antiaircraft batteries, and the effective conning of the carrier in combing through and evading nearly a dozen torpedo tracks saved *Enterprise* from the fate of her two sisters.[7] By 1052 the *Zuikaku* torpedo attack was over, and John Crommelin thought he might be able to reopen the flight deck to take aboard a host of *Enterprise* and *Hornet* planes desperate for fuel and ordnance. With the number one elevator machinery known to be damaged, planes would have to be lowered on elevators numbers two and three, both required to be in the up position for landing aircraft. As the *Enterprise* radar once again was out of commission, neither Crommelin nor Griffin knew yet another attack was only fifteen minutes away. The situation was not entirely known to Jimmy either, but he too was only a few minutes away from joining dozens of fuel-starved planes waiting to land on a damaged flight deck. As Jimmy approached *Enterprise,* she again came under attack by enemy planes, and her deck was made all the more dangerous by several hundred "friendly" guns from CV-6 and screening ships firing at anything in the air.

Return to Reaper Base

The flight back to TF 61 for Reaper One and the strike group after attacking the enemy required nearly two hours. There was little time to think about Reaper Six, the missed opportunities, and the destruction of the Zero. Paramount attention had to be given to scanning the sky for more enemy planes, plus keeping a close watch on fuel consumption and power settings. A miscalculation on fuel by Jimmy could put himself and his other three Reapers in the water. By 1115 Jimmy knew he was nearing the task force. Involuntarily, he briefly relaxed, realized energy had drained from his body, and mused how enjoyable it would be to drink a coke, eat a sandwich, and light a cigarette. But by 1130 all consciousness of relaxation, hunger, and nicotine dissipated as he could see shell bursts mixed with the large but broken gray and white cumulus clouds. Arriving only minutes earlier, dive-bombers from the fourth enemy carrier, *Junyo,* were attacking *Enterprise.* Now, Jimmy's only hunger was for fuel and ammunition.

Within sight of *Enterprise* and her attending warships, Jimmy ordered Reaper One to move abreast and initiate the mutual beam defense tactic to which he had converted only two months earlier. Could Witte, with Coalson in support, time turns to be in the correct position to fire on an intruder? If Jimmy had to shoot, did he have enough .50-caliber shells to down or drive away a Zero? Did his wingman have any ammunition left? To the great relief of Jimmy, Russ, Cliff, and Ed—the tactic worked so well that the one enemy fighter to challenge them gave up after several passes even though no shots were fired. After the war, the enemy pilot remarked that Reaper One's "teamwork was very good."[8] After this experience of confronting a Zero with little ammunition and a 50 percent power setting, Jimmy believed he had earned the landing signal officer's flag to set down on Reaper Base.

At noon Jimmy's four-hour ordeal was over. His broken foot had not seriously impeded the handling of his aircraft, BuNo. 5053. Still he did not fly again until 7 November. In his log for the twenty-sixth he wrote, "The Battle of Stewart Islands; shot down (1) one Nagoya Zero and strafed enemy cruiser and battleship." Apparently later (blue ink as opposed to the usual black), he returned to the same page in the log to write, "Officially known as Battle of Santa Cruz Is."

Assessment

It did not take long back aboard *Enterprise* to discover that things were little better there than they had been in the air. "The Big E" had taken a damaging near miss and two bombs, one well forward that had holed the flight deck and exploded alongside the port bow, and a second that passed through the flight deck just behind the number one elevator. The second bomb apparently broke in half with one explosion on the hangar deck and another on the second deck. Forty-four of the crew were dead and scores wounded while much of "officers' country" was destroyed. Some of the staterooms belonged to the Reapers and other officers of Air Group Ten. Ordinarily, Jimmy would have offered an oral report to Gaines, but Gaines was still waiting to land. And ordinarily Crommelin also would have wanted and received at least a quick report; but he still had his hands full trying to oversee the landing signal officers (LSOs)—

Lts. (jg) Robin Lindsey and James G. Daniels III—highly successful signals to land too many planes on too little deck in too little time. Consequently, Jimmy grabbed anyone he could find who might provide a quick briefing on which Reaper divisions were still flying CAP. Finding few who could shed light on his questions, he headed below amidships to find Reapers who were aboard. Moving forward on the still smoking second deck, he discovered his own stateroom had escaped damage, but many of the compartments immediately forward, including several squadron offices, staterooms, and mess facilities were either no longer extant or inhabitable.

After joining other Reapers, it was obvious no one really knew all that had happened and was happening.[9] Nearly a dozen Reapers were missing, and reports from section and division mates added little to resolving their fates. Initial oral reports indicated several were believed to be in the water near either *Enterprise* or *Hornet*. If they were seen, it was a good bet that the downed flyers would be picked up by a screening ship (usually a destroyer). While the prospect was encouraging, all could see the wounded *Enterprise* was moving away from the dormant, burning *Hornet*. With other attacks possible and several escorting ships damaged—particularly the destroyer *Smith* (DD-378) and the cruiser *San Juan* (CL-54)—there would be little opportunity for a proper search pattern to find downed aviators. Hopefully, search planes would locate aviators, and PBYs could pick them up. Having served a long prewar tour in flying boats, Jimmy simultaneously felt encouraged and concerned. The Catalina was a very capable plane for both search and rescue, but Zeros now controlled the air over the water where American aviators bobbed in their small rafts or life jackets. (Unfortunately, the approach of Japanese ships prevented all from being picked up at Santa Cruz.)

As the long day passed, more information became available, and except for learning that Reapers Kane, Eckhardt, and Ens. M. Phillip Long were picked up by destroyers, most of the news was not good. Additional attacks were expected, and with surviving *Hornet* planes roosting on *Enterprise,* both the hangar and flight decks were too congested for effective CAP operations. Designed to operate seventy-two planes, *Enterprise* now hosted nearly a hundred, many still on the flight deck, as only the two elevators aft of the island were operable. A majority of the Reapers had lost everything as the junior officers' quarters took the brunt of the second bomb hit on their carrier. There was no water, and so many things taken for granted were suddenly a struggle. Routine was no longer routine for Air Group Ten pilots, and now—although happy to accommodate—they needed to share space and their few amenities with *Hornet* pilots. Survival and trying to keep body and soul together became paramount for all the Reapers.[10] Even conversation was strained. Lt. Commander Elias "Benny" Mott, the assistant gunnery officer who so effectively had helped direct the carrier's antiaircraft batteries during the morning actions, could not speak of the missing aviators who shared staterooms near his. Denying his worst fears, he spoke instead of the damage to his sword (presented to him on his Naval Academy graduation), which he retrieved from his gutted quarters.[11] Likewise in a state of semi-denial, Hal Buell of VB-10 lamented the loss of all his flight logs in the destroyed squadron offices.[12]

Hours after *Hornet*'s billowing smoke disappeared astern of *Enterprise,* the carrier's crew and refugees from CV-8 could only ponder her fate. A "War Information Bulletin" printed on 28 October aboard *Enterprise* offered battle details, much of which proved correct from both Japanese and American records in postwar analysis. The bulletin correctly reported that Lt. S. Birney Strong and Ens. C. B. "Chuck" Irvine had attacked an unnamed enemy carrier without even encountering fighter opposition. In fact, one 500-pound bomb that hit aft before 0800 closed *Zuiho*'s flight deck for the day—a major contribution—but the two VS-10 SBDs encountered fierce combat with Zeros on their way out. The bulletin correctly identified *Shokaku* and *Zuikaku* and noted, "At least three 1,000 lb. hits were made on either the *Zuikaku* or *Shokaku*" by the *Hornet* attack group. In fact, it was *Shokaku,* and though severely damaged—just as she was at Coral Sea—she would fight again. The bulletin correctly reported the loss of the destroyer *Porter* (DD-356) and damage to other ships—except *San Juan*—and stated only "serious damage to the *Hornet*." In fact, *San Juan* had taken a direct hit that required a trip to Sydney, Australia, for repairs, and *Hornet* was gone. A little over three hours after CV-8 disappeared from sight of TF 16, a final air attack found no protecting fighters over her, and the sitting-duck carrier again took bombs and one more torpedo against her already wounded starboard side. After escorts attempted to sink her with gunfire and torpedoes, she was left adrift, burning throughout her 827-foot length. Japanese destroyers found the flaming derelict that evening, launched additional torpedoes, and the carrier that launched Doolittle's B-25s against Tokyo finally submitted to the sea after midnight.

Although Jimmy understood why the "War Information Bulletin" published on the twenty-eighth might not mention the loss of *Hornet,* he knew she was gone. He also knew the battle was a tactical loss for U.S. forces, just like Coral Sea. He could only hope that in the larger frame of reference the battle had been a strategic victory—also like Coral Sea. Even though the Japanese did not lose a carrier, two (*Shokaku* and *Zuiho*) required major repairs due to combat damage, and a third (*Hiyo*) required mechanical repair. As at Coral Sea, *Zuikaku* escaped damage, but her aircrew and aircraft losses were severe. *Junyo* also suffered appreciable losses, and in sum the Japanese were unable to capitalize upon their tactical victory. A combination of battle damage, aircraft losses, aircrew casualties, and a belief that they had swept all U.S. Navy carrier air power from the region, led to the withdrawal of Japanese carriers. However, Henderson Field was still a viable American base, *Enterprise* was still afloat, and the contest for Guadalcanal was by no means over or ultimate Japanese victory assured.

The same 28 October bulletin also provided a fairly accurate description of Jimmy's escort flight, and listed VF-10 losses as eleven planes and nine pilots. Continuing, the bulletin stated that "personnel losses may be considerably reduced when full information is available." Indeed, those few words were Jimmy's deepest thought, and while thinking about all the concerns a squadron commanding officer had to handle, his overriding concern was the missing Reapers.

Unaccounted for were three members of Reaper Six: John Leppla, Dusty Rhodes, and Albert Mead. Jimmy was especially worried about these three because their battle was at least sixty miles from TF 61, and Don Miller had gone down on the twenty-fifth even further west. Also missing were ensigns Gordon F. Barnes, Gerald V. "Jerry" Davis, James E. "Slim" Caldwell Jr., and Lyman J. "Jim" Fulton.

A month after the Battle of Santa Cruz, it was apparent to Jimmy that none of these Reapers was coming back. Beginning on 22 November he began the sad task of writing letters to the next of kin. To Mrs. Addie Davis, Jerry's mother, Reaper Leader wrote, "No one knows the exact circumstances under which your son disappeared . . . [he] took off by himself in the last remaining plane . . . [and] was instrumental in warding off numerous attacking Japanese planes."

To Mrs. George Barnes, Gordon's mother, the message was similar, "We know little of the circumstances under which your son was lost. . . . He did, however, engage with distinction and bravery. . . . Gordon personally made a great and a significant contribution towards the winning of this naval air battle which, I am convinced, will prove to be one of the turning points in the war in the Pacific." To Mrs. Lavina Mae Fulton, Jim's mother, he wrote that her son "deliberately flew through a hail of antiaircraft fire . . . shot one [dive-bomber] down . . . and we believe that he was shot down while making [a] brave attempt almost single handed to ward off [another] attack."

To Don Miller's wife, Margaret, Jimmy wrote, "I had confidently trusted that it would never be my duty to write you such a letter . . . Don . . . was a most capable pilot . . . it is definitely known that his engine failed in darkness." To Mrs. James E. Caldwell Jr., he wrote "Slim . . . was not seen to crash . . . as his friend, I can only say that my heart is broken . . . he gave his life in battle in defense of you and his parents . . . those of us who are left behind are more determined than ever to destroy the enemy."

And to Mr. and Mrs. George W. Leppla, Jimmy went into great detail of John's desperate battle, a part of which he had witnessed: "I must write . . . of how much John meant to us, not merely as an officer and a pilot, but as a friend and companion. . . . His unfailing cheerfulness and good nature, his quiet but unflinching courage were ever a rallying point for the morale of the whole squadron . . . I can only say that no fighting unit ever suffered a more severe loss. . . . He . . . was our outstanding naval aviator. . . . Our loss is very great, but our determination to wipe out our common enemy is stronger than ever for having known and loved your son." Two months later, Jimmy sent a formal request to the navy requesting a destroyer be named in honor of Lt. John Leppla.[13]

While all the letters carried similar phrases, each was written as though it was the only letter he had to write. Still, each closed with the same thought, although altered slightly for each individual. One example: "God in His divine wisdom calls us when He wants us. I confidently hope that when our call comes, we will find your son waiting for us in Heaven. When we do meet him, again he will be the same smiling, gentle but strong man that remains now in our memory."

Jimmy's letters to Mr. and Mrs. R. C. Mead and Mr. W. C. Rhodes left no doubt that he believed both Al and Dusty were dead. "I wish I could hold out some hope for Al, but the odds are greatly against his returning," and "I assume that Dusty's wife has told you of the . . . circumstances of Dusty's tragic death." However, before the war was over, Jimmy and other surviving Reapers learned both had been picked up by the Japanese and were in prisoner of war camps. In 1953 Swede Vejtasa received a message inviting all Grim Reaper pilots to a gathering at Los Alamitos, California. Arriving from China Lake in a Corsair, Swede was moved to see many other pilots winging in from everywhere. It turned out that Jimmy Flatley had arranged the event, and although all were guests of honor, the presence of Al Mead and Dusty Rhodes ensured an especially warm and friendly reunion of the original VF-10.

In the more than fifty years since 26 October 1942, no one can say with certainty what might have happened to Fulton or Davis, but later it was believed Caldwell was seen to parachute from his plane: if so, he probably died in his life raft. Gordon Barnes was reported to have made a successful water landing and was seen in a life raft. Sailors aboard *Maury* (DD-401) believed it was Barnes they were preparing to rescue when another attack required the ship to resume its antiaircraft duties.[14]

Two months later—and after yet another battle—Santa Cruz was still very much on Jimmy's mind. "Did I tell you that we have ordered gold wings . . . for all the wives and mothers of our missing pilots," Jimmy wrote to his wife on 20 January 1943. "I'll include a squadron picture too. I don't recall sending you one, but anyway it was taken just two days before we lost our beloved squadron mates in battle. I am sending a copy to all the wives and mothers. The other written material ('Prayers . . .') is what I gave to each one of these boys before their first battle. They took it all very seriously, and I like to think that they are all in Heaven as a result. Anyway, I shall always feel that as their commanding officer, I did all I could for them in every way."

The retrospective of time has revealed Santa Cruz to have been a strategic victory for the Allies. But in spite of that, and despite the downed Zero plus the overall fine performance of his Reapers in their first battle, Jimmy always remembered the Battle of Santa Cruz in the context of his closing in letters to the families of his lost Reapers— "Sincerely and sorrowfully yours."

8

The Grim Reapers at Guadalcanal and Rennell Island

Before retiring on Monday evening 26 October, Jimmy and John Crommelin sought out the assistant FDO, Ens. George Givens, to go over fighter direction problems throughout the Santa Cruz battle. Jimmy knew from his Coral Sea experience that the paramount problem had been too few fighters for interception. At Santa Cruz the *Enterprise* and *Hornet* had enough fighters in the air to do the job, but as at Coral Sea, they were not positioned where needed. The problem was recognized by all concerned, but a solution was more complicated than Jimmy acknowledged to Givens, Griffin, or even to himself in the first hours and days after Santa Cruz.

Decidedly unhappy over what they considered an unsatisfactory result for the aggressive effort on their part, most Reapers soon gave up the discussion over interception and strike problems and began a search for water, clothes, toiletries, and sleeping quarters. Still near the bottom of the pecking order despite downing an enemy dive-bomber before it could attack, Whitey Feightner joined other junior officers, first in the chiefs' quarters and later in a narrow passageway under the 5-inch starboard guns, where bunks were welded to the bulkhead. A highlight for Whitey during the three-day voyage was the use of Jim Billo's stateroom to shave and look out a porthole. A "lowlight" for the entire crew was general quarters (GQ), with everybody piling out of the bunks at the same moment, and the noise of the guns in train.[1]

On 27 October *Enterprise* continued on a southerly heading toward Noumea, New Caledonia. Well southeast of Guadalcanal, Noumea offered relative safety both from enemy land-based planes and submarines. Before the carrier arrived in the harbor, many of the planes prepared to fly to Tontouta airfield north of Noumea, but Jimmy remained aboard with several other pilots. The plan was for "The Big E" to undergo repair at Noumea rather than return to Pearl Harbor, this despite the fact that everyone knew the ship needed to be dry-docked for proper repair. Emphasis would have to be placed on restoring the hangar deck forward, and repairing the malfunctioning radar and the forward elevator. Other damage, including significant repair of officers' country, was assigned lower priority. Barring an emergency, a tentative schedule called for major repairs to be complete by 21 November.

On 1 November Jimmy, still limping slightly, left *Enterprise* with a handful of other pilots. Leaving the "tent city" that had risen within the damaged area of the carrier for an outdoor tent city about forty miles northwest at Tontouta, Jimmy and the others packed all the personal items they could carry for their rustic adventure. Each brought a pillow, which was too much temptation for the six-foot-five-inch former football player—and future ace—Ens. Roy M. "Horse" (later "Butch") Voris. Voris, who had already endeared himself to Jimmy by helping break his foot, asked the relatively diminutive Reaper Leader if he was taking his mattress ashore. Only the affable, fun-loving Voris could tease Jimmy in such a manner. Although Jimmy returned a scowl, inside he was laughing as hard as the other Reapers.[2]

At Tontouta Jimmy was the last VF-10 pilot to get in some flying time, recording 1.8 hours on the seventh for tactics and 2 hours of gunnery practice on the eighth. His foot was healing quickly, and he felt stress on the foot only while braking at the end of a flight. Despite the rustic accommodations, a moderate climate and other amenities were a welcome change, plus Jimmy found walking much easier on soil than the steel and wood decks of a carrier. Thoughts of death were much further away than the forty miles then separating Air Group Ten and

Enterprise. But, a carrier was a much dryer place to live and it had no dust clouds. Plus, there was no substitute for a shower and the carrier's wardroom food was particularly missed.

Back Aboard

Somewhat surprised to be so quickly notified of orders on the tenth, the Reapers were in the air on the morning of the eleventh for three hours. Jimmy and the other pilots flew south from Tontouta to Noumea, but found the carrier still in the harbor. But when the Reapers returned to Tontouta, word then came that the ship was under way, and Air Group Ten was back aboard after another one-hour flight. Aware that he and his Reapers were about to fight again, Jimmy led his squadron aloft on the twelfth for 2.9 hours of gunnery practice. An infusion of pilots from VF-72 brought Fighting Squadron Ten to full strength even if the carrier wasn't. The VF-72 pilots had arrived discouraged, an understandable condition in light of the loss of their carrier and discomfort with former leadership. Attitudes changed, however, as they got to know the even-tempered, confident, and sympathetic new commanding officer.

Japanese plans for a significant troop reinforcement had been intercepted and Admiral Halsey, commander of the South Pacific (ComSoPac) —who already had a reinforcement and supply mission of his own under way—was quickly pulling together every ship and plane he could find to counter the enemy thrust. Unknown to Halsey, the Japanese buildup was actually preparation for a major offensive to take Henderson Field and adjacent airstrips the following month. But the misreading of enemy intentions proved a blessing. There was no question in Halsey's mind that the Japanese—confident of victory in the belief they had erased major naval opposition off Santa Cruz—would have battleships and cruisers to support this new operation. And certainly there would be enemy carriers, but how many or how they might be employed was not known. ComSoPac did know that he would commit the only two battleships, *South Dakota* and *Washington* (BB-56), available to him, and that *Enterprise* would fight despite her state of disrepair. Indeed, a repair crew remained aboard CV-6 struggling to repair the forward elevator.

On both the eleventh and twelfth, Japanese air attacks materialized over the U.S. Navy warships and transports delivering personnel and supplies to Guadalcanal. The intense but mostly ineffective air raids against the U.S. Navy ship concentrations off the disputed island on these two days only reinforced belief that a decisive battle was imminent. Such moments brought out the best in Halsey. His ability to communicate absolute and adamant confidence in the face of overwhelming danger made him an American legend. Even though removed by many miles of ocean, his belligerent-toned orders communicated emotions as well as battle specifics. One of many Halsey disciples along with Crommelin—who considered Halsey "the greatest"—Jimmy was about to rise to the occasion, and he began the process of inspiring the Reapers to rise to their best along with him.

Before the Battle of Santa Cruz, John Crommelin had gathered Air Group Ten in the wardroom, promised to get all pilots back aboard after the battle, and expounded at some length on what the next day's battle meant to Guadalcanal, the U.S. Navy, the United States, and the whole world. "John Crommelin was an intense warrior, one who would get out in front and say, 'come on, let's go.' When you have a war on, he's the kind of guy you looked for."[3] While "The Big E" pounded on toward Guadalcanal, Crommelin again gathered the air group on the evening of the twelfth for a repeat of his pre–Santa Cruz speech ("either we win this thing or the United States is going to be in deep trouble"). Having heard that "Uncle John" had already told mess attendants to cook every steak in the lockers "because tomorrow evening they may be on the bottom of the ocean," the pilots were "all ears."[4] For Whitey Feightner the Crommelin speeches, in combination with tutorials from Jimmy, fully explained for the first time why he "was out here." To himself Whitey determined that he wasn't going to live to be twenty-five, but he was going to make it count.[5]

Jimmy's preparations for the pilots were communicated in a quieter, more matter-of-fact tone, but he too stressed the expanded significance of the coming battle. The bottom line was that a successful enemy attempt to land troops, food, and munitions could tip the land battle in Japan's favor. Once defenders were pushed away from the landing fields, the loss of air cover spelled sure defeat not only for Guadalcanal, but also the possible loss of bases from Samoa to New Caledonia. And the fragile ties to Australia would certainly break. Before the Reapers took to their planes on Friday 13 November, they fully appreciated the weight of the burden riding with them.

Deciding not to test *Enterprise*'s forward elevator, Crommelin ordered Lt. Albert "Scoofer" Coffin to lead his nine TBFs on a sweep of the waters north of Guadalcanal whereon a furious surface battle had raged in the dark morning hours of the thirteenth. Escorted by six of the new Reapers, Coffin was to land on Guadalcanal after his early morning sweep, this to facilitate flight operations aboard the carrier rather than add planes to CACTUS, the designation for Guadalcanal-based aircraft. Upon landing, however, marine aviators greeted them as reinforcements, the "welcome mat" placed before them even before all the marines present learned the VT-10 pilots had attacked the Japanese battleship *Hiei* on the way in.[6] Seriously damaged in the night battle, *Hiei* circled north of Savo Island with a jammed rudder and spent most of the day attempting to repair damage while battling U.S. Army Air Force B-17s, Marine SBDs, TBFs, F4Fs, and yet another attack by VT-10. Best evidence is that VT-10's torpedo hits during their afternoon second attack inflicted sufficient damage to put the twenty-six-year-old battleship on the bottom of the sound after dark. In the twenty-four hours since the battle began, Japan had lost *Hiei* and two destroyers while the lighter-gunned American force had lost the light cruiser *Atlanta* (CL-51) and four destroyers. Although a tactical defeat on the first night of what would become known and renowned as the Naval Battle of Guadalcanal, the gallant effort of the U.S. Navy cruisers and destroyers had prevented a bombardment of the airfields. Further, the battle gained a precious day for Task Force Sixteen comprised of *Enterprise, Washington, South Dakota,* and their escorts to approach Guadalcanal.

While TF 16 moved northwest on the thirteenth, Jimmy spent four hours in the air on combat air patrol. As Jimmy remained over the force, Swede Vejtasa took his own division to track down an enemy search plane. The ensuing kill was the Reapers' only combat for the day, somewhat of a surprise as enemy carriers were suspected to be near. Later it became known that the only enemy carrier in the area was *Junyo*, which remained some two hundred miles north of Guadalcanal for the duration of the battle.

In the early morning hours of 14 November, a Japanese cruiser and destroyer force found no surface opposition between them and the airfields they so coveted. Although the island of Guadalcanal measured some ninety miles in length with a maximum breadth of twenty-five miles, the few square miles near Lunga Point with the airfields were the prize. Bombardment alone could not secure the airfields for the Japanese, but it could destroy some planes, damage runways, and disrupt flight schedules. Although highly discomforting to the defenders, especially to the newly arrived Torpedo Ten crews and the six Reapers, this most recent shelling resulted in relatively light damage to runways and aircraft.

As the cruisers and destroyers that had attacked the airfields steamed west just before dawn, TF 16 drew close enough to begin launching. Jimmy and ten Reapers roared down the deck and into the air to escort Cdr. Bucky Lee and seventeen SBDs on a search and attack mission.[7] When first ordered back to the carrier on the tenth, Jimmy assumed he would again be fighting enemy carrier aircraft. On the morning of the fourteenth that possibility was still valid, but the main objective was enemy transports. Flying with Jimmy's Reaper One were Lieutenant Reiserer, Ens. "Cliff" Witte, and Ens. Phil Souza (VF-72). Lt. Swede Vejtasa led Reaper Seven with Lt. "Tex" Harris, Ensign Reding, and Ens. William H. "Hank" Leder, while Reaper Three was comprised only of Lieutenants Ruehlow and Voris.

Soon after leaving *Enterprise* just before 0800, two Reapers (Reding and Leder) went after a contact, lost it, and then lost their way back to the attack group. Continuing on with seven Wildcats in addition to his own, Jimmy followed Bucky Lee, who was receiving radio updates from the carrier and from other SBDs launched earlier. Unknown to any of the escorting Reapers, one of the enemy cruisers—*Kinugasa*—had been pounded by marine and *Enterprise* SBDs (morning patrol), and Lee had orders to seek other ships in the same area. Known to the Reapers was the fact that the distance to their targets might take them too far from the carrier for a return. Consequently, Lee's strike group could elect to land at Henderson Field upon the completion of the mission. After attacking several cruisers without positive results, he did land at Henderson, but Jimmy's Reaper One was not with him. Unable to communicate by radio, Jimmy missed one of Bucky's turns, and after a lengthy search for Lee, he turned and headed back to the carrier, touching down just before noon. Nearly an hour later Reding and Leder also found the carrier, the only bright moment for a morning escort that had been utterly frustrating. Jimmy's four Reapers had separated from the strike group; Reding and Leder had also separated from the strike group and needed help from *Washington* to locate the carrier; and the whereabouts of Ruehlow and Voris were not known for sure. Fortunately, both had landed at Henderson for fuel.

The Slot

Intent on attacking the retreating enemy cruisers during the early morning flight, Lee apparently had not spotted the expected Japanese transport convoy. Neither had Jimmy, but before he headed back to *Enterprise,* several sightings by marine and *Enterprise* aircraft confirmed the convoy's location. Eleven transports, ranging in size from fifty-four hundred to nearly ten thousand tons and escorted by eleven destroyers, were steaming straight down the Slot between islands toward Guadalcanal. Aboard were over seven thousand troops and tons of critically needed supplies.

As Jimmy neared *Enterprise* at the end of his frustrating morning, marine SBDs, Coffin's VT-10, and two VB-10 SBDs were preparing to lift off Henderson Field for the first of many attacks against the transports. Throughout the day these planes, in addition to Lee's SBDs, flew shuttling flights against the transports. B-17s from Espíritu Santo also joined in, and just after noon *Enterprise* prepared to fly most of the remainder of Air Group Ten into the battle and depart. For this flight the four pilots of Reaper One were joined by Reaper Two (Lt. Albert Pollock and ensigns Whitey Feightner, Steve Kona, and Ed Coalson) plus Reaper Eight (Lt. "Fritz" Faulkner and ensigns Philip Long, Don Gordon, and Lynn E. Slagle).

While his plane and others were hastily refueled, Jimmy was ordered to lead twelve fighters and eight SBDs against the convoy and then join the two dozen other Air Group Ten planes already at CACTUS on Guadalcanal. Although there had been time for a quick lunch, orders for takeoff left the Reapers no time to grab a toothbrush or extra ammunition for their .45s, items soon to be missed. As with the morning flight, the fighters climbed several thousand feet above the eight SBDs and headed northwest of Guadalcanal.

Before Jimmy's formation arrived over the convoy, combined marine and Air Group Ten attacks from CACTUS had resulted in fatal damage to four transports. Unlike the previous day, the sky was clear over the lower Solomons, and Jimmy had no difficulty locating his targets or determining which ships were already damaged. Lt. (jg) Red Carmody, one of the first *Enterprise* SBD pilots to find the convoy that morning, was also one of the first to spot the convoy again about 1500. But Carmody also saw several Zeros that were higher than Jimmy's escorts, then flying at twenty-two thousand feet.

Noting a tone of alarm in Carmody's transmission, Jimmy came on the air. "Okay, everybody, quiet down. The Zeros haven't seen us, and I don't want any wing rocking or canopies flashing. We're going to concentrate on defending the bombers and hitting the transports." Then Jimmy began to assign targets, ordering Carmody to "take the number one transport on the right side," and directing others to specific targets. "The idea was to keep all the SBDs from ganging up only on one, as he knew all the enemy transports had to be hit." Jimmy's voice and directives calmed all. "In combat, Jimmy was unflappable."[8]

As Carmody recalled, "We were able to make steady dives without having to worry about the Zeros." Having flown west of the convoy, the SBDs were able to approach the convoy from astern. Never celebrated for quick maneuverability and steaming at ten knots, the thin-skinned transports were not difficult targets. "The greatest impediment was enemy fighters, and they were not in position to interfere during the 14,000-foot descent." The result of this attack was severe damage to two transports that contributed to their eventual sinking.[9]

While Carmody and the other SBD pilots dived on their targets, Jimmy led the three Reaper divisions down to cover the bombers and to strafe. Before pulling out at fifteen hundred feet, Jimmy could see the carnage wrought by the formation's bombs and .50-caliber slugs. Firing first at a transport, Reaper One then loosed rounds on a destroyer before pulling up to gain altitude.[10] As usual, this was not the time to reflect on pain and injury his ordnance was inflicting. Any temptation to do so was quickly precluded by the sight of another group of Zeros at low altitude preparing to engage. As Feightner remembered, "There was so much chaos in combat that one could not keep attention on one target for very long. We were in a target rich environment and didn't have to hunt for trouble. Consequently, we had to know the overall tactical plan. During battle we were alone except for our wingman, so we shot, turned, and looked for someone else as we were often outnumbered. Intensity was such that there was no time for fear. Even though it was so hectic, there was time to think, and there were so many things to think about. The brain really speeded up, and the world seemed to go into slow motion."[11]

As there was no time for fear, neither was there time for jubilation. Even though he had to pull up at one thousand feet before he could see his bomb explode on his chosen transport, Red Carmody knew his attack was a success. But before any awareness of satisfaction could pervade his senses, his rear-seat gunner shouted the presence of Zeros. The enemy fighters Red had seen at thirty-thousand feet did not give chase, but now he too discovered the Zeros at low altitude. "Jinking at 100 feet as ordered by my gunner, one of Jimmy's fighters suddenly appeared to shoot down our nearest pursuer, and before the other Zero could pull up, my gunner shot him down in flames."[12]

There were a few other quick aerial combats between the Reapers and Zeros as the American fighters pulled away from the two burning transports. Slagle and Coalson each downed Zeros while no Reapers or any of the SBDs were lost. By 1630 Jimmy's formation of twenty fighters and bombers were on Guadalcanal.[13]

Air Group Ten Joins the CACTUS Air Force

Members of Air Group Ten who had considered Tontouta rustic now had to rework their definition of the word. On Guadalcanal the aviators were indeed further back to nature, back to the most primitive living conditions (including an even greater leap backward for answering the call of nature), but not back to a more temperate climate, and certainly not back to a place of serenity. At Tontouta the rats had been a real nuisance, especially at night when they joined the aviators in their cots. But on Guadalcanal the rats had guns. The only reason the intermittent shelling of the airfields was accepted with relative calm was the greater fear of being bombarded by enemy surface units. Even the food was worse. Still, as Swede recalled, "Skipper Flatley knew all the Marine Generals and Colonels in the South Pacific . . . and we enjoyed the best that they had to offer, and there was nothing like a good bit of chow and a bunk with mosquito nets at night. The Marine in charge would see that Jimmy's boys were taken care of . . . and often a bit of bourbon would find its way to the table."[14]

Although Swede wasn't sure if tactics were discussed when Jimmy was with his marine friends, Joe Foss remembers most conversations with Jimmy eventually included discussion of tactics.[15] Always instructive, always give and take, such conversations were necessary as well as enjoyable. However, Jimmy's first conversation with an old marine friend became memorable not for the content of the conversation, but as much for the remembrance of seeing a friend for the last time. The incomparable Lt. Col. Harold W. "Indian" Joe Bauer, an ace with eleven kills whom Jimmy had known since his second year at the Naval Academy, was preparing to take off just as Jimmy landed. Climbing onto Bauer's wing, there was time only for a few quick barbs and a promise for a later visit. Even though Bauer was going to where Jimmy had just been, neither probably had any doubt that they would share more time together after darkness drew a curtain on the day's aerial combat. But it was not to be. After downing one more enemy plane, "the coach" was seen alive in the water, but darkness arrived before Foss and others could locate him again.[16]

Around midnight as the very long Saturday the fourteenth of November became Sunday the fifteenth, the distant muted explosions of another surface battle awakened Jimmy and others. No one knew what was happening or who was winning, but after 0100 majority opinion seemed to be that U.S. Navy units must have done well because there was no enemy bombardment of the airfields. Despite the vested interest in what was happening well out in the sound near Savo Island, conversations trailed off and sleep overcame efforts to stay awake. Later, all learned that *Washington* had caught the Japanese battleship *Kirishima* occupied with *South Dakota,* and had scored enough 16-inch shell hits to put *Kirishima* under. By dawn the victorious *Washington* and wounded *South Dakota* had withdrawn, leaving three escorting destroyers behind on the bottom with the *Kirishima* and one Japanese destroyer. Victory arrived with the dawn of the fifteenth, but that fact was not then known to friendly forces on Guadalcanal, back on the *Enterprise,* or by Com-SoPac Halsey.

Now residents of Guadalcanal, Jimmy and the Reapers awoke to the explosions of artillery shells dropping around the airfield on the morning of the fifteenth. Not immediately required in the air thanks to their marine hosts who flew the morning missions, Jimmy managed to obtain some information on the status of the battle. Of the eleven transports that had started down the Slot toward Guadalcanal, seven had either been sunk or were in a sinking condition. The other four had been run aground well west of the airfields in an attempt to land as many troops and supplies as possible. While many of the nearly two thousand troops landed by dawn could move inland, from there they could not unload the transports. But there were many attempting to unload the ships, and no aviator could hope for better targets.

Shortly after noon Jimmy was again in the air with Reaper One and Reaper Two, each division including the same pilots as when the battle began two days previous. Charged with defending Henderson Field and the two adjacent fighter strips, Jimmy was also directed by First Marine Air Wing Operations to cover *Meade* (DD-602). The scrappy destroyer had used her four 5-inch guns to good effect against the beached transports and with other friendly vessels was rescuing survivors from *Preston* (DD-379) and *Walke* (DD-416), both lost in the night battle with *Kirishima.* Pulling 266 survivors from the water, *Meade* was a sitting duck, but the protecting Reapers did not have to intervene on her behalf. Still, the threat was real. Soon after the gritty destroyer steamed back across the sound to Tulagi, radar detected enemy planes. Reaper Three (Ruehlow, Voris, and Slagle) and Reaper Eight (Faulkner, Long, Gordon, and Ens. James H. Dowden) quickly took off to assist Reaper One and

Reaper Two, which were near the end of their fuel endurance. Also rising from CACTUS in a purloined Marine F4F was the recent hospital escapee, Bobby Edwards—bad knee and all—as a self-appointed Reaper division of one. Although the last to leave the ground, Edwards was the first to engage, having flown directly into a group of seven Zeros flying cover for a bomber formation of equal size. In the short battle that followed, Jimmy overshot the one Zero he attacked, Russ also missed, but Witte and Souza destroyed the one post-battle claim that held up in postwar analysis. Bobby Edwards fought all seven Zeros, expended all his ammunition, and landed back at CACTUS to receive a reprimand from a marine officer for stealing one of his planes. After the reprimand the marine aviator told Jimmy, "We need more like him." Having already written a recommendation for a Silver Star for Bobby, Jimmy, with a smile, agreed.[17]

By 16 November it was apparent the Japanese reinforcement effort was finished as search planes located no enemy ship movement in the lower Solomons. A section of Reapers made one final strafing run on the beached transports on the sixteenth, and then those pilots followed others of Air Group Ten off Guadalcanal. The *Enterprise* flyers had pleased the marines when the flyers unexpectedly arrived before the battle, and now they helped the marines once again by leaving. With the immediate threat diminished, the marines and army air force could once again divide the limited human resources of CACTUS. Many of the air group's planes, however, were left at Henderson while others were flown to Espíritu Santo. Jimmy was one of only six Reapers to fly Wildcats back to Espíritu Santo, arriving near the same time as the *Enterprise* dropped anchor well south at Noumea. Exceedingly unkempt and too tired to take immediate measure of their contributions to victory, food was the first priority for the returned flyers followed closely by soap, water, and sleep.

Interlude

From 25 November and extending into January 1943, Air Group Ten was based again at Tontouta, Espíritu Santo, and aboard *Enterprise*. Despite the acquisition of new planes, Jimmy registered nearly all his

32.2 hours in December and January's 22.5 hours in the same F4F-4 (BuNo. 11661) that he had flown consistently before and since Santa Cruz.

Well behind in his paperwork due to the stress of battle in mid-November, Jimmy and the other Reapers attempted to write reports and update their flight logs. Jimmy's preoccupation with combat is apparent in his log entries for the period. After his first flight on 14 November, for the first time in his career he could not remember—if he ever knew—the bureau number of his Wildcat for the remaining flights on the four-teenth through sixteenth. Neither was he sure of the exact number of hours he had been in the air after the first four-hour flight on the four-teenth. Rather than record precise information not within his grasp, he listed fifteen hours to cover his flight time for the remainder of those three days. Obviously penned several days after, Jimmy gave his own name, the "Second Battle of the Solomons," to what history remembers as the Naval Battle of Guadalcanal. Inked in small print, he wrote:

> Led attack Group 8 SBDs and 12 VF against enemy transports approach-ing "CACTUS." Scored bomb hits on 5 AK and AP. VF strafed 2 trans-ports, 2 DDs. Set transports afire. Shot down one Zero. All planes arrived CACTUS safely. Next day Reapers shot down 8 Zeros in defense of CACTUS. Lost none.

That Jimmy's calculations on how many enemy planes were shot down "next day" do not match postwar analysis is not surprising. As Whitey Feightner recalls, "There were many versions of the battle . . . you would think we had all fought a different war when reading the post battle accounts."[18] Of course, what happened most often is that one pilot would damage a plane, lose sight of it, another pilot would attack, see smoke, and naturally report the hit as a result of his own guns, and so on. But even postwar accounting confirms the Grim Reapers more than held their own in the air above Guadalcanal. And the SBDs and TBF Avengers from Air Group Ten accounted for the sinking of at least four transports in addition to considerable damage to cargo in or near the four beached transports.

In some respects postwar adjustments do not account for the mag-nitude of emotions at the time of battle. Writing to "all Cactus based First Marine Aircraft Wing units and other attached units [including the squadrons from Air Group Ten]," Brig. Gen. L. E. Woods, the commanding officer, wrote on 16 November that he believed the CACTUS planes had stopped thirty thousand enemy troops from landing on Guadalcanal. Vice Admiral—within days Admiral—Halsey's messages on the eighteenth and nineteenth to South Pacific commands that had "derailed the Tokyo Express" did not mention enemy numbers but did convey his emotions: "My pride in you is beyond expression. Magnificently done. To the glorious dead—Hail heroes and rest with God." Admiral Nimitz, ever a master of restrained emotions and a man who carefully chose his words, signaled Halsey on the seventeenth, "You have earned the undying gratitude of all who share our righteous cause." On the nineteenth his message to *Enterprise* read: "On 13–15 November the Air Group of *Enterprise* wrote finis to many of the enemy and his ships. This is what I, CINCPAC, have come to expect of planes bearing the honored name of our veteran fighting carrier."

General Wood's estimate of the enemy stopped short of Guadalcanal later proved to be inflated. However, his assessment that the pilots and ground crews had "insured us the possession of this island, and the final defeat of the enemy" stands eternally correct.

Operational Reflections

As discussed above, combat—particularly a protracted battle such as the convoy attacks over the Slot—left Jimmy and the Reapers too preoccupied to worry about paperwork. Flight log entries often were delayed for days, and while action reports were required within hours of battle, the result was initial-handwritten and final-typed copies revealing anger, frustration, exhilaration, and other emotions expressed by exhausted bodies and tired hands. Nonetheless, battles were fought, and won or lost to a significant degree by paperwork, particularly as it related to communicating lessons learned and logistics. Indeed, a decisive factor in the battle for control of Guadalcanal was logistics. The antagonist who could adequately supply and maintain garrisons should have been—and was—victorious.

Paperwork was a major element revealing reflective thought, listings of technical problems, and analysis of how equipment limitations or potential bonded with tactical implementation. Poor performance by submarine and aerial-launched torpedoes constantly defeated sound tactics and an abundance of courage for U.S. forces throughout 1942. In the air, bombsights fogged while SBDs descended from cold air into tropical humidity. Radar was still in its incipient stage, but its limitations, and great potential, were being rapidly addressed, as were the problems with grossly inadequate radios in aircraft. Radios were critical to direct attack, but poor transmissions and a thirty-mile range did not meet the need.[19] Estimates on *Enterprise* indicated that no more than 15 percent of transmissions were received during combat.[20] Wildcat guns jammed as ammunition belts slid from poorly designed trays during violent rolls, spins, and loops. And it was discovered that the .50-caliber guns in the F4Fs also jammed if there was oil on them when they got cold at high altitude (solved by daily cleaning).[21]

There was, of course, an urgent need to resolve matériel and operational problems. In the two month period between the Naval Battle of Guadalcanal and the action off Rennell Island, Jimmy caught up on his paperwork while maintaining a training schedule ashore and on the carrier. With some time to think, he offered several lengthy written opinions on operational policy, two concerning significant issues.

The first was a 5 December letter through proper channels to Captain Hardison on the matter of utilizing fighter pilots as standby fighter director officers. Despite having been quite critical of the fighter direction after Santa Cruz, enough time had passed for Jimmy to better think through all the variables that had contributed to the less than desired interception performance on 26 October. First, Jimmy objected to Dave Pollock being detailed for such training, believing him "not temperamentally adapted for the position." Doubtless, Dave encouraged Jimmy to offer the opinion, as he had no desire to trade the cockpit of an F4F to be locked up in a closed compartment. That aside, Jimmy did not champion the idea of any fighter pilot being trained as a fighter director officer. Jimmy acknowledged that fighter pilots, himself included, had been overly critical of FDOs, and that "we have not struck the proper balance in the relationship of the FDO to the fighter leader in the air." Continuing, Jimmy noted that "the pilots themselves have been the prime offenders . . . because . . . the FDO is simply there to pass on to the fighters the information given to him by his radar operators. Further, if he [pilot] receives it and acts without some attempt at evaluation, he is very liable to be wrong. The pilots are in a position to supplement what they hear with what they can see, such as clouds and visibility conditions . . . they must help in keeping the FDO informed." Attempting to strengthen his debate position on a matter he thought to be critically important, Jimmy called attention to the fact that the landing signal officer was not held responsible when a pilot ignored his signals and crashed.

Jimmy offered an opinion that the fighter pilot was 75 percent responsible for his effectiveness on combat air patrol. Still, he did not believe a fighter pilot could be effective as an FDO because a pilot "would instinctively be attempting to visualize conditions in the air from a coop on the ship, and . . . would be trying to fly his plane for him." Finally, Jimmy offered praise for Ens. George Givens, the same young nonaviator officer he and Crommelin had grilled on the night of 26 October. Jimmy wrote that Givens radar-plot work and experience as standby FDO to John Griffin and other FDOs "would make him an excellent fighter director officer . . . and I'm willing to risk my reputation on him."

Knowing that ideas from above did not disappear easily when questioned by lower echelons, Jimmy courteously acknowledged such in his last paragraph writing, "If this recommendation is not accepted, I suggest that an aviator other than a fighter pilot be selected for the reasons outlined above." And then to strike one last blow for his cause, Jimmy ended his discourse with, "As a matter of interest, the Fighter Director Officers at Guadalcanal are not aviators."

For the short run Jimmy's argument did not carry the day. Captain Hardison placed Lieutenants Ruehlow, Pollock, Edwards, and Kilpatrick under instruction to be FDOs on 20 December, and in the next air battle, Stan Ruehlow was on duty in the "coop" rather than in the air. For the long run, however, Jimmy was correct and the navy chose and trained nonaviators as fighter directors.

On a second matter of long-term relevance, Jimmy engaged in an interesting exchange of ideas with Lt. William I. "Bill" Martin, a tall, dark-haired, always distinguished looking 1934 Academy graduate from Missouri. Martin strongly championed the use of radar in a TBF Avenger to serve as a reconnaissance aircraft, and proposed immediate implementation. Having logged most of his combat time in SBDs, Martin knew the SBD was too small and cramped to handle the sixty-plus pounds of the early airborne radar units.

Martin's 30 October and 4 December 1942 memorandums were forwarded up the chain through Commander Gaines, who on 9 December endorsed them to ComSoPac and to the commander of the air force in the Pacific Fleet. Even though not in that chain of command, on 16 January 1943 Jimmy authored a five-page letter to the executive officer of Scouting Ten in response to the use of radar for night and all-weather flight operations. Martin, unquestionably well ahead of most contemporaries and destined to become one of naval aviation's great innovators, may well have wished he had discussed his proposals with Jimmy before releasing them. Jimmy was not quite as far-sighted, but he nonetheless offered some relevant questions and practical considerations.

"My first advice to you is to confine your interests entirely to instrument training of CV pilots and to developing CV aircraft radar . . . I do not mean to discourage your interests in other phases of carrier aircraft employment, but it is extremely difficult to do any important job well unless you devote all of your time to it." Following this opening statement, Jimmy then addressed Martin's thesis point by point.

1. MARTIN: A radar guided TBF could find an enemy force in bad weather. FLATLEY: If a scout plane can not see the enemy, how can other planes see to attack the enemy?

2. MARTIN: Bad weather in the Pacific is brief and localized as opposed to the protracted, large weather systems in the Atlantic. Therefore, a radar-equipped plane could determine whether only allied forces were under clouds while the enemy was in the clear. FLATLEY: What if the radar plane is lost? And, extant SBDs could determine local weather.

3. MARTIN: A radar-equipped plane could locate enemy planes at night. FLATLEY: Only a fighter plane could respond to such a threat. [In his response, Jimmy questioned whether or not

sufficiently advanced equipment would ever be available to accomplish such a mission. It was, and sooner rather than later.]

4. MARTIN: The radar plane could amplify uncertain contact reports. FLATLEY: Unless the radar plane was in the immediate vicinity of a contact, a reconnaissance plane would arrive too late to be useful. [Jimmy also commented that the Japanese had proved to be better scouts to that time in the war.]

5. MARTIN: A radar plane could locate the enemy and make an initial attack. FLATLEY: Only radar-equipped planes could attack, and discovery of our reconnaissance plane may give away our position. [In 1944, Martin's radar equipped Avengers made the first offensive night attack at Truk.]

6. MARTIN: The radar reconnaissance pilot could be the attack director at the scene of action. FLATLEY: This is the function of the senior pilot, and he should be the Air Group Commander.

7. MARTIN: The radar pilot could be a formation navigator and guide for all night operations. FLATLEY: A guide, yes. Navigator no, because he may crash. Individual pilots need to do their own navigation.

While the overall tone of Jimmy's letter was professional and thought provoking, he did end his epistle on a negative note taking issue with Martin's advocacy of using low-level daylight and glide attacks. Alluding to the extremely heavy casualties to both U.S. Navy and Japanese low-level attack aircraft, Jimmy added, "Let's not complicate our present problem until we have mastered the fundamentals of our present attack methods. I have yet to see VS-10 or VB-10 deliver a satisfactory dive-bomb attack. I have never seen them look half good in a glide-bomb attack." Martin, who later turned his visionary ideas into reality during a distinguished wartime career and then advanced to command of the U.S. Sixth Fleet before retiring as a vice admiral in 1971, accepted Jimmy's comments in a positive light. Writing on 20 March 1976 to the Green Bay, Wisconsin, committee honoring Jimmy, Martin wrote, "There may be those who knew Admiral Flatley more years than it was my privilege to know him, but there are none who had more admiration and respectful affection for him."

The Air Battle off Rennell Island

In the two month period after the Naval Battle of Guadalcanal, Jimmy landed aboard *Enterprise* six times on training exercises. Repairs continued on the carrier throughout the period, the forward elevator was made operational again, and watertight integrity was restored to most of the second- and third-deck areas damaged at Santa Cruz. Underwater restoration was still required, but "The Big E" would have to wait for a period in dry dock for that work and numerous other needs. Still, by late January progress was such that she could risk damage in another battle. On 28 January 1943 *Enterprise* and Air Group Ten again went to sea, not looking for trouble but ready for it if it came. Departing Segond Channel with one light cruiser—*San Diego* (CL-53)—and five destroyers, the carrier landed thirty-five Wildcats, twenty-six SBDs, and thirteen Avengers for the voyage.

Along with four other task groups built around a carrier, battleships, or cruisers, *Enterprise* was ordered to be in position to defend a convoy carrying troops to Guadalcanal for the relief of the First Marine Division, a unit that had written a new chapter in the annals of valor. While ensuring the safety of the distant convoy, the *Enterprise* and Air Group Ten were scheduled to continue training exercises, some with *Saratoga*'s TF 11. However, plans for tactics and gunnery were quickly pushed aside in the late evening hours of 29 January when an urgent, plain-language message arrived from Rear Adm. Frederick C. "Ted" Sherman, now commanding Task Force Sixteen. Just after sunset one of the other four task forces in the area, TF 18—comprised of six cruisers and six destroyers—had been attacked by enemy torpedo planes, and the heavy cruiser *Chicago* (CA-29) had taken two torpedoes on her starboard side. A survivor of the disastrous Battle of Savo Island on the night of 9 August, when her bow was damaged by a surface-launched torpedo, *Chicago* had just returned to the war zone after repairs in San Francisco. Now down at the stern and without propulsive power, the cruiser not only could not move out of enemy air-attack range but also was hard pressed to evacuate water from her hull. A sister ship, *Louisville* (CA-28), took *Chicago* in tow around midnight and worked up to four knots, a speed maintained by the tug *Navajo,* which took over the tow after sunrise. Aboard the slow-moving *Chicago* and the rapidly closing *Enterprise*—nearly 350 miles south at midnight, there was no question whether the enemy would strike again; it was a question of when.

Although Sherman was not celebrated for his modesty or charm, Jimmy was nonetheless pleased to have his former *Lexington* commanding officer involved. Sherman was explosive, demanding, and irritable, but also an intelligent tactician who loved battle and—like Jimmy—was calm and totally focused during battle.[22] As important to many of the Reapers, Sherman was an aviator. Kinkaid, though competent at Santa Cruz and Guadalcanal, was not.

Two of Bucky Lee's SBDs located TF 18 at sunrise, and Jimmy assigned a combat air patrol to cover the seven warships of TF 16 while he led another CAP to a station above the larger TF 18. The sun had barely appeared before an enemy scout was sighted, but it didn't linger as its pilot saw all he needed to see. After four hours in the air, Jimmy landed, ate lunch, and conferred with Gaines and Crommelin—now executive officer. Then with other Reapers, Jimmy waited for information on enemy planes. While waiting he mixed several blends of tobacco Dotty had sent him for Christmas with "an ordinary brand we have aboard . . . makes a good smoke."[23] As the early afternoon became midafternoon, none believed the day would pass without incident, but a few wondered aloud why the Japanese were taking so long to respond to a wounded cruiser. Wonder ceased at 1504 when a message from Guadalcanal alerted Sherman that eleven unidentified planes were heading in his direction. At 1530 Jimmy, still fighting his first head cold since leaving California, was back in the air leading Reaper One to ten thousand feet.

Navajo and *Chicago* inched on, encircled by only six destroyers as *Wichita* (CA-45) and the three new *Cleveland*-class cruisers had been detached. In less than thirty minutes since the signal from Guadalcanal, the CAP over *Chicago* and *Navajo* discerned a two-engined Mitsubishi G4M1 "Betty" approximately twenty miles to the west. Killer Kane retained his wingman, Ed Coalson, over the cruiser and assigned several ensigns—Leder, Maurice N. Wickendoll, Albert G. "Cowboy" Boren, and Frank T. Donahoe—to give chase. After a long-running battle the four F4Fs overtook and claimed the lone bomber, but with *Enterprise* then only forty miles from *Chicago,* the enemy pilot most likely reported the position of both ships. At 1654 the recently damaged and maligned radar on "The Big E's" masthead picked up the incoming raid at sixty-seven miles, and the carrier quickly accelerated from twenty-one to twenty-seven knots. Ten minutes later the fighter director officer instructed Lt. Macgregor Kilpatrick to intercept the incoming planes twenty miles distant. Mac quickly sighted the torpedo-armed twin-engine Bettys descending in line abreast. That the enemy planes were armed with torpedoes and approaching at low altitude was no surprise, but Mac was momentarily surprised to see that they were heading for *Enterprise,* and him, rather than the crippled *Chicago.*

Unlike at Santa Cruz, "The Big E's" radar was functioning perfectly; the fighter director officer had the Reapers in position to intercept well away from the carrier, and the Reapers had altitude. Kilpatrick and newly assigned Ens. Robert T. "Bob" Porter roared to altitude and position on one side of the approaching Bettys while Ensigns Gordon, Slagle, Kona, and Feightner were doing likewise on the other. The leader of the enemy land attack planes could see the Reapers ahead and above, smoothly moving into position to strike from both sides. Apparently determining he could not fight his way through to the carrier, the decisive enemy aviator ordered his charges into a sharp 150-degree left turn toward the disabled cruiser.[24] The long line-abreast formation became two lines of six each, as the Bettys emerged from a hasty but smooth turn. While this maneuver ensured the carrier's safety, four of the Reapers lining up for attack were no longer favorably positioned. A long tail chase was now their only option. However, Mac Kilpatrick and Bob Porter were between the Bettys and *Chicago,* and neither missed the opportunity placed before him. In textbook position both executed overhead high-side attacks and scored heavily with their deflection bursts. Pulling out, the two then attacked from the opposite side in the same manner. Between the two Reapers, three drab-colored Bettys crashed into the sea—their ordnance contributing only to the flaming pyre and cascading water marking their graves.

Despite their skillful attacks, Mac and Bob could not stop the entire formation and eight or nine surviving Bettys roared over the defending destroyers toward *Chicago*. Hit twice the previous evening while maneuvering at high speed and illuminated only by flares and the light of burning planes, the immobile cruiser was now no challenge in the broad daylight of 30 January. Having picked up speed from 160 knots to an estimated 250 knots as they headed downhill to their release point, the Bettys placed at least six torpedoes into the sea. Running true, four more torpedoes crashed into the same starboard side of the ship. Great columns of water rose high as the masthead concussion reverberated to nearby destroyers, and within twenty minutes the twelve-year-old *Northampton*-class treaty cruiser capsized and disappeared. Ten percent of the crew of twelve hundred did not survive the earlier attack that had crippled *Chicago* and later sinking. Another torpedo holed the fast-firing *Fletcher*-class destroyer *La Vallette* (DD-448) and killed twenty-two, but she survived.

Flying well above the detached cruisers moving east of *Chicago* (north of *Enterprise*), Jimmy and his division (Reiserer, Witte, and newcomer Ens. Peter M. Shonk) could see what was happening. But it was quickly apparent that they, like four pilots in Kilpatrick's six-plane division, also had a stern or stern quarter chase. Just as the Bettys picked up speed as they descended, so did the Wildcats. Following standard procedure, all the Reapers reached to charge their guns and release drop tanks. Their guns charged but at high speed—and with fuel in the external tanks—the drop tanks had a propensity not to drop. On this day consistency reigned, and only one Reaper succeeded in getting rid of a burden that reduced speed and spoiled aim. Even had the tanks dropped, Reaper One could not have caught the bombers in time to gain favorable beam position. Consequently, all ten Reapers reached the bombers just as they crossed the destroyer circle. Blazing away, the Reapers expended eleven thousand rounds of .50-caliber shells; Bettys burst into flame, crashed straight in, performed cartwheels, or broke apart. Despite the Reapers point-blank range, and enthusiastic gunnery from the destroyers, four Bettys were still flying as they exited on the opposite side of the destroyer ring. One of the burning wrecks short of the opposite side of the destroyers fell to Jimmy's guns. As usual there was no time to think of the downed Betty as Jimmy realized he was surrounded by friendly antiaircraft fire. As he later noted in his action report, he didn't mind being shot at while approaching the destroyers or while he was within their defensive circle, but he very definitely did not appreciate the gunfire that followed his egress.

With nearly a dozen Reapers now in pursuit—and in the midst of the destroyer's antiaircraft fire—concerns for defending *Chicago* and the destroyers now turned to attacks of revenge. Due to a balky engine, Whitey Feightner arrived over the destroyers out of position with his Reaper division, but he was in good position to blast away at the Bettys. Passing over the destroyers, he found himself abeam Jimmy's division and soon abeam of Jimmy himself. Without the burden of ordnance the surviving Bettys picked up speed, and much to his chagrin Jimmy could not catch his second target of the action. "Jimmy pulled his nose up and fired tracers over the guy which got him to turn toward a cloud." The Betty escaped into the low broken clouds whereupon it flew into a break in the mist directly in front of Whitey. The young ensign either had to shoot the Betty down or fly through it. Seeing the burning Betty dropping out of the clouds toward the water, Jimmy flew up alongside Whitey and flashed him a big smile and thumbs up. In like spirit Russ Reiserer, who later in the war over Saipan shot down four enemy planes in one action and chased a fifth with such tenacity that it surrendered to a water landing, continued pursuit of another surviving Betty despite having expended all his ammunition. "The Betty had one engine smoking, and Russ was not about to let it get that close to destruction and still get home. So he dropped his tail hook and made several passes trying to hook the tail fin and dump him in the water."[25]

Only one Reaper was lost on 30 January, and Jimmy's heart sank again as another bright light with boundless potential was prematurely extinguished. Popular Silver Star recipient Bobby Edwards, who had literally escaped from a hospital and then purloined a plane to get back into combat over the Slot in November, lost power just as he approached *Enterprise* after three hours on CAP. At 1343, two hours before Japanese torpedo planes threatened TF 16 and *Chicago,* Bobby "struck the sea[,] nose down and with considerable force" in the carrier's wake, and although his plane remained afloat, he made no attempt to leave the plane.[26] None of the Reapers were lost in the battle, and Jimmy recorded in his action report and flight log that the Grim Reapers had downed twelve of thirteen torpedo planes.[27] Disappointment in not saving *Chicago* was tempered with realization that *Enterprise* was not attacked due to the Reapers presence and positioning,[28] and that the Reapers had proved to be more "wildcats" than the Wildcats they flew. Jimmy recommended medals for Kilpatrick, Witte, Leder, Porter, Gordon, Wickendoll, Slagle, Reiserer, and Feightner. Landing aboard at 1735 after the Battle off Rennell Island Jimmy walked over to Whitey and said, "You're a fighting fool, aren't you!" That comment was for Whitey as great a tribute as the Distinguished Flying Cross and Air Medal he received for downing three planes on that day.[29]

Jimmy could not recommend medals for himself, but Gaines, Crommelin, and Hardison could and did. "For heroism and extraordinary achievement" Jimmy received a Distinguished Flying Cross for leading Fighting Ten in the 13–15 November 1942 attacks on enemy transports plus their aerial and surface escorts. For his part in the 30 January 1943 action off Rennell Island, Jimmy originally was awarded the Air Medal, but it was later recalled in lieu of a second Distinguished Flying Cross. Additionally, he received Presidential Unit Citations awarded both to *Enterprise* and to the First Marine Division, Reinforced.

On the evening of 30 January, Jimmy did not know he had led his Reapers into battle for the last time. Just over a week later (8 February), he had orders to the United States to take command of a new air group. An announcement on 11 February that the Japanese had evacuated Guadalcanal helped ease Jimmy's discomfort at departing the fighter squadron he had built from less than a dozen officers and planes into a squadron that Commander Gaines had promised months before "would make the Japanese regret their existence." Still, the man who was renowned by his men for being "unflappable in combat" could not summon the courage to speak to his squadron before leaving the *Enterprise*. Instead he wrote a letter, handed it to Killer Kane, and asked that it not be read until after he departed. On 13 February, Kane read the following to the Reapers:

> I can't find it in me to make a farewell speech. I'm afraid I'd get all choked up.
>
> I want you to know that I take my leave of you with deep regret. No squadron commander, anywhere, has ever had a gang like you serving

with him. I'm so darn proud and fond of everyone of you that my heart's about to bust.

If I could have had the pick of the Navy for my relief, it would have been the "Killer."

Take care of yourselves. Stick together and don't forget to respect that airplane. Every time you see a Jap, remember Leppla, Mead, Rhodes, Caldwell, Davis, Fulton, Barnes, Miller, Edwards, and Von Lehe.

One parting word of advice. There is a definite tendency on the part of every one of you to throw caution to the wind every time you meet the enemy. We've been lucky as hell so far. But, it's dumb. We've spent hours and hours on tactics, designed not only to destroy, but also all to protect ourselves. Keep that thought foremost in your minds. Rip 'em up and down, but do it smartly.

I trust our paths will cross in the near future. Meanwhile, keep your chins up and don't forget that little guy who called himself

Reaper Leader

9

Air Group Five Commander on *Yorktown* (CV-10)

WHILE AIR Group Ten shuttled between *Enterprise,* the New Hebrides, and New Caledonia in the first weeks of 1943, Jimmy caught his first glimpse of the new escort carriers converted from tanker hulls. Longer than most other escort carriers that followed and blessed with greater range, two of the four *Sangamon*-class carriers had supported the November 1942 invasion of North Africa. Due to the critical carrier shortage in the Pacific, they had traversed the Panama Canal to bolster fleet operations in the lower Solomons region. As interesting to Jimmy as the sight of *Sangamon* (CVE-26) and *Suwannee* (CVE-27), however, was the sight of an old friend. Capt. Joseph James "Jocko" Clark was commanding officer of *Suwannee* before her commissioning, during her first combat off North Africa, and was still on the bridge 4 January 1943 when the carrier arrived at Noumea, New Caledonia. Within days, however, Jocko had orders to command a large new fast carrier, and he invited Jimmy to be his air group commander.

Jimmy did not hesitate to say "yes." At Jacksonville in late 1940 and early 1941, Jimmy had proved indispensable to Jocko, and both men were eager for the new opportunity before them. Of course it wasn't official until orders arrived in Jimmy's hands, and he knew better than to count chickens before they hatched. Still, he could not keep himself from sharing the possibility, writing Dotty on 20 January, "You know, my pilots are continually dreaming up rumors that we will get back to the States soon. It's the inactivity that breeds rumors. Actually, they won't get back [in] under a year and neither will I unless they want me for something else."

On the day after his letter to Dotty, a war information bulletin announced the launching of a new *Essex*-class carrier at Norfolk, Virginia. In the early stages of CV-10's construction she was to become *Bon Homme Richard,* but the navy changed her name to *Yorktown* in honor of the gallant carrier (CV-5) lost at Midway six months earlier. Even though Jocko was not present for the launching, it was his ship. And within two weeks, it was Jimmy's.

After 8 February when Jimmy's orders to command Air Group Five arrived, he lost little time making his way back to California. His plans were to have Dotty leave their three sons in Coronado for a few days and meet him in San Francisco. The navy, however, had other plans thereby preempting Jimmy's welcoming party of one. Constantly promising Dotty an enjoyable celebration upon his return, Jimmy didn't get the mid-February timing he wanted, but a fourth son, David Michael, born 19 December 1943, attests to the joy of their early March reunion.

The navy's plans were to fly Jimmy to Pearl Harbor (18 March), put him on the not-fast-enough SS *Calarares* on the twentieth, and have him in San Francisco on the twenty-eighth. From San Francisco Jimmy rode a train down the coast to San Diego and home. Aboard the train he carried nearly as many papers as clothes and toiletries, not a great problem as the train offered enforced leisure. Official mail included notification of permanent promotion to lieutenant commander, the temporary rank he had carried since 2 January 1942.[1] Reflecting on his academy graduation in 1929, he would have then quickly accepted a promise to rise to that exalted rank by retirement. Just as quickly, his thoughts turned to promotion to full commander. Another promotion would surely be his barring a disastrous performance as commanding officer of Air Group Five, which had just been commissioned on 15 February, the same day Jocko arrived aboard *Yorktown*. But not all the reading was pleasant. On the same two-page promotion list with his name were the names of good friends John Collett and Lem Massey. Jimmy and the navy knew they were dead, but since their bodies were not recovered, by regulation for one year they were only "missing in action."

On 2 March Jimmy reported to the commander of Fleet Air on the West Coast at NAS San Diego for temporary duty. On the fifth he was in the air for a two-hour familiarization flight in an SNJ-4, a newer version of the trainer he had first flown while with Jocko at Jacksonville. Despite his permanent exalted rank and an assignment to become an air group commander, the first four hours flying time for the month were ferry flights. But, on 24 March, he got what he came for, a two-hour familiarization flight in the new Grumman F6F-3 Hellcat fighter (BuNo. 06140). After repeated calls from Jimmy Flatley, Jimmie Thach, Butch O'Hare, Joe Foss, and nearly everyone else flying F4F Wildcats in the Pacific, Grumman had produced "something that would go upstairs faster."[2] In the following two years it proved to be the "war winner" naval aviation needed.

New Plane and a New Ship for a New Air Group

The experimental XF6F-1 Hellcat appeared on Grumman's design tables in June 1941 as a replacement for the F4F Wildcat. Significantly improved performance was not possible with the Wildcat, and the new design held great potential on paper. Suggestions from O'Hare, other fighter pilots, and Grumman's own test pilots quickly prompted the company to replace the original sixteen-hundred-horsepower Wright Cyclone engine in the experimental models with a more powerful two-thousand-horsepower Pratt & Whitney Double Wasp. The eighteen cylinder R-2800-10—the same engine powering the new F4U Corsair—and subsequent power-plant versions—enabled the F6F to hold its own with the Zero in climb, and to surpass the nimble Mitsubishi fighter in overall speed. In short, the more powerful engines converted potential to performance.

A Zero had been captured in the Aleutians, but it played no role in the design of the new Hellcat since the XF6F-1 first flew on 26 June 1942, a month before the Zero was recovered. The most significant contributions of the captured Zero were not mechanical modifications to the Hellcat but knowledge that enabled navy pilots to understand the enemy plane's limitations in combat tactics.

While the Zero still had an edge on turns and maneuverability at lower altitudes and lower speeds, it retained no other meaningful advantage over the first F6F-3 models produced in the late fall of 1942. All the earlier proven attributes of the Wildcat were improved and incorporated into the new fighter, including seatback armor, superior visibility over the nose, and self-sealing fuel tanks. Nearly double the weight of the Wildcat, the F6F featured the largest wing fitted on an American single-seat fighter during the war. The new wide-track landing gear folded into the wing, and a toggle switch replaced the hand crank required to raise the landing gear in the Wildcat. Speed increased to 376 mph, 56 mph faster than the Wildcat and the Zero, and the much larger Hellcat could carry 150-gallon drop tanks for much greater range. As with the Wildcat, the Hellcat could easily dive away from a Zero.

Well remembering the days before the war when he flew gunnery practice with ammunition in only one gun—and remembering the days when fighters had only two guns—Jimmy was not as vociferous as younger fighter pilots complaining about the reduced firing time between the four-gun F4F-3 and six-gun F4F-4 Wildcat models. Still, the new Hellcat not only offered six guns but an increase of 160 rounds per gun (400 each). Firing time increased from twenty seconds to nearly forty. All these improvements in combination with the declining quality of enemy pilots resulted in a nineteen to one kill ratio for the Hellcat by the war's end. Although Grumman was consistent with its policy of naming fighters for cats, the new F6F might have been more appropriately named "Vanquisher."

While airborne in the Hellcat for only two hours on 24 March, the effect of the flight lasted much longer. All the Hellcat's new features and exhilarating performance drew a wide smile on Jimmy's face, and for one of the few times in his life he took the job home with him. Amid so much bad and sad news he had been sharing with Dotty and his parents, it was a great change of pace to offer some good and exciting news.

A week after his Hellcat familiarization ride, Jimmy, Dotty, and then youngest son Brian boarded a train for Norfolk, Virginia, leaving nine-year-old little Jim and seven-year-old Patrick with Jimmy's parents and Jeanette. How long Dotty could be with Jimmy in Norfolk was unknown, but both wanted every day they could squeeze from the navy and the war. On 7 April Jimmy reported aboard *Yorktown* to assume command of Air Group Five. Being quite familiar with Norfolk, he knew he was not going to find all his squadrons in one place. Pilots of the thirty-six plane Fighting Squadron Five had been at Oceana, but on 8 April they moved to Creeds airfield as Oceana was temporarily closed to lengthen runways and enlarge the complex. Jimmy was pleased to hear that some of his fighter pilots had earlier traveled to Bethpage, New York, and successfully persuaded Grumman to allocate some early production Hellcats to Fighting Five that were to have been assigned to the *Essex* and Air Group Nine.[3] Torpedo Squadron Five was already equipped with eighteen Avengers, and on 11 April Jimmy flew an SNJ to Pungo field to meet the pilots and get a briefing on status and needs. Not unexpectedly, the greatest needs were for spare parts and combat experience, which the pilots lacked. The same report came from the thirty-six-plane Bombing Five, which had formed in California and was new to Norfolk.

There was a natural tendency for Jimmy to spend an inordinate amount of time with Fighting Five rather than Bombing Five or Torpedo Five. Temptation to do so, however, was eased by several factors. First, the commanding officer of Fighting Five was Lt. Cdr. Charles L. Crommelin (USNA 1931), the third Crommelin brother Jimmy had served with in less than a year. Like Richard and John, Charles was highly motivated and cut from the same warrior cloth. Consequently, Jimmy knew he could best serve VF-5 by letting its competent squadron commander run his own show. Moreover, Crommelin and two other squadron pilots—Lt. Melvin C. "Boogie" Hoffman and Lt. Edward M. Owen—had been involved in the initial tests of the Hellcat. Plus, Hoffman had flown the captured Zero and could share performance strengths and deficiencies with squadron mates.[4] Consequently, Jimmy contented himself by selecting a Hellcat—with oo side numbers—as his personal air group commander (CAG) mount.

Lt. Cdr. Richard Upson, commanding officer of Torpedo Five, was not a candidate for a congeniality award, but he too was quite capable.

Bombing Five, led by Lt. Cdr. Robert M. Milner, was more of a challenge as there was an internal dispute concerning the choice of a squadron commander between the two small units that had been combined to form the squadron. Adding to Bombing Five's personality problems was their new plane—the Curtiss-built SB2C Helldiver. The "beast" was well deserving of its appellation in the spring of 1943. Intended to be a successor to the battle proven SBD, it was experiencing many of the same mechanical problems then plaguing the F4U Corsair fighter. Most disconcerting for both planes in their early stages was their tendency to literally come apart during carrier landings.

Jimmy knew he could do relatively little to solve mechanical problems, and the overall lack of experience in the squadron was an equally serious problem. Training he could address, and by emphasizing training and squadron tactics he expected personality problems—especially those in Bombing Five—to be relegated to the bottom of everyone's priority list. Having just left a squadron commander's billet, he knew how important it was for his three respective squadron commanders to handle their own internal problems. Delegation of responsibility and attendant authority was not an overwhelming problem for Jimmy. In fact, he fully expected his squadron commanders to assume and demonstrate leadership. While not content to become solely a cheerleader, he understood he must still inspire as well as teach. But transition required Jimmy to cope with the change, and in some respects he felt like he had given up a fatherly role for that of a grandfather. Too, Jimmy now had to acclimate himself to the policy that air group commanders observe or direct battles rather than attack. Just as Dick Gaines flew at Santa Cruz as an observer without ordnance, now Jimmy was expected to do the same. Later in the war, some commanding officers and air officers would not allow their air group commanders to even leave the carrier without direct permission.[5]

On 21 April enough Hellcats were available for Jimmy to claim one for himself, and on the twenty-second he led group tactics for the first time. The 2.5-hour exercise was about what Jimmy expected for the first such effort, but it was a start. Paperwork consumed his time for the remainder of the month, but aerial training intensified in May. On 1 May Jimmy led the group for carrier qualification landings on two escort carriers in Chesapeake Bay, and on 6 May he made the first landing aboard the new *Yorktown*. The landing took much less time than the public relations requirements, a matter of no concern to the smiling air group commander. With his Hellcat chocked abreast the island Jimmy dutifully, and happily, smiled into cameras, first from the cockpit and then with his left foot on the edge of the cockpit. Stepping onto the wing, he was asked to pose again, but this time he was all smiled out. However, a smile reappeared when Jocko and others hauled a cake onto the flight deck. A few more smiles, a few more pictures, and a few quick bites later, "Double Zero" was moved forward, Jocko went back to the bridge, the carrier accelerated into the wind, and other planes high above the secure bay dropped down onto the Douglas fir flight deck.

On 15 April Jimmy stood on *Yorktown*'s flight deck with the 450 officers and men of Air Group Five along with some twenty-five hundred ship's company to participate in the carrier's commissioning. The day was overcast, windy, and cold, but the ceremony captured more attention than the weather. Of the planned two-dozen *Essex*-class carriers, only the *Essex* and second *Lexington* (CV-16) had been commissioned earlier, but none of the three were ready for combat. *Essex* had completed her shakedown cruise, but *Lexington* and *Yorktown* had that important test before them.

Of necessity, Jimmy was preoccupied with air group matters and had little time to wander about *Yorktown* for inspection purposes. A radically different pyramid island structure distinguished the *Essex*-class carriers from earlier carriers, but the overall design was not greatly different from the preceding *Yorktown* (CV-5) class. Staterooms, offices, and ready rooms were about the same size. The wardroom seemed smaller and not as elegant. But the differences between the first *Yorktown* and the second were especially important to an air group commander. The flight deck was a little longer in footage (872 versus 809), but more important was the width (148 versus 110), which when seen from the air was especially comforting. On the hangar deck, planes could pass each other more easily, and the new arrangement of the number two and number three elevators greatly accelerated deck operations. The number two elevator for the *Essex* class was abreast the island and outboard the flight deck. The third was immediately aft of the island but well forward from the stern. Planes landing on the old *Yorktown* class—of which only *Enterprise* still lived—touched down near both elevator number two and three. And while engineers specifically appreciated the greater fuel capacity, all who had earlier served on CV-5, CV-6, or CV-8 were especially pleased to know that the *Essex*-class carriers had alternating boiler and engine rooms. This arrangement, which might have saved the first *Yorktown* and first *Hornet*, contributed to saving the second *Lexington* and *Intrepid* when they took torpedoes in December 1943 and February 1944, respectively.

There was one major design change Jimmy appreciated as a naval officer but not as an air group commander. The new *Yorktown* sported twelve 5-inch guns, four more than the first carrier to bear the same name. However, eight of them were in mounts immediately fore and aft of the island. As long as they were fired to starboard, there was no problem. However, when the guns were trained to port, the muzzle blasts ripped metal skin from fuselage and wings. The only solution was to keep planes as distant as possible from the guns. Later in the war, time did not always allow for securing aircraft, and the rapid firing 5-inch guns damaged deck-bound planes while the guns were blazing away at enemy attackers.

Cruise to the Caribbean

While Jocko Clark and a very small group of regular officers attempted to mold over two thousand green sailors into a smooth functioning team, *Yorktown* prepared to steam south to Trinidad in the British West Indies for a shakedown cruise. Air Group Five intensified training at their shore bases, landing on CV-10 only twice before leaving on the mandatory ship trials to the Caribbean. With spring in full force at Norfolk, few looked forward to a tropical sojourn. And no one expected Jocko to make the trip a pleasure cruise.

Having been in the Pacific before the day of infamy, Jimmy had to shift gears in his thinking and planning from Japanese conduct of war to that of Germany, and keep a daytime antisubmarine patrol over the ship during the southerly voyage. Trinidad's Gulf of Paria should be secure for the ship and training exercises, but safe passage down the Atlantic coast had to be earned. The sight of burning merchant ships off Virginia, North Carolina, and other eastern seaboard states had been an all too familiar sight. Few in the Norfolk military and civilian communities had not been affected to some degree by the German U-boats. Apprehension was pervasive and justified.

Before leaving Norfolk, Jimmy tried to clear his desk and mind of all matters not related to the impending four-week voyage. A letter from Stanley Johnston arrived on 8 May confirming "our agreement that I am collaborating with you on writing the story of the Grim Reapers." The book was to cover naval actions in the Pacific and would be printed in installments for the *Chicago Tribune* Press Service syndicate. Noting that the idea for the project was his, Jimmy wrote to the Navy Department that, "it will outline to the public just how their sons are trained, how they are led and how they fight and die." Sales of the book were to net Jimmy fifty percent of all income after deduction of handling costs. As a naval officer, Jimmy did not have authority to act upon Johnston's letter without permission. It is not clear whether or not Jimmy knew of an earlier problem between Johnston and the navy pertaining to a leak of information after the Battle of Midway. Regardless, in letters to the Navy Department, Jimmy requested permission to proceed with the project, requested direction pertaining to navy censorship—to protect the navy and himself, and offered assurance that Johnston would forward the finished manuscript to the Navy Department before it was published.[6] The Office of Public Relations in the Navy Department was well aware of, and pleased with, Johnston's earlier syndicated articles.[7] On 14 July Jimmy received a letter from the Office of Public Relations informing him that the collection of articles comprising the book were officially cleared. The letter went on to say, "The articles focus on the squadron more than they do on you personally, which is right."

Another public relations endeavor was also right. Traveling with *Yorktown* to Trinidad were photographers to film a documentary, and another crew from Twentieth Century Fox was aboard to film a commercial movie. Footage shot during the Caribbean voyage was later used in two feature-length movies, one being *The Fighting Lady* which won the 1944 academy award for best documentary. The other footage was for *Wing and a Prayer,* a movie (very loosely) based on the Battle of Midway. Having nearly a full month to work on the project, the documentary photographer Dwight Long—working under Lt. Edward Steichen, USNR, had time to highlight several members of the crew. Jocko, of course, got considerable attention and no written material can ever capture the essence of him better than *The Fighting Lady.* In one segment, the frustrated commanding officer abandoned the bridge to give a loud, hands-on demonstration on how to arrange planes on the flight deck. As *Yorktown* veterans recall, most of the crew had no frame of reference for ship captains, so they accepted his dynamic, profanity-laced instructions as normal procedure. As many of the crew were former athletes, Jocko was just one more coach. Officers who were recipients of his outbursts maintained respect for what he was attempting to accomplish but did not hold much warmth for the man. A smaller group of officers, however, revered Jocko. That group, which included Jimmy, were those who knew their jobs, knew what was required to obtain necessary results, and complained only that there were too few hours in a day to get it all done.

The Fighting Lady featured several other officers: Jimmy was captured on film (the only known audiovisual remembrance of him), speaking in the wardroom to fighter pilot Lt. Elisha T. "Smokey" Stover and torpedo pilot Lt. James "Pop" Condit. In time, portions of the film covering Smokey became significant as he was later shot down over the Japanese stronghold at Truk in the Caroline Islands, captured, and executed. Pop Condit was also shot down less than two months after camera crews filmed him. When the movie was released, both Smokey and Pop were reported as missing and believed dead. At war's end, however, Pop came home from a POW camp, but Smokey and others did not.

While public relations projects were moving smoothly and proving "right," the new SB2C Helldivers were anything but smooth or right. As *Yorktown* passed through the torpedo nets from Chesapeake Bay into the grayish green Atlantic on 21 May, Jimmy knew he would have to keep planes in the air over the carrier. During daylight hours the aircraft searched to find U-boats before they could get in position to attack the carrier and her three escorting destroyers. Long scheduled to be the replacement scout-bomber for the battle-proven SBD, the Bombing Five

Helldivers were constantly proving themselves unworthy, both for the pilots of Bombing Five and as a replacement for the venerable Dauntless. The larger SB2C did offer greater maximum speed (295 mph versus 245) and faster cruising speed (158 mph versus 144), but gains in range (still about 1,100 miles) and ordnance capacity (two thousand pounds versus sixteen hundred) were negligible. For most air group commanders, the only advantage of the Helldiver over the SBD was folding wings that allowed more scout-bombers to fit into hangar decks. Jimmy was generally satisfied with his 1.2-hour familiarization flight, but he could not turn a blind eye to the continuing mechanical problems plaguing "the beast." Curtiss engineers and mechanics accompanied CV-10 on the shakedown trip to assist with modifications and repairs. However, nearly every Helldiver touchdown on the flight deck was a promise of a tailhook failure or a collapsed landing gear. Worse was a tailhook that held, but separated the plane into two parts, and the Helldiver's engine had a tendency to stall when approaching the deck. Few wanted to fly such a plane. When *Yorktown* made her return voyage from Trinidad, the SB2Cs remained behind and Bombing Five enjoyed an unscheduled break in training. Upon their return to Norfolk, they happily climbed back into new SBD-5s. The final decision to abandon the Helldivers was Jocko's, but Jimmy offered no dissenting voice. Later in the war, extensive changes and refinements to the SB2C resulted in an effective scout-bomber that provided commendable service.

Training over and around Trinidad's Edinburgh and Xeres airfields from 26 May to 13 June (sister-ship *Lexington* was also in the Gulf of Paria for shakedown) went much better for Fighting Five and Torpedo Five. After recording only thirteen hours in April with his new air group, Jimmy was aloft for 30.5 hours for group tactics and gunnery. But the air group flew aboard the carrier only three times, as Jocko was preoccupied with the task of turning his green volunteers and conscripts into a coordinated team. Little needed to be said to ship's company or the air group regarding the reason for the exacting training to which they were being subjected. Object lessons before them were the several training and operational accidents in Air Group Five. From the date of the group's commissioning in February to its first combat in late August, over a dozen planes of all types were lost and over a half dozen pilots were killed. Tragic as these losses were, their occurrence added impact to the words of Jocko, Jimmy, and other officers that anything less than perfection in completing all tasks potentially carried a penalty of death.

Back in Norfolk on 16 June, Air Group Five continued training from its shore bases, and Jimmy spent what few hours he could find with Dotty. Attempting to clear paperwork from his desk before heading to sea again, he dashed off another letter to the Navy Department. All the letters that passed from Jimmy to the Office of Public Relations crossed the desk of one of his old friends, Cdr. Frank W. "Spig" Wead. Spig was an early naval aviator who had been seriously injured in a fall. Leaving the navy, Wead succeeded in Hollywood as a screenwriter, especially excelling in stories on naval aviation (especially one on himself, portrayed in the movie by John Wayne). Recalled to active duty early in the war, he remained until 1944, signing all his wartime correspondence with "Ret." (Retired) after his name. Knowing that Spig loved the navy as much as he did, Jimmy did not hesitate to ask his help on matters unrelated to the proposed Grim Reaper book. (Permission to go ahead with publication of the book was totally separated from Flatley's requesting Spig to add his voice to Jimmy's in proposing that CVLs carry fighters exclusively.)

Jimmy wrote Spig on 24 June clearly asking him to step into operational matters well beyond his role as a public relations specialist. Noting that he was not alone in his opinions, Jimmy broached the matter of aircraft allocation for "cruiser conversions" (*Independence* class). Noting that the new *Independence*-class carriers' thirty-six plane complement included twelve Avengers, twelve SBDs, and twelve Wildcats (soon replaced with Hellcats), Jimmy complained the CVLs did not have enough planes of any type to do any job satisfactorily. After stating that the fixed-wing SBD created operational problems (inferior range and speed compared to their Japanese counterparts), in addition to reducing the number of planes a carrier could accommodate, Jimmy championed an "ideal combination [of] one or two *Essex* class [carriers] accompanied by one CVL . . . carrying nothing but fighters." Solidly convinced on the merit of his argument Jimmy wrote, "We can realize such a set-up right now if the powers-that-be would recognize the value and act. Inevitably they will be forced into it. I'd like to reduce the time lag." Finally, he wrote that he was headed to Jacksonville over the weekend to see Jimmie Thach, no doubt to seek his assistance in spreading the same word. Six weeks later the matter was addressed at the highest level in the navy, but Spig's thoughts on the matter, whatever they were, didn't carry the weight Jimmy hoped it might.

On 6 July *Yorktown* again passed from Chesapeake Bay into the Atlantic for another southerly cruise, but this time there was no return to Norfolk. Emotions rose and fell for Jimmy during the first few days of this excursion. Training did not cease, and thoughts of yet another difficult departure from Dotty did not cease. On the eighth, a submarine alert was no drill. On the ninth he received word that he had been promoted to the temporary rank of full commander. After passing through the Panama Canal, a planned stop at San Francisco—and perhaps one more quick visit with Dotty—was canceled, and the carrier sped on toward Hawaii. On the twenty-second Air Group Five flew ashore to Barbers Point. Emotions now in relative abeyance, Jimmy turned all thoughts to combat preparations. On 22 July he did not know exactly where or when he would again see the enemy, but he knew it would come soon.

Raid on Marcus Island

In the six month period between May and late October 1942, the United States Navy and the Imperial Japanese Navy had fought four major carrier-versus-carrier battles (Coral Sea, Midway, Eastern Solomons, and Santa Cruz). By late August 1943, nine months had passed since the last of these four battles. The lull was necessary for both antagonists to build replacement flattops for those lost in 1942 (four United States, six Japan), repair damage to surviving carriers, and train new air groups.

While there was a lull in carrier battles, there was no combat lull in the Pacific. Gen. Douglas MacArthur's forces were steadily pushing north from Australia through New Guinea. Admiral Halsey made maximum use of his still relatively meager resources by carefully choosing strategic targets in the central Solomons. And though not directly engaged with the enemy, Admiral Nimitz kept central Pacific garrisons

tied down as he marshaled new ships and troops. The Japanese anticipated a thrust into the central Pacific in the summer of 1943, and did
have plans to commit at least one carrier division to the defense of the
Marshall Islands as well as the Gilbert Islands immediately to the southeast. The two strongest bases for Japanese naval power in the region
were Truk in the Caroline Islands and Rabaul at New Britain. From
Truk, enemy naval units were roughly equidistant from the Marianas,
Palau Islands, New Guinea, the Solomons, Marshalls, and Gilberts.
The Allies had no land bases near Truk. Rabaul, however, was within
range of land-based aircraft. Consequently, in the late summer of 1943
Japanese planners had to balance a desire to commit their carriers
against an American incursion into the central Pacific or commit their
carrier air groups to the defense of Rabaul. After some vacillation the
Japanese decided the immediate pressure on Rabaul had to be top priority. Therefore, three air groups were transferred from their carriers to
Rabaul's airfields. That decision and action was unknown to Nimitz at
Pearl, but it had little significance regarding his plans. When he had
gathered sufficient strength, especially carriers, he was determined to
begin the long awaited offensive through the Marshalls and Gilberts. In
late August he had what he needed.

The offensive into the Marshalls and Gilberts was planned for
November. Before moving forces west to occupy selected enemy territory in the two island groups, there were to be two trial runs, Marcus
Island on 31 August and Wake Island on 5–6 October. Isolated and
little, Marcus Island had no strategic value beyond serving as a weather
station and small airfield. Wake Island had sentimental value as it had
been overwhelmed in the first month of the war despite a particularly
gallant defense by marines. But possession of Wake, or Marcus, was
not necessary to secure or facilitate the advance to Japan. Jimmy would
be detached from Air Group Five before the attack on Wake, but he was
about to see a lot of Marcus.

Training continued unabated for Air Group Five with much of it at
sea. On 13 August, *Yorktown* and *Independence* (CVL-22) were conducting exercises when a Fighting Squadron Six pilot from *Independence*
rolled his Hellcat into the port catwalk while landing. The heavy fighter
could not be pulled out of its precarious roost and the new light carrier

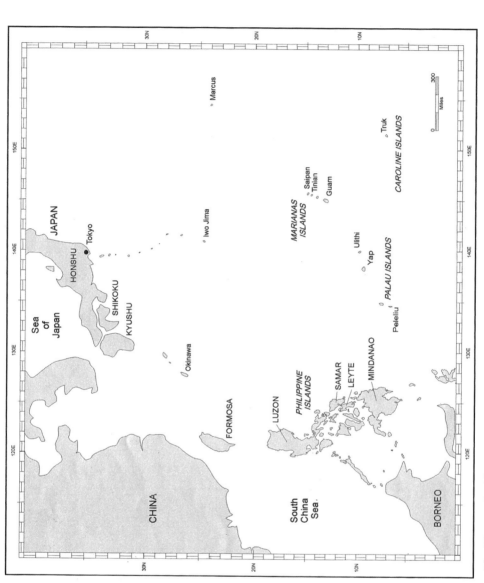

The Western Pacific

had to cancel air operations. A few VF-6 pilots in the air had to land on *Yorktown* before returning to NAS Puunene, one being the squadron commander, Lt. Cdr. Butch O'Hare. Jimmy did not fly on the thirteenth and therefore had a few minutes to share a cigarette and pleasantries with Butch while his F6F was being refueled. The meeting between Jimmy, the former instructor, and his student was short but Jimmy remembered it well. In the Gilbert Islands operation three months later, Butch was killed while leading a successful night interception from *Enterprise* off Tarawa. It was the first such operation from a carrier.

On 22 August *Yorktown* left Pearl for what most aboard believed to be yet another training exercise. By the next day it appeared to be about a three-day training exercise as *Yorktown* steamed with two other carriers, *Essex* and *Independence,* the new fast battleship *Indiana* (BB-58), two light cruisers, eleven destroyers, and a fleet oiler. Under the command of Rear Adm. Charles A. "Baldy" Pownall, the training group was in fact Task Force Fifteen. All three carriers operated together within the same screen, a cruising disposition on trial just like the new Hellcats and their carriers. On the twenty-third Jimmy and other officers with a need to know, learned TF 15 was to attack Marcus Island. *Enterprise's* air group had hit remote Marcus—only a thousand miles southwest of Japan—on 4 March 1942. The purpose of the 1942 mission, which first struck Wake Island, was to build morale. Any damage inflicted was a bonus, as it was known the enemy could replace planes, guns, and men without difficulty. In August 1943 the purpose of the raid was to provide battle experience for the air groups. Yet, even though damage was a peripheral consideration within the minds of strategic planners, aboard the three carriers it was the paramount consideration (then and over fifty years later).

Although he could not forward mail to Dotty until he returned to Pearl, Jimmy began a series of letters describing his mood and thoughts as the task force headed on a circuitous northerly route to the target, which was almost due west. "We are really a good outfit, ready and rarin to go," Jimmy wrote on the twenty-fourth. "We're out here for a training cruise and looks like it's going to be strenuous training. Well, we're fit. That's all I can say. Tojo is going to take an awful licking."[8]

By the twenty-seventh nearly everyone knew this was not an ordinary training cruise due to the distance already traveled from Pearl and pattern of flight operations. There was always a combat air patrol during daylight hours and SBDs or Avengers patrolling for submarines. There were no group tactics until the twenty-eighth when Jimmy joined the air group aloft for a three-hour flight. On the thirtieth, attack plans were announced to the crew, and everyone seemed to move just a little quicker and with a little more purpose. One who had not been moving too fast was Jimmy. "Everyday all the young bloods put me to shame by taking a lot of strenuous exercise. I've decided to stay away from it. All I do is get hurt. Anyway, I seem to be strong enough."[9]

Being strong was the essence of a commander, and Jimmy had to be strong on several fronts. "The days are long . . . each one is a new experience in some way. . . . A different problem to solve. . . . A new personality to become acquainted with. . . . A crooked soul to comfort. My office is the crossroads of the Pacific. I must have a kind face."[10] To keep himself strong Jimmy reported, "I go to mass every afternoon . . . at 4:45 p.m. . . . It gives me a new lease on life." Despite their long and close relationship, Jimmy could not convey the strength of his inner peace to Jocko. "We're getting farther 'n farther away from anywhere. . . . Each day I go up to see Jock, and each day he becomes more lovable [sic] and obstreperous." Determined to succeed in combat, Jocko continued the noisy and agitated conduct he had displayed since taking command of CV-10. Indeed, he was giving nearly everyone around him ulcers like the ones that had plagued him for several years. He worried about every detail, and despite knowing he had and was giving everything within him, he could not know how everyone aboard would react when the real trial came. But wrote Jimmy, "One thing is certain. We will never disappoint him."[11]

Upon receiving word of the mission, Jimmy immediately conveyed maps and other data to his squadron commanders, who in turn informed their pilots and invited each pilot to submit an attack plan. Subsequently, Jimmy joined Crommelin, Upson, and Milner for a meeting to agree on an attack procedure that was then submitted to Admiral Pownall. A conference for all pilots was then held for a general discussion with specific emphasis on the role of each squadron, an especially beneficial exercise for the inexperienced pilots before their first combat. As a result of this conference, all pilots had a definite idea of not only their own course of action over Marcus, but also what others were to do. Conference over, pilots then held classes in their ready rooms for identification of friendly planes and ships and those of the enemy.[12]

On the evening of the thirtieth, Jimmy gathered his pilots in the wardroom for a final conference. In similar earlier meetings he always solicited input from the pilots, but for this last meeting Jimmy held the floor in a more fatherly tone. The attack plan was addressed in detail with Jimmy stressing the need for coordination of effort in order to obtain the maximum effect with the least number of combat losses. Crommelin, Upson, and Milner then explained the part their pilots were to play and how they were going to execute it. Finally, Admiral Pownall assured the pilots of his confidence in their ability to perform their task efficiently. Wrapping up the tactical instructions ("Your best defense is a strong, accurate, determined attack"), admonitions ("Don't get excited"), cautions ("Keep together), and encouragement ("We are the best"), Jimmy closed the meeting in the same manner he had nine months earlier aboard *Enterprise*. "Got all my kids to say their prayers this time without too much talking. Just said . . . say your prayers tonight. Thank God you are given the chance to fight for the heritage He left you. Tell Him you're sorry for having offended Him by violating in any way all the things you are fighting for. . . . Or words to that effect. . . . Actually, I said it a little smoother than that, but it got over and they all said their prayers, thank God."[13]

Having passed well to the north of Midway, and away from enemy patrol planes flying from Wake, TF 15 had turned south into cloudy and rainy weather after refueling on the twenty-seventh and twenty-eight. Flagship *Yorktown* and the other ships turned southwest for final approach on the thirty-first, which was already 1 September on local calendars at Marcus. Final operational orders—including tactical recommendations from Jimmy and his pilots—drawn up by Capt. Herbert S. Duckworth ("Ducky" to Jimmy and other longtime close friends) and Capt. Wallace M. Beakley, called for dawn strikes by Air Group Five and Air Group Nine aboard *Essex*. Air Group Six on *Independence* was assigned combat air patrol and air-search missions.

Awake at 0200, Jimmy joined the other pilots for a breakfast of steak, eggs, milk, and coffee. The last cigarette out, he stood in an air-conditioned ready room watching the ticker tapes provide readings on weather and navigational data. From their high-backed leather chairs, pilots watched with stone faces at information mostly to their liking. Visibility was no problem, but a calm sea also meant little or no wind over the deck. Escorted to his plane in the predawn darkness, Jimmy had plenty of time to observe the takeoff, as his "Double Zero" was to be the last plane off for the first strike.

One Pratt & Whitney R-2800 was enough to drown out any voice or speaker system. When four dozen started and began warming up, thought itself was a challenge. At 0422 a VF-5 Hellcat rolled down the deck and into the air. Then Avengers lifted off and headed for the pre-determined rendezvous. Then a delay as one of the SBDs suffered an engine failure. Another delay as one Hellcat got in the way of another. Finally it was Jimmy's turn. On the horizon he could see the artificial horizon of truck lights at the top of destroyer masts. Down the deck were the muted lights, and at the sight of a green light he roared down the deck, lifted off just short of the bow and turned left into the vesper of wind. Crommelin's fighters, Upson's Avengers, and some of Milner's SBDs were already on their 130-mile flight to Marcus as Jimmy gained altitude. He would have preferred to have led the formation, but on this day his assignment and responsibilities were different. No less important, but different.

Forty-five minutes after the first plane was launched, Upson left his assigned rendezvous sector and departed for the objective with other aircraft behind. Climbing gradually to fifteen hundred feet so search radar could follow the strike-group track out to fifty miles, the planes then dropped to five hundred feet until they were fifty miles from Marcus when a climb to eight thousand feet commenced. As *Yorktown* remained on her launching course twenty minutes longer than estimated, a course change of 12 degrees was transmitted to Jimmy via VHF and was in turn relayed to Upson. Upson's radar-equipped Avenger made contact with Marcus eighteen miles out, and at 0603 he could see the small, triangular-shaped island, half obscured by clouds. No Japanese planes were aloft. No antiaircraft guns fired. Surprise was complete.[14]

At 0608 eighteen Avengers began the attack. Each VT pilot had been given a definite point of aim with reference to a known feature on the island. Aiming point had been worked out by dropping angle, altitude, and trail with a wind allowance of ten feet for every knot of wind. Approaching from different paths, each division attacked from a different side of the triangular island. The first Avenger in each division was loaded with six clusters of incendiaries and two 500-pound bombs; the others with two 1,000-pound bombs with either daisy cutter fuses or .01 delay fuses. Incendiaries dropped by the division leaders illuminated the gray dawn effectively, and no following aircraft had difficulty seeing assigned targets. For nine hours, bombs and bullets rained on Marcus, *Yorktown* and *Essex* delivering two deck loads of aircraft each and *Independence* one.[15]

Hellcats supported the initial attack with twelve F6F-3s employed to harass antiaircraft positions to divert fire from the Avengers. Knowing the glide path of each division of Avengers, the fighters were able to work at right angles to the glide to carry out their mission despite lingering darkness. Four other Hellcats arrived and remained at twelve thousand feet as cover in case Zeros were airborne. Twenty miles east of the island the Avengers gathered at five hundred feet before returning to CV-10. As the Avengers departed, the dozen Hellcats flew out of antiaircraft range, but stayed close enough to prevent enemy aircraft from taking off.

Next to arrive were the dive-bombers at 0635, still twenty minutes before sunrise. Only six SBDs attacked (the others incurred a rendezvous problem), but the results were good. Following immediately was Crommelin's division of four Hellcats. Spotting seven Betty medium bombers in a line abreast some one hundred feet apart, Crommelin drew down from eight thousand feet upon the neat row and attacked in a series of strafing runs down to fifteen hundred feet that lasted nearly ten minutes. In what Jimmy described as "the highlight of the day," the four Hellcats—under fire from all directions—set all seven enemy aircraft afire, their distinct pyres of black smoke rising for most of the morning.

By the time Air Group Nine from *Essex* arrived over Marcus at 0720 for the first of four attacks (at 0720, 0845, 1235 and 1430), the major damage to military targets was complete. But the training mission went on. Orbiting at six thousand feet, Jimmy's orders for the day called for him to "observe and direct the attack." At Coral Sea over a year earlier, Jimmy had included comments in his action report calling for a strike coordinator. The need had become obvious within naval aviation and many others voiced Jimmy's May 1942 thoughts. In the air for nine hours Jimmy returned to CV-10 only once to refuel as his Hellcat carried a fuel load of 516 gallons. The regular gasoline capacity of 250 gallons was augmented by one 150-gallon belly tank and two 58-gallon stub wing tanks. Accompanied by wingman Ens. Ted Schofield for protection, Jimmy observed (with the help of binoculars) and directed attacks as the numerous formations arrived over target. And he took photographs with an army K-25 camera mounted in the fuselage in a horizontal position. By pointing the trailing edge of the wing tip at an object and actuating a spring-loaded switch in the cockpit, Jimmy was able to photograph the action and brought back excellent film to be developed. Other pictures were available from camera guns but none from Jimmy's six .50s. There were, however, a few moments when Jimmy was terribly tempted to take his fingers off the camera switch, drop the nose of "Double Zero," pick out an antiaircraft battery through his illuminated gun sight, and give, as he and his wingman had received. Both returned to *Yorktown* with shrapnel damage to their planes.

Directing the first, second, and fourth attack groups from his own carrier, and the first and third attacks by *Essex,* Jimmy was relieved by the commander of Air Group Nine for nearly three hours while he flew back to CV-10 to refuel and report. At the end of the day Jimmy reported 85 percent of fixed installations destroyed along with all seven aircraft on the island, and that the performance of all air groups "was gratifying." For the first time in his combat experience radio discipline and air discipline "were above average." But not all was perfect. Bombing Five's rendezvous problem was one, with that and other delays upsetting a schedule that called for hourly attacks to prevent the enemy from replenishing ready ammunition and extinguishing fires. Glide bombing by the TBF Avengers was executed at too shallow an angle; the TBFs were also flying too close behind each other and exposing themselves to protracted and zero deflection ground fire. And post battle analysis concluded that bomb damage to the very wide runways on Marcus was meager, and that future attacks should relegate bombing of runways to low priority.[16] Still, "Marcus proved to be an advanced training mission, a confidence builder for the more important actions which were to follow."[17] Jimmy recorded essentially the same thought in the final words of his action report, noting the "courage and determination of the leaders and . . . pilots . . . was inspiring to behold . . . the Japs are in for a rough time in future actions."[18]

Returning to *Yorktown*, Jimmy talked first with combat intelligence officers and then with Charlie Crommelin. Two of Charlie's pilots, Ens. Oren C. Morgan and Ens. Floyd A. Towns, were missing, but only one was seen to have crashed. Torpedo Five had lost a TBF; the crew had been last seen in a life raft and a rescue submarine was looking for them. Returning to his stateroom, Jimmy realized for the first time during the day that he was exhausted. Before turning in early, he recorded in his flight log, "Participated in attack on Marcus Island this day. . . . Night take off. . . . First landing back aboard was 400th career landing." After entering his two flights of 5.5 and 3.3 hours, he was quickly asleep. The next morning he wrote to Dotty, "I'm down, dog-tired, but I'm not out. Tojo is. Serves him right for messin' around with good 'ole country boys."[19] After finishing his eleven-page action report, which took two days to complete, he turned his attention to a letter reminding the air group not to discuss any aspect of the raid with anyone until the navy released the story. Next up was the pleasurable task of writing citations. Despite his overall satisfaction with Air Group Five's conduct under fire, he nonetheless acknowledged, "This war certainly separates the wheat from the chaff."[20]

On the seventh as the task force neared Pearl, Marcus was still very much on his mind. "The training cruise is over. From now on it's the real thing. . . . The significance of the above statement is tremendous."[21] To himself he remembered that he had told Dotty that he and his air group would not disappoint Jocko Clark. All things considered, he felt Air Group Five had done reasonably well for its first combat. Overall Jocko was pleased with the air group, his major displeasure being with the problems within Bombing Five. But he most certainly was not disappointed with Jimmy's efforts and performance as evidenced by a recommendation for Jimmy to receive a second Navy Cross. Jocko's superiors decided instead on a third Distinguished Flying Cross, but Jimmy nonetheless had documented proof he had not disappointed his old friend. On the bridge of *Yorktown* the evening before the Marcus attack, Jimmy and Jocko had leaned over a splinter shield on the bridge. Looking into the setting sun Jocko had said, "Jimmy, we've waited a long time for this; we've worked and slaved. I know we won't fail."[22] Indeed, the two were about to share in two years worth of victories, of which even though it was a training mission, Marcus Island had proved a good beginning.

More interested in social life and extracurricular activities than books, Jimmy—"the little rogue"—graduated in the bottom quarter of his 1929 Naval Academy class. *Flatley Collection*

In 1933 Jimmy was one of the first naval aviators to fly the new Grumman FF-1 ("Fifi") fighter including the experimental XFF-1. The squadron insignia represents VF-5B, then attached to *Lexington* (CV-2). *Flatley Collection*

A Boeing F4B makes a practice carrier landing at Corry Field, Pensacola, Florida. Jimmy recorded most of his hours in the F4B while an instructor at NAS Pensacola from 1939 to 1940. *Flatley Collection*

Omaha (CL-4) rides at anchor in the harbor at Villefranche-sur-Mer. While in the Mediterranean the Flatleys rented a house on the hill beyond the ship.
Flatley Collection

Almost always the shortest man in the fighter squadrons in which he served, executive officer Jimmy stands, *fifth from the left,* next to commanding officer Paul Ramsey in this autographed picture of VF-2 aboard *Lexington* in December 1941. Within a year six of these pilots were dead. *U.S. Navy*

Jimmy does not appear in this picture of VF-42 taken early in the war, but the squadron was intact when he served as VF-42's executive officer operating from the first *Yorktown* (CV-5) during the Battle of the Coral Sea. *U.S. Navy*

While Pearl Harbor shipyard personnel and *Enterprise* crewmen work to repair damage below decks from the 24 August 1942 Battle of the Eastern Solomons, Vice Adm. William F. Halsey pins the Navy Cross on Jimmy during a 30 September ceremony. A few months later Jimmy would earn the Distinguished Flying Cross for action in the Naval Battle of Guadalcanal. The Navy Cross recognized Jimmy's exploits in the Battle of the Coral Sea. *U.S. Navy*

Six Japanese flag decals adorn Jimmy's F4F-4 Wildcat aboard *Enterprise*. The decals represent Jimmy's aerial combat victories at Coral Sea, Santa Cruz, the Naval Battle of Guadalcanal, and Rennell Island. *U.S. Navy*

With the VF-10 banner draped as a backdrop on *Enterprise*'s island, the original Grim Reapers pose three days before the Battle of Santa Cruz. For eight pilots it would be their first and last battle. *Front, left to right* (*dead): *Barnes, Leder, Dowden, Harris, Vejtasa, *Miller, Wickendoll, Eckhardt, Kane, Axelrod, Witte, Reiserer, Flatley. *Middle:* Feightner, Slagle, Gordon, Long, Faulkner, *Caldwell, Billo, Blair, Edwards, Packard, Kanze, Voris, Ruehlow. *Back:* Greene, Harman, Coalson, Boren, Kilpatrick, Rhodes (POW), Reding, Mead (POW), *Leppla, Kona, *Fulton, *Davis, Pollock. *U.S. Navy*

The Grim Reaper banner records aerial victories from Santa Cruz through the battles off Guadalcanal. *Front, left to right:* Whitey Feightner is second from the left; Jimmy kneels fifth, and Killer Kane is immediately to his left. *Middle, left to right:* Jimmy's favorite antagonist, Butch Voris, stands second from the left. Jimmy's "greatest fighter pilot," Swede Vejtasa, stands second from the right in the middle row. *Flatley Collection*

On 6 May 1943 Jimmy made the first landing aboard the new *Yorktown* in a F6F-3 Hellcat. Assisting Jimmy with the "Happy Landing" cake were *left to right:* Lt. Cdr. Charles Crommelin, Capt. Jocko Clark, future CNO Cdr. George Anderson *(behind mess attendant),* and CV-10 executive officer Cdr. Raoul Waller *(second from right). U.S. Navy*

A tireless teacher of aerial tactics, Jimmy demonstrates combat maneuvers to pilots of VF-5 before their attack on Marcus Island. *U.S. Navy*

As Air Group Five commanding officer, Jimmy flies his "oo" Hellcat toward an attack on Marcus Island, 31 August 1943. *U.S. Navy*

Rear Adm. (and cousin) Gerry Bogan congratulates Jimmy for his third Distinguished Flying Cross (Marcus Island attack) prior to both joining the fast carrier task force. Bogan served as a task group commander, and Jimmy joined First Fast Carrier Force commander Vice Adm. Marc Mitscher as task force operations officer. *U.S. Navy*

Left to right: Commander of the Second Fast Carrier Force in the Pacific, Vice Adm. John S. McCain, studies a map with his operations officer, Cdr. Jimmie Thach. Longtime friends, Thach and Jimmy Flatley worked closely as the First and the Second Fast Carrier Force staffs alternated combat operations during the last year of the Pacific war. *U.S. Navy*

Bunker Hill (CV-17) aflame on 11 May 1945 after taking two kamikaze hits. When this picture was snapped, Jimmy was immediately below the flight deck searching for wounded and leading them to safety. *U.S. Navy*

On 12 May 1945 survivors of Admiral Mitscher's staff posed for a picture aboard their new flagship, *Enterprise*. Two days later the staff transferred to *Randolph* after "The Big E" was severely damaged by another kamikaze. *Front, left to right:* Jimmy is seated third from the left; Chief of Staff Arleigh Burke is fourth; Mitscher is fifth. *U.S. Navy*

A happy reunion for Jimmy and his parents in early June 1946 just after the end of World War II. Joining the family at Pensacola are, *left to right,* former Grim Reaper pilots Albert Mead and Dusty Rhodes after their release from a Japanese POW camp. Three years earlier Jimmy, believing they were dead, had written condolence letters to their families. *Flatley Collection*

One of the most prolific speakers in U.S. Navy history, in the early days of the Cold War Jimmy nearly always carried the large polar-view map of the world to stress proximity to the Soviet Union. The religious banner in this picture is a coincidence, but Jimmy's speeches were always a combination of geopolitics, religion, country, and the navy. *U.S. Navy*

USS *Block Island* (CVE-106) was Jimmy's first carrier command from July 1952 to July 1953. The escort carrier served in a hunter-killer group in the North Atlantic and Mediterranean while Jimmy was on her bridge. *U.S. Navy*

When he was in the Mediterranean as commanding officer of the *Block Island* and *Lake Champlain* (CV-39), Jimmy made arrangements to have as many sailors as possible receive the Sacrament of Confirmation at St. Peter's Basilica, Rome. Here Jimmy stands near Pope Pius XII during *Block Island*'s visit 8–13 June 1953. *Flatley Collection*

USS *Lake Champlain* (CV-39) dockside at Norfolk. Sailors spell an "E" on the flight deck as the carrier received the 1956 Battle Efficiency Pennant. To that date Jimmy was the only commanding officer to have won the coveted award for two different carriers. *U.S. Navy*

Old *Yorktown* friends gather at Annapolis for a reunion in 1951. *Front, left to right:* Jimmy is seated next to John Crommelin. James T. Bryan Jr., the reunion association founder, is seated seventh from the left next to Vice Adm. Jocko Clark. *U.S. Navy*

The Flatley family circa 1957. *Front, left to right:* David, Dotty, and Brian. *Back:* James H. III, Patrick, and Jimmy. *Flatley Collection*

Jimmy Flatley as many remember him: the enlisted man's officer. *Flatley Collection*

At Chincoteague Air Station on 28 May 1954, Capt. Jimmy Flatley awards the Distinguished Flying Cross to Lt. Cdr. James L. Holloway for combat in Korea. Holloway later served as chief of naval operations from July 1974 to July 1978. *U.S. Navy*

10

Task Force Operations Officer

Battle of Leyte Gulf

"ISN'T IT ABSURD. The triumphant warrior returned to his lair not even mounted on a jackass," Jimmy wrote Dotty on 3 September as *Yorktown* headed back to Pearl Harbor from the Marcus raid. "I'm laid up with a bruised leg . . . it happened at a dance. I was jitterbugging . . . in a dream. . . . You and I were at one of those big dance balls . . . and I got too fancy. . . . Wham! . . . I woke up [and] thought my leg was broken. It came down on the sharp edge of the bunk." Three days later Jimmy was still nursing his latest wound, and he reported to Dotty that someone else would have to fly his plane ashore.[1]

Before *Yorktown* arrived at Pearl, the recently promoted Jimmy learned that Charlie Crommelin had also been promoted to commander, and Jimmy knew that either he or Charlie would soon leave the air group. Back in Pearl on the seventh, *Yorktown* took on fuel and supplies and was back at sea on the ninth for a fast logistics run to San Francisco. Jimmy was still aboard, but instead of being air group commander he was a passenger with orders to report to the Bureau of Aeronautics in Washington. Although he had written Dotty on 3 September that he might "work on Ducky [Duckworth] to get me a billet at Jacksonville," Jimmy formally asked for assignment as an operations officer as first choice, Jacksonville second. Arriving in San Francisco on the thirteenth, he traveled to San Diego by rail and reported there on the eighteenth for temporary duty through 7 October with Fleet Air Command, West Coast.

Temporary duty with Fleet Air, West Coast, soon became permanent. Now there were eight people living in the three-bedroom house at 817 G Street in Coronado—the family having moved from the rental at 823 G to purchase the larger house on the same street—and a ninth was expected in December. Although a little crowded with Jimmy's parents and Jeanette, there was nonetheless a satisfying comfort in having all the family together. Despite his busy schedule, Jimmy found time to teach his oldest son and Charles H. Quinn Jr., another ten year old and son of a naval aviator, to play golf. To the greatest degree possible Jimmy attempted to live a normal life with a normal schedule, and for the war years this was the one period in which he was relatively successful.

Fear of invasion along the West Coast diminished by late 1943 even though blackouts continued. In the evenings Jimmy often eschewed the radio in favor of music boxes acquired while in Europe just before the war. Spring-wound with cylinders that could be changed for different music, the mahogany music boxes provided a unique sound both Jimmy and Dotty loved. With four children and her volunteer duties, Dotty's time for enjoying the music was as limited as it was for Jimmy. Along with many other navy wives, Dotty was very active with the Red Cross, and along with numerous officers' wives she assisted enlisted wives. Standard practice and expectation was not to contribute financially, but rather help with sick kids or look after children while their mothers worked. As Dotty recalls, "Some wives worked and the rest took care of the kids."[2]

Staff Member Fleet Air, West Coast

Fleet Air Command, West Coast, was established 9 January 1942, and the first commanding officer appointed was Rear Adm. Charles Pownall. Although the command prepared officer specialists for landing signals, combat information center (CIC), arresting gear, catapults, and gasoline handling—especially for the new escort carriers—Jimmy was charged with preparing newly formed aviation units for combat. The command also allocated and distributed personnel, coordinated overhaul schedules for aircraft and engines, and distributed aviation supplies including aviation ordnance and photographic equipment. Jimmy, of course, was quite familiar with the command via his experience with the formation of Replacement Air Group Ten.

On 6 August 1943 Rear Adm. Marc Mitscher relieved Pownall, who went out to command carriers in the Pacific. Mitscher had already seen considerable combat as commanding officer of *Hornet* for the Halsey-Doolittle raid on Tokyo and the Battle of Midway, and had commanded land-based air in the Solomons during part of the Guadalcanal campaign and the subsequent move into the central Solomons. Not surprisingly, he wanted his staff training officer to have combat experience. Indeed the function of Fleet Air, West Coast, was to put recent flight school graduates into the type of planes they would fly in combat and teach them how to fight.

Having reported for duty on 18 September 1943, Jimmy was quite pleased to find Bill Leonard, a fellow VF-42 Coral Sea veteran. A 1938 Academy graduate, Bill had two Navy Crosses and three Japanese planes (five by the end of the war) to his credit before being transferred back to share his combat experience with new pilots. As happy as Jimmy was to see his former squadron mate, twenty-seven-year-old Lieutenant Leonard was even more pleased to see thirty-seven-year-old Commander Flatley, as Bill was holding down a job normally assigned to one of more senior rank. A brief conversation between Jimmy and Mitscher led to a discussion on 7 October 1943 between Mitscher and Vice Adm. John Towers, commander of the air force of the Pacific Fleet, resulting in Jimmy being named staff training officer with Bill Leonard as his assistant. Until 29 August 1944 Jimmy was the de facto director of training, but the official title as the director of training was not assigned until September 1944 when Capt. John Crommelin arrived to take over Jimmy's former duties.

There were some sixty squadrons—fighters, bombers, and torpedo planes—spread between San Diego and Seattle, and it was Jimmy's responsibility to supervise the training of all new squadrons preparing to go aboard both fleet and escort carriers.[3] Supervision was Jimmy's operative word for the twelve months between late September 1943 and mid-August 1944, as he helped fight the war from a desk rather than a cockpit.

USF-74B

Fleet Air, West Coast, was well established before Jimmy arrived, and Admiral Pownall was an excellent administrator. A separate syllabus was in place for each of the three squadrons to which a new pilot might be assigned (fighters, bombers, and torpedo aircraft), plus a syllabus for instrument training. Just as in initial flight training, most days were divided between classes on the ground and application in the air. Not unexpectedly the heaviest emphasis in preparing pilots for operations was gunnery, bombing, and tactics.

While flights in a Hellcat or the new General Motors–built FM Wildcat kept Jimmy proficient in the cockpit (in addition to being fun for him), his major responsibility was training. The job required know-how and authority, along with the ability to write. Grabbing Leonard and three bomber-torpedo pilots, Jimmy began a rewrite of the current tactical orders and doctrine for carrier squadron operation, "United States Fleet 74 Revised' (USF-74). Dating from 1941, USF-74 stated how to operate air groups and squadrons on carriers; but in late 1943 much of it, reflecting a naval-air mentality more in tune with biplanes and single carriers operating alone, had become outdated. Jimmy had been part of the new multicarrier formation at Marcus, and the success there was soon repeated off Wake Island in October 1943, the Gilberts in November, and the Marshall Islands in January 1944. Consequently, the rewrite needed to reflect changes in organization and command. By this time the new *Essex*-class carriers could operate a total of ninety planes comprised of thirty-six fighters, one squadron of bombers (thirty-six SBDs or SB2Cs), and eighteen torpedo planes plus spares of all types. Twenty-four fighters and nine TBFs were standard for the fast light carriers of the *Independence* class, and composite squadrons for escort carriers operated up to twenty-four Wildcats and twelve Avengers. Whereas in 1942 missions most often involved only six to twelve fighters, now groups as large as thirty-six or more might operate together in a formation for attack or defense.

Jimmy, Bill, and the other pilots formulated policy and training plus management and control of all aspects for preparing new squadrons for combat. Flight patterns were diagrammed, tactical signals were standardized, and task force operations and training were discussed. Cruising instructions, scouting and attack doctrine, communications and airborne radar utilization, aerial mining and antisubmarine doctrine were updated. Paramount among Jimmy's objectives in rewriting the "book" was standardization of practice (the term "uniformity" had often been interchanged with standardization in the original) for as many aspects of training and combat operations as possible. Due to increasing carrier strength, standardization or uniformity of tactics was essential as task groups joining at sea on short notice for concentrated attack had no time for interchanging a mass of special instructions. The document acknowledged in its preface that "continuous change and improvement in types of aircraft, accessory equipment and armament demands a constant change in air combat tactics," and that the need for flexibility was recognized. Flexibility indeed! After reviewing action reports from the invasion of the Marshalls, Jimmy stated that replacement pilots could be effective only by virtue of "standardization of tactics, which we are approaching."[4] Although the time spent on the USF-74 rewrite was consuming and took the pilots away from flying, the project was critical, as the book and the current reality were different.[5]

While rewriting USF-74, Jimmy and his colleagues needed to translate what had long been theory into standardized practice. One of the more pressing problems was close air support, the need for which was being demonstrated in amphibious landings throughout the Gilberts (where there had been a very disappointing deficiency in close air support at Tarawa), and the Marshalls. Pilots needed training in how to read terrain maps, how to use and recognize different colored smoke, and how to use signal lights to identify front lines; pilots assigned as forward air controllers also needed a special vocabulary to use when directing air support efforts. Jimmy and Bill well knew that the developing doctrine and tactics could save a lot of lives, and the training process had to show pilots and squadrons how to conduct such attacks. Additionally, both recorded time in the air on training exercises showing squadrons how to fly close air support, watching them do it, and upon returning to the ground, encouraging the pilots to spread the good ideas around.[6] Further, there would be a need as well to provide glide and low-level bombing attacks at night as well as during the day, and doctrine for such was addressed. Night attack and defense doctrine for fighter squadrons was also addressed, but technological innovations, such as smaller, lighter radar that could be carried on fighters, moved faster than modifications to written doctrine. These, however, were problems more welcome than the overwhelming frustrations earlier in the war when matériel was not available to meet the most basic combat needs.

Despite all the changes, some long-held practices were not altered. Altitude advantage was still an axiom; straggling and losing a wingman remained major sins. One statement in USF-74B, however, did stand out. The section on leadership noted, "Air Combat, to a greater degree than any other form of warfare, is dependent on competent and aggressive leadership. Therefore, tactical control of units will be given to the best qualified pilots regardless of rank," a significant difference from Japanese policy. Following (in all caps for emphasis) was the comment, "Combat experience proves that any pilot in a formation may be called upon to assume tactical control of his unit at any time. The success of a mission may depend on the ability of the junior pilot to assume command." Indeed, many a junior pilot—often a reserve officer—distinguished himself in just such a role throughout the last two years of the Pacific war.

In the Air

For his year at Fleet Air, West Coast, most of Jimmy's flight time was usually a means of traveling from one meeting to another up and down the coast. Averaging just less than thirteen flight hours a month for the year, most of his flights were in an SNJ, but when it was possible, he flew a Hellcat. Among his test flights were hours in the new General Motors (Eastern Aircraft Division, Trenton, New Jersey) FM-1 and FM-2 versions of the Wildcat. Marked improvements over the earlier Grumman F4F series, the FM Wildcats were assigned primarily to new escort carrier air groups. Utilizing a more powerful 1,350 hp Wright R-1820-56 engine, the FM-2 was only slightly faster in level flight but had nearly double the speed in climb (3,650 feet per minute versus 1,950 for the F4F-4) and had 130 more miles of range.

In late 1943 and into mid-1944 there was a tremendous increase in aircraft numbers, quality of aircraft, and the number of pilots. The quality of these pilots was partially Jimmy's responsibility. The increase in combat aircraft was critically needed at Fleet Air, West Coast, as the early shortage in aircraft kept some pilots from preparing for operations in the type of plane they would actually fly. In contrast to the approximately seventeen-hundred combat planes in the navy's inventory in December 1941, there were some eighty-seven hundred in December 1943 and projections were for over twenty-two thousand by December 1944. Pilot numbers had jumped from four thousand in 1941 to over twenty-one thousand in 1943, while similar quantum leaps were evident in aircraft and ordnance technology. Improvements in radar and communications equipment were especially appreciated by all associated with carrier air groups.

The new technology and the old was realistically utilized when Fleet Air, West Coast, cooperated with other commands to take advantage of naval vessels operating near San Diego. When formations of battleships or new carriers approached from the East Coast via the Panama Canal, they were often met with simulated combat. Multi-engine search planes and carrier aircraft would make a series of simulated attacks. Personnel in navigation, radar, formation flying, and in every phase of combat flying obtained invaluable experience. Even the officers and men of the ships benefited as they had realistic training for defense against aircraft attack and snoopers.[7]

Just as training with surface units increased proficiency in skills, training programs were coordinated to provide maximum return from the time available. When bomber squadrons were in the air, simulated fighter opposition was supplied to the advantage of both. And within squadrons, improved results were obtained by assigning a training mission more than one subject. As an example, a mission that earlier might have emphasized only navigation would now also include radar. Still, throughout Jimmy's tenure, gunnery and rocket training was hampered by lack of sufficient ranges, the concentration of training planes leaving inadequate space over the Pacific Ocean.[8]

Everyone aboard the carriers, battleships, and all other surface ships felt more secure with the invention of the variable time (VT) proximity fuse. Developed in association with British researchers and available to the Pacific Fleet in 1943, the proximity fuse enabled 5-inch antiaircraft batteries to fire a 55-pound shell nearly ten miles (horizontally) that would explode when a radio impulse from the shell reflected from an enemy plane. The detonated shell threw fragments over three thousand square feet and "helped blaze the trail to Japan," according to Secretary of the Navy James V. Forrestal.[9]

While U.S. Navy pilots were pleased that their navy had the proximity fuse and the Japanese did not—best evidence is that the Japanese did not know of this secret fuse until after the war—these pilots, naturally, were more interested in the rapid advances in their own aircraft. On 24 August 1944 Jimmy left the ground for a 2.2 hour flight in the experimental XFR-1 Ryan Fireball jet-propelled fighter (BuNo. 48232, first of the three experimental models). The experimental fighter had a 1,350 hp Wright R-1820-72W radial engine up front and one sixteen hundred pound s.t. General Electric J31 turbojet in the rear of the fuselage. Greatly resembling the Wildcat in overall appearance as well as having essentially the same engine and armament up front, the Fireball had a top speed of just over four hundred miles an hour, about eighty-six miles per hour faster than any F4F-4.

When Jimmy took the Ryan Fireball into the sky over San Diego on 24 August 1944, he was not only familiarizing himself with it, but also thinking how it would perform against the Japanese Zero. He had become even more familiar with the Zero when the enemy fighter recovered at Adak in the Aleutians in August 1942 was returned to San Diego in the spring of 1944. Having been repaired at North Island in August and September 1942, the plane was then thoroughly tested at San Diego and flown to Anacostia, located in southeast Washington, D.C., for further test flights. Tests completed, the enemy plane then sat in Washington, D.C., gathering dust. Bill Leonard's request to bring the plane back to San Diego was approved, the only requirement being that a pilot be sent to fly it back. Jimmy and Bill Leonard took over the plane on its arrival back in San Diego, and being the fighter training officer, Bill was the first to fly the plane. Demonstrating the Zero for new pilots, Leonard flew the plane gently at first, then moving the plane into zooms and hard turns, so that his students the new pilots could "see what it looked like in the air." It was a good education, practice always being better than theory.[10] The Zero proved to be a great plane, but Hellcats and Corsairs were better, and newer planes like the Ryan Fireball and Grumman F8F Bearcat promised to be even more superior than the Mitsubishi A6M2 fighter. (Did Jimmy get a chance to fly the Zero? His family says that he did, but there is no record in his flight log book indicating that he did so.)

While remaining Jimmy's assistant, Bill Leonard also continued to serve as fighter training officer, which put him in the air more than Jimmy; but Jimmy also had a few occasions of particularly enjoyable moments in the cockpit of his new FM-2 Wildcat. While flying into a training base at Astoria, Oregon, he joined up on an old F4F Wildcat in the landing pattern. But when the F4F cut to land, Jimmy went to full throttle and put on an air show with his fast climbing FM-2. "The young pilots were awe struck . . . [and] the morale of the squadron leaped forward from that moment."[11]

Not as enjoyable were occasions when Jimmy had to sit in judgment of officers' conduct of training exercises. He did not tolerate irresponsibility and strictly graded those who did not measure up. Still, he was very supportive of those who tried, always wanting and expecting the best anyone had to give. Although Southern California's Mediterranean climate provided mostly favorable flying conditions twelve months of the year, there were always notable exceptions. Unable to directly challenge more senior officers that insisted on endangering pilots and equipment in dangerous weather, Jimmy on several occasions did support air group commanders against complaints from higher authority.

Never enjoyable were the too frequent reports of training accidents and loss of life. Away from combat, Jimmy was not away from danger. Even at home tragedy was a pervasive occupant. On many occasions Dotty, in company with another navy wife, joined an officer to carry the bad news of death to a nearby family. Jimmy and Dotty both went to the home of Cdr. Finley E. Hall in early December 1943 to inform his wife that he had been lost in the sinking of *Liscome Bay* (CVE-56) on

24 November during the Gilbert Islands operation. Commander Hall, who was serving as executive officer aboard the ill-fated escort carrier that succumbed to a Japanese submarine, with a loss of 646 officers and men, was a fellow 1929 Naval Academy classmate and longtime friend.

Task Force Operations Officer

While Jimmy was with Fleet Air, West Coast, the fast carriers were performing wonders in the Pacific. When Jimmy left *Yorktown* after the Marcus Island raid, there was another similar practice raid on Wake Island, and then forays into the Marshalls. These early raids demonstrated a need for more aggressive leadership, and in January 1944 Marc Mitscher was given the opportunity to provide it. Bold almost to the degree of being audacious, Mitscher proved the great potential of the fast carriers with raids and support of island assaults through the Marshalls, New Guinea, Marianas, and Carolines. Even before the 19–20 June Battle of the Philippine Sea, Mitscher was highly respected by superior officers, peers, and subordinates. Having given an order to "turn on the lights" to help his task force pilots find the carriers in the dark upon their return from attacking the Japanese fleet during the Battle of the Philippine Sea, he was elevated by all to near deity status. The "Bald Eagle," as he was affectionately known, was renowned as a fighter and for taking care of his men, always assuring his pilots that if they were down at sea, he would search for them with planes, submarines, and the entire fleet if necessary. Most often Mitscher, who was a short, frail-looking man, was seen aboard his carrier flagship riding backwards on the flag bridge (to keep the wind out of his face), where he sat most of the time on a high deck-mounted chair, wearing a baseball-type cap to shield the sun. A man of few words and not known for his oratory, he was exceptionally eloquent in conveying his thoughts with facial expressions. And although not known for being especially brilliant, he possessed an abundance of common sense. Once Mitscher was convinced that his pilots and planes were better than the Japanese, he was particularly successful in convincing all around him of justifiable confidence. The size of his reputation was almost matched by the number of new fast carriers steadily arriving to join his armada. But because their size was increasing, his carrier force, escort, and support ships required more detailed and meticulous attention.

By the late summer of 1944 Jimmy anticipated another assignment. That he received orders to become operations officer for the new carrier task force was no accident or whim. Jimmy consistently requested such duty throughout his year at Fleet Air, West Coast. The three rear admirals Jimmy served under at San Diego were Mitscher (6 August 1943 to 4 January 1944), William K. Harrill (4 January 1944 to 25 March 1944, plus 2–29 August 1944), and former *Lexington* CO Ted Sherman (25 March 1944 to 1 August 1944). In August 1944 Mitscher was commander of the First Fast Carrier Forces in the Pacific Fleet (Task Force Fifty-eight). Sherman was heading back to the fleet from command of Fleet Air, West Coast, to assume command of a task group under Mitscher; and Harrill had just returned to Fleet Air, West Coast, after commanding a task group under Mitscher. On fitness reports Mitscher had rated Jimmy "an outstanding officer in every respect," Sherman noted his "fine qualities of leadership . . . and . . . excellent job of training squadrons for combat duty," while Harrill not only complemented Jimmy's "outstanding" work but also stated, "He . . . is much better qualified for operational duty."

Jimmie Thach also thought Jimmy Flatley should be transferred back to operational duty. Having just left a similar training tour at Jacksonville, Thach had been appointed as Vice Adm. John S. "Slew" McCain's operations officer. McCain—commander of the Second Fast Carrier Task Force in the Pacific—was scheduled to relieve Mitscher later in the year or early in 1945. In late May, Thach joined McCain on Adm. Raymond A. Spruance's flagship, USS *Indianapolis* (CA-35), to observe the Marianas operations. (When Spruance was in command the designation was Fifth Fleet and when Halsey commanded the same ships it became Third Fleet.) During the May–June operations Thach made it a point to seek out Mitscher's chief of staff, Capt. Arleigh A. Burke, to "strongly recommend" that Jimmy Flatley take the job of operations officer for Mitscher. "I . . . told him how good Jimmy Flatley was. Also, Jimmy and I thought a lot alike, and it was easier to relieve when we rotated, so we were able to meet a few times and agree on the task force instructions." Later, Thach recalled that he and Jimmy Flatley had "been very close all our Navy lives, and this was a very fortunate thing because we knew how each other was thinking. We worked very well together, very closely, and whenever he discovered something that he thought would be useful to us, he passed it to me immediately . . . and I did the same thing."[12]

Wasting no time to get back into the war, Jimmy hurriedly packed as soon as he received his orders to join Mitscher as operations officer. On 29 August he piloted a JRB from San Diego to Alameda, and on the thirtieth he was aboard a PB2Y for sixteen hours, headed for Pearl Harbor. On the thirty-first he was aboard a thirty-passenger, four-engine Douglas R5D-1 Skymaster for another sixteen-hour flight from Pearl to Manus (Admiralty Islands), sitting in as copilot for four hours. On 1 September Jimmy hopped a ride in Red Carmody's SB2C for a 2.4 hour flight from Manus to *Bunker Hill* (CV-17), and the next day he arrived aboard *Lexington,* Mitscher's flagship, as a passenger in a TBM Avenger.

Mitscher's first operations officer had been Cdr. Gus Widhelm, a highly decorated hero of Midway, Santa Cruz, and Philippine Sea, and a long-time friend of Jimmy's. Mitscher had hand picked Gus to be his operations officer, the two having served together aboard the first *Hornet.* A character among characters, Gus's opinions were always immediate and expressed in a colorful mix of English and profanity. Because of their days together on *Hornet,* Widhelm's combat record and success as operations officer, he and Mitscher enjoyed a very good relationship. But Gus had been in or near combat for much of the war and was overdue for rotation. Although he could handle the details required for the task force he had served, details and routine were not his greatest interests. Interest was critical now, however, as there were more details each day to be managed. Reporting as training officer on the staff of the commander of fleet air at Quonset Point, Rhode Island, he was soon promoted to captain, but Widhelm's brilliant career was cut short when he died at age forty-five in a 19 July 1954 plane crash.

Reporting aboard, Jimmy was cordially greeted by Mitscher. There was no need for formalities or extensive briefings. Absent from each other for only six months, each knew what was expected and the two were comfortable together. Jimmy had successfully faced the enemy in direct aerial combat, as had Widhelm, and Marc Mitscher made no secret of his respect for such men.

Jimmy well appreciated Mitscher's aggressive use of carrier aviation and loyalty to his staff and pilots. But he especially appreciated the admiral's delegation of responsibility. Speaking on the subject of delegation, Mitscher once said, "I tell them what I want, not how."[13] Jimmy knew how, and like any competent staff officer, he aspired to no greater expression of faith. Mitscher proved innovative in the use of carrier strike forces, particularly with the idea of ordering fighter sweeps before bombers and torpedo planes arrived over a target. Jimmy knew that for understanding the big picture of how to use a multicarrier force, Mitscher was the best. However, Jimmy also knew that Mitscher was not especially given to a rapid change in thinking on some tactics. Among the earliest naval aviators (Naval Aviator No. 33, 1916), Mitscher's piloting experience was mostly before carrier squadrons came into being, and he didn't have a feel for actual dive- and torpedo-bombing.[14] Additionally, he demonstrated a reluctance to use night fighters, in part to reduce pressure on his pilots by not interfering with their rest, in part because he questioned their chances for success. This meant he leaned heavily on subordinates like Capt. Truman J. Hedding (an aviator and the chief of staff he inherited from Pownall), Widhelm, and now Jimmy. Still, Jimmy knew one of his difficulties might be convincing his admiral on the use of some new technology and associated tactics. For the first two months, though, there were no significant debates or disagreements.

Mitscher, however, was not Jimmy's immediate superior. Commo. (in August 1944) Arleigh Burke, a tall, wavy-haired 1923 Naval Academy graduate of Swedish descent, had been appointed Mitscher's nonaviator chief of staff in March 1944, much to the chagrin of both. Mitscher did not want a nonaviator in such a critical staff position, and Burke, who had earned one of the most deserved reputations ever for his combat operations in destroyers, had no desire to serve on a carrier staff. The determination that aviators would have nonaviators as chiefs of staff and vice versa was a decision made by Admiral King, and throughout most of the spring, Mitscher and Burke endured a mutually frosty relationship. Mitscher once half-seriously told his marine orderly to keep an eye on Burke while a destroyer was close aboard their carrier for a delivery. However, by the Marianas operation each of the two had recognized the talents of the other, and a strong professional relationship developed. By the time Jimmy came aboard, the professional relationship between the two who had been forced together was secure, and what would become an especially close personal relationship was budding.[15]

Although Burke (who ten years later would become chief of naval operations) respected and appreciated the work of Gus Widhelm, he was not sorry to see Jimmy arrive as Widhelm's replacement. For much of Gus's time as operations officer, Mitscher went directly to fellow aviator Gus instead of going through Burke. Also, Jimmy was very low key compared to Gus, and nowhere as pugnacious or confrontational. There were times when Jimmy and the admiral had discussions just between themselves, but Burke was not offended, as he knew neither was keeping anything from him. Jimmy "took an instant liking to Arleigh and attached himself to him as colleague and disciple."[16] Flag Plot, where the task force brain trust determined the course of ships and directed the order of battle, became much quieter, at least in tone. As time went on, however, the Jimmy Flatley who perennially was noted in his fitness reports for being so quiet, became more loquacious. As Burke recalled, there were times when he talked too much.[17] Still, Jimmy was brought on board because in addition to combat experience, he had new ideas on how to get the job done.[18] And in the final analysis, Mitscher, Burke, and Flatley had no major philosophical differences. Mutual respect between the three made them a team, and all members of the staff shared their spirit of teamwork.

Pacific Battles from Late 1943 through the Philippine Sea

During Jimmy's sabbatical year with Fleet Air, West Coast, the Pacific war had changed drastically. When Jimmy left Fighting Ten and the war zone in February 1943, the United States Navy had only two large carriers in the Pacific. Now in September 1944 there were at least fifteen available for combat, three others undergoing repairs or overhaul, plus another dozen in various stages of construction. Additionally, there were dozens of escort carriers in this theater, and nearly one hundred commissioned aircraft carriers were projected by the end of the following year. And as Jimmy well knew, pilot production was being reduced, as there were already more than enough in the pipeline to meet expected needs.

Although Jimmy had been away from combat for only a year, in attitude it seemed like a century. Leaving Air Group Five and the fleet in September 1943, he along with many other pilots knew the U.S. carrier force had scored only two tactical victories in carrier-versus-carrier battles although all four were strategic victories. But, boundless optimism among all U.S. Navy pilots in September 1944 was justified by a string of uninterrupted and overwhelming aerial victories throughout the previous year. On 5 November 1943 air groups flying from *Saratoga* and *Princeton* (CVL-23), Ted Sherman commanding, had attacked heavily defended Rabaul to disable several heavy cruisers that threatened Halsey's landings at nearby Bougainville. Concerned that he might lose both carriers and many of his carrier-borne planes to enemy land-based air, Halsey had no choice but to attack the enemy heavy cruisers that could outgun his surface units protecting the landings in the upper Solomons. To the surprise and great relief of all, the Hellcat pilots proved over Rabaul that the lopsided Hellcat victories over Wake Island the previous month were no fluke.

Based on the successes over Wake, Rabaul, and the Gilberts, five carriers again struck Rabaul on 11 November 1943, their Hellcats blasting defending fighters out of the air, burning them on runways, and then defending the carriers from retaliatory strikes. Over the Marshall Islands in February 1944 aerial opposition was again less than expected, and Truk, "the Japanese Pearl Harbor," was attacked on 17 February. Losing only 17 planes for some 250 enemy aircraft in the air and on the ground, an emboldened task force steamed west to the Marianas on 21–22 February. As the enemy was alert to the raid, Mitscher's carriers had to fight their way in but the results were the same as they had been over Rabaul, Truk, and the Marshalls. Two months later on 29 April the carriers returned to Truk and destroyed most of the enemy planes flown in since the February raid. And in June, TF 58 had attacked and invaded the Marianas, destroyed over four hundred enemy planes on 19–20 June, and sunk one Japanese carrier (*Hiyo*). Despite the overwhelming victory, Mitscher and other naval aviators were unhappy that nonaviator Spruance declined Mitscher's request on 19 June to chase the enemy carriers, in favor of retaining the fast carriers to cover the assault beaches. Unknown at the time, however, submarines *Albacore* (SS-218) and *Cavella* (SS-244) had sunk, respectively, two additional large carriers, *Taiho* (Japan's newest fleet carrier) and *Shokaku* (veteran of Pearl Harbor, Coral Sea, Eastern Solomons, and Santa Cruz). Landings on Saipan began on 15 June, and the big island fell in July. A month later Tinian and Guam fell, and on 24 November the first of the Army Air Force B-29 raids took off for the Japanese homeland.

In studying the several carrier actions from October 1943 through the Battle of the Philippine Sea, Jimmy noted several axioms then current in carrier operations that were unthinkable during his last carrier battle. First, the practice of sending fighters to sweep enemy fighters from the sky before attack aircraft arrived—unthinkable in 1942 due to paucity of fighters—had proven highly effective. Second, communications and radar technology, though still not perfect, had greatly improved over the past year. It was not good enough to remove human eyes from the horizon and beyond, but it was sufficiently improved to be incorporated with more confidence in operational planning. Third, rockets demonstrated considerable potential for close air support, even though the necessary long glide toward a target left the attacking aircraft vulnerable to ground fire. Fourth, the quality of enemy pilots was obviously not what it was when he had confronted them over the Coral Sea and lower Solomons. Consequently, he would now have to caution pilots against overconfidence as opposed to his previous perpetual attempts to build confidence. Of course there were other lessons and principles, but 1942 was a distant memory . . . and happily so.

First Operations

There was very little time for Jimmy to get settled into his new job. Although he spent about eighteen hours a day in Flag Plot (located on the second level up from the flight deck inside the island structure), his stateroom was one level (second deck) below the hangar deck, immediately at the bottom of a nine-step ladder. That put five ladders between his stateroom and Flag Plot. Normal quarters for Admiral Mitscher was his sea cabin immediately aft of Flag Plot (starboard), while Burke was assigned to the relatively luxurious admiral's in-port cabin immediately beneath the flight deck (portside). Most other flag staff officers were quartered in staterooms in officers' country on the second deck forward of amidships.

During the first week of September Jimmy got acquainted with the few flag staff officers he did not already know. Among these were reserve intelligence officers Lt. Cdr. E. C. Cheston and Lt. Byron R. White. White, a former All-American athlete was later appointed to the U.S. Supreme Court. There was no occasion to visit Jocko Clark—a rear admiral since March and now a battle-proven carrier task group commander—who was aboard *Hornet,* or to visit his cousin, Rear Adm. Gerry Bogan, who had moved up from the escort carriers to command a fast carrier task group. As Admiral Halsey had relieved Admiral Spruance on 26 August, designation changed from TF 58 to TF 38. The ships were the same, the only change being a different commander and his staff. A similar policy would hold for Mitscher and McCain. When one relieved the other, it was again the same ships, just different commanders and their staffs; but the task force designation changed only when Halsey and Spruance came or went.

Operations were under way when Jimmy reported for duty, so he had to jump in immediately. Actually Task Force Thirty-eight had left Eniwetok in the Marshalls on 28 August headed for Morotai, just north of New Guinea, and Peleliu in the Palau Islands southeast of the Philippines. The strategic plan was to assault and take the Philippines. To achieve the strategic objective, Third Fleet struck targets as far north as Chichi Jima and Iwo Jima, as far to the east as Wake Island, and as far south as the Palaus. From September sixth through the ninth, the task force concentrated on the Palau Islands, particularly Peleliu, Ulithi, and Yap. On the ninth and tenth planes were over Mindanao in the Philippines and raids in the central Philippines followed on the eleventh and twelfth. As aerial opposition over the Philippines was considerably less than expected, Halsey forwarded a recommendation up the line to abort plans to land on Mindanao, the large southernmost island comprising the Philippines. By the fourteenth, approval of Halsey's recommendation was back in the fleet, and Jimmy was directed to immediately begin planning for an assault at Leyte in the central Philippines and Luzon to the north. Target date for Leyte was 20 October, two months ahead of schedule.

Preparing plans for Leyte did not relieve Jimmy of his other day-to-day responsibilities, especially those of drawing up attack plans for raids that preceded the Leyte landings. On the fourteenth fast carrier task groups hit Mindanao and Visayas (Philippines) while others covered the invasion of the Palaus and Morotai on the fifteenth. On the twenty-first the target was Manila on the western side of Luzon and the Visayas. Approaching from the eastern side of Luzon on the twenty-first, heavy weather surrounded the carriers. Veteran pilot that he was, Jimmy expressed his concern to Mitscher. However, Mitscher noted radar contact with an enemy plane in the direction of Luzon and said "If the Japs can fly in this, so can we."[19] It was the correct decision as the skies over Luzon were clear and targets were bountiful.

While Jimmy was off Luzon from 21–24 September, the conquest of the Palaus and Morotai continued. Opposition on Morotai was relatively weak, but Peleliu was a killing ground equal to the anguish encountered at Tarawa and later at Iwo Jima and Okinawa. Still, the excellent anchorage at Ulithi was occupied on 23 September. Located in the northern Palaus to the southwest of Guam, it provided yet another base for supplies and rest. Rest, however, was about to become an unfamiliar concept as the At Sea Logistics Service Group comprised of fleet oilers, escort carriers, and destroyers/destroyer escorts was being formed to carry fuel, supplies, and replacement planes to the carriers. While pilots and sailors felt the pressure of constant operations, the pressure on the enemy was even more intense.

The value of the Philippines to Japan was critical. Without command of the skies and seas in and around the Philippines, the crucial raw materials—especially oil—from Southeast Asia were unavailable. Consequently, the enemy had to commit major military resources to retain possession of the islands that had been under their control since the Japanese had expelled American forces in May 1942. Throughout September and early October, TF 38 had destroyed hundreds of Japanese planes and nearly a hundred ships. Unlike battles on small Pacific atolls and in the battle for the Philippines, the Japanese seldom knew when or where U.S. Navy carrier planes would strike—and surprise quickly translated into Japanese aircraft lost while sitting on the ground. Even when the Japanese did know where and when, the results were usually overwhelming losses as under-trained pilots fell before Hellcat guns.

Battle of Leyte Gulf

By the end of the first week of October, Task Force Thirty-eight was ready to begin attacks to isolate the Leyte landing area, so the carriers began working over enemy airfields from north to south. Attacks on Okinawa were followed by attacks on Luzon and Formosa. Unknown to the U.S. Navy, the Japanese concentrated air power to meet the Formosa (Taiwan) strikes from the twelfth through the fifteenth. Successful in damaging two cruisers, *Canberra* (CA-70) and *Houston* (CL-81), the Japanese were unsuccessful in interrupting the Allies' timetable and lost five hundred more planes during the four-day battle. Particularly significant was the loss of pilots critically needed for carrier air groups. Recognizing their relative impotence in the air, the Japanese drew up a new plan to challenge the Leyte landings.

Realistically evaluating their strengths and weaknesses—despite joyful and optimistic Japanese news reports of a great victory in defense of Formosa—the new Japanese plan called for the following. First, a (northern) force of four decoy carriers, and escorts, with only two-thirds of their normal aircraft complement aboard, were to entice TF 38 away from the Leyte landing beaches. Second, a (center) force comprised of battleships, cruisers, and destroyers would approach Leyte through the Sibuyan Sea and San Bernardino Strait. Another (southern) force of battleships, cruisers, and destroyers were to steam toward Leyte through Surigao Strait. This plan assumed that TF 38 would leave Leyte and continue to follow the decoy carrier force north. Then, the center force, which included super-battleships *Yamato* and *Musashi,* would approach the Leyte beaches—hopefully undetected; and the southern force would outfight a much larger U.S. Navy surface force that included six prewar battleships. It was a desperate plan, but the Japanese were desperate.

Even though the Japanese plan was desperate, it was formalized, written on paper and distributed to relevant commanders. To the contrary in Task Force Thirty-eight, Admiral Halsey, aboard his flagship *New Jersey* (BB-62), preferred to maintain maximum flexibility and operate more by dispatch rather than a detailed written plan.[20] As aviator Halsey would control all fleet movements and assume tactical command whenever the task groups were separated, Mitscher was rendered all but superfluous except when the carriers were operating together. But Mitscher, understanding the need for short lines of communication and the desirability of as few communications as possible, accepted this command arrangement better than his chief of staff and Jimmy.[21]

On 20 October Task Force Thirty-eight began concentrating on the Leyte beaches to secure the general area from aerial counterattack and to cover Gen. Douglas MacArthur's landings. Opposition in the air was light, and despite consistent rainy weather dozens of enemy planes were burned in their revetments. By the twenty-second it was apparent to Halsey, Mitscher, Burke, and Jimmy that their carriers needed replenishment, especially ordnance, and that many pilots needed rest. McCain's TG 38.1 was therefore ordered to Ulithi, and his five carriers departed. *Bunker Hill* was also heading to Ulithi for additional aircraft, leaving the task force with eleven of its seventeen fast carriers. Early on the twenty-third, Jimmy learned submarines *Darter* (SS-227) and *Dace* (SS-247) had found the enemy central force in the Sibuyan Sea and shortly after 0630 had torpedoed three cruisers (heavy cruisers *Atago* and *Maya* were sunk and *Takao* damaged). Later that day Admiral Kinkaid conveyed word through circuitous channels to Admiral Halsey that the Leyte beaches might soon see enemy surface units. The circuitous channels were necessitated by a divided command: Kinkaid, the commander of Seventh Fleet, answering to MacArthur and Halsey, the commander of Third Fleet, answering to Nimitz. Back through the same elongated communications route, Halsey acknowledged the possibility that the Japanese might attempt to disrupt the landings. As Jimmy turned in late on the twenty-third, he and everyone else in the task force knew that the decisive Pacific battle that planners had anticipated since early in the century when Japan was identified as a possible antagonist was imminent. Early on the twenty-fourth, Jimmy plotted two forces on his maps, identifying a large center and a smaller southern force.[22] A carrier force was expected from the north but had not been located by the early morning hours of the twenty-fourth. Any competent officer could see the logic of the developing Japanese plan, as there were only three natural sea routes to Leyte. By 0930 the Japanese were known to be on course over two of those routes—their speed indicating both forces could arrive off the Leyte beaches at dawn on the twenty-fifth—and a third force was undoubtedly just out of sight. Certainly, Jimmy and Burke reasoned, the Japanese would not commit such large surface forces without also committing their carriers, which were believed to be in home waters to the north. For the two American officers at work in flag plot, it was only a matter of locating the enemy carriers. Convinced they were en route and heading south, Jimmy included them in his calculations. And indeed, nine enemy battleships (two with small flight decks but no planes), one large carrier, three light carriers, more than a dozen cruisers, and attending destroyers all steamed toward Leyte.

McCain's TG 38.1 was quickly recalled to rejoin the three task groups which were then widely separated. Sherman's TG 38.3—with Mitscher and Jimmy aboard *Lexington*—was east of Luzon and about 150 miles north of Bogan's TG 38.2, which was east of San Bernardino Strait. Nearly 150 miles south, Rear Adm. Ralph E. Davison's TG 38.4 was east of the Leyte beaches. From midmorning Bogan and Davison's planes attacked the Center Force in the Sibuyan Sea, and by early afternoon reported one enemy super-battleship (*Musashi*) sinking and considerable damage to other ships. Sherman's TG 38.3 aircraft eventually got in some blows, but first had to ward off a series of air attacks.

Despite another overwhelming Hellcat aerial victory in defense of their ships, one enemy plane did work its way through the overcast skies to drop a bomb on *Princeton*. Jimmy knew immediately that the light carrier had armed strike aircraft in the hangar and was therefore not surprised by the multiple explosions. Nor was he surprised when *Lexington*'s air officer and commanding officer decided against reopening magazines to arm Air Group Nineteen's planes with armor-piercing bombs and torpedoes.[23] Sherman, aboard *Essex*, elected to remain by the disabled carrier when she dropped out of formation, all the while continuing to ward off additional air attacks and fly off strikes on Center Force. At 1524, however, fires on *Princeton* reached a magazine and a horrific blast blew off the stern and aft flight deck. *Birmingham* (CL-62), which was standing by to fight fires, lost 237 officers and men. Attention to the tragedy aboard *Princeton* and *Birmingham* was diverted less than twenty minutes later as search planes reported contact with the expected Northern Force. Hour later reports confirmed the presence of enemy carriers some two hundred miles beyond the first ships. Jimmy, however, combined both on his maps as "Northern Force."[24]

Halsey issued directives and information as the four task groups were still separated. For much of the twenty-fourth and twenty-fifth, Jimmy did not have all the necessary information to see the big picture since Halsey and his staff were making the decisions. Jimmy did know that Kinkaid's Seventh Fleet would intercept the Southern Force, most likely in narrow Surigao Strait. He also knew Halsey planned to form Task Force Thirty-four, led by four battleships from the six available, to intercept the Center Force. But as the overcast twenty-fourth gave up the last signs of daylight, Jimmy did not know that Halsey was rethinking his plans. Believing Center Force to be as weakened as action reports stated and noting that it had reversed course to the west after the several air attacks against it, the commander of Third Fleet began to concentrate his plans on the Northern Force and its enemy carriers. Mitscher, Burke, and Jimmy were working on a proposal to have all six battleships under Vice Adm. Willis A. "Ching" Lee Jr. speed north for a night action, but before this idea was communicated Halsey issued a directive for all of Task Force Thirty-eight to head north. Before midnight a number of senior officers in TF 38 began to suspect that Northern Force was a decoy, but Halsey's staff had considered that possibility. The bottom line was that Halsey understood his primary mission to be the destruction of enemy carriers; that Kinkaid and Rear Adm. Jesse B. Oldendorf had sufficient battleship and escort carrier strength to guard the Leyte beaches; and that most ships had already unloaded supplies to support the invasion. On this occasion Halsey was determined he would not suffer Mitscher's great disappointment off the Marianas four months earlier, when Spruance delayed releasing Mitscher to pursue and destroy the enemy carriers. This opportunity would not be missed.

The run north on the night of 24–25 October was anything but smooth for Jimmy, Arleigh Burke, and other members of Mitscher's staff. In the last hours of the twenty-fourth, reports from night-carrier *Independence* (whose crew had been given special training to conduct night operations) first indicated and then confirmed that Center Force was again heading east toward San Bernardino Strait. Alarmed, Jimmy and Burke awoke Mitscher, who asked Jimmy if Halsey had the information. Answering that Halsey did, Mitscher then told Jimmy and Burke that Halsey would ask for his advice if he wanted it. Shortly thereafter, Jimmy and Arleigh were back in the admiral's sea cabin with another problem worthy of waking him. As Task Force Thirty-Eight was pulling its separate groups together Mitscher's staff assumed they would have tactical command and the sleep-deprived admiral adamantly confirmed the understanding. However, after Halsey's staff countermanded several of Burke's orders, it was apparent that the Third Fleet's commander was not going to relinquish tactical command.[25]

An expected night engagement between the enemy and Lee's six battleships, seven cruisers, and eighteen destroyers did not materialize. Just before the early gray dawn, Jimmy quickly briefed pilots who were to conduct search and attack missions. The exact location of the Northern Force was not known, but was expected to be within range of the task force aircraft. One hour after launch the Northern Force was located approximately 150 miles distant, and by 0730 attacks were under way. Under attack off Cape Engano were one large carrier (*Zuikaku*); three light carriers (*Chiyoda, Chitose*, and *Zuiho*); two battleships with eight 14-inch guns and short, aft flight decks (*Ise* and *Hyuga*); three light cruisers (*Isuzu, Oyodo*, and *Tama*); and eight destroyers.

For the next seven hours Jimmy was on the battle circuit to Cdr. Hugh Winters, Air Group Nineteen's commanding officer. Winters later recalled, "Jim Flatley was just one of us, an old fighter pilot . . . young enough to have flown some tough missions against the Jap Zeros in their prime, and a close friend." On 25 October 1944 "as two fighter pilots, we said enough with few words."[26] Winters led his planes off

Lexington after other task force aircraft found and attacked the Northern Force. By the time his group arrived, one enemy carrier, *Chitose,* was already sunk, and what little aerial opposition the Japanese had offered was destroyed. In addition to leading his air group, Winters was one of two target coordinators for most of the battle off Cape Engaño, and he had a powerful radio to transmit what he saw to Jimmy. As soon as Jimmy received information, he turned to Burke or Mitscher, or both, to describe what Hugh told him. Soon after arriving over the enemy, Winters told Jimmy that a second carrier, *Chiyoda*—like *Chitose* a converted seaplane carrier—was seriously damaged and moving at only four or five knots. *Zuikaku* and *Zuiho,* however, were steaming north at twenty knots.

Admiral Nimitz had made no secret that one of the greatest days of his life would be the one when he received word that *Zuikaku,* last survivor of the Pearl Harbor raid, Coral Sea, Eastern Solomons, Santa Cruz, and Philippine Sea, was no more. "Zui" was no stranger to Jimmy, who had faced her planes over the Coral Sea and off Santa Cruz. At that time he did not know the planes that ambushed his Reapers at Santa Cruz were from *Zuiho,* but he did know *Zuiho* had been among the enemy carriers for that October 1942 battle. For similar and different reasons Jimmy, Burke, and Mitscher were overly anxious for confirmation that those carriers had been destroyed.

More Task Force Thirty-eight strikes arrived, and Hugh Winters coordinated their attacks. *Zuikaku,* having taken several bombs and torpedoes, gently rolled to port and slipped beneath the surface at 1414. *Zuiho,* her flight deck camouflaged to resemble a battleship, lived another hour before succumbing to multiple hits. Winters then radioed, "Jim, they are not burning, or smoking, or sinking now—these two carriers are under the water." Shortly thereafter, about 1600, Hugh provided a course change to approaching cruisers from TF 38 toward *Chiyoda.* After advising the cruisers, which he could see, that he was directly over *Chiyoda,* he circled long enough to see their first salvos finish the last enemy carrier.[27]

While Winters was guiding planes to their targets, ensuring photographs were taken, and sending verbal reports to Jimmy, many of the ships around *Lexington* began to change course from north to south just before noon. By dark the eight carriers remaining with Mitscher turned southeast while an accompanying cruiser force continued the stern chase with the Northern Force, finishing off a destroyer before midnight.

Later, Jimmy learned that the enemy Southern Force had been overwhelmed in Surigao Strait by destroyers, PT boats, and Oldendorf's old battleships, five of which had been sunk or damaged at Pearl Harbor and later repaired. Both Japanese battleships, *Fuso* and *Yamashiro*, were sunk before sunrise on the twenty-fifth. Not too surprising was the news that Center Force had indeed arrived near the Leyte beaches just after dawn. In what became known as the Battle off Samar, Center Force, led by four battleships including the remaining super-battleship *Yamato*, surprised the six escort carriers of Taffy Three, northernmost of three escort carrier groups, and attending destroyers and destroyer escorts. There ensued one of the most heroic actions in United States Navy history—seven destroyers and destroyer escorts charging a Japanese surface force of two dozen ships led by four battleships. Despite the magnificent display of courage one escort carrier, *Gambier Bay* (CVE-73), was sunk by gunfire along with two destroyers, *Hoel* (DD-533) and *Johnston* (DD-557), and one destroyer escort, *Samuel B. Roberts* (DE-413). Aware that Southern Force had been destroyed and that two of his cruisers were sinking from aerial counterattack, the Center Force commander, Admiral Kurita, ordered a withdrawal back toward San Bernardino Strait. Among the other factors influencing his decision was an approaching force of carriers believed to be part of TF 38. Some of the planes attacking his formation were from McCain's TG 38.1, but the force he sighted was actually another escort carrier group.

For the remainder of Jimmy's life, memory of the four separate engagements that comprised the Battle of Leyte Gulf was primarily a remembrance of a great victory. The "what ifs" and "could have beens" were recalled and discussed, and Jimmy knew within himself that he had done all he could to influence Mitscher to join the several other senior commanders who attempted to modify Halsey's decision to leave San Bernardino Strait open to Kurita's advance. Since Jimmy's passing and Halsey's death a year later, however, the memory of victory at Leyte Gulf has been considerably diminished by debate, derision, and conjecture over the commander of the Third Fleet's decision to complete his primary mission: destruction of the Japanese carrier force.[28] This aside, Leyte Gulf was a clear and significant victory. Between 23 and 26 October, Japan lost three battleships, one large carrier, three light carriers, six heavy cruisers, and three light cruisers plus several escorts. After Leyte Gulf, no Japanese carrier force steamed to challenge invasion beaches or carriers. And with the exception of *Yamato*'s suicide foray toward Okinawa in April 1945, no major Japanese surface force again sought a conventional sea battle with the U.S. Navy.

The New Unconventional Battle

Arguably the main reason why Jimmy and other members of Mitscher's staff did not immediately devote a majority of their time to the four engagements just won was the onset of a new and highly disconcerting element of combat. On 25 October the Japanese introduced aerial suicide attacks. Inspired in part by typhoons (divine winds) which destroyed invasion fleets from the Asian mainland over six hundred years earlier, the kamikaze attacks were desperate attempts to reverse the tide of war. Realistic Japanese naval officers understood after the Formosa battle in mid-October that conventional tactics in the air were doomed to failure, inadequate pilot training being a major contributing factor. Without command of the air, surface units had little hope of success, as Leyte Gulf proved. For the Japanese, the probability of their few remaining operational aircraft in the Philippines succeeding after so many others had failed was faint at best. As maximum results were imperative, the informal, occasional practice of ramming an opponents' plane transitioned to a formal plan to utilize human senses to guide a bomb-laden plane into an enemy ship. Approved only days before the Leyte assault, Japan's original goal for crash diving into flight decks was to neutralize the U.S. Navy carriers for one week. Such destruction, it was thought, could provide sufficient time for Kurita's Center Force—devoid of air cover—to reach the Leyte beaches.[29] Although this initial goal was not achieved, the suicide attacks on the twenty-fifth against the escort carriers were successful, and few in Japanese planning circles argued against expanding their use.

The first victim, struck just before 0800, was *Santee* (CVE-29), which lost sixteen killed. *Suwannee,* Jocko Clark's first carrier command, was hit shortly after with severe damage to its flight deck and over 270 killed or seriously wounded. Both escort carriers were steaming with Taffy One some 150 miles south of Taffy Three. At about 1100, Taffy Three absorbed the next suicide attacks. *Kitkun Bay* (CVE-71) took little damage as did *Kalinin Bay* (CVE-68), but *St. Lo* (CVE-63) was not as fortunate. In only thirty minutes the escort carrier went under.

For Jimmy and all involved in operations, the introduction of the kamikaze complicated tactical planning, a process that continued daily even when Mitscher's staff was relieved by McCain and his staff. Communications passing between Jimmy and Jimmie Thach during the period, while Mitscher's staff was planning future operations and McCain's staff was in combat, did not fail to mention "the special attack boys." There was sufficient challenge without this threat not only for planning offensive operations, but also for maintaining morale and confidence among all officers and men. The psyche of the American sailor initially approached a state of anomie, a loss of norms, a loss of knowledge of one's place and purpose in war. The rules of the war had suddenly changed, and as in any contest failure to operate by known and accepted procedures, even rules, produced a disconcerted disposition. In the following months, however, anomie dissipated, replaced by an incongruous attitude of stoicism and determination to be as ruthless in combat as the kamikaze. But for Jimmy, attitude was only one element of combat. Now he had to modify his operations' plan to allow practically no enemy planes within range of ship guns. The VT fuse in 5-inch guns had performed wonderfully, and until 25 October most were pleased with the performance of the 40 mm and 20 mm. The "forties" and "twenties" could do the job against conventional tactics, but neither had enough punch to absolutely destroy a plane without a hit on pilots, fuel tanks, or ordnance. Bigger caliber guns with more range plus faster and improved directors were needed, and they were being developed. But they were not available to the fleet in October 1944, and they would not be for a long time.

In the weeks following Leyte Gulf several changes were made to meet the new threat. The number of fighters was increased to fifty-four on the large fast carriers in late 1944 and to seventy-three in early 1945. Marine Corps squadrons, with their fast F4U Corsairs, were placed on several fast carriers while other squadrons took their Corsairs aboard escort carriers to support their landing forces. And the June 1944 cutback in pilot training was reversed. Attrition projections led to the cuts, but in early 1945 fatigue joined the kamikaze threat as reasons to produce more fighter pilots.

Victory at Leyte Gulf was most welcome. But, thanks to questions regarding leaving San Bernardino Strait unguarded and to the new kamikaze threat, the fruit of victory had no sweet taste.

11

Task Force Operations Officer

Iwo Jima and Okinawa

ADMIRAL MITSCHER, Arleigh Burke, and Jimmy piled into a PB2Y for a ten-hour flight from Ulithi to Eniwetok just after the momentous Battle of Leyte Gulf. From Eniwetok to Johnston Island required six hours, and another twelve hours in the air took the group to Pearl Harbor. Joining the three for the flights were Cdr. Frank Dingfelder, the communications officer, and Lt. Cdr. Charles Steele, Mitscher's aide and flag secretary. Admiral Halsey remained with the fleet off the Philippines so it continued as Third Fleet, but the flattops became Second Fast Carrier Force as Admiral McCain assumed command of Task Force Thirty-eight in Mitscher's place. Just as Arleigh and Jimmy were seldom more than a few steps away from Mitscher, so it was that operations officer Jimmie Thach was always near McCain. And always near or with Jimmie Thach was one of his little black books with notes to pass on to his opposite, Jimmy Flatley.

While Halsey, McCain, Thach, and Bill Leonard—now Thach's assistant operations officer—continued operations to secure the Philippines, Mitscher's staff was ordered home for leave before reassembling at Pearl Harbor to complete plans with Admiral Spruance's staff for the invasions of Iwo Jima and Okinawa. As the two assaults were scheduled less than three months apart, plans had to be devised and written while the two staffs were at Pearl. There would not be sufficient time for such a conference between the two invasions.

When Mitscher and Burke boarded another plane for their flight to the United States on 1 November, Jimmy remained behind for ten days to work on plans with Spruance's staff. On the tenth he borrowed a Hellcat and flew alone to Maui, particularly interested in replacement air groups and new fittings for rockets and napalm. The assault on Peleliu, like Tarawa, offered tragic lessons that promised further expression on both Iwo and Okinawa. Initial objectives met, on the eleventh he boarded an R5D for transportation to Alameda. From there he joined task group commander Rear Adm. Jocko Clark, also on leave, in a smaller JRB for a three-hour flight to Los Angeles. Bidding farewell to Jocko, Jimmy was on to San Diego and home.

From 3–5 December 1944 Jimmy, Burke, Mitscher, and the few other staff members with them, retraced their path from San Diego to Pearl. For the rest of the month, Jimmy poured over maps and mountains of other papers putting together operational plans for Iwo Jima and Okinawa. Christmas Day was just another twelve hours in an office as was part of New Year's Eve and New Year's Day. Writing plans and drawing maps were interrupted, somewhat pleasantly, on two occasions when Jimmy loaded Arleigh into a GB-1 and SNJ, respectively, for short hops over to Maui. Arleigh, too, needed to become acquainted with some new ordnance expected to see considerable utilization. The 5-inch rockets had already proven valuable, but there was no consensus regarding the newer 11-inch "Tiny Tim" rockets. Jimmy was particularly unhappy with them, noting in a 10 December 1944 letter to Thach that they required too much storage space aboard carriers, carried too little explosive, and that accuracy left much to be desired.

On 25 January 1945 Jimmy arrived at Ulithi after 19.5 hours in the air and boarded Mitscher's new flagship *Bunker Hill*. Only five days after Jimmy, Arleigh, and Mitscher disembarked from *Lexington* (5 November 1944), a kamikaze dove on "The Blue Ghost" and crashed the starboard side of the island, killing forty-seven. Quickly repaired, *Lexington* stayed at sea and supported the Iwo landings before leaving for overhaul, but she would miss the Okinawa campaign. Originally the assault on Iwo Jima had been scheduled for mid-January, but delay in consolidating gains on Luzon impacted the schedule. Landings on Iwo were now set for 19 February. The plans he had worked on written and printed for distribution, Jimmy prepared to resume the combat routine at sea.

A Typical Day in the Life of a Task Force Operations Officer

Jimmy fully grasped what was required of an operations officer. It was a difficult and demanding job requiring considerable experience, an ability to write clear directives, and when in combat, an ability to function without adequate sleep. In short, he had to know his stuff and possess the capability to communicate it to everyone else.

If combat operations were not scheduled, the day began at 0530. When strikes were scheduled, the day began about 0315. Jimmy, and everyone else on the staff of 130 officers and men, remained at their posts until dark but were on alert twenty-four hours a day, every day at sea. The only sit-down meal was enjoyed in the flag mess after dark when most flight operations ceased and the threat of enemy attack lessened. To stay awake everyone on the staff—except the force fighter director, Lt. Cdr. Joseph R. Eggert Jr.—drank coffee. Eggert, a reserve officer who successfully coordinated the fighter directors of each task group during the Marianas Turkey Shoot, insisted on tea. Although a reserve officer who returned to the banking business after the war, Eggert was highly respected for his demonstrated competence. Another habit that may or may not have helped the sleep-deprived multitude was smoking. Nearly everyone from Mitscher—who could light a cigarette in a typhoon—on down the roster of officers smoked, and smoked a lot. Jimmy acknowledged thirty cigarettes a day during his 1 May 1945 physical, but no one tallied, or cared to tally, one of the few pleasures available to the staff at sea.

Jimmy did not have to worry about the strategic direction of the war. That was a matter for the Joint Chiefs of Staff in Washington and the chief of naval operations (King). The next level was the commander of the Pacific Fleet (Nimitz), then the commander of the Third Fleet (Halsey) or Fifth Fleet (Spruance), and finally the commander of the First Carrier Task Force (Mitscher). Each command, including the task groups comprising the task force, had its own planning and operations officers. Though Jimmy was near the bottom in this command pyramid, it was his responsibility to determine and write the plans for combat implementation. Throughout his tenure as operations officer, Jimmy drew up the plans. Chief of Staff Burke approved or modified the plans, and the final version was then submitted to Mitscher who was not given to reading operations plans. He expected Arleigh or Jimmy to provide him with a verbal synopsis. After Mitscher nodded assent, it was Jimmy's responsibility to ensure that everything was printed and then conveyed to air group commanders.

Air group and squadron commanders flew aboard the flagship for early morning briefings with Jimmy. At the beginning of a new objective, Mitscher and Burke usually stepped into the meeting to say a few words. As the admiral and his chief of staff headed out of the flag mess, Jimmy began the meeting in earnest. On one occasion, however, Jimmy could not resist telling the assembled air group commanders, "Now that you've listened to all that _____, here is what we're going to do." The comment drew a laugh from the pilots, a smile from the departing admiral, and a shake of the head from Arleigh. Not only did everyone understand no disrespect was intended, all knew that the Mitscher-Burke-Flatley team was just that, a team. Still a team usually has a captain, and despite the burdens of command on the shoulders of the admiral and his chief of staff, the pilots saw Jimmy as a contemporary who could totally identify with their needs. In the opinion of then-Cdr. R. Emmett Riera who had an air group with the task force, "Jimmy really ran the show."[1]

The meetings between Jimmy and the air group commanders featured considerable give and take. All were well trained, and by late 1944 it was not unusual for air group commanders to have combat experience commensurate with Jimmy's. Having shared the rigors of combat formed a base of mutual respect. As important to seal the bond of mutual respect, however, was Jimmy's expectation that everyone express his true thoughts. Though very forceful Jimmy was also very considerate of ideas not necessarily in concert with his own.[2]

Jimmy was very adamant that everyone understand objectives. Planning was meticulous because it had to be. As part of his planning, however, Jimmy constantly asked air group commanders to share their concerns in full. In short time, both air group and squadron commanders noticed a distinct difference in philosophy between Jimmy Flatley and Jimmie Thach. Thach tried to bring everyone up to his level whereas Flatley stated, "Let's do what the ordinary pilot can do." While not challenging Thach when McCain was leading the fast carriers, some commanders nonetheless operated on the basis of Flatley's philosophy.[3]

Before a specific attack, discussions included intelligence reports so that everyone would know what he might expect. High on the list of concerns throughout the final year of the war was the same issue that had been a major concern on 7 December 1941: What pattern of attack was the enemy using in attacking the task force? From his observations directing the fighter engagements, Eggert confirmed what the pilots already knew—the Japanese practice of approaching at low altitude for a period followed by higher and higher attack altitudes. Other subjects of concern during the meetings included the type of ordnance that was most effective for certain targets and Japanese efforts to conceal their aircraft on the ground. These two subjects were usually intertwined since some ordnance, like cluster bombs, worked better on hidden aircraft; for such instances, a direct hit was not necessary to destroy the target.

No meeting failed to cover weather, numbers and types of aircraft best suited for specific missions, and communications problems. More specific discussions covered the benefits of re-assigning the same pilots to strike certain areas where feasible, since familiarity with a target promised better results. With surface targets rapidly diminishing and more fighters needed for protection against kamikazes, some air group commanders suggested placing former bomber pilots in Hellcats, their experience making them potentially more valuable than new replacement pilots directly from training. Always high on the list for discussion was the amount of time pilots should be expected to fly combat missions. Many believed that three consecutive days was the maximum before fatigue rendered pilots more dangerous to themselves than to the enemy.

Air groups usually spent six months in a combat area, but very soon the intensity of combat necessitated rotating air groups every four months.[4]

Some suggestions and recommendations seemed obvious, but Jimmy could only listen. He agreed that training rockets did not have the same ballistic characteristics as service rockets, but that was a subject that had to be handled back at Fleet Air, West Coast, and other training centers. Observations that destroyer pickets were not always where they were supposed to be proved an irritant. That, however, was something Jimmy could address.

Once the air group and squadron commanders departed for their respective carriers, Jimmy could turn his attention to his many other daily responsibilities. First, he had to be aware of orders from a higher echelon. If strikes were ordered for the following day he had to prepare one last operation order, ensure that targets were assigned, a specific number of planes designated, and list exact bomb loads. Next came consideration of how large a combat air patrol was necessary and whether or not any special searches or fighter sweeps were required. Were night operations necessary or ordered, and if so, how many and in what areas should they be assigned? Did the carriers have sufficient planes aboard? If not, when and where would replenishment occur? Were friendly submarines within range of task force aerial operations, and were any special dispatches required concerning downed pilots?

Being responsible for the flight operations just noted might seem to be enough on anyone's plate, but it was only half for a task force operations officer. Jimmy also had to worry about the ships of the task force. Seldom did many consecutive days go by without a ship departing or joining the force. Point option (where ships would be at a given time) had to be issued daily to all ships, as did the designation of the duty task group. Fueling plans had to be reviewed daily as heavy weather or unexpected combat could increase fuel consumption. Especially throughout the kamikaze period, destroyer scouting lines had to be in place, fighter director stations assigned, and aircraft approach sectors determined. Night orders had to be provided to the ships, mail deliveries scheduled, and the task force staff had to know how operations of other allied forces might affect the next day's carrier operations. Finally, Jimmy had to prepare a daily report for the fleet commander. These things done, and no enemy ships or planes on radarscopes, Jimmy could hit the sack (usually about 2100, but midnight was not unusual).

The Impact of the Kamikazes on Planning

Although the first kamikaze attacks occurred while Mitscher's staff was engaged off the Philippines, Admiral McCain and Jimmie Thach had to deal with the threat daily as they assumed command of the fast carriers on 30 October 1944. Within a month *Lexington, Franklin,* and *Belleau Wood* (CVL-24) were heading east for repairs inflicted by kamikazes. Attacks intensified in January 1945 as MacArthur landed on Luzon, the northernmost island in the Philippines, and damage to TF 38 ships mounted alarmingly. Kamikaze tactics varied in both numbers and approach to the target. Whether intended or not, these variations added additional stress and problems for the U.S. Navy. In response to the effective suicide attacks, as well as continuing conventional aerial attacks, Thach devised some training exercises termed Exercise Moose Trap. Essentially the idea was to copy a practice method used by football teams when they had one of their units assume the offensive or defensive formations of an upcoming opponent ("scout team" in more contemporary language). Thach would have friendly planes try to discover the disposition and size of the task force combat air patrols and then fly the routes suicide planes could be expected to use. Consequently, Hellcat pilots rode down the nulls of the radar, "attacked" in pairs (one high and one low), or approached low on the water. Further, Thach put a combat air patrol over picket destroyers, especially those in the direction friendly strikes would be returning and from which the enemy might follow. This CAP was in addition to those always above the carriers when they were in a combat zone. And knowing that night fighters most often flew too high to see enemy torpedo planes approaching low on the water at dusk, Thach addressed this problem (Operation Jack) by having a spread of fighters fly low at dusk to catch the intruders before they could reach the task force.[5]

Another defensive tactic was a requirement for returning pilots to fly to their carriers over the picket destroyers "so they could get deloused" as enemy planes sometimes hid beneath the incoming planes. Clear areas —zones through which the enemy most likely would approach—were delineated to pilots, who were told that even they would be shot down if they flew through such an area instead of prescribed routes to the task force. While pilots did manage to stay out of clear zones for the most part, there were two problems that bedeviled both Thach and Jimmy Flatley. First was the continuing failure of pilots to turn on their IFF, thereby causing numerous intercepts of friendly planes. Second was the constant unnecessary use of radios that kept essential information from getting to pilots in position to intercept oncoming Japanese planes.[6]

Another constant in the minds of the two operations officers in combating kamikazes was the axiom that bad weather was a friend of the Japanese and an enemy of friendly aircraft. Poor visibility allowed both well-trained and inadequately trained Japanese pilots to approach the task force unseen. When emerging from low clouds, there was sufficient time to guide a plane into a ship while American antiaircraft gunners had too little time to get on target.

Long after the war, Jimmie Thach said he thought "Mitscher wasn't very quick to pick up a new untried idea for a solution to a problem, such as the kamikazes. . . . He liked to depend on antiaircraft fire and the fighters." Regarding the Moose Trap disposition, Thach stated, "I know that Jimmy Flatley was all in favor of it, and little by little he would attempt to persuade Mitscher, but Mitscher was reluctant to take up new ideas, just as he was in the night fighter business." Thach did think, however, that Jimmy Flatley persuaded Mitscher to adopt the three-strike system (Flatley did but it was late in the Okinawa campaign and used only sparingly). Named and remembered as "The Big Blue Blanket," the three-strike system was designed to not allow enemy planes off the ground. Previously, the two-strike system allowed bombers and torpedo planes to hit targets after fighters had swept enemy fighters from the sky. Considering the time necessary to prepare and launch planes, half a deck load was launched, and when it was on the return flight the second half arrived over a target. But given the kamikaze danger, enemy planes could not be allowed off the ground at any time that carriers were near enough to be attacked regardless of deck loads to be launched. Precise timing was required both to keep fighters over enemy fields and to have the carriers heading into the wind as they launched and recovered planes. When properly executed, the three-strike system maintained Hellcats and Corsairs over most major enemy airfields in the area throughout a day. When *Enterprise* and *Saratoga* were available as night carriers, enemy planes could be kept on the ground both day and night.[7]

Although there is some justification of Thach's criticism of Mitscher, it must be seen in context. First, Thach was as loyal to McCain as Jimmy Flatley was to Mitscher. In his oral history, Thach deflected praise assigned to him in favor of McCain.[8] Despite this understandable loyalty, available documentation appears to support the argument that Thach had more influence with McCain than Flatley had with Mitscher. Second, the kamikaze attacks were considerably heavier against Mitscher than McCain (as many as 355 on two days against Mitscher in early April 1945 as opposed to 424 for the entire Philippines campaign), and third, Mitscher operated in a smaller area while off Okinawa than did McCain while off Luzon. Further, attempts to destroy enemy planes, particularly while they were still on the ground, were included in the plans drawn up by Jimmy Flatley while working with Spruance's staff before the attacks on Iwo Jima and Okinawa. Two major carrier sweeps were planned against the Tokyo area, one on 16–17 February to coincide with the pre-assault bombardment at Iwo and the second on 25 February while the battle was still being fought. Finally, despite their close personal and professional relationship plus the constant sharing of information and tactical instructions, the Mitscher and McCain teams had numerous differences of opinion on the conduct of air operations. In addition to variances in addressing the kamikaze threat, Jimmy Flatley did not agree with McCain's suggestions to replace SB2Cs with F4U Corsairs for dive-bombing missions.[9] Several extant letters and memos originated by McCain and Thach from the period have "do not agree" penciled on by Jimmy Flatley. Thach's disagreement with some of Mitscher's practices is already noted. Finally, McCain—though recognized as a courageous fighter—was not as highly regarded as Mitscher by some task group commanders. Confusion resulting from McCain's "orders, counter-orders, and disorder" to some degree deleteriously affected other ideas and recommendations emanating from his flagship.[10]

Iwo Jima (Operation Detachment)

Impressed by the effective suicide attacks off the Philippines, members of Admiral Spruance's staff needed very little persuasion from Jimmy and others of Mitscher's staff to support the Iwo Jima assault by attacking airfields in Japan, Formosa, and other nearby islands. Rather than standing off the volcanic island comprising less than twelve square miles, the fast carriers would use their greatest asset, mobility, to counter aerial reprisals. On 30 January Mitscher relieved McCain; and as Spruance had already relieved Halsey, the designation was again Task Force Fifty-eight.

Iwo Jima was desired for several reasons. After capture of the Marianas, Japanese planes managed several successful raids against B-29 air bases on Tinian. It appeared the enemy planes had staged through Iwo Jima and the loss of the big bombers while sitting on the ground was not acceptable. The distance between the major Army Air Force B-29 bases on Tinian and Tokyo was fifteen hundred miles: Iwo Jima was approximately half way between the two. Possession would not only eliminate enemy fighters that rose from completed airfields on the island to raid the Marianas or intercept B-29s en route to Japan, but also would provide landing strips for friendly fighter escorts. The great distance between the Marianas and the Japanese homeland required the big B-29s to carry more fuel than bombs. And Iwo Jima could also serve as an emergency landing field for bombers unable to complete a round-trip mission. By the end of the war, Iwo proved its value as nearly twenty-five-hundred bombers made emergency landings with their standard crews of ten or eleven officers and men. Still, the island cost seven thousand soldiers and marines killed in action to eradicate twenty-three-thousand determined defenders between 19 February and 26 March 1945.

In writing the operations memorandum to the pilots for the Tokyo attacks on airfields and aircraft facilities in support of the Iwo Jima assault, Jimmy stressed the same basics he had preached since the beginning of the war.[11] Aware that nearly half the fighter pilots on these missions were new to combat, he admonished the pilots to never let their section break down, maintain at least 160 knots, pull out of strafing runs at one thousand feet, and not to attack an enemy plane without looking above and around.[12] Further, he advised the pilots to keep a hundred rounds for the return trip, to fire only short bursts in order to avoid stoppages, and to use the weave "in a tough spot." The fighter sweeps were to arrive with high cover at twenty thousand feet, an intermediate cover at fifteen thousand, and the other third of the fighters lower. If no air opposition was encountered after twenty minutes, even the high-cover bomb or rocket-armed fighters were to attack. As it turned out, the two big air attacks against the home islands on 16–17 February and 25 February were only partially successful because of bad weather. High expectations attended the first carrier strikes against the enemy home islands since Halsey, Mitscher, and Doolittle visited nearly three years earlier. It was not surprising that the several hundred enemy planes destroyed in the air and on the ground—most in the first attack, but both using the foul weather procedure delineated in the operations plan—failed to satisfy the task force staffs or pilots.

Between the two strikes, Task Force Fifty-eight stood off Iwo for the 19 February landings, keeping an eye on radar for major enemy aerial counterattacks and supporting the assault with continual napalm, rocket, bomb, and gunnery attacks. Every bomb, rocket, and bullet was needed as the deeply entrenched Japanese contested the landing beaches and every square yard beyond. On the twentieth, however, Mitscher ordered the fast carriers northwest back toward Tokyo. The timing proved fortuitous for the enemy as their one and only major aerial assault arrived at Iwo on the evening of 21 February. *Saratoga,* left behind to provide night support and protection for the amphibious force, was struck by several kamikazes and put out of the war.[13] Escort carrier *Bismarck Sea* (CVE-95) also fell victim to kamikazes just after dark and was sunk. Mitscher, Burke, and Jimmy had no choice but to detach *Enterprise* and send her back to Iwo while the other fast carriers continued on toward Tokyo. As it turned out "The Big E" was not missed off Tokyo due to the early termination of the weather-plagued raids. But Cdr. Bill Martin's Air Group Ninety proved invaluable off Iwo by having planes continuously in the air for 174 hours from 23 February to 2 March.

After the abridged 25 February Tokyo raid, Admiral Spruance returned to Iwo with heavy units while Mitscher headed to Okinawa with three of his four task groups. On 1 March carrier planes raided the sixty-mile-long island and then headed to join the fourth task group at Ulithi, arriving on the fourth. Photographs obtained were of even greater significance than the damage to enemy targets. Stereo photos were especially important as they could provide more of a three-dimensional perspective of enemy strongholds. Of lesser importance to Jimmy and intelligence analysts were photographs for the press, but informing the public was also an important front.

While they were steaming toward Ulithi, assignments had been made for Operation Iceberg, the code name for Okinawa. Jimmy's responsibility was the employment plan. His assistant, Lt. Cdr. Frank B. Quady (USNA 1938), took air-sea rescue while others assumed primary responsibility for photographic requirements, communications, intelligence, friendly air-search, target charts, logistics, task organization, movement plan, and special instructions.[14] When completed the information was compressed as both Burke and Jimmy were advocates of saying much with few words. Indeed, each officer was advised in writing how many pages he was allowed for the compositions. Several of the areas of responsibility were restricted to one mimeographed page or chart. Communications was allowed five mimeographed pages and intelligence up to ten while Jimmy was allowed up to twenty-two pages for the employment schedule, cruising instructions, and air operations. In addition to drawing up the employment plan, which was to be distributed on 5 March, Jimmy was also assembling rough-draft comments and recommendations for inclusion in the operations action report for Iwo Jima.[15]

Okinawa (Operation Iceberg)

Only 350 miles from Japan (the "Empire"), China, and Formosa, Okinawa was a natural staging location for the invasion of Kyushu, the southernmost of the four main islands of Japan. As a staging area Okinawa offered protected anchorages and numerous airfields for the scheduled 1 November 1945 Operation Olympic which would precede

Operation Coronet; the invasion of Honshu, Japan's largest island and site of the nation's capital, Tokyo.

With 485 square miles along her 60-mile length, Okinawa offered several advantages to the nearly two hundred thousand invaders approaching in over fourteen hundred ships. Okinawa's elongated shape, ranging in some places from two to ten miles, exposed considerable areas to naval gunfire. Still, there were numerous advantages offered to the Japanese for their defense of the island. Annexed by Japan in 1879 the 450,000 residents of the island spoke Japanese as the official language, and by no means did they welcome the impending assault. Japanese planes could fly to Okinawa from Kyushu to the north, from China to the west, and from Formosa to the southwest. Ashore, hilly topography and heavy spring rains would aid the 130,000 defenders, plus the Japanese would commit everything they had to this battle.

Operations Plan 2-45 (for Iceberg) recognized the above in addition to noting extensive minefields protecting both the Inland Sea and Sea of Japan, alerted all ships to be prepared to tow or be towed, and stated the correct presumption that the Japanese knew an assault was coming. Further noted was the assumption that the tactical situation might require the task force to be in the operating area "for an extended period." By this time in the war the Japanese knew an absence of carrier raids meant the task force was at some forward base—in this case Ulithi—replenishing and preparing for another landing operation or preparing strikes directly against the Empire. Attendant with the absence of carrier aircraft was an increase in land-based bombing attacks. While the exact date of the attack was only surmised, it made little difference as the Japanese forces were in place, and they did not intend to challenge the landings or landing beaches. Having already experienced the telling effect of naval gunfire, the enemy retreated inland, dug tunnels, erected small fortifications, and prepared for a defense in depth. As at Peleliu and Iwo Jima, every yard would be contested. And again, navy and marine pilots would find napalm and rockets especially effective and photographic reconnaissance critically significant. But also again, the battle would have to be won on the ground with M-1 rifles, bayonets, hand grenades, and flame-throwers.

Anticipating a protracted and heavy kamikaze assault, multi-page appendices were written at the task force and task group echelons pertaining to fighter direction and radar doctrine. Every detail was addressed. Fighter direction control sequence was explicitly defined as to daily responsibility and shifting of tactical command in case the flagship was damaged. Communications and landing instructions were even more precise, and combat air patrol procedures became even more complicated. A pilot's intelligence and memory were now perhaps more important than courage.

All the task force preparations were needed as the Japanese had expanded the kamikaze effort. Planes, rocket-powered baka bombs, boats, ships (including super-battleship *Yamato*), submarine and airborne commandos could be employed. Ten major aerial kamikaze formations and smaller groups would be launched in the coming weeks resulting in 930 being expended.[16] Volunteers had made up the initial kamikaze special attack units, but peer pressure had become necessary to recruit some that would die over and off Okinawa. Many of the new kamikaze pilots were college graduates. Notably missing in great numbers were experienced pilots who had graduated from the Japanese naval academy (Eta Jima). Someone had to lead, even if it was from behind.

Even before Task Force Fifty-eight steamed from Ulithi on 14 March, a small, long-range kamikaze attack resulted in damage to *Randolph* (CV-15). The extreme aft end of her flight deck was destroyed and twenty-five were killed. On the eighteenth the task force's planes initiated strikes on Kyushu airfields, but few planes were found, as they were en route to attack the carriers. *Enterprise, Yorktown,* and *Intrepid* took minor damage, and the three carriers combined lost only seven killed. However, on the morning of the nineteenth, *Wasp* (CV-18) lost just over a hundred of her crew to a kamikaze and within minutes *Franklin* took two bombs in a conventional attack. In the process of launching fully loaded planes, "Big Ben" was quickly aflame from amidships to her stern. In the following hours she lost some eight hundred officers and men, the largest casualty list for any carrier during World War II.[17]

Steaming to Okinawa from the shores of Kyushu, the fast carriers quickly replenished, repaired, and prepared for pre-invasion raids on Okinawa from 23 March through 1 April (Easter Sunday) when the first troops sloshed ashore. Then began the period for the task force to remain near enough to provide air support. As expected, the kamikazes appeared from the first day of the landings and continued to rain havoc throughout the month of April and into early May. Because the fast carriers did not expect to be tied to the Okinawa area for the protracted period of three months, an expression was coined: "The Fleet that came to stay." The army's slow construction of airfields was a major contributing factor to the extended stay. But a second reason developed to ensure that the above expression would always be associated with Operation Iceberg. Off Okinawa the U.S. Navy lost some one hundred vessels sunk or put out of action. Thirty-six were sunk, including 15 destroyers—12 to kamikazes—while 368 were damaged and nearly five thousand sailors were killed. The battle on land and sea became a slugging match with attrition determining victor from vanquished.

While no fast carrier was lost, several absorbed serious damage. *Hancock* (CV-19) and *Essex* were hit in April while *Enterprise* and *Intrepid* again took damage. Watching the attacks, Jimmy could not help but be frustrated by some practices that seemed impossible to resolve. If a carrier was making a turn in response to orders given to a task group, the move might place the targeted carrier in a position where she could not bring the weight of her own guns to bear. Suggestions abounded including placement of heavily armed *Atlanta*-class light cruisers or *Sumner*-class destroyers off the especially vulnerable sterns of carriers. But there was one inescapable fact: only the target ship itself was in good position for defense, as it did not have to allow for deflection shooting. The VT fuse, heretofore so widely applauded, now became a subject of criticism for its premature detonation and problematic reliability; there were too many duds. And many of the newer gun directors were not living up to expectations for finding enemy planes in low clouds.

After a month off Okinawa nearly all aboard *Bunker Hill* looked as though they had been at general quarters for a year. Fatigue and strain could and sometimes did translate into accidents. Admiral Mitscher looked and felt terrible, and it was speculated that he might have suffered a heart attack. Arleigh Burke did not miss the few pounds he lost, but Jimmy did miss the pounds he did not need to lose. Never over 130 pounds during the war, by May he was under 120 (and by June he was on the sick list). The ships that had escaped sinking or damage were also showing literal signs of wear and tear. On carriers, catapults broke down. The retrieving gear of the port catapult on *Yorktown* failed on 20 April, and it then became necessary to pull the piston back to battery with a tractor after each shot, thereby introducing a considerable delay in launching the next aircraft. Soon after, the starboard catapult failed completely after 1,529 successful shots. It was apparent that for prolonged and continuous operations, the catapults required conservative use, and full pressure shots needed to be held to a minimum.[18]

There were victories, notably the 7 April sinking of *Yamato,* the cruiser *Yahagi,* and four of eight attending destroyers. With Mitscher ailing, Arleigh Burke and Jimmy organized the strikes that sent the six ships to the bottom. The enemy force was headed on a one-way mission to the Okinawa landing beaches to destroy as much shipping as possible before being sunk. For once, Jimmy was not unhappy about having his pilots risk danger to obtain photographs sent to the press on Guam, Nimitz's new headquarters since 29 January. But that satisfying event aside, most hours of each day were spent watching for kamikazes, attending to the routine of air support, writing never-ending reports, searching for replacement destroyers for those sunk or damaged, and occasionally wondering about the future. The war in Europe ended the first week in May. Maybe that would free some destroyers, officers, and men for the Pacific, but how long would it take for them to arrive? When would TF 58 be relieved? When would Leyte replace Ulithi as a major replenishment base? When would fast carriers undergoing repairs or upkeep return to the task force? When was the next amphibious operation? Where would it take place?

Ordeal on Bunker Hill and Enterprise

In his lengthy action report written at the end of his tour of command off Okinawa, Admiral Mitscher wrote quite candidly in evaluating everything from tactics and logistics to decisions made in Washington, D.C., on the location of the combat information center. In the original designs for the *Essex* class, CIC was to be located in the island structure near

Flag Plot. When the first of these carriers were commissioned CIC was built into the island structure. Mitscher's earlier flagship, *Lexington*, had CIC in the island. But despite adamant opposition from Vice Adm. John Towers, Mitscher, and others, CIC in later units of the class were located on the gallery deck immediately under the flight deck. And as early members of the class, including *Bunker Hill,* returned from operations for overhaul, CIC was relocated from the cramped spaces of the island to the gallery deck. In his action report Mitscher complained that his operations officer needed to have immediate access to information to conduct offensive operations, and that either his chief of staff or operations officer needed to be in CIC for defensive actions. Voice tubes, phones, and talkers lengthened lines of communication when time was critical. Further, neither Jimmy nor Arleigh could immediately see lines being drawn on plot boards in CIC. Of course the two officers could not be in CIC and Flag Plot at the same time on *Bunker Hill,* so both spent nearly all their time in Flag Plot. Lastly, Mitscher noted that even air-conditioning did not keep CIC cool enough to prevent the heat of electronic equipment from contributing to malfunctions or to cool operators during the long stressful hours in combat zones.

At 1000 on the morning of 11 May, Jimmy was in flagship *Bunker Hill*'s combat information center immediately below the flight deck. One of the major kamikaze strikes was in the air, and there were reports from CIC that some of the enemy planes may have followed the carrier's returning first launch back to the task force. Attempting better to assess this information, Jimmy had gone directly to CIC. An explosion aft on the flight deck announced the reality that CIC had suspected.

Stepping out of CIC, Jimmy made a sharp right turn and ran about twenty-two feet aft along the starboard gallery deck to a ladder that led to the flight deck level. At the top of the ladder, which faced forward, he turned 180 degrees and ran aft thirty feet within the base of the island structure toward another ladder which led up to Flag Plot and the flag bridge. As his foot reached the first of the steps, sheets of flames blasted through the open door only two feet behind him and climbed his back. Slightly burned, Jimmy jumped the remaining steps and dashed into Flag Plot. There he found Arleigh and others, but smoke was quickly filling the compartment. Evacuating forward toward the bridge, several peered over the side to see the damage in the area of CIC and the flames that were reaching for the radio room one level below them. Returning down the hot, smoke-filled narrow ladders that he had just ascended, Jimmy and Arleigh joined Frank Dingfelder to pull and drag out the radio room's stunned and injured occupants. This accomplished, Arleigh rushed back up the ladder to the flag bridge.

Rather than return to the flag bridge, Jimmy descended to the gallery deck toward CIC ordering several uninjured enlisted men to follow him. The gallery deck was filled with smoke, but in he went. Stumbling through the blinding smoke, he felt his way through the passageway into CIC. Grabbing the first man he came to, he led him back to a man behind him with orders to take the choking man about twenty feet to an open door on the starboard side of the ship. Gulping fresh air, he turned and headed back in an attempt to help others.

Fortunately, the commanding officer of the carrier turned the ship to allow the wind to carry the smoke aft. This did not immediately clear the smoke in the gallery deck area but it did provide clear air down two ladders to the hangar deck. From there the injured could be led well forward away from danger. Emerging from the gallery deck destruction, Jimmy's heart began to sink as he realized members of the staff in the flag office along with pilots in ready rooms aft of CIC and the flag office could not possibly survive the clouds of smoke.

Later, Jimmy received a commendation ribbon and citation for his "coolness and leadership . . . voluntarily [leading] parties below decks to rescue personnel who had been overcome in the smoke filled compartments." The award, however, became only a painful reminder of yet another painful day. Two kamikazes had struck the carrier, the first slamming across the flight deck just aft of the island and number three elevator, igniting many Corsairs waiting to take off. The first suicide plane, a fighter, carried over the port side while its bomb penetrated the flight deck and port side of the ship, detonating in the air close aboard. The second plane, a bomber, dove less than a minute later and struck the port side of the flight deck amidships. This was the source of the fire that burned Jimmy's back. Its bomb, released before the plane's impact, penetrated the flight deck and detonated on the gallery deck near the Fighter Squadron Eighty-four ready room, resulting in death for those who had just returned from the morning's first launch. While the bomb blast took its toll, the severe gasoline fire ignited by the two kamikazes plus the many burning Air Group Eighty-four planes gutted gallery deck compartments and the hangar deck below between frames 82 and 165. Later it was apparent that smoke was responsible for most of the deaths.[19]

Initial mustering indicated some 400 dead or missing, over 250 wounded, and many aboard other ships after leaping from the burning carrier. The pilots of Air Group Eighty-four had received a special commendation from Mitscher for their outstanding performance on 25 February when they had pressed home attacks on Tokyo to a greater degree than other air groups.[20] Now, twenty-two pilots of VF-84 were dead. Those who died quickly were fortunate. One of the more tragic pictures of the war shows bodies piled four high in a passageway where smoke had overcome the victims. Movement of squadron ready rooms below the hangar deck from the vulnerable compartments immediately under the flight deck had been recommended but not required.[21]

Jimmy was not sure whether his assistant operations officer, Frank Quady, had died quickly or not. Indeed, he did not want to know. Found dead in the stateroom reserved for the flag chief of staff was flight surgeon Capt. Raymond W. Hege, apparently asleep in the bed Arleigh Burke would have used had he chosen to use the compartment. Flag secretary and aide to Mitscher, Charles Steele, was also dead. Eleven enlisted men of the staff were dead or missing, all killed alongside Quady, Steele, and Hege in or near the gallery deck flag office. While fires were still being fought aboard *Bunker Hill*, the destroyer *English* (DD-696) was ordered alongside to transfer Mitscher, Burke, Jimmy, and more than a dozen other staff to *Enterprise*. Others followed as soon as possible. On "The Big E," Flag Plot was a deck higher than on *Bunker Hill* and other *Essex*-class carriers, but at least its CIC was in the island. By late afternoon the staff could do little but stand high on the island of *Enterprise* and mournfully look two and a half miles across the water at the still smoldering former flagship.

On the morning of the twelfth, Mitscher resumed command of the task force. Jimmy recommended the task force head north to attack airfields on the home islands of Kyushu and Shikoku. Mitscher and

Burke were also in a mood for a fight. By the morning of the fourteenth, the task force was back on station off Okinawa. So were several kamikazes. As occurred so often, low clouds made the deadly hide and seek game frustrating for the combat air patrol. On this morning one Zero fighter repeatedly escaped danger while others with him were found and destroyed.

Following task force orders for hard turns to port, *Enterprise* had just emerged from the second of two such turns and the Zero pilot saw the venerable carrier straighten her course. The wind stream in this position did not favor the experienced gunners on the carrier, holding the acrid yellow and white smoke over their guns and interfering with vision. But the gunners could nonetheless see the brownish-green fighter dive toward them out of the low clouds. With both ship and plane now in the clear, all antiaircraft guns that could bear opened fire. Jimmy, hearing the relative silence instantly broken by the thunderous noise, stepped out on the port side of the flag bridge, looked up and astern, and then unceremoniously dived back through the door yelling, "Hit the deck!" Everybody except Mitscher did. The admiral's luck held, but that of "The Big E" did not.

The nimble Zero dove from astern off the port quarter. Apparently believing he would miss the ship or that it might turn hard to port causing him to miss, the pilot rolled over to port and smashed upside down into the carrier's flight deck fifteen feet behind the number one elevator. Astonished onlookers from other ships in the formation, many of whom had movie cameras in hand, watched—and filmed—a large sheet of red flame rise from the carrier. As the flame rose it turned yellow and then transformed into white and black smoke. At the top of a column of fire and smoke was most of the number one elevator on its way to a height of five hundred feet above the ship. As the remains of the elevator crashed back down into the sea, and clouds of black smoke rose from the flight deck and hangar bay, the carrier steamed on as before. Unlike *Bunker Hill*, *Enterprise* was at general quarters and in twenty minutes the fires were out and only wisps of smoke trailed the flattop. *Enterprise* having been in more combat than any other ship in the U.S. Navy and having been hit more than a dozen times, her well-prepared crew lost only fourteen of their own.

The large hole behind the elevator and the loss of the elevator itself made it immediately obvious that Mitscher and his staff would need to move again. Advance repair bases could do wonderful work, but repairing this damage would require a major shipyard. Mitscher's first words after impact were, "Jimmy, tell my task group commanders that if the Japs keep this up they're going to grow hair on my head yet."[22] About an hour later an announcement was made to all the crew to bring any pieces of the Zero to the flight deck for examination and tagging. After that was complete, anyone who wanted a souvenir could come and pick it up. The admiral expressed interest in having a memento from the pilot's papers found on the remains of his body. For nearly fifty years, readers of World War II history knew the Japanese pilot as "Tomi Zai." However, a mistake in translation was made on 14 May 1945. Actually, he was Lt. Shunsuke Tomiyasu, a college graduate and member of the 306th Squadron, 721st Air Group.[23]

For the second time in four days Jimmy prepared to leave a carrier flagship and reestablish operations planning. "If we get hit again I'm coming over to *Hornet* [CV-12]," Jimmy wrote to Jocko Clark's aides, Lt. Herman Rosenblatt and Lt. (jg) Robert "Bob" Reynolds aboard Clark's flagship (CV-12) on 23 May.[24] This time, however, the stop was on *Randolph* (CV-15), repaired from her 11 March kamikaze damage. At 1636 on 15 May Mitscher, Burke, Jimmy, seventeen other officers, and twenty-five enlisted men were transferred from *Hickox* (DD-673) to CV-15, a process requiring an hour and a half. Air support for the amphibious forces continued as before as did the kamikaze attacks. Progress ashore also continued, but not at the pace allied planners had hoped. That fact plus the stress and strain to the command staff prompted Admiral Nimitz to direct Halsey to relieve Spruance on 27 May. McCain relieved Mitscher on the twenty-eighth, and after Mitscher, Burke, and Jimmy met with Halsey on his flagship, *Missouri* (BB-63), they returned to *Randolph* for a ride away from Okinawa and the Pacific. Jimmy, however, was to remain. Having learned he had been promoted to captain (message dated 28 April to rank from 30 March) he understood that he probably would be transferred from his job as task force operations officer. Jimmie Thach was on the same promotion list, so his days as operations officer for McCain also appeared numbered. On 28

May Jimmy shot off a letter to Jocko Clark, who was still serving as a task group commander aboard *Hornet*. Announcing his promotion, he inquired if Jocko "could use a junior Captain at Corpus Christi," Jocko's next assignment. Additionally, he told his good friend that his wife Dotty had just joined the Catholic Church "which makes me very happy."

Sudden Peace

As fighting on Okinawa drew to a close during the last week of June, Halsey took his Third Fleet up and down the coast of Japan, carriers striking targets of opportunity while battleships and cruisers trained their guns on industrial sites. Fewer kamikazes came out to challenge than before, but they did sortie and die without significant success.

The first week in June, Jimmy flew back to Pearl Harbor via Guam with Mitscher, Burke, and a few other members of the staff—again taking the controls of their plane for four of the thirty-three hours in the air. Returning to San Diego for temporary duty, he was placed on the sick list for treatment and recovery from general exhaustion and a related illness. Feeling much better the last week of July, he rejuvenated his spirits with familiarization flights in the latest version of the Corsair (F4U-4) and the new Grumman Bearcat (F8F). Plans were for the 446-mph Corsair to serve as a carrier's primary interceptor against kamikazes until the fast-climbing, highly maneuverable Bearcat was available in sufficient numbers.

Planning for Operation Olympic, the invasion of Japan, had been under way for some time with estimates of Japanese strength fairly balanced. One B-29 incendiary raid in March had killed some eighty-thousand people, but the Japanese Army still had millions of men in uniform. Information from a prisoner indicated the Japanese were so deficient in aviation fuels that gasoline was being mixed with 30 percent alcohol. Further, castor oil was being used in place of lubrication oil, the combination of these practices prematurely ruining engines. But it was also noted that even trainer type aircraft could and would be armed for kamikaze use.[25] Opinions varied, of course, as to how many would die in Operation Olympic, but those like Jimmy who had been in daily combat with the enemy knew an invasion of the Empire would be catastrophic for both sides. Postwar analysis solidly confirmed the trepidation. The Japanese were short of petroleum and food for the general population, but they had plenty of soldiers, ammunition, and over seven thousand kamikaze pilots awaiting an invasion. Nonetheless, all these considerations became moot in early and mid-August just as Jimmy started his last wartime assignment.

On 6 August—the same day a B-29, *Enola Gay,* released the world's first atomic bomb in anger—Jimmy was on a twelve-hour flight from San Francisco to Pearl Harbor. On the eighth he continued on to Guam in accordance with 31 July orders to join Admiral Nimitz's staff as aviation plans officer and liaison officer with Far Eastern Air Force, a great assignment indicating Nimitz's confidence in him. In this capacity Jimmy would work with representatives of the army air force. Surely this would be an assignment he would find rewarding. With the European war over, full resources could be devoted to defeating Japan, or so he and many other navy planners thought. But Japan was now cut off from resources from Southeast Asia; submarines had devastated her merchant marine; and by mid-August aircraft and mines imperiled even her coastal waterway traffic. A second atomic bomb released on the ninth in combination with a Soviet Union declaration of war on the same day drove the enemy toward surrender. In less than a week the Japanese agreed to surrender unconditionally.

With the sudden end of the war Jimmy found himself assisting Admiral Spruance, whom he had gotten to know during planning sessions in the last days of 1944 and several face to face meetings during the Okinawa campaign. But rather than planning air operations, he was helping with occupation details.

Jimmy received recognition for his service during the final months of the war. In addition to the Commendation Ribbon Jimmy received from Admiral Spruance for leading rescue parties on *Bunker Hill,* Admiral Mitscher awarded him the Bronze Star and Legion of Merit. Jimmy appreciated the decorations, the kind words, and a fitness report rating him as 4.0 on his present assignment and administration. But more than the decorations, the words, and the fitness report, Jimmy most treasured an invitation by both Mitscher and Burke a few months later to join them as they took command of the Eighth Fleet in the Atlantic and Mediterranean. Then already assigned to Jocko Clark at Corpus Christi, Jimmy was not available, but the invitation was as high a compliment he could have received from the navy's foremost fast carrier commander and a future chief of naval operations.

12

From Combat to Cold War

Combat Evaluation

A T C O R A L S E A , Santa Cruz, Guadalcanal, Rennell Island, and Marcus Island Jimmy Flatley directly engaged in combat and emerged with a Navy Cross and three Distinguished Flying Crosses. As executive officer (Coral Sea), squadron commander (Santa Cruz, Guadalcanal, and Rennell Island), and air group commander (Marcus), he enjoyed success. There was no question in his mind that he could handle greater responsibility, and the navy needed officers in positions of responsibility who had proven combat records. In this self-evaluation he was correct as more decorations were added in his subsequent assignment of greater responsibility as operations officer for Admiral Mitscher during the furious last year of the war. Before Jimmy moved on to his command assignments, it is instructive to revisit and evaluate his combat experience and combat leadership performance.

Throughout Jimmy's career, the two-page Bureau of Naval Personnel forms for reporting the fitness of officers were relatively consistent in listing the qualities to be graded by superior officers, usually the commanding officer of a ship or squadron. Since the early 1960s these fitness reports have changed in design and wording for evaluating personal and professional qualities. Nonetheless, the composite fitness evaluation of Jimmy that follows is restricted to the time frame of World War II and the qualities valued in that time period. It should be understood, however, that more than one quality is often incorporated within the examples cited. Quite often, it is not possible to totally separate the qualities, particularly intelligence, judgment, and moral courage, in any officer's combat leadership experience.

The original forms of the World War II era listed thirteen qualities; these qualities were presented in a different order from the one presented below; moreover, they did not prioritize the order in which the qualities were presented. One quality, "Military bearing and neatness of person and dress," is not evaluated in the following presentation, which includes twelve items, as the "reference to dignity of demeanor, correctness of uniform, and smartness of appearance" had little relevance in combat. Of course, that didn't inspire the Bureau of Naval Personnel to edit out that quality or to preclude superiors from grading tidiness. At least that last column on the form must have brought ironic and perhaps bitter smiles to those evaluators sitting in the heat and mud at Guadalcanal, or looking at the smoldering remains of uniforms near the burned out officers staterooms aboard *Enterprise* and other battle-damaged ships.

The following discussion is primarily an analysis of the thirteen qualities valued in an officer; but it is based on actual comments that were recorded on a number of Jimmy Flatley's fitness reports. The material at the head of each section was printed on the fitness report forms.

Intelligence

With reference to the faculty of comprehension; mental acuteness

Jimmy Flatley was not a candidate for a Nobel Prize in science, literature, or the arts. Graduating in the bottom quarter of his academy class was more a matter of lack of application than lack of inherent intelligence. Still, for promotion to lieutenant he had to take the Marine Engineering test a second time. And in understanding fighter squadron tactics, he was not quick to see the advantages of the mutual beam defense along with its necessary organizational change from three-plane to two-plane sections.

Exceptional intelligence for one application does not necessarily transfer to another. And lack of exceptional intelligence in one discipline does not mean one cannot display extraordinary talent in another. While Jimmy was arguably above average in overall intelligence, his special gifts were not associated with academic brilliance. But he did demonstrate intelligence during his combat experience when it was critically needed.

In defending the three-plane division, Jimmy believed the presence of six planes was more advantageous than four. The favorable disposition of British pilots in early combat helped strengthen his conviction. Even after becoming separated from his wingman at Coral Sea, he saw the problem as air discipline rather than tactical formation. But after further discussions with Jimmie Thach and then Butch O'Hare in the summer of 1942—and with more time to cogitate, weigh, and balance, he fully grasped the antithesis of his position and then never wavered in its adoption, implementation, advocacy, and instruction. As noted before, when he saw the light, he really saw the light.

Jimmy seemed to have a realistic appreciation for his potential and limitations. When he believed he was correct on a matter he was very open on the subject, especially to his wife. When he accomplished a goal he was matter-of-fact in acknowledging it. And when he could not measure up to a situation or his own standards, he was equally matter-of-fact. Such admissions to Dotty were usually made in a humorous vein, his lamentations on aging and getting hurt too often during exercise periods serving as an example. Comprehension of potential and limitations is an understanding and accommodation of oneself often lost on otherwise intelligent people in all walks of life.

While being consistently realistic to himself and those close to him, Jimmy also demonstrated considerable intelligence, and good judgment, by staying true to himself. A case in point was his association with John Crommelin. Both men were warriors, but their approach to combat was entirely different. In no manner did Jimmy possess Crommelin's flamboyance. In *Enterprise*'s wardroom before Santa Cruz, Jimmy felt no jealously as he listened to the Alabama native speak. "Uncle John's" serious facial expressions while speaking profundities and profanity in a pronounced Southern accent not only inspired one to rise and fight but also tempted one to laugh with a joy to fight. John Crommelin had no intention of evoking humor, and certainly no one laughed or overtly expressed a joy to fight when he spoke, but emotions rose. Although Jimmy was known to enjoy humor, nothing in his manner or speech even hinted at humor in his approach to combat.[1] Still, those who remember the dark days in the Solomons recall John Crommelin and Jimmy Flatley as a great team, both effectively communicating why they and everyone else "were out there."[2] Jimmy's approach to motivating his men never relied on emotion. It worked for Crommelin, Halsey, and others, but Jimmy made no appeal to the emotions. To the contrary, he used organization, cogent lectures, attention to administrative detail, and a father-son, one-on-one approach even when there were many in the ready room or wardroom. In short, he had the good sense, intelligence, and judgment to always stay within himself and the boundaries of his personality, especially in combat or preparing for it. That consistency went a long way in providing a stable atmosphere for his pilots.[3]

Although Jimmy stayed within himself as a leader, he nonetheless underwent a transformation during the war. On numerous fitness reports before the war, Jimmy was cited as being a "quiet" person. But Rear Adm. Osborne Hardison remarked on Jimmy's 13 February 1943 fitness report, "He is aggressive, outspoken." The word "outspoken" was repeated again and often on fitness reports and in correspondence throughout the remainder of his career. Having been in many of the major carrier-air actions for the first two years of the war, he knew he had an obligation to speak out on his experience, confirm what was right, and challenge practices that needed to be corrected or improved. Jimmy grew to comprehend both the art and science of aerial combat at multiple levels. Such understanding translated into the training process, such as his recognition that former SBD dive-bomber pilots brought no bad flying habits as they transitioned into new roles as fighter pilots in Fighting Squadron Ten.[4]

Many who knew him believe Jimmy's greatest expression of intelligence was his perceptiveness. Acknowledged as having "an almost tele-pathic rapport with his pilots,"[5] Jimmy seemed to know exactly who needed encouragement or commiseration—or someone to listen to them—and when they needed it. In the ready room aboard *Enterprise* after Santa Cruz, dejected pilots did not need a ranting discourse from their commanding officer on all that had gone wrong during the battle. They were doing that among themselves. What they needed, and got from Jimmy, was a soothing tone. His men came to talk to him, and his office did become the crossroads of the Pacific as he reported in a 26 August 1943 letter to Dotty. During wartime nobody came to score points; they came for help knowing Jimmy cared and had solutions to their problems. This same perceptiveness was equally applicable to "separating the wheat from the chaff." A number of pilots from the several squadrons Jimmy commanded were transferred because they were more a danger to them-selves and their squadron mates than to the enemy. Such transfers were not matters of anger or even disappointment; they were simply matters of applied intelligence.

Judgment

With reference to a discriminating perception by which
the values and relations of things are mentally asserted

Despite his overall calm demeanor in combat and his daily life, Jimmy was nonetheless subject to periods when not all his frustrations could be contained. While he was particularly adept at perceiving other's emo-tional stress before or after combat, he sometimes could not contain his own emotions in combat reports, usually written within hours after battle. In his section of the Santa Cruz action report, Jimmy's uneven comments appear to be a catharsis for his frustrations along with a combination of clear perspective and objective judgment. Although he quickly learned his carrier's radar failed more than once during the battle, and later learned that it did not pick up the enemy as early as some other ships in the formation, he nonetheless did not qualify his criticism of the day's interception. He left the brunt of the blame for inadequate performance on the fighter direction officer. His comment that division and sections leaders "are not required to bluntly follow all orders of the Fighter Director Officer" leaves no doubt of his feelings. In the action report's concluding statement Jimmy wrote:

> The most valuable weapon we have, if properly used, is the radar. If not properly used, it only compromises the ship. The fighters could be much more effective without it. To date, we have lost three carriers and others have been damaged because of inefficient fighter direction. A heavy price to pay just because a valuable piece of equipment has been inefficiently used.

The Santa Cruz catharsis also included a perhaps overstated comment concerning the "inexcusable . . . disregard for our planes" by *South Dakota* antiaircraft gunners as a result of "improper training," plus an overly pessimistic observation "that enemy planes were avoiding detection by acting on information given to [fighters by the FDO]."[6]

Given more time and distance, Jimmy doubtless would have realized his statement that fighters could have been more effective without radar was a contradiction of the main theme of his argument. Broken clouds at both Coral Sea and Santa Cruz would have influenced interception with or without radar, and the Japanese aviators were better than Jimmy might have then acknowledged. Radar technology available to the U.S. Navy in 1942 could not provide precise altitude, but Jimmy nonetheless expected better interpretation. "By using a little common-sense and practical experience and knowledge of enemy tactics, any Fighter Director Officer should be able to estimate altitudes closely if the operator is capable of detecting raids at or near maximum distance."[7] The operative word "estimate" in his written statement reveals a state of mind influenced as much by opinion as scientific fact.

Nevertheless, Jimmy was undeniably correct in the Santa Cruz action report—and Coral Sea—that some directives from the FDO were confusing, especially relative-bearing vectors given while the carrier was weaving furiously to counter enemy attacks. Everyone was on the same page regarding the necessity to intercept the enemy at least twenty miles away from the formation being defended. And Jimmy was particularly perceptive in noting that one or more surface ships could be stationed approximately forty miles in the direction of the enemy as radar pickets. These ships could not only detect an incoming flight but also provide an assessment regarding the critical determination of altitude. As an operations officer two years later, one of his daily responsibilities was the use and placement of destroyer radar pickets.

Veterans of Air Group Ten recall that Jimmy knew exactly when to be assertive, when to intervene, and when to remain silent. Always insisting on air and radio discipline, Jimmy's calm tone and instructive comments concerning the Japanese transports heading down the Slot toward Guadalcanal on 14 November 1942 served to settle the dive-bomber pilots and maintain focus. In that instance, Jimmy displayed unusually keen judgment in estimating the situation and making a sound decision how to conduct the impending combat.

Veterans of Air Group Five recall the August 1943 Marcus raid as though it was last week. And after fifty years—plus a few drinks at their annual reunion aboard *Yorktown*—someone will still yell, "Beat the *Essex!*" Jocko Clark invented the competition against the class leader as an artificial incentive to inspire his green recruits and officers to ready CV-10 for on-time commissioning, successful shakedown, and early entry into combat. Most members of the *Essex* crew could have cared less about the competition as their ship was commissioned nearly four months earlier, completed shakedown earlier, and arrived at Pearl Harbor two months earlier than *Yorktown*. That *Yorktown's* Air Group Five attacked Marcus minutes before Air Group Nine from *Essex* can be attributed more to the task force commander flying his flag from *Yorktown* than Jocko's exhortations. Jimmy recognized Jocko's tactic as a good motivating tactic, but he did not adopt it to any meaningful degree as an incentive for Air Group Five. It just did not fit his style, and he knew all too well that *Essex* was not the enemy. His judgment was, as always, to create no artificial competition but rather to deal with the practical details of tactics and specific challenges presented by combat.

Far more important to Jimmy than the *Essex* ploy were the problems within Air Group Five. Fighting Five and Torpedo Five enjoyed high morale, but Bombing Five had problems beyond those of their plane, the SB2C Helldiver. Two smaller squadrons were combined to form Bombing Five, and the squadron commander was chosen from one of the two groups thereby leaving the other unhappy. As personality problems were at the core of the squadron's unhappiness, Jimmy decided not to dictate happiness. He knew he did not have sufficient grounds to transfer half the squadron, which was apparently the only viable solution. Consequently, he basically ignored a battle he knew he could not win, and rather than attempting to channel personalities and emotions, he concentrated focus on training. Although Bombing Five did acquit itself admirably during the Marcus attacks, it did not form up according to plan during the predawn rendezvous, and that did lead to a change of squadron commander.

Initiative

With reference to constructive thinking and resourcefulness;
ability and intelligence to act on own responsibility

It is difficult to locate any fitness report for Jimmy after 1941 that does not contain a favorable reference to initiative in the "remarks" section of the form. Still, his initiative on one matter, though very much appreciated by his pilots and immediate superiors, was not well received at higher echelon, particularly Vice Adm. John Towers, commander of air forces in the Pacific (ComAirPac). In his 3 September 1943 Marcus Island action report, Jimmy wrote:

> The left turn after take-off is strongly recommended in preference to the right turn because it is easier and safer for the pilot of a heavily loaded modern plane to turn to the left at speeds near the stalling point. This is true because instead of fighting to overcome engine torque as is necessary in turning right, the torque is used to help the pilot turn left. This results in removing the slipstream from the bow area more quickly and will reduce take-off intervals by an average of five seconds with a well-trained group. It is recommended that all carriers investigate.

Neither *Yorktown* commanding officer Jocko Clark or task force commander, Rear Admiral Pownall, had any problems with the left turn maneuver. However on 5 August 1943, three weeks before the Marcus raid, Admiral Towers had forwarded the following message to Pownall:

> After due consideration it has been decided that any advantages resulting from take-off procedure involving aircraft making a left turn after leaving the deck are not sufficient to justify a change in the already established procedure for carriers of the U.S. Fleet . . . *Yorktown* comply with the latter procedure.

With no prevailing wind off Marcus on the morning of the attack, Jimmy requested permission to use the left turn to obtain every advantage possible for safe launchings. Clark and Pownall agreed. On 19 December, however, both Clark and Pownall received a letter from Towers stating that his 5 August letter was "a definite and categorical order which has not been subject to any subsequent modification. Commander Air Force, Pacific Fleet, not only expects, he demands compliance with orders, and directs a prompt explanation." Of course both responded to Towers with "we're sorry, it won't happen again" letters, but neither could resist defending the procedure one last time. Clark wrote, "It is a fact that pilots of this ship have preferred the use of the left hand turn, and . . . this ship has indicated certain advantages to be gained by its use." Pownall wrote, "The *Yorktown* when using it was habitually faster in her take-off procedure than were other carriers, which decidedly enhanced her tactical value to the Task Group."

Jimmy lost the "left hand" battle, but his initiative later proved to be yet another plus on his record. Such innovative and rational thinking endeared him not only to pilots in his command, but also enhanced his standing, as will be seen later, with aggressive task force commanders like Vice Adm. Marc Mitscher.

Admiral Towers (Naval Aviator No. 3) could well appreciate the proposed innovation, but he also knew that standardization of procedure was necessary. In time Jimmy became a champion of standardization, beginning with a plea to create a standardized system for assigning calls to combat patrol divisions. Such a system should be much simpler for the pilot and the FDO. In sum, Jimmy recognized an early need for standardized procedures to facilitate many of the innovations required to meet the ever-changing demands of war.

Force

With reference to moral power possessed and
exerted in producing results

During the Battle of the Coral Sea, F4F Wildcat fighters and fighter pilots were in short supply. Lt. (jg) Scott McCuskey lost contact with *Yorktown* (CV-5) and then lost two Wildcats by leading Ens. John Adams —who did have contact—to a forced landing on a desolate beach. Squadron commander Lt. Cdr. Charles Fenton subsequently grounded McCuskey for ignoring Adams's signals, and relieved him as section leader. With enemy planes inbound on 7 May, McCuskey, knowing the critical need for fighter pilots, ran to the flight deck, climbed into a Wildcat and prepared for takeoff. Scott desperately wanted to fly, and Jimmy very much wanted a pilot with Scott's skill and enthusiasm in the air. But Jimmy, then VF-42 executive officer, shook his head to indicate "no" and later recalled, "As much as I wanted to take him, I knew that to relax discipline at this point would ruin the whole idea behind punishment.[8] After Jimmy took off, Scott found another F4F being serviced, pleaded his case to Fenton (who rescinded the disciplinary action), and got a plane.

In 1992 retired Capt. Scott McCuskey, USN (Ret.), who had also earned a Ph.D. along the way, traveled to the second carrier *Yorktown* in Charleston Harbor to participate in a fiftieth-anniversary Battle of Midway symposium. Spotting Jimmy's eldest son in the audience, he momentarily digressed from his prepared remarks to recall the Coral Sea incident just related. McCuskey told the audience that in his opinion, no greater officer ever served the navy than the senior Flatley. At Coral Sea in a moment of extreme duress, McCuskey had learned a life-long lesson that transgression had a price. Time and again throughout his own military and education careers, Scott McCuskey cited Jimmy Flatley's calm, firm but compassionate administration of "moral power possessed and exerted in producing results." Jimmy knew the difference between compassion—which he had for Scott—and the dangers of empathy in a military context. Fenton, as was his prerogative, allowed McCuskey to fly, but Jimmy taught Scott a lesson for life.

Rear Admiral William Leonard recalled that "Jimmy was personal with hard-pounding ideas." The problems with radar during the Battle of the Coral Sea "bothered Jimmy and he was in an excited state of mind to do something about it." Never shy during World War II about expressing an opinion as to what was right or wrong, Jimmy did not drive people away by expressing his thoughts, in part because he was very easy to talk to and because he cultivated people. "We either agreed with him, cheered him on or argued with him." When Jimmy left *Yorktown* to form the Grim Reapers, Leonard remembers that all were sorry to see him leave.[9]

Moral Courage

With reference to that mental quality which impels one to carry out the dictates of his conscience and convictions fearlessly

Just as Jimmy proved to be a model and mentor for Scott McCuskey, he served in the same role for many others. Whitey Feightner recalled that after he shot down several planes—particularly one that he and Jimmy both chased—Jimmy said to him, "You're a fighting fool, aren't you." That was as close as Jimmy came to discussing killing the enemy. While Whitey dutifully read Jimmy's letter addressing religious matters the night before Santa Cruz, he equally grasped the depth of Jimmy's moral courage and convictions from the brief conversation after Rennell Island.

On another occasion Jimmy did speak at length on the subject of killing the enemy with another officer. While visiting the Von Tempsky ranch on Maui, a submariner—and future vice admiral—Lt. James F. Calvert, engaged Jimmy Flatley in a deep philosophical discussion about the "real world." Acknowledging he was aching for a better understanding of the killing and why it had to be done, Calvert asked which world was real, the kill-or-be-killed life aboard his submarine or the luxurious, leisurely dinners and warm company at the Von Tempsky ranch? In his 1995 book, Calvert recalls Jimmy's quick and memorable response.

Look, . . . why do you think these people have asked us over here to share their homes? We're here so they can express some of their gratitude for what we are doing for them . . . don't feel guilty about what we are doing in this war. I, too, feel sorry for those oil-soaked seamen, just as I do for the aviators we shoot down. But don't ever forget that the Japanese asked for this war, and unless we go after them hammer and tongs, the opportunity for this peaceful life on Maui . . . will be gone. . . . Take my advice and stop worrying about it.

Calvert heeded Flatley's words and after fifty years considered that conversation the most important part of his visit to the Hawaiian paradise.[10]

Another aspect of Jimmy's moral courage was honesty in reversing his position 180 degrees. While it is difficult for some to admit changing their mind on a policy or practice, Jimmy followed the dictates of his new understanding and conviction as fearlessly as he had defended an earlier, opposite position. The aforementioned Thach weave was one occasion. Another was written praise for formerly maligned Fighter Director Officer John Griffin. And less than a year after downplaying Bill Martin's ideas on certain uses of airborne radar, Jimmy wrote in his Marcus Island action report, "The island was located by airborne radar. Every effort must be made to perfect night radar scouting and bombing."[11]

Cooperation

With reference to the faculty of working harmoniously with others toward the accomplishment of common duties

While Jimmy did not consider his 1929 classmate and disputed VF-42 commanding officer, Lt. Cdr. Charles Fenton, a mentor, he nonetheless was pleased with Fenton's magnanimous spirit and high praise for Jimmy in his 25 May 1942 fitness report. Fenton recognized his executive officer's cooperative spirit by writing that Jimmy was "extremely capable . . . his services have been invaluable from the standpoint of both morale and tactical instruction . . . [and] he possesses the attributes of leadership in the highest degree and instills confidence in his subordinates."

Just as Fenton greatly appreciated Jimmy's cooperative spirit, so did his next immediate superior, Cdr. Richard Gaines. Gaines is not remembered as a warrior (some may not have known he had orders limiting his combat role), but he was a good administrator, cheerleader, and had the good sense to delegate to his squadron leaders. Further, he strongly championed ideas forwarded from his pilots on up the line. Gaines recognized his limitations and made the most of his strengths. Still, a definite sensitive touch and understanding were required of Jimmy in this relationship. While Gaines can be commended for delegating and deferring, Jimmy had the good sense not to take advantage, overstep the discretion informally ascribed to him, or to belittle his superior officer, directly or indirectly.

Cooperation with Fenton and Gaines depended upon Jimmy's understanding of conduct with superiors. Upon becoming commanding officer of Air Group Five, cooperation depended upon Jimmy being able to adequately delegate to squadron commanders working for him. In many respects, delegation of duties and responsibilities is more difficult than assuming or sharing responsibilities with a superior. With Fenton and Gaines, Jimmy was accepting an invitation "to eat more of the cake." With Air Group Five he had to give up portions of the cake—which he was tempted to keep for himself—to others. Without doubt, Jimmy had to make a conscious effort on numerous occasions to stay away from Charles Crommelin's Fighting Squadron Five. Mitigating Jimmy's intrinsic motivation to be more involved with the fighter pilots was his confidence in Crommelin. But just as good an illustration of Jimmy's cooperative spirit was his abstaining from interfering in the problems of Bombing Squadron Five.

While staying away from the internal matters of all three of his squadrons in Air Group Five, Jimmy nonetheless actively built a spirit of cooperation among all pilots by directly involving them in the most important issues pertaining to their success in combat and safety. Before teamwork can exist there must first be a team. By inviting all pilots in all squadrons to be directly involved in creating the comprehensive Marcus Island combat plan, Jimmy helped create the team and teamwork. During these meetings it was apparent to all that their air group commander was not only inviting but requiring input, that he wanted substance, that he was listening to suggestions and openly evaluating ideas. In short, Jimmy rated high marks for cooperation by knowing his own place on the team, and by creating a place on that team for all others by developing meaningful interaction.[12]

Loyalty

Fidelity, faithfulness, allegiance, constancy—all with reference to a cause and to higher authority

There is no better sample to document Jimmy's "fidelity, faithfulness, allegiance, constancy—all with reference to a cause and to higher authority" than the two separate letters he wrote to his wife on 20 January 1943. Earlier it was noted that religion, family, and the navy were not only components of his life but they were his life. The interrelationship between those components and his loyalty to them is best described here by his own words.

Darling, I notice a little bit too much impatience in some of your letters. Please don't. You know it's just as difficult for me to be away from you as it is for you to do without me. The biggest thing in the history of the world is happening. My part in it is infinitesimal as in every individual. However, working together, we are going to achieve victory in the shortest possible time. I must be where I can contribute the most to that effort. It is not for me to say where my post will be, but if it's near or on the front line, we must accept it. Let us not worry about the future. Rather let us be thankful for all the happiness of the past. It may be that I will be employed behind the lines. That, of course, will be wonderful. However, I know the needs of naval aviation as well as anyone today. I know the strength and character of our individuals. I know the record of each man who had combat experience. Actually there are very few. I know that my knowledge and leadership should be utilized in combat operations because it will win victories and save lives at the same time. I am not going to ask for any particular duty, but I am going to make sure that if I am not selected for training duty that I will be given a new air group to train. I fully expect that in the near future I will be given another job. I expect to get an opportunity to get home. However, if that new job involves getting an outfit ready to come back out and fight, I want you to be happy and thankful that we will have at least a few weeks or months together. As I have said before, our most difficult days are behind us.

[In the second letter he says:] Write and tell me that you will not be unhappy whatever comes to pass. You know that I love only you. I live only for you and you alone. But I am a naval officer, my solemn duty is to do all I can to help our nation win this war. That's my profession in addition to being my obligation. Think of the millions of men, volunteers, draftees, etc. Okay sweetheart. I know you are ten thousand percent in every way. I know it is difficult for you at times to accept the hardships imposed by war. So it is for all of us. Let us all be brave and patient, and put our trust in God.

After the war Jimmy traveled to Lima, Ohio, to visit with John Leppla's parents, and later with the families of other lost squadron mates. A 1953 party he organized at Los Alamitos, California, for all the Grim Reapers (with former POWs Albert Mead and Dusty Rhodes as guests of honor), fully demonstrated not only his loyalty and continuing care for his people but also reinforced the demonstrated principles he had imparted in earlier years.[13]

Perseverance

With reference to maintenance of purpose or undertaking
in spite of obstacles or discouragement

"Purpose . . . in spite of obstacles or discouragement" best describes the essence of Jimmy Flatley's life. In sum, Jimmy persevered because he had learned several of life's lessons the hard way.

One excellent example of perseverance related to combat is Jimmy's written farewell letter to the Grim Reapers. While some might initially dismiss that letter as only a sentimental epistle, there is within evidence of perseverance. While expressing genuine feelings for his men, he did not miss an opportunity to instruct them one last time. The salient principle Jimmy conveyed was that despite all their training, and all his lectures, *the pilots still reverted to basic instincts in combat rather than fighting together as a team.* In his autobiography, *A Proud American,* Joe Foss wrote that he studied Jimmy's tactical doctrine and praised him as a pilot and tactician. However, in his book and in the 28 April 1943 interview at the Marine Corps Public Relations Office, Foss describes his combat and that of his squadron mates as mostly individual dogfighting. The Thach, O'Hare, Flatley weave appears to have been used by most Reapers and the early marines on Guadalcanal only when required for defense. Still, the point is that Jimmy identified a primary issue of relevance and taught it literally to the last moment.

Reactions in Emergencies

With reference to the faculty of acting instinctively in a
logical manner in difficult and unforeseen situations

The ambush at Santa Cruz stands as the foremost example of Jimmy's capability to act "instinctively in a logical manner in difficult and unforeseen situations." Despite excruciating pain evoked as he watched squadron mates and friends fall out of formation, he was sufficiently steeled to function effectively as a fighter pilot and as a squadron leader. Had he not been "unflappable in combat," and always able to have coolly reacted to emergencies, he might not have survived Coral Sea, Santa Cruz, or later battles.

Emergencies were not restricted to combat. During a 1943 training exercise about 40 miles off San Diego, Jimmy, Bill Leonard and another pilot flew out to observe carrier landings. The third pilot, however, developed engine problems and went into the water. Jimmy quickly ordered Bill to leave the exercise and follow him. Flying low over the downed pilot, Jimmy could see the flyer was out of his plane but without his life raft. Jimmy extracted his own raft and with flaps down, dropped it. The struggling pilot, however, could not get to it, so Jimmy ordered Bill to stay over him while he flew off to a nearby ship for help. Regrettably, a ship arrived too late to save the man's life, but the sad result was not for lack of immediate and positive reaction to the emergency. In recalling the story, Leonard added that Jimmy would have suffered a similar fate had his engine quit, as he no longer had a life raft.[14]

Endurance

With reference to ability for carrying on under any and all conditions

Conduct during the Battle of Santa Cruz attests to Jimmy's endurance as well as to his ability to react in an emergency. With a broken bone in his foot he had a good excuse not to fly. Fortunately he had a boss (John Crommelin) who would give him benefit of the doubt in such situations.

Equally important was Jimmy's ability to carry on after emotional injuries. The episode with VF-42 could have caused a lesser man to have sulked and harbored feelings of disappointment, frustration, and discouragement. Jimmy actually turned a negative into a positive by volunteering to remain with the squadron as executive officer, by performing admirably in combat, and by impressing all not only with his fighting spirit but also his spirit of cooperation.

Industry

With reference to performance of duties in an energetic manner

The greatest regret shared by all members of Jimmy's family was his untimely and premature death, but a near unanimous second regret was the great amount of time Jimmy was away from his family. Recognized as a skillful pilot, an innovator of fighter tactics, and among the first to know the enemy in combat, he voluntarily forfeited many rest and recreation periods in order to teach young pilots how to win in combat and how to survive. Admiral Carmody noted that Jimmy "was a tireless instructor and spent much time with each of our three squadrons providing all the lore and experience he had acquired in his engagements with the Japanese."[15] While Jimmy held his family dear, his pilots were a second family, and the war was a threat to both. The long hours he was more than willing to expend on behalf of his navy placed him in a highly critical position for the last year of the war. His boss for that year wrote, "The success of the carrier operations in the many campaigns . . . was due in large part to Commander Flatley's knowledge, his planning ability, and above all—his willingness to work day after day around the clock."[16]

Leadership

With reference to the faculty of directing, controlling, and influencing others in definite lines of action

JIMMY FLATLEY'S CONCEPT OF LEADERSHIP

It is helpful to note Jimmy's thoughts on leadership via his own words. That he deemed "leadership" the major attribute for all members of his Grim Reaper squadron is evident by his placing it first among "the attributes necessary to ensure the success of a fighting squadron and its effectiveness." In his July 1942 "Combat Doctrine," he wrote under the heading of leadership:

> The degree of effectiveness attained by a squadron depends on the quality of the leadership to which it is subjected. Good leadership is based in part on certain intangibles inherent in the individual such as personality, patience, understanding, loyalty to others, aggressiveness, and the will to win. It is also based on piloting ability and a thorough professional knowledge of the problems involved. Every man is not blessed with the intangible qualities to the same degree, but he can win over natural shortcomings and develop into a good leader if he applies himself.
>
> In the air, good leadership requires that the formation leader, be he only a section leader, possess a high degree of initiative and skill, and that he be able to judge instantly when and how to attack the enemy in the most effective manner. (p. 5)

PERSPECTIVES ON JIMMY FLATLEY'S LEADERSHIP SUCCESS

Only those who served with Jimmy could determine whether or not he was an effective leader and explain why and how. Hal Buell remembers: "As a leader, Jimmy had some good answers to the pressing problem that the Zero was not invincible. We all wanted a genuine winner and Flatley (along with Thach, Foss, and Capt. Marion Carl, USMC) was one of the few whose demonstration in the air caused us to listen. We

[SBDs] felt that if we held a tight formation and did not panic, if a Zero made a pass on us we had a chance. Jimmy Flatley was positive, and made us feel we were going to be winners."[17]

Whitey Feightner, one of only a few who enjoyed first-hand knowledge pertaining to the differences in leadership between Jimmy Flatley and Butch O'Hare, recalled that Jimmy's "age had something to do with it," and the experience difference between the two was noticeable.

> Jimmy was a deeper thinker and more attuned to the broad picture of why we fight wars. Butch was more into the practical flying concerns although both had spirit and drive. . . . Jimmy was always very serious, and he thought deeply about life. War was no game to him. Often for the younger pilots, life was a day-to-day proposition, but Jimmy integrated what was happening today with what would happen tomorrow, next year and beyond. He saw big picture. At Guadalcanal, he knew what 11 transports could mean to the overall battle, and that's why he wanted to stop them all. He integrated strategic and tactical considerations.[18]

Off Guadalcanal, Jimmy not only controlled and directed his pilots with his instructive short radio speech while approaching the transports on 14–15 November but also instilled calm and confidence. On numerous combat occasions he demonstrated an unusual ability to simultaneously give directions, motivate, and calm. Unquestionably, this capability was a significant key to Jimmy's leadership success.

To Control, Direct, and Influence: Success and Failure among Jimmy's Contemporaries

During World War II there were a number of officers in all ranks who had proved themselves to be adequate to excellent pilots, staff officers, and leaders before the war. In combat most continued to perform satisfactorily while many excelled beyond expectations. One of Butch O'Hare's academy roommates and closest friends knew Butch would do his duty in peace and war, but was surprised when he won the Medal of Honor in his first aerial combat and then went on to additional distinction both as a warrior and leader.[19] Other naval officers were surprised at the wartime exploits of a few heroes, but there were some officers with excellent peacetime records whose combat performance rose neither to their own expectations nor to those of the navy.

As Task Force Fifteen approached Marcus Island on the last day of August 1943, Capt. George R. Fairlamb Jr., commanding officer of the *Independence,* became physically ill on the bridge of his ship and for a time was unable to command. Rear Adm. Samuel P. "Cy" Ginder also lost a meal off the Palau Islands in March 1944, suffered an apparent nervous breakdown, and could not continue to function. During the 1942 Guadalcanal campaign, Vice Adm. Robert Lee Ghormley kept his meals down but was not optimistic or aggressive in his conduct of operations. And off Marcus in August 1943, and again in the Marshalls in October, Rear Adm. Charles Pownall acted irrationally and with a dispiriting sense of caution. As a result of these problems, all four were relieved from their command. While one might be tempted to write off these officers as simply lacking courage, such single factor analysis does not do justice to the internal fortitude of the individuals or to the dynamics involved.

Admirals Ginder and Pownall demonstrated personal courage as aviators many times during their career, and Ginder had earlier performed well in combat. Fairlamb did not want to be relieved of his command and contested removal. And Ghormley's problems were not associated with personal courage. Impacting all, however, was the knowledge that their decisions affected the lives of hundreds to thousands. Being willing to risk their own lives was one thing; risking the lives of many was another. Indeed, higher command equated to greater potential for loss of life. The responsibility for so many lives in conjunction with sleep deprivation, diet, and overall health pushed stress levels beyond Fairlamb and Ginder's capability to perform. Flight surgeons were required to assist administratively in Fairlamb's removal, while Pownall was doubtless affected by the pacifist teachings of his Quaker background. Ghormley, like Pownall, apparently had difficulty understanding the value of aggressive action. After losing the South Pacific command in October 1942, Ghormley's pessimism and defensive attitude found further expression in early 1943 when he championed the building of costly bomb shelters at then relatively secure Pearl Harbor.[20]

During the early months of the Pacific war there were several competent carrier fighter squadron commanders. Lt. Cdr. Paul Ramsey with VF-2 and Lt. Jim Gray with VF-6 were quite effective. But the names Jimmy Flatley, Jimmie Thach, and Butch O'Hare rise to a peak of special distinction when that period of the war is revisited. Flatley, Thach, and O'Hare stand apart from the others on the basis of (1) exceptional competence; (2) their creative insights in developing aerial tactics; (3) their recognition of a need for change; and (4) their remarkable ability to transfer personal confidence and manner of combat to their squadron mates.

Flatley, Thach, and O'Hare had eighteen aerial victories in the first fourteen months of the war; and as a group they had earned by 1 February 1943 one Congressional Medal of Honor, one Distinguished Service Medal, three Navy Crosses, and two Distinguished Flying Crosses. Many more decorations were awarded to the trio for later service. Although O'Hare never had an opportunity to fly in any of the four major carrier-versus-carrier battles in 1942, Jimmy Flatley fought in the Coral Sea and Santa Cruz battles while Thach fought at Midway. Their collective experience was invaluable not only for future combat, but also for training.

While Jimmie Thach must be recognized as the most creative innovator of the three, his tactical insights needed validation from proven fighter pilots of equal esteem for these insights to achieve full results. Jimmy Flatley and Butch O'Hare possessed such status in mid-1942, primarily due to their demonstrated competence. Their adoption and adaptation of Thach's innovations quickly spread implementation of the successful tactics to other fighter pilots. The ultimate result was confidence among pilots of individual and collective victory.

Change is seldom easy. Before and during World War II, change in thought as well as actions was difficult for many naval officers. Secure within himself as a person, a pilot, and as a naval officer, Jimmy Flatley consistently did not let the path to an ultimate objective be derailed by refusing to consider another line of thinking. The paramount example was his willingness in the summer of 1942 to abandon the six-plane division in favor of four. This not only documents his ability to see a need for change (albeit not immediately), but also his willingness to change even when there was potential for extreme embarrassment. Jimmy had made a navy-wide argument for the six-plane division in "The Navy Fighter" letter. To Jimmy's everlasting credit, when Butch O'Hare convinced him of the value of the four-plane section to facilitate the mutual beam defense, he promulgated it with the same enthusiasm as his previous hypothesis.

Flatley, Thach, and O'Hare shared a number of similar distinguishing characteristics that enabled them to successfully transfer their personal confidence and combat tactics to others. Thach related through an almost overwhelming personality of ebullience and ability to communicate. O'Hare, though a very pleasant person, was a man of few words, his leadership more often evident by actions rather than words. Jimmy Flatley possessed neither the enjoyable flamboyance of Thach nor the endearing shyness of O'Hare, but his paternal style of teaching and deft personal counseling served him well. But paramount among the personal similarities of the three officers was their inner security that allowed them to delegate both responsibility and authority, each of which is worthless without the other.

Flatley, Thach, and O'Hare's personal security and self-confidence greatly facilitated the training of their pilots. Choosing the right moment to delegate responsibility and authority was a gift possessed by all three. Delegation allowed for individual pilots to develop discipline within and grow to the limit of their respective capabilities. Once given responsibility and authority, subordinates could clearly see the goals that needed to be met and have a clear understanding of their role. A role with responsibility defined status, thereby helping a subordinate maintain esteem—how he viewed himself; and prestige—how he viewed himself through the eyes of others. High morale and productivity was the result as each subordinate had meaningful control over his own vested interests of security, both physical and social. And although probably not given much thought at the time, there was a peripheral benefit of eventual favorable remembrance that accrued to Jimmy Flatley and other officers of the era who understood how to delegate.

In viewing the benefits of being remembered favorably that Flatley, Thach, O'Hare, and others enjoyed, it may be advantageous to look at illustrations wherein one's legacy of leadership is not now what an individual would have preferred or intended. Any Naval Academy graduate is familiar with the term "ring knocker." Officers assigned this derisive appellation are those who take themselves and their roles in the well-defined navy society quite seriously, and are quick to remind others of their real or self-perceived exalted status. Strict protocol, discipline, and formality characterize such persons. They could further be defined as adhering to the ideal expressed in Plato's *Republic* of "the philosopher king," a member of the elite expected to lead by having a personal knowledge of that which is good and right. Some less inclined to defining this sort of person along sociological or philosophical lines refer to "a blueblood aristocracy." Regardless of the definition, many officers remembered for their elevated sense of their own worth have had successful careers, even great careers, but their legacy invites consideration. One example illustrates how too great a concern with status and self-esteem resulted in a tainted and prejudicial remembrance.

For many years after the Battle of Midway, some survivors of *Hornet*'s air group were reluctant to discuss their air group commander, Cdr. Stanhope C. Ring. The main reason was to keep focus on the exceptionally heroic sacrifice of the twenty-nine pilots and gunners lost from Torpedo Squadron Eight who flew into battle from *Hornet,* and the sixteen lost from the same squadron (detached) who flew from Midway Island. Other reasons include respect for Ring's personal courage, his family, and an inclination not to complain about the weight another person has had to bear. Ring had good reason to take himself seriously. He had been an outstanding student at the academy (class of 1923), was a good boxer, and handsome. Under his yearbook picture in the Naval Academy's 1923 *Lucky Bag,* the text begins with the sentence, "Isn't he handsome?" Capt. Albert K. "Bert" Earnest who was the only survivor among the six VT-8 (detached) TBF pilots that flew from Midway during the battle recalled in 1996 that Ring "looked better than Gregory Peck on a good day."

Before the war, Ring demonstrated courage during rescue operations while assigned to patrol planes, and was awarded a Navy Cross after the war began for attacking a cruiser off Midway on 6 June 1942. But Ring's bearing, formality, and insistence on protocol while the air group were training and on the first day of the critical Midway battle served him poorly. Just before leaving Hawaii before the Battle of Midway, he had a near mutiny on his hands, some of his men telling him to his face how little they thought of him.[21] He "was mean to his people, and had a low threshold for criticism."[22] These documented incidents suffice to make the point, but there are troubling reports from survivors of the Battle of Midway pertaining to the degree of disagreement between Ring and Lt. Cdr. John Waldron, VT-8's CO, as to the location of the enemy carriers on 4 June.

It is well known that Waldron found the enemy without difficulty and that Ring not only did not find the enemy, but also lost all ten escorting fighters due to fuel exhaustion. Ring's lack of combat experience was a factor in not locating the Japanese, but some students of the battle will continue to question Ring's perception of leadership that might have betrayed him in not deferring to Waldron's insightful advice. Further, these students well know that the large *Hornet* strike group, had it found the enemy, could have attacked the one carrier that survived the near simultaneous *Enterprise-Yorktown* morning air assault that fatally damaged *Akagi, Kaga,* and *Soryu.* Even one bomb on the deck of *Hiryu* during the morning of the fourth could have precluded the attack launched from her deck that led to the loss of *Yorktown.* In sum, Ring's emphasis on formality and protocol did not help morale on the eve of battle and may have contributed to his command failure on the first day of the Battle of Midway. Even though promoted to rear admiral in 1950 and advanced to vice admiral on the basis of combat decorations at retirement, his otherwise successful career is clouded by his manner of leadership and failures on 4 June 1942.

The lengthy examples above demonstrate that Jimmy Flatley, Jimmie Thach, and Butch O'Hare controlled and directed their pilots in definite lines of action by demonstrating competence and conveying a genuine interest and respect. Their method of leadership was effective and thereby influenced those serving with them to adopt their leaders' characteristics and then pass them on. By contrast, Commander Ring was not as competent at Midway as some of his subordinates, attempted to control his people by fear and insistence on protocol, and was therefore unable to direct effectively.[23]

"In the history of mankind there have been those rare individuals who seemingly have been created and endowed with unusual qualities but somehow held in reserve, to arise at the time of urgent need to exercise the qualities of leadership and dedication so necessary for national survival. Such a man was Jimmy Flatley."[24] Another pilot stated,

> Those few days of combat action (Guadalcanal, November 1942) will long be remembered by all of us. Our survival is a testament to the leadership and dedication of our coach, Jimmy Flatley. Little did we realize that his lessons in leadership would be repeated many times by those of us who returned for second tours during World War II. In my case I'm sure I emulated these leadership qualities throughout my career in the Navy. Despite the fact that Jimmy was relatively short in stature, I always think of him as being a giant among our leaders in World War II.[25]

Jimmy Flatley would unquestionably be humbled by the words of Vejtasa, Leonard, Burke, Buell, Feightner, Carmody, and many others who equate his name with leadership. But perhaps the words most meaningful to someone who never knew him might be Jimmy's own words recorded in the two letters written to his wife on 20 January 1943. In reference to his lost Reapers at Santa Cruz, Jimmy alluded to his "suggested prayers" letter and then confided to Dotty, "I shall always feel that as their commanding officer, I did all I could for them in every way." Indeed, how many other officers, then and now, can say the same for those they have led or may lead into combat?

Cold War

Corpus Christi

In October 1945 Jimmy loaded Dotty and their four boys into a 1941 Plymouth and set out from Coronado for Corpus Christi, Texas. Although the car could carry eight passengers, only six made the journey. Longtime friend, housekeeper, and nursemaid Jeanette Ebelmann married and remained in Coronado. Jimmy's eighty-two-year-old father and sixty-seven-year-old mother journeyed to Wisconsin from California, but rejoined the family later in Texas.

On 22 October Jimmy again joined Jocko Clark. The irony of being together in a training command (Jacksonville) just before World War II and then again immediately after the war was not lost on the two. But that was only a passing thought. What interested both was the fact that Jimmy enjoyed handling many of the administrative details that Jocko didn't, and Jocko was very happy to have a self-starter as his director of training—especially since nearly all his wartime staff had left the service or been otherwise reassigned. Though unspoken, the friendship between the two was now even stronger as a result of their time together on the new *Yorktown* and on the same combat team for the last year of the war. Also unspoken was their mutual appreciation for knowing each could count on the other to do whatever was necessary. In many respects the tour at Corpus Christi was almost a sabbatical for both from late 1945 until Jocko was reassigned in September 1946 to Washington, D.C., as assistant chief of naval operations (air).[26] Jimmy remained at Corpus Christi another ten months after Jocko left and served under Rear Adm. C. A. F. Sprague, a renowned combat veteran and personal friend as well as professional colleague.

Corpus Christi was still an intermediate training base in late 1945, taking students from primary training to relieve pressure on those bases and preparing fledgling pilots for the next phase, advanced training. With the end of the war, demobilization led to amalgamation of the Primary and Intermediate Training Commands, and Jocko traded his "Chief of Naval Air Intermediate Training" title for "Chief of Naval Air Basic Training." Pensacola and Corpus Christi were retained for all flight training except for advanced training, which remained at Jacksonville. As director of training, Jimmy settled into his job to help produce twelve thousand graduates a year, a substantial number but many less than the fifty thousand required had the war continued. In addition to producing new pilots, the command also provided training for flying boat and multi-engine aircraft, mostly on satellite fields—auxiliary naval air stations—at both Pensacola and Corpus Christi.

After 1 November 1945, Primary Training, Intermediate Training

Command, Advanced Training, Technical Training for Aircrewmen, and Naval Air Reserve Training formed the Naval Air Training Command with headquarters at Pensacola. At Pensacola in the director of training billet was Jimmie Thach, so once again the two former task force operations officers worked together in a complementary relationship. Both Jimmy Flatley and Jocko were constantly in the air, flying to meetings or graduation exercises at Pensacola, those flights comprising most of Jimmy's hours to maintain flight pay. Within months of his fortieth birthday, Jimmy was content to occasionally take the controls of a multiengine plane or the single-engine two-seat SNJ. For the remainder of his career he lifted off the ground only three times in a fighter: twice in a Hellcat (administrative) and one last time on 8 October 1947 for a familiarization flight in the Grumman F7F Tigercat twin engine fighter.

Among Jimmy's contributions at Corpus Christi was his role in eliminating one plane from the navy's inventory and assisting with the development of the navy's most visible recruiting program. Before Jocko departed for his next assignment, Jimmy personally initiated and began supervision for the transition from the Stearman biplane to the low-wing monoplane SNJ as the primary trainer. Citing earlier elimination of inept students, radical reduction in accident rates both in training and in the fleet, and noting that once naval aviators earned their wings they would not again fly biplanes, Jimmy had no difficulty converting Admiral Sprague.

For the immediate postwar years the greatest challenge was to find a method to maintain national defense with fewer people and dollars. Demobilization and greatly reduced budgets were especially painful to naval aviation. Still, there was a need to present a favorable public image and to recruit new pilots and sailors. The idea of a flight demonstration team was not new, the "Three Seahawks" and other teams having performed long before the war. But on 24 April 1946, Fleet Adm. Chester W. Nimitz, then chief of naval operations, ordered Vice Adm. Frank Wagner, chief of naval air training (Pensacola) to organize a navy flight exhibition team within the Naval Air Advanced Training Command. Later the team would become the Blue Angels, the name inspired by a New York nightclub. Selected to lead the team was Butch Voris, one of Jimmy's original Grim Reapers who had survived the war and risen in rank to lieutenant commander. Another former Reaper on the team was Lt. Maurice Wickendoll. Former Reaper Dusty Rhodes, released from a Japanese POW camp where he had been since the October 1942 Battle of Santa Cruz, joined in 1947.

In the team's first shows only three Hellcats were used in the air with a fourth plane, an SNJ, painted to look like a Japanese Zero. The routine usually ended with the SNJ releasing smoke and diving as in a crash. To make the show more realistic, Voris decided to have the pilot of the "Zero" bail out, a stunt easily performed as the SNJ was a two-seat trainer and the man in the second seat could throw a flight suit filled with sand from the plane. On one occasion, however, the man in the other seat—apparently never trained in aerial ordnance—dropped the dummy directly onto the VIP section, hurting none of the scampering VIP's but seriously damaging several folding chairs and navy pride. Voris, well known for his humorous antics, anticipated retribution from the attending brass but instead received only a plea to reduce realism. A few years later an unintentional sonic boom created during a show after the "Blues" transitioned to jets broke glass over much of the host city. A local newspaper noted on the following day that "if these were the angels, how bad could it get when the devils showed up?"[27]

While the early shows were great crowd pleasers, Admiral Wagner ordered a change. Jimmy Flatley and Thach reminded Wagner that the basic fighter formation was still four planes in two sections. Consequently, the Blues were instructed to develop a routine using four planes and to add the Thach Weave to their program. While propeller-driven Hellcats, Bearcats, and SNJ's along with the Thach Weave are long gone from the Blues program, the four-plane diamond formation was still in use at the end of the century.[28]

The Challenge of Communism

After two years at Corpus Christi, Jimmy was ordered to the Air War College at Maxwell Air Force Base, Montgomery, Alabama. Again the family loaded into the faithful Plymouth for a two-day drive east. Before another move, however, the family would be smaller as Jimmy's father passed away in 1948 at age eighty-five.

Arriving on 4 September 1947—ironically only fourteen days before the United States Air Force became an independent branch of the military—for a full year, Jimmy could concentrate on studying and writing about two of his favorite subjects: communism and unification. Although in an academic setting, Jimmy was far more interested in having his written ideas communicated to the larger audience of the navy and the nation rather than writing just for the staff at Montgomery. Papers written at the Air War College formed the basis for innumerable later articles, letters, and speeches.

Before Jimmy went to Europe in 1937, he had expected the Soviet Union to be the greatest threat to the United States. Chief among his concerns was that the economic philosophy of communism incorporated atheism. As the economic philosophy of communism transferred into political expression in the Soviet Union, Jimmy believed it was only a matter of time before "godless" communism and Christian democracies would engage in combat. World War II, he thought, was only an interlude in an existing and ongoing conflict. Among the files Jimmy carried to Montgomery was a twenty-five-page confidential report dated 16 April 1942, which he had written and which had been distributed by the vice chief of naval operations. The report, titled "Communist Party Propaganda and Espionage," discussed communists in the United States armed forces; and their activities within labor unions, private industry, local government organizations, and within the Negro community.

Jimmy, like most Americans of that day, truly believed that the communists in the Soviet Union meant exactly what they said when they spoke of transforming the world into a socialist utopia. It was not necessary to listen closely to communist pronouncements, as the actions of the Soviet military in Eastern Europe spoke eloquently regarding the destruction of democratic forms and way of life. On 13 May 1948 Jimmy submitted a twenty-one-page paper to the Air War College titled "Remarks Concerning Integration of Psychological Action in our National Effort to Defeat Communism." Drawing on the 16 April 1942 document noted above, Jimmy's thesis was that human relationships were the root of happiness and sorrow, success and failure. Extrapolating from this basic thought, he argued that world stability rested on man's ability to defend his freedom, and for the present (1948) he must prevail in the "Cold War" (which Jimmy defined as a psychological war). Not surprisingly, he introduced his views on the significance of Christianity and the role of the military. In sum he wrote, "It is reasonable to assume a nation's instinct to survive (including the USSR) is stronger than the impulse to invite certain destruction." Like many contemporaries, he believed "weapons of mass destruction and the totality of modern war" dictated "the futility and absolute impracticability of war." Missing from his analysis—again like that of so many others in the late 1940s—was the concept of limited wars and the role the navy could or would play in conflicts short of nuclear war.

Unification

In 1947 the Soviet Union did not have nuclear capability, but Jimmy's Air War College papers presumed the inevitability of what actually did occur later when the Soviets exploded their first atomic bomb. That explosion—detected in early September 1949—plus the Berlin Airlift in response to the Soviet closure of roads around that city (24 June 1948–12 May 1949), cemented the "we" versus "them" relationship between the free world and communist world. And coincidentally, the explosion of the Soviet nuclear bomb occurred during the height of the acrimonious verbal explosion between the U.S. Navy and the new United States Air Force ("The Independent Air Force" as Jimmy and many other naval officers termed it).

The concept of unification was well known long before 1947. As aviation developed in the army and navy after World War I, there were numerous discussions in the military and in Congress pertaining to unifying aviation into a single force. In 1925 the Morrow Board (the president's aircraft advisory board) report to President Calvin Coolidge and the House of Representatives' Lampert Committee addressed military aviation and rejected the idea of unifying army and navy aviation into a separate air force. But the idea did not disappear. On 6 December 1928 —Jimmy's last year at the Naval Academy—Rear Adm. J. M. Reeves, then commander of aircraft squadrons in the Battle Fleet, forwarded a lengthy letter to the chief of naval operations on the subject of "a Department of National Defense and a Unified Air Service." Reeves noted that the proposal under consideration would have the army, the navy, and "an additional department, comprising the air forces of the United States . . . [that] are supposed to be 'co-equal,' and are to be coordinated under the Secretary for Defense." Eighteen single-spaced typed pages later he concluded, "To summarize . . . I believe this proposed re-organization to be unsound in its basic conception, unsound in its detailed arrangement, unsound from the narrowest to the broadest point of view, and fraught with the gravest danger to the development of our national defense." Rear Admiral W. H. P. Blandy prepared a similar letter in October 1943, right in the middle of World War II. The views of Reeves, Blandy, and others expressed the U.S. Navy's majority opinion right up until 26 July 1947 when the National Security Act created the Department of Defense and the United States Air Force (18 September 1947).

Prior to 1939 motivation in Congress for unification centered primarily on the isolationist attitude following the Treaty of Versailles debacle after World War I and the severe depression that dominated the 1930s.[29] Great Britain and Italy set precedent by combining their aviation services before World War II, but the United States Navy could point to less than desirable results from those initiatives. Shortly after unification became a reality, Jimmy attempted a pull-together attitude in another Air War College paper, but he still expressed concern and misgivings by writing, "We can't afford a big Army, a big Navy, and a big Air Force . . . in peace or war . . . an insufferable situation.

Jimmy had begun his earnest battles to defend the honor and autonomy of the navy and naval Aviation in July 1942. Incensed then by an article in *Aero Digest* that had given undeserved credit to army air force B-17s and B-26s for their role during the Battle of Midway, Jimmy began a lifelong series of letters directly to national magazine editors and writers. By the time the unification debate surfaced in Congress just after World War II, Jimmy was well known to many of the major magazine and newspaper editors of that time (plus a number of congressmen). Jimmy's directness in his writing ("Seldom have I read a more vicious, biased, unfounded report on any subject . . . it is simply another step in the drive for a separate air force") got him off to an unfavorable relationship with several editors.[30] But over time, professional encounters with editors led to personal relationships with many of them. As a recognized war hero and later as an officer of flag rank, Jimmy and his letters were not dismissed. Further letters from Jimmy followed replies of substance, and he developed solid lines of communication through the unification debate, the "revolt of the admirals," and his several air station and ship commands. That these professional relationships became personal is best documented by the volume and tone of the remembrances offered at the time of his death.

Still, Jimmy and the navy initially believed they lost the unification battle. Jimmy's thoughts and reasoning on the matter are best stated in his own words in a 12 June 1947 confidential letter (sent through official channels) responding to a request for input from Congressman W. S. Cole. "I think that initially the main purpose behind all the 'merger' and unification talk was to create a separate Department of Air." That said and elaborated upon, Jimmy then changed course to say that the military budget would be spread too thin to ensure quality. Given that, he suggested that all military aviation could flourish only as part of the new air force to "let it be the best . . . for national security." Jimmy suggested a system of joint procurement, education, and common basic training in boot camps, colleges, military academies, and aviation training.

Revolt of the Admirals

In July 1948 Jimmy completed his tour at the Air War College and was back in operations as assistant chief of staff, United States Atlantic Fleet, at Norfolk, Virginia. When the roles and missions debate of the respective services and consequent budgetary issues resulting from unification came to a head in 1949, Jimmy was only peripherally involved. But the debate was central to him and every other officer in the navy. Economy was a major factor because the rapidly shrinking postwar budget could not meet the desired levels of the three services or allow duplication of effort. A second major factor was the general attitude that any future war would be nuclear. Given the continuing deterioration of relations between the communist and free world, it was generally accepted that the Soviet Union would be the enemy to be met in combat (the 1949 communist takeover in China being too recent for in-depth consideration). The air force argued convincingly that the only deterrent to war was their capability to deliver nuclear weapons.

In early 1949 the United States Navy was unquestionably on the defensive. Although the National Security Act promised maintenance of the Marine Corps in the navy and the continued existence of naval aviation, major proposed budget cuts indicated otherwise. And statements from Louis A. Johnson, the new secretary of defense, seemed to confirm the navy's fears. The air force not only had proven its ability to deliver the heavy, 10,000-pound atom bomb, but also argued that the navy had no such capability, and for reasons of duplication should not develop the function. Whether or not duplication was desirable was a subject for debate. Navy capability was demonstrated by flights of the P2V-3C Neptune and—late in 1949—the new AJ Savage. Carrying ten thousand pounds, these two propeller-powered planes launched from *Midway*-class carriers and flew over five thousand miles. Further, there were plans on the drawing boards for new jet aircraft with markedly increased capability, plus there was authorization for a new aircraft carrier—*United States* (CV-58)—that would be large enough to accommodate and launch future nuclear-capable aircraft. Construction on the new carrier began on 18 April 1949. However, on 23 April, Johnson canceled construction without consulting either the chief of naval operations or the secretary of the navy, John L. Sullivan. Disgusted, Sullivan resigned. A political crony of Johnson's, Francis P. Mathews, was appointed as a successor. Owing his appointment and loyalty to Johnson, the new navy secretary was also burdened by lack of a navy background. Thus, many in the navy felt they had no sympathetic ear at the top in a time of political and economic crisis. Jimmy was offered the opportunity to become Mathews's aide but declined, privately referring to Mathews as "that stubborn, stupid Irishman."[31] Unlike former president Roosevelt, current president and former army officer Harry S. Truman did not have a full appreciation of naval aviation. He did, however, have an appreciation of the country's desire for military budget reduction and he expected his cabinet and military subordinates to find ways to economize.

From his first week of duty with the Atlantic Fleet in August 1948,

Jimmy had been active in putting together public relations programs with the navy reserves, newspapers, civic groups, and politicians at all levels to present the navy's value to national defense. Having just left a year of duty on an air force base, he had an understanding and appreciation of that service. In his 1948 "Training of Armed Forces Aviators" paper he had advocated combining basic training for all services—a far-reaching concept that has not yet been totally renounced. But he knew the air force leadership was so focused on obtaining funding for their service that they either did not understand, or want to understand, the still relevant role of the U.S. Navy. The Atlantic Fleet at the time was primarily occupied in providing a presence in the Mediterranean and Atlantic to counter communist initiatives. That function was mostly flag showing as the Soviet Union had not yet begun major construction of a blue water navy to threaten either of the two large navies still extant: the United States Navy and the Royal Navy. Still, the Soviets did have some three hundred submarines that could threaten commerce. Consequently, the second basic function of the Atlantic Fleet was to provide hunter-killer groups to counter the potential threat from beneath the surface. Training was the order of the day, but budget constraints limited effectiveness of all operations.

In August 1949 fallout from the unification debate and funding priorities came to a head in Washington, D.C. Jimmy had direct access via personal relationships or recent combat association to all navy representatives who were preparing to present the navy's case to Congress. Admiral Radford was to be the most effective witness before the House Armed Forces Committee while Capt. Arleigh Burke headed a special section (Op23) to research responses countering the effective air force public relations effort. Many others on the "Washington" team were close personal friends. One scheduled to speak before the committee in August was Capt. John Crommelin, but before he could be heard the hearings adjourned.

With the loss of brothers Richard and Charles in the closing months of the war, and having narrowly escaped death himself on both *Enterprise* and *Liscome Bay*, John Crommelin was in no mood to be silent. Convinced the navy, and especially naval aviation, was about to be politically and economically bled to death by Congress and the air force, John went public with a personal press conference on 10 September. Mathews then issued a 14 September directive that comments should be forwarded through proper channels. Among those who did so were Jimmy's cousin, Vice Adm. Gerry Bogan, then commander of the First Task Fleet. Bogan's confidential letter clearly stated that morale in the navy was at an all-time low. Admiral Radford's endorsement noted that most officers in the Pacific Fleet agreed with Crommelin and Bogan. In the end, Chief of Naval Operations Adm. Louis E. Denfeld did not disagree with the opinions of his subordinates. By the end of September John Crommelin had copies of Bogan's letter with Radford and Denfeld's endorsements. Emboldened with documentation for some of his earlier statements, Crommelin leaked the letters to the major national press organizations. Newspapers in Washington and throughout the country carried stories on Bogan's letter with a result that congressional hearings were reopened. Crommelin had told Jimmy "what his plans were," that Jimmy should keep his name out of the papers, and "that he hoped that a few of us would come through this crisis clean."[32]

Soon after, Gerry Bogan decided to retire. While there is no documentation to support his belief that he was being or was about to be forced to retire, he went to his grave in 1973 convinced the navy would have retired him had he not beaten them to it. In a 14 January 1950 letter, Jimmy wrote his cousin to say, "I believe it was a wise decision on your part to leave the service at this time and I am glad you are going out with your flag flying. I am no more satisfied with conditions today than you are."

When the hearings ended in October 1949, few initially felt the navy had won its case to save naval aviation or to secure adequate budget funding. But neither had the air force totally won as the inadequacies of its B-36 bomber had been exposed, and both services incurred embarrassment from the debate, hearings, and media accounts. Happily for the navy a new super carrier (CV-59) was approved on 30 October 1950 and named for former secretary of the navy and first secretary of defense, James V. Forrestal. In September 1950 Secretary Johnson was replaced, and most of the anguish and despondency of 1949 was forgotten in the summer of 1950 when the cold war became hot on the Korean peninsula.

13

Commanding Officer

NAS Olathe and USS Block Island

NAS Olathe

ON 10 APRIL 1950 Jimmy received notification to proceed to Naval Air Station Olathe, Kansas, and to assume duty as commanding officer effective 14 July. His immediate superior would be the chief of Naval Air Reserve training, NAS Glenview, Illinois.

This was not the assignment Jimmy was hoping to receive. On 5 June 1950 he wrote to the chief of naval personnel requesting a command at sea. Acknowledging that his staff duty with the Atlantic Fleet was technically sea duty, he nonetheless expressed "the hope that I would be given command of a ship before going to shore duty. It is true that after I was informed . . . that I was not to get a ship command I requested a command ashore and was given my present orders. However, this was done in order to obtain some consideration for a command billet and should not be interpreted as nullifying my expressed and continuing desire for a ship command at this time." Vice Adm. Felix B. Stump endorsed Jimmy's letter on the same date stating, "That such a Naval aviator of his qualifications desires most of all command of a seagoing ship as a preparation for future higher command and rank is proof of his own sound judgment." But, a letter from the chief of naval personnel on 22 June 1950 denying the request noted, "Having completed two years in a sea billet you are due for a shore tour . . . there are many more qualified officers than there are sea commands now available."

During a quick visit to Olathe in late June, Jimmy inspected his family quarters, directed minor changes to floor space, and got a briefing on extremes in climate, sandstorms, and windstorms. His initial impression of NAS Olathe was favorable and he reported, "I hope I can stay here long enough to enjoy the command and maybe make a few improvements, rename the streets after heroes of World War II and give each building a street number."[1]

On 18 August Jimmy again "let off a little steam" to Stump as he learned some juniors were receiving orders to command ships as a result of the Korean emergency. But he also admitted to another officer that he was happy with the Olathe assignment: "I feel that this experience as command experience is much more valuable to me than fighting paper in Washington." In the same October letter he expressed the view that the Korean War was over.[2] That, however, was before the Chinese intervened some six weeks later.

Purpose of the Base and Operations

One of twenty-seven stations located throughout the country when Jimmy arrived, the Naval Air Station at Olathe was a member of the Naval Air Reserve Training Command. Established 1 October 1942 as a primary training base, it was then utilized as headquarters for the Continental Division of the Military Transport Service before being converted to a Naval Air Reserve Station in 1946. After 1946 the primary mission had been to maintain the combat readiness of organized reserve squadrons. At Olathe the navy was not alone in 1950. Along with the Naval Air Technical Training Unit (Ground Control Approach School and Aircraft Control Tower Operators' School), NAS Olathe also hosted a Marine Air Reserve Training Detachment (MARTD) and two air force commands (2472nd Air Force Reserve and 130th AC&W Squadron). The Aircraft Control and Warning Squadron was an operational unit of the Air Defense Command and from late 1951 operated on a twenty-four-hour basis. The air force had no flight training program at Olathe when Jimmy arrived.

In spite of the rapid turnover of air force personnel, about fifteen hundred servicemen were aboard. Naturally for a reserve station, Saturday was the busiest day of the week. Nearly everyone hailed from Kansas, Missouri, and Nebraska, and as reservists they were civilians first and warriors second. Jimmy knew that reservists and civilians had won World War II, and he had to gauge the civilian mind-set to be effective in upholding navy standards. While not unhappy to work in such an environment, he nonetheless missed the interaction with professional peers. Reams of paper passed through typewriters as he filled that void with a stream of letters to peers at Norfolk, Washington, and world-wide locations ashore and afloat.

A major function of NAS Olathe, and therefore a responsibility for Jimmy, was to select men for the naval aviation cadet program. The quota for Kansas was usually about thirteen each month, a goal difficult to meet as the air force was accepting high school graduates for flight training. Some quota periods proved to be more difficult than others during Jimmy's tenure at Olathe, but he always sold the program with enthusiasm. Recruitment was directed to native-born or naturalized unmarried men, eighteen to twenty-seven years old, physically, mentally, and morally fit, and who had at least two years of college. If accepted, a cadet reported to Pensacola—earning $105 a month plus housing, board, medical, and uniform benefits—for sixteen weeks of preflight indoctrination followed by eighteen months of basic and advanced flight training. Successful completion earned the new ensign "wings of gold," and $350 a month plus permission to marry. An additional $80 went into the paycheck to support a wife. Two years of active duty were required with an option to join an organized reserved squadron. Twenty years of active association with the reserves made the officer eligible for retirement benefits at age sixty. Recruitment was facilitated by the National Selective Service Act as healthy young men knew they had to meet their military obligation in one manner or another. But, there was concern that too many AvCads would rise over time into command positions without the benefit of a four-year degree. Expansion of ROTC programs relieved this worry in coming years.[3]

Compounding Jimmy's procurement problem was the fact that not all companies in the eastern Kansas and western Missouri region were aware of the Universal Military Training and Service Act of 19 June 1951. The legislation required employers to grant a leave of absence to employees for the purpose of performing training duty in the armed forces of the United States and their reserve components. The problem was sufficiently acute that when army Lt. Gen. Maxwell D. Taylor was invited to speak during Armed Forces Week in May 1951, Jimmy asked his guest to address the reserve program, since discrimination existed in business, not only in job placement but also in advancement. Occasionally, Jimmy had to write letters referring employers to the Department of Labor, Division of Veterans Reemployment Rights. Additionally, some reservists found it difficult to find employment in the region because of their reserve training obligations. Therefore, Jimmy solicited help from the *Kansas City Star*. His message was that in addition to lack of patriotism involved in discriminating against reservists, there was a great danger that young men would be afraid to join any of the armed forces reserve organizations. The newspaper agreed that if the problem continued it could result in a national calamity.

For Jimmy's entire tenure at Olathe, the major concern was rapid growth and expansion primarily due to the Korean War. When he took command, the station's runways were too short to handle jets, and new lights for runways and approach were needed. Both the navy and air force wanted new barracks and aircraft hangars, not to mention additional housing and recreational facilities. In the summer of 1950 there were adequate quarters only for the CO and XO, and no married enlisted men lived on the station. Growth required more adjacent land, and before he left in July 1952, Jimmy had overseen a multimillion-dollar program of acquisition and construction plus plans for improved highways between Olathe and Kansas City.

Although planning and implementation for the station's growth took most of his time, Jimmy made time to address personnel concerns. Policy at Olathe had been for station medical and dental clinics not to provide care to dependents. Jimmy opened these services to dependents on a "not to interfere" basis, but the dental officer took particular offense. Consequently, Jimmy referred the matter to his boss, Rear Adm. A. K. Doyle, who responded in November 1950, "You are the senior officer on the spot and are in the best position to judge your needs." Another problem was handling marital problems, a matter Jimmy could draw upon his own past for direction. Believing the navy shared responsibility with the parents of minors for their proper supervision, Jimmy experienced several occasions wherein his counseling and position precluded young sailors from marrying under extenuating circumstances. And as more and more youngsters were required to fill the reserve squadrons, Jimmy moved to retard exposure of alcoholic beverages on the station to underage sailors.

VF-884 and the Korean War

When Jimmy requested command of a ship in his 5 June 1950 letter to the chief of naval personnel, he was thinking of a carrier. But one of the reasons he had not received orders to command a carrier was the paucity of carriers in commission. In June 1950 only fifteen carriers were active. The three battle carriers of the *Midway* class rotated duties throughout the North Atlantic and Mediterranean. Four *Essex*-class carriers, four *Independence*- and *Saipan*-class light carriers, and four escort carriers rounded out the available slots for carrier commanding officers. Jimmie Thach had one of the escort carriers, *Sicily* (CVE-118). As Thach was two years senior to him, Jimmy could partly understand why Thach had one of the coveted posts, but the other part of him could not shake the memory that both he and Jimmie Thach had received temporary promotion to captain at the same time.

Carriers were not the only ships in short supply. Since the end of World War II manpower was insufficient to keep ships of all types fully manned. Ships in commission only two years were showing rust to a degree unseen during World War II, and some ships missed deployments due to personnel problems. Naval aviation had forty-one thousand planes when the war ended but was down to fourteen thousand in June 1950. While the navy did have fifteen carriers in commission, only one—*Valley Forge* (CV-45) was in the Far East. Three other *Essex*-class carriers were on the West Coast along with Thach's escort carrier. This was the carrier deployment and availability when the country unexpectedly found itself with another war in the western Pacific.

Attention had been so focused on the Soviet Union and Eastern Europe since the end of World War II that the communist takeover in China in 1949 came as a surprise to many Americans. With two strong communist allies at her back, North Korea invaded her neighbor to the south, and North Korean troops streamed across the thirty-eighth parallel into South Korea on 25 June 1950. A Japanese protectorate after the Russo-Japanese War of 1904–1905, the country was annexed by Japan in 1910 and then divided in 1945 into a northern zone occupied by the Soviets and the southern zone occupied and administered by the United States. All parties had agreed to the eventual reunification of Korea, but the communist influence in the north and democratic experience in the south, the 1950–1953 "police action," and the following decades of animosity have rendered that goal all but unrealistic.

Despite not being on a carrier stationed off the embattled peninsula, Jimmy watched with great interest and more than a little satisfaction as many of his predictions and those of other naval officers materialized. Budget woes began to disappear, and the major worry among some officers was that the conflict would end before they could get into the fray.[4] Early North Korean success in nearly pushing an unprepared South Korean army and handful of American advisers into the sea was reversed by the brilliant 15 September 1950 Inchon landings and counterattack leading to the subsequent march up the peninsula almost to the border of China. The hastily assembled United Nations forces, primarily comprised of American troops led by Gen. Douglas MacArthur, justified their march deep into North Korea to destroy an aggressor army. China, concerned with an advance to her borders, gave warning of intervention unless the United Nations troops returned to the thirty-eighth parallel. Their dismissal of the warnings led to Chinese intervention in late November 1950, and the fighting did not conclude until July 1953 after President Dwight D. Eisenhower threatened to use nuclear weapons.[5]

The Korean War placed the unification conflict in abeyance for reasons beyond mere economics. Coming so soon on the heels of the August and September 1949 congressional hearings, Korea presented hard cold facts to counter the theoretical arguments presented by the air force. First, despite geographical obstacles, a hostile population, and lengthening lines of communications (including lack of control of the air and no navy worthy of the name), North Korean forces had marched some two hundred miles south in the first two months of war. Air force B-29s rained tons of bombs on the enemy's troop columns and transportation nodes vulnerable to air attack, but strategic bombing did not stop the advance. A second lesson was the realization that neither the air force nor army could get to Korea without the navy, and that the growing naval armada was the force that protected the flow of logistics. Certainly, no ground troops wished for a diminished carrier force that was incapable of quickly providing tactical support. The navy's seagoing artillery, so recently forgotten by the army, again demonstrated its value, often turning the enemy's flank near the coast in addition to disrupting rear-area communications and destroying tanks and artillery. The economics of casualty rates also drew notice, as surface ships were all but immune from enemy reprisal.[6]

Although he would have preferred being at the helm of a carrier in the Yellow Sea off Korea's western coast or the Sea of Japan to the east, Jimmy did participate from far away Kansas as one of the reserve units in his command entered combat. Before the war was over he did obtain command of a newly activated escort carrier, but it was not one of the sixteen carriers that did operate off Korea over the three years of war.

During Jimmy's tenure at Olathe, Fleet Air Service Squadron (FASRON) 885 and Marine Air Reserve Fighter Squadron VMF-215 were recalled to active duty from his command. FASRON 885 transferred to NAS Alameda while VMF-215 reported to El Toro, California. But Olathe's VF-884, called to active duty in August 1950, was ordered to sea duty aboard the USS *Boxer* (CV-21) and to combat in early 1951. Assimilation into the operating fleet was not smooth, but the "Bitter Birds" of VF-884 nonetheless distinguished themselves in combat. Flying F4U Corsairs with TF 77, the VF-884 pilots destroyed scores of enemy ground targets. During their eight months over and off Korea, the squadron flew over fifteen hundred missions.

Although Jimmy had to fight the war from Kansas, he was not as far removed from some of the more unwelcome tasks of war. Once again he was writing letters to young widows and mothers, only this time they were neighbors, and he had to assist with the return of remains and funerals.

As reservists joined their units for active duty, families were left behind. Wives (VF-884 had a particularly effective Weekend Warriors Wives Club) and other family members naturally looked to the station for news concerning not only husbands and sons, but also news concerning the welfare and activities of the units. Jimmy lobbied for a closer working liaison within the navy for improved and more frequent personal news dispatches from the operating squadrons. The improvement eventuated, and a better flow of communication disseminated to families lifted morale both at Olathe and off Korea. Still, the loss of six pilots in combat, one quarter of the squadron's pilots, caused Jimmy to question the advisability of sending squadrons of the organized reserve to combat duty as units. His thinking was that regulars should first be called to meet the new combat needs in Korea.[7] In a letter requesting information on the F9F's performance in combat he added, "I hope that if we are going to order more organized squadrons to duty that we won't wait until the last minute to let them know. . . . They need all the lead time they can possibly get."[8]

When VF-884 returned from combat, Jimmy worked with Kansas City officials to set up a parade and formal luncheon to honor the squadron on Armistice Day in November 1951. Jimmy had also planned to announce during the luncheon that he had convinced the navy to name the airfield for Lt. Cdr. Glenn F. Carmichael, the squadron's former commander. Carmichael, who was a resident of Kansas City, had been killed in action 24 May 1951. The navy, however, declined Jimmy's suggestion for the reason that selections for such an honor should be based on only a few personnel worthy of distinction. But the navy was amenable to the return of recovered bodies (including Carmichael), a decision that proved a boost for local morale. Ironically, the unnamed field was later named for Jimmy after his death.

Floods, Speeches, and Departure

In several early Olathe speeches Jimmy said, "I consider civil defense to be the first requirement of any national security plan because for the first time in our history our base of operations, the continental United States is vulnerable to attack from other continents."[9] As it turned out,

Jimmy's most significant association with civil defense did not involve anything radioactive. Heavy rains precipitated flood conditions around Lawrence, Kansas, a city of twenty-two thousand at that time, situated just over thirty miles northwest of Olathe. The rain fell between 23 June and 1 July 1951, and then again 11–20 July. Over half a year's normal rainfall fell in less than a month, causing local rivers to rise as much as twelve feet above flood stage. Requests for assistance in repairing and reinforcing dikes and levees along the Kaw River resulted in 210 men from NAS Olathe joining the battle against the flood waters. This number did not include Jimmy, who of necessity abandoned supervisory functions and spent one night filling sandbags, along with his oldest son. Reinforced dikes generally held during the first flood, but the second was too much for the efforts of man. Business and civic leaders in Lawrence attributed the effort of Jimmy's sailors, marines, and airmen to have been largely responsible in holding damage to the city to a minimum. In addition to answering calls for assistance for specific projects, Jimmy's troops provided drinking water, soup kitchens, electric power necessary to continue sandbagging the levee, medical emergency stations, ambulances, flood lights, trucks, radios, life preservers, bedding supplies for shelters, and even clothing. Active in evacuating families in the threatened areas before the dikes broke and took over forty lives, the Olathe naval personnel were even more active and courageous in braving raging flood waters in boats to save lives. In the weeks after the floods, letters of thanks and commendation from the navy, governor of Kansas, Red Cross, local chamber's of commerce, and even the air force arrived on Jimmy's desk.[10]

Within days of his arrival at Olathe, Jimmy had written to a friend, "I am not a particularly competent speaker, but I do have some very definite ideas and . . . the confidence of my own convictions."[11] Jimmy's professional peers knew he had definite ideas, confidence, and convictions, and despite his deprecating assessment, they also knew he was an effective speaker. In the next two years over three hundred civic and college groups in the Kansas and Missouri region were soon to learn the same. With the Korean War only weeks old and interest high, Jimmy was in constant demand. He soon wrote his boss, "As a result of the article in the *Star* . . . I am being deluged with requests from all around the compass. I will comply to the limit of my time."[12]

Speeches were extremely important in Jimmy's thinking.[13] He strongly believed in maintaining an alert, informed citizenry and was particularly concerned about a false sense of security. Convinced the United States had a moral obligation to lead the world to real peace, he stated that "our future security depends on the men in our country who make public opinion."[14]

Having a message to share, Jimmy set out to influence local public opinion. Among his topics were Navy Supply Corps operations highlighting not only how the navy accomplished its objectives in a commendable manner, but also how the navy worked with the civilian sector in procuring and distributing everything required to meet the needs of ships, planes, and people. Jimmy knew that people were interested in other people so human interest stories comprised a significant part of his speech material.

As usual Jimmy stayed abreast of social, economic, and political factors that influenced decisions on the military. Reading several leading newspapers and magazines, he also pored over impending legislation relative to the armed forces. In speeches throughout the Kansas City area he stressed the strategic importance of Formosa in the Far East. Always carrying along a map of the world, he pinned it on a wall or set it on an easel before going into a point-by-point discussion. Chief among his subjects was push-button war, followed closely by avocation for a national psychology against communism. His standard speech—which President Truman heard about and requested a copy—was titled "World Power." Topics covered were geopolitics, industrial and military power, Soviet objectives and strategy, and American postwar foreign policy. The speech culminated with comments on success requirements to maintain peace.[15]

Jimmy made innumerable thirty-minute speeches at college and university fraternity houses pertaining to the Naval Aviation Cadet Training Program. Most presentations were made at the University of Kansas, Kansas State, and the University of Missouri; but he was just as happy to travel to smaller colleges. But all of the running around cost money, and over time Jimmy began to feel the pinch, enough so that he recommended the navy take a cue from Col. W. Oscar Brice (soon to become the director of Marine Corps aviation) on how the Marines had obtained an allowance of $100 a quarter for a public relations fund.

Over four hundred friends, including the top business and civic leaders from the greater Kansas City area, gathered at the Hotel Muehlebach to pay tribute to Jimmy and his wife at a farewell dinner, the highlight of the 1952 Armed Forces Week. This time the region chose to honor him instead of having him set up a program, for he had become one of the most highly visible and active leaders in the Kansas City area. Cited in a series of three-minute "words of praise and appreciation," Jimmy listened to speeches regarding his "quiet courage, his great ability and just plain good-neighborliness." Jimmy responded, "You are friends of the Navy and through me you are honoring the Navy. I accept it, but only for the men of my command, the Navy, Marine Corps and Air Force men at the air station who are ready to do anything at anytime for their community."[16]

Jimmy had championed the idea of naming streets within the growing complex for naval aviators from the region lost during World War II. Before leaving Olathe he personally conducted the dedications, one being Ault Road in honor of Cdr. William B. Ault, *Lexington*'s air group commander who died in the Battle of the Coral Sea. After his departure, the navy recognized Jimmy's achievements by presenting him with The Naval Air Reserve Award, "In recognition of the outstanding contribution made to the Naval Air Reserve Program by NAS Olathe under your command." The presentation made him one of only three individuals to receive the award in the first seven years of its existence, and the first individual to be recognized. The Blue Angels were a later recipient of the award.

USS Block Island (CVE-106)

When the Korean War broke out in June 1950, Jimmy thought he should have been on the bridge of one of the four escort carriers then in commission. Though he came to enjoy his duty at Olathe, he had let nearly everyone in the navy know he wanted a ship, "preferably one that floats." Knowing his oldest son would be entering the Naval Academy soon and that all the family liked Norfolk, Jimmy hoped he could command a ship operating from the East Coast.[17]

In April 1952 Jimmy learned he was about to receive command of an escort carrier, but he was not happy with the specifics. His ship was USS *Block Island,* and instead of a letter of thanks or appreciation, he quickly shot off a letter to the Navy Department to complain. "I am very unhappy about my ship assignment, having just learned that *Block Island* will be in the Navy Yard for three months during the short time that I will have command." After noting a classmate was about to take command of his third ship, Jimmy offered to take a ship on the West Coast if that would get him to sea sooner. He also offered suggestions as to who should take his place at Olathe.[18] Despite Jimmy's "suggestions," the navy stuck to its plan, and he was ordered to *Block Island* effective 26 July 1952. After completing a short course on damage control in Philadelphia 14–18 July, he was off to Boston on 21 July to complete a one-week course, Senior Officer's Combat Information Center Familiarization. From Boston he traveled to Norfolk and on 31 July relieved Annapolis classmate Capt. Arthur S. Hill as commanding officer.

The crew of CVE-106 nicknamed their ship "FBI" for "Fighting Block Island." Their pride was justifiable. The first *Block Island* (CVE-21) was the only United States Navy carrier lost in the Atlantic during World War II. Part of a hunter-killer team to search and destroy German U-boats, the *Bogue*-class CVE-21—normally operating twelve Avengers and twelve Wildcats—was credited for the sinking of two U-boats with her planes, and her aircraft shared credit for two others with screening destroyers and destroyer escorts. On 29 May 1944 the carrier was torpedoed and sunk by U-549. The German U-boat had little time to celebrate, however, as it was quickly destroyed by two of the carrier's screening destroyer escorts. The second escort carrier to bear the name was a larger (11,373 versus 7,800 tons) and longer (577 versus 466 feet) *Commencement Bay*–class escort carrier. The second *Block Island* (CVE-106), like the first, earned two battle stars, with those for the new carrier of that name earned off Okinawa and Balikpapan in 1945.

Off Okinawa CVE-106 carried a marine group usually flying eighteen Hellcats and fifteen Avengers to cover amphibious landings and fight Japanese ships, aircraft, and submarines. In 1952 the threat was Soviet submarines that had the potential to attack shipping off American ports, threaten or close sea lanes, and possibly launch missiles against civilian and industrial centers. Like CVE-21 during Atlantic operations in World War II, CVE-106 operated as part of a hunter-killer team with destroyers and destroyer escorts. Wildcat fighters that flew from the first *Block Island*, Hellcat fighters that flew from the second (longer deck), and Avenger torpedo-bombers that flew from both were weapons of the past—although some Avenger variants served in operational status until the summer of 1954. The front-line aircraft for the Korean War–era antisubmarine escort carriers was the Grumman-built AF-2 Guardian.

The single-engine, four-blade propeller Guardian offered the speed (317 mph), range (fifteen hundred miles), and punch (up to four thousand pounds of ordnance) to hunt and kill enemy submarines. Its most significant negative, however, was that two Guardians were required for a single mission. One (AF-2W) carried a very large APS-20 radar and crew of four to search for submarines while the second (AF-2S) carried a crew of three to attack. The AF-2S attack version carried a smaller radar plus sonobuoys (sound waves to locate a sub), a searchlight, depth charges, and homing torpedo or bombs. Attack Guardians produced after Jimmy's tour with CVE-106 also carried a magnetic anomaly detector—trailing aft on a long boom to minimize interference from the plane's own metal—that could sense the minute disturbance between the submarine and the Earth's magnetic field. While at sea, Jimmy usually had seventeen Guardians aboard.

Block Island was in the yard for Jimmy's first two months as commanding officer. At least it was in the New York Navy Yard, a location well appreciated by the crew. The crew, however, presented some immediate problems for the new CO. Jimmy knew that as a result of growing up in a time of great tension and war, the young sailors in his crew did not find security in the military. And he knew also that many sailors in the early 1950s, even though they had joined the navy, were not attracted to military life. Prior to World War II everyone was a volunteer, but "today we have had to force the majority of our youngsters into uniform [all were subject to the draft] and they don't like to be forced." Jimmy favored higher pay and a tougher attitude instead of babying youngsters too much. And he advocated more patriotic education.[19]

Jimmy could not help but wonder upon assuming command how his "tough attitude" and prospect of higher pay via promotion might work. He knew he could count on his chief petty officers to guide young-sters. But formal education was another matter, and he worried about the 57 percent of the crew that were not high school graduates. Conse-quently, he "asked" his ensigns to conduct a "High School Afloat." He encouraged crew members to participate in the all-volunteer ship's band and to increase attendance at church services. Immediately he began to demonstrate a tough but fair attitude. This approach was apparent when he mustered the entire crew on deck after the acts of a homosexual were discovered. Jimmy personally escorted the accused through the remain-der of the crew with orders to identify all others with the same sexual orientation for discharge. And before the ship left the yard he began preparing articles addressed to the crew in the ship's newspaper.[20] Pre-sented as "Captain's Corner," many of these articles would be used again in future commands as they addressed the most basic problems con-fronting all sailors.

Competitive exercises during the period 15–26 September 1952 were not especially pleasant for Jimmy due in large part to problems with the chief of staff to the commander of Carrier Division Eighteen, untimely transfers of air department personnel, and poor performance by one maintenance officer. More enjoyable was a seven-week cruise to the Caribbean in January and February 1953. The *Block Island* sailed in April with three destroyers, three destroyer escorts, and one submarine on a two-month hunter-killer cruise with Carrier Division Eighteen. Comprising the carrier division along with *Block Island* were two sister ships, *Kula Gulf* (CVE-108) and *Salerno Bay* (CVE-110). Steaming as flagship, *Block Island* carried seventeen of Air Antisubmarine Squadron Thirty's Guardians.

Perhaps the most memorable cruise, however, was from 17 April through 25 June 1953. Upon arriving off Europe, the seven-ship task group completed joint exercises with the Royal Navy. Jimmy was quite pleased with the exercise as his carrier maneuvered in such a manner that the British OTC determined that a torpedo could not have been fired at CVE-106. On the first day of the British-run convoy escort prob-lem, it was determined that one torpedo could have been fired from nine thousand yards. Later it was determined that two of thirty-three ships could have been lost, but Jimmy noted that was possible only because he was steaming "the British way with the CVE in the box." For the remainder of the problem Jimmy operated detached but in support of the convoy and no more torpedoes were fired. At the conclusion of the problem, he thought his unit sank at least six submarines. Above all, he was pleased that all seventeen planes aboard performed well, in no small part due to outstanding work by the maintenance crew. Damage to the Guardians was limited to two barrier crashes—requiring replacement of both spare engines aboard plus two props—and they occurred en route rather than during the exercise. Jimmy was also impressed with newly promoted Rear Adm. Ira E. Hobbs (USNA 1925) who flew his flag from Jimmy's ship. Jimmy "had to remind him a couple of times that this was my ship . . . [but noted that Hobbs's] judgment is very sound, he never gets excited, and there is never any vacillation."[21]

Exercises during the spring cruise were interspersed with shore visits to Bangor, Maine; Londonderry, Ireland; and Plymouth, England. While sailors went ashore for both formal and informal visits, the warships also hosted guests, including 170 children from nearby orphanages and residential homes— for tea, a movie, and a ride on the "FBI" aircraft elevator, after which Jimmy requested further information as to how his crew could assist orphans. The cruise then continued on to southern France and Naples, Italy, before returning to Norfolk. Before entering ports in Ireland and Britain, education information was officially disseminated primarily to highlight places of historical interest. As the cruise moved into the Mediterranean, however, official information —especially on how to bargain with Italian merchants—was supplemented with warnings pertaining to political practices. Unofficial advice from CPOs usually reinforced official information on what not to buy, eat, or drink; where not to go; and with whom not to fraternize ("Italy has one of the highest venereal rates in the world").[22]

On 12 May Jimmy had written to Monsignor Romulo Carone concerning the carrier's visit to Naples 8–13 June. Arrangements were made for the visit, and Jimmy took 250 Catholic boys to Rome on 10–11 June. A highlight was the Sacrament of Confirmation for sixteen sailors from Escort Destroyer Squadron Two, which took place in the Chapel of the Canons, at St. Peter's Basilica, Rome. With a hand on the shoulders of kneeling sailors, Jimmy added his personal touch for the moments he considered the best in life. But when things are at their best, it can be expected that the opposite will inevitably occur. On the French Riviera, some sailors were less interested than others in the historical points of interest and had a definition of "enjoyment and betterment" not in keeping with Jimmy's expressed goals of the visit. Excess of liquid spirits and social interaction resulted in court-martial and loss of hard-earned rates. Jimmy was especially concerned about proper deportment while his ship was in Naples. Elections were being held during the visit, and he expected some verbal abuse from radical groups. "If you feel you haven't got the necessary self-control, I advise you to stay aboard . . . if you fail to conduct yourself properly, you leave me no choice but to deal with you harshly before the Mast."[23]

Antisubmarine warfare exercises continued in the Mediterranean as the carrier and escorts continued the cruise. The day began at 0345 with reveille for the air department and squadron. At 0430 Guardians, in teams of two, were being catapulted—zero to eighty-five miles per hour in three seconds—an hour and a half before the ship's crew was rousted from their bunks. While some aircraft searched for a real threat, others dropped ordnance on practice targets. Aboard ship the crew was kept busy with normal routine and duties but always alert for various announced and unannounced drills. Some drills were similar to those of World War II, but most of the crew were not veterans of that conflict. Consequently, smoke bombs were added to fire drills to better simulate realism. The atom bomb drill, which emphasized speed in taking cover and spraying radioactive contamination, did not require artificial realism. In the 1950s the expression "atom bomb" created internal responses both conscious and semiconscious.[24]

At the end of the European cruise, and the end of Jimmy's tour as commanding officer of the carrier (22 July 1953), laudatory messages flashed to and from *Block Island*. On 20 June Jimmy sent an expression of gratitude to USS *Eaton* (DDE-510) citing outstanding to excellent performance "in comparison with ships from three other DESRONs [destroyer squadrons] we have worked with previously." Messages coming in were more numerous as *Block Island* stood first in battle efficiency for CVL/CVE-class ships assigned to the commander of the air force in the Atlantic Fleet during the fiscal year 1953. The award of the Battle

Efficiency "E" demonstrated leadership and ability in contributing materially to the exemplary performance. Documentation included a record of no injuries, no lost planes, availability of aircraft when required, and not one parted line during a six-month period of heavy operational demands when over two and one-half million gallons of fuel were passed to and from the carrier. Satisfied with the hard work, good supervision, state of training, and readiness, Jimmy's boss wrote, "His ship is without exception the smartest looking CVE in the Atlantic Fleet." Cognizant that Jimmy's carrier never sent a message that something could not be done, other superiors agreed that few CVEs could equal and none surpass CVE-106.[25]

Walking away from *Block Island,* Jimmy was disappointed that his "Captain's Corner" articles and other efforts had not resulted in a higher reenlistment rate, but he did feel good about the state of his relationship with the enlisted men. Assisting with the organization of a navy theatrical group to provide musicals navy-wide had been a lot of fun for everyone. But primarily Jimmy believed he had helped many during father-son type conversations. In this belief he was correct. For the remainder of his life, correspondence continued from sailors. Some wrote to ask for promised recommendations, some wrote to thank him for advice that had proven sound, some wrote just to say hello, and some wrote to ask him to stand in as best man for their wedding. Indeed, being a commanding officer had its downside, but the upside more than made up for the disappointments.

14

Commanding Officer

Safety Activity, NAS Norfolk, and USS Lake Champlain

NAS Norfolk, the Safety Challenge, and the "Flatley Report"

IMMEDIATELY AFTER serving as commanding officer of the *Block Island,* Jimmy returned to NAS Norfolk on 22 July 1953 as the officer in charge of naval aviation safety activity.[1] This assignment had personal significance as well as professional. On a cold rainy night in February 1951, Jimmy was riding in the back of a Douglas R4D—the navy version of the famous DC-3/C-47—on his way home to NAS Olathe, Kansas, from Chicago's NAS Glenview. Belted with him in the uncomfortable aluminum bucket seats was his oldest son, aboard by virtue of his status as a seaman recruit. Alone in the twenty-seven-passenger compartment, the two had been informed by the copilot that due to poor weather conditions at Olathe, the plane would make a ground control approach. If the pilot failed to contact the ground when he reached ground control approach minimums, he would proceed to an alternate airport at Springfield, Missouri. Jimmy thanked the copilot for the information and then returned to conversation with his son. However, only a few minutes later the wheels of the R4D caught the top of a Quonset Hut well forward of the NAS Olathe runway. Slowed, the plane dropped a wing, struck a pile of lumber and then plowed through a chain-link fence. In another instant the stricken transport was sliding through the mud sideways toward the runway and continuing to leave parts of itself behind. Fortunately no one was hurt.

The next day a still disgusted Jimmy pieced together what had gone wrong. He learned that the pilot, despite being on final approach, had taken his eyes off the instrument panel to look for the ground when told by the tower that he was at ground control approach minimums. Realizing he was nose-high and too slow, the pilot advanced power, but this particular plane was equipped with needle props, and there was an appreciable delay between the application of power and the taking hold of the props. Consequently, the R4D dropped eighty-seven feet below the glide path. This was not Jimmy's first crash, but it did give him a first-hand reminder of what was happening too often in naval aviation. But his interview with the two reserve pilots was as important as the experience itself. Like so many other accidents, this one should not have happened. And it was apparent that pilot training was the primary problem.[2]

Exclusive of combat action during Fiscal Year 1953, on average one of every 4.4 navy aircraft was involved in an accident. One of six suffered major damage, and 5 percent of the 14,051 operating navy aircraft (714) were destroyed. For personnel, 423 naval aviators died in 248 separate accidents. While no cost estimate could ever be made for the lost aviators, it was estimated that the cost of replacement aircraft and damage repairs was 500 million dollars. In 1953 dollars, 500 million dollars was equivalent to over thirty carrier air groups, and this included the higher costs of new jet aircraft. Of the 2,266 major accidents, 22 percent (493) were judged to have been avoidable. Had the avoidable accidents been eliminated, the dollar value would have covered the cost of seven carrier air groups. And lurking in the back of navy officers' minds was the knowledge that the air force safety record was so exemplary that service might make yet another argument to Congress alleging it could better ensure the best use of defense dollars.

On 3 September 1953 Jimmy forwarded a confidential letter of some sixty pages to OP-53 in the office of the chief of naval operations. Titled "Review of Naval Aviation Accident Prevention Methods," the letter emphasized deficiencies of the naval aviation accident prevention program. In time the letter became known simply as "The Flatley Report." In his one-page cover letter Jimmy, no doubt remembering his own 1951 crash, called attention to the recent 17 July 1953 crash of another Douglas transport at NAS Whiting Field just outside Pensacola, Florida. That crash killed all forty-four aboard, the cause listed as undetermined. A review of the Whiting crash disclosed that both pilots were lacking in night-flying experience. Jimmy concluded that whatever the cause of the accident, the assignment of unqualified pilots to such a mission indicated a serious lack of supervision some place in the chain of command. Further, he noted that his letter was "restricted to classes of accidents considered to be avoidable and susceptible to better control . . . [and that] organizational changes [were] deemed necessary if such control is to achieve the maximum degree of effectiveness in reducing aviation accidents." In short, Jimmy stated that naval aviation was its own worst enemy regarding safety. His documentation was too strong to ignore as evidenced by his statement that after forty years naval aviation did not have a single trained crash investigator who could be produced on request.

Had Jimmy Flatley never engaged in combat he nonetheless would have earned a special remembrance for his contribution to naval aviation safety. On his 15 October 1953 fitness report Rear Adm. Lester K. Rice wrote that Captain Flatley "stirred up more interest in the [safety] program and was responsible for more progress in that activity than had been in evidence during the whole year prior to his arrival." Ironically, this assignment was the shortest of his long career—only two months. But in that time he identified a problem crippling the service. Many of Jimmy's peers considered his work between 6 August and 8 October 1953 to have arguably saved naval aviation. Certainly he pointed the way for naval aviation to save itself.

Having just returned from commanding an escort carrier and having spent considerable time with air force officers at the Air War College and then later with the operational exchange program while with the Atlantic Fleet, Jimmy was well equipped to visualize the navy's problem and offer solutions. Despite his continuing misgivings regarding relations with the air force, Jimmy knew that the service had set and maintained extremely high safety standards. With a liaison officer within his office working with the USAF Safety headquarters at Norton AFB, Jimmy could obtain all the background information he needed for a comparison between the two services.

As important as the cogent arguments Jimmy made in the report was its tone, a tone also evident in written comments to old friends while he was in charge of the safety program. "Our Aviation Safety Program is so weak, it is a national disgrace," Jimmy wrote on 8 September 1953 to Capt. Jimmie Thach. Admitting to Rear Adm. Arleigh Burke in a 11 September 1953 letter that "my temperament is incompatible with this job (but maybe something constructive will come about before I go off my rocker)," Jimmy nonetheless called it as he saw and felt it. His written presentation in his report was direct and critical, but he conveyed the depth and seriousness of the problem without being mean-spirited. Expressed best in the words of a peer, "It took a Jimmy Flatley to shake a lethargic Navy into doing something about aviation safety."[3]

Awakened by Jimmy's frank epistle and fully recognizing the problem, the navy soon expanded the safety "activity" into the U. S. Naval Aviation Safety Center and placed a rear admiral in charge of an enlarged staff. Although not always in the form Jimmy suggested, most of his ideas were translated into policy. The results were, and have been, exceptionally dramatic. The 1953 fiscal year major accident rate was 51.22. Two years after "The Flatley Report," the rate dropped significantly to 38.18, continued a steady decline to 3.3 in 1984, and declined even further in the 1990s. From the period immediately after Jimmy's report, the navy implemented a standardized system of training and information to ensure that everything possible will have been done to save lives and prevent damage to aircraft. NATOPS (Naval Air Training Operating Procedures Standardization) provides all pilots with standard safety procedures for each aircraft, for all training and emergencies. Before authorizing a pilot to take a navy plane into the air, the pilot must have passed safety tests and must undergo annual testing and a check ride to maintain flight status.

Rear Admiral Rice sagely observed in his 15 October 1953 fitness report that Jimmy "gets things done and has a penchant for cutting red tape." Later as a flag officer Jimmy followed up on his safety concerns by championing a policy to put pilots in the cockpit and leave them there. Such a practice, as he saw it, would not only serve the interests of safety but also produce an even better trained pilot. Too often, he noted, assignments took pilots out of the cockpit for years and when they returned in leadership billets, the result was rusty pilots attempting to train untrained pilots. To these perspectives the navy again turned a receptive ear to Jimmy's voice. Although his influence continues to be felt in other areas of operations and training, an argument can be forwarded in regard to naval aviation safety that Jimmy Flatley is still on active duty.

Commanding Officer Norfolk Naval Air Station

By virtue of having spent so much of his naval career in Norfolk both before and after World War II, it was nearly as much a home as Green Bay. Certainly there was no disappointment when he learned in late September that he would succeed Capt. Fitzhugh Lee—class of 1926 just promoted to rear admiral—in the dual role as commanding officer of the Norfolk Naval Air Station and as the commander of naval air bases in the Fifth Naval District. After both Lee and Jimmy read their orders on 8 October at historic Chambers Field before two thousand NAS personnel in dress blues and another one thousand guests, Jimmy pledged in his short speech to perpetuate his predecessor's program and policies.

Olathe's challenge was to oversee a major expansion. *Block Island* was a challenge to achieve and maintain potential combat effectiveness in a noncombat but nonetheless dangerous environment. At Norfolk the first of many challenges was to effectively grasp the needs of a very large military complex. A major base since the beginning of the United States Navy, the air station dated from 27 August 1918. Facing historic Hampton Roads, it covered nearly two thousand acres and was a headquarters from which supplies, overhauled and repaired aircraft—one thousand planes and fifteen hundred engines annually—and trained sailors were sent to ships, squadrons, and naval air bases through much of the world. Some sixteen thousand civilian employees fell under Jimmy's jurisdiction along with over two thousand regular navy personnel and six thousand squadron transits. Another eight thousand naval personnel of the Atlantic Fleet units lived aboard ship, but spent considerable time ashore on the station or in the city. Cessation of hostilities in Korea in July 1953 ended combat but not the threat of continued war or the draft of young men into the military. Consequently, there was a daily challenge to remind conscripts and volunteers alike that they were the one's upon whom the fragile peace rested. And there was a daily need for Jimmy to remind all the sailors under his command, and any others he could reach, that most of the world was not free.

Never hesitant to enlist the assistance of others to reach a goal, Jimmy wrote a three-page letter to the family of newly assigned sailors. Promising his best effort to see that sons or daughters enjoyed "health, safety and happiness," Jimmy reminded parents that their continuing support was required to ensure positive morale and spirit "in these critical times in world history." Responsibility, then, became a three-way proposition: the navy, parents, and sailor. Specifically, Jimmy asked parents to write their children frequently.

Chief problems were absence without leave and automobile accidents. Often one or both of these problems were due to family problems at home. Jimmy asked parents to write to their children in the service and tell the truth, and explain what was being done to resolve the matter. In short, he was asking the parents not to make their child chose between the navy and the family. Automobile accidents were often caused by young men trying to visit homes too far away. At the end of 1953, the Shore Patrol headquarters reported twenty-three fatalities in 980 traffic accidents; 1954 fared no better, so Jimmy asked parents to discourage sailors from stretching leave time or liberty.

Jimmy's initial letter to parents, ending with an invitation to contact a chaplain or himself, was only a beginning to address problems. Weekly he wrote a new "Captain's Corner" article for the station newspaper, *The Dope Sheet,* or submitted a still-relevant article printed earlier in the *FBI Daily Press*. Regardless of the main topic, in some manner he managed to tie it to how the navy could help the sailor and the sailor could help the navy. And he continued his message through the comments of teachers aboard the station in an invigorated education program.

After the experience as commanding officer at NAS Olathe and aboard *Block Island*, Jimmy had a solid grasp of the productivity potential and limitations of the navy's enlisted men. After listening to countless charges and explanations during sessions before the Captain's Mast, it became apparent to Jimmy that one of the most common threads through the multitude of problems of enlisted men was lack of education. For many, deficient education resulted in insufficient knowledge even for basic occupational requirements. But even those who had a reasonably good command of basic educational skills encountered limitations of opportunity due to absence of a diploma. A high school education, in essence a "union card," did not guarantee an open door, but for many occupations it allowed one to knock on that door.

For nearly all his sailors in difficulty, Jimmy came to believe that the dearth of knowledge and want of a formal document recognizing a significant plateau within the educational system lowered self-esteem among those regularly cited for personal and professional problems. Although he had four sons in school during this period, their commendable performance did not signal the challenges he found in their peers. Not uncharacteristically, he moved resolutely to simultaneously help his sailors and his navy.

NAS Norfolk was not just another naval air station. Not only the largest naval installation on the East Coast, NAS Norfolk with its department for overhaul and repair comprised one of the largest industries in the state of Virginia. And Jimmy was its commanding officer. Recognizing the symbiotic relationship between the military and civilian economy, Jimmy began to formalize intensive education practices. In late 1953 he recruited volunteer instructors, particularly Wave officers, to teach English, math, history, and other classes required for high school graduation. The classes operated two nights a week on an alternate-night basis so as not to interfere with duty, and enlisted men who had not completed a high school education, were encouraged—before the Mast and through other channels of communication, to attend. Within a year over six hundred attended classes prescribed by the United States Armed Forces Institute (USAFI) and graduates received either a diploma from their former high school or a high school equivalency certificate. In some cases, sailors took leave to march with other graduates at their hometown high school. Before Jimmy left Norfolk in June 1955, over fifteen hundred graduated.

Jimmy was so relentless in promoting his educational program that it soon became known as "Flatley High School." It was unofficial as far as the navy was concerned, and was in fact an activity of the NAS Norfolk Education Division. But, that division had never enjoyed so much activity or recognition until Jimmy placed his own mark on it. His first step was to require new arrivals on the vast complex that were not high school graduates to take tests to determine educational deficiencies. Second, analysis of the tests determined which of the nearly thirty courses offered were required to remove deficiencies and meet graduation requirements. Third was his recruitment and encouragement of the volunteer instructors, fourteen serving regularly with another twenty in reserve. Given defined and attainable objectives, instructors reveled in having maximum personal encouragement from the station's commanding officer and students who for either intrinsic or extrinsic reasons (advancement in rating, pay, and privileges) were anxious to learn and graduate. Standardized tests passed at Norfolk met the standards of respective states and thereby opened the possibility of pursuing further education in college.[4]

Community leaders, the local media and the navy took considerable pride in reporting and praising the many benefits of "Flatley High." Morale and esprit de corps rose, as did self-esteem among those who volunteered to improve their lives. A collateral benefit of the program, one which neither Jimmy nor his peers overtly discussed or announced to the public, was that a more educated crew might prevent accidents aboard ship or be able to save them in future combats.

Jimmy's idea to more effectively communicate with his crew via his "Captain's Corner" articles was an unqualified success aboard *Block Island*. He knew the effort was successful due to the countless numbers who made their way to his quarters or just talked with him where they found him aboard ship. The specific matters he addressed, he had long since discovered, served primarily to open dialogues. While little more was added to what he had already written, ensuing discussions allowed a personal touch and demonstrated expression of genuine interest. Logically, he expected his "Captain's Corner" articles to accomplish the same ends at Norfolk.

At Norfolk, *The Dope Sheet* was published weekly and distributed free-of-charge throughout the Norfolk naval complex. Included were articles on national issues, military matters, base and national sports, movies, special events, and a calendar for base enlisted and officers' clubs. Jimmy's "Captain's Corner" would provide status reports on the Cold War and add perspectives on hard work, honesty, basic courtesy, loyalty, and a host of other positive attributes he believed his sailors should demonstrate, practice, and enjoy.

Jimmy prepared his articles in his first month as commanding officer. On more than one occasion his article appeared opposite another page with a headline calling attention to the latest graduates from "Flatley High." Although each article carried a different title, often tied to seasonal or national holidays, nearly all were directed toward five themes: religion, citizenship, family relations, geopolitics, and the navy with special emphasis on why a sailor should re-enlist. The vast majority of his articles were sermons with absolutely no disguise. Taking no chances on a lack of comprehension when writing on the Ten Commandments as the basis of a code of ethics, Jimmy paraphrased the commandments into everyday English (doing this several years before the rewordings of the King James Bible into a more modern idiom).[5]

Articles on religion and citizenship were intended to raise the moral tone among sailors. Jimmy knew from countless experiences before the Mast that many young men had been raised in good homes and had attended church prior to entry into the navy. But, away from home for the first time and encountering heavy peer pressure "to be a man," many found their pursuit of manhood resulting in a detour to official trouble with serious consequences. Jimmy's mixing biblical quotations with selected sections from the U.S. Constitution and national law reflected his conviction that the United States was a Christian nation, and that obedience to the absolutes of the Bible and laws of the nation were required for individual happiness.

A favorite topic was family relations. Jimmy did not refer directly to his own problems as a young man, and despite his many friends in the navy only Dotty could relate the words from his articles to certain events and failures of the past. However, there was a certain fervor found in the flourish of words pertaining to economics, dating and marriage, unfaithfulness and drinking. At a conscious level and perhaps another in the subconscious, he was addressing his past as well as the present and future of his young readers. And though always direct in his written expressions, he was crystal clear and very direct on the topic of marriage and the family. On economics he wrote, "Don't take on the responsibility of a family until you attain 2nd class petty officer. You can't support a family any sooner . . . you aren't old enough."[6] Regarding infidelity, Jimmy first noted it violated the sixth commandment and added, "The big strong he-man who says his wife doesn't understand him. The big coward who can't take the cares and responsibilities that children impose . . . The playboy . . . who can't resist the coyness of some good-for-nothing little hussy."[7] And on the excessive use of alcohol Jimmy, with no fond remembrance of its role in his 1933 annulment, provided figures from a study indicating the single greatest cause of divorce was drinking.[8] Aware that most liquor smuggled aboard ship occurred in the morning from market boats rather than liberty parties, Jimmy served unequivocal notice that taking liquor aboard a ship would be dealt with severely as it threatened loss of life and perhaps loss of the ship.

Geopolitics continued to be Jimmy's favorite theme while speaking to civic clubs in the Norfolk community, and the subject often found its way into the "Captain's Corner." His basic message stated that the greatest crisis in modern civilization has caught most Americans completely unprepared, morally and intellectually, . . . [and that] our frontiers of defense had to be established far beyond our coastlines."[9] His only compliment for the Soviet Union was that they had better sense than to start World War III by first using nuclear weapons.[10]

Articles on geopolitics usually centered on the U.S. military, always led by the navy: "If we can't control the seas our Army and Air Force can't be put where they can fight and be kept there."[11] And the navy needed the help of every sailor. Jimmy noted more than once that two-thirds of those who wished to re-enlist were being rejected, and that the navy had learned that only 65 percent of first enlistees had the potential to move up in rating to petty officers.[12] These were the sailors the navy needed to have re-enlist and remain for a career. He shared a host of statistics with his readers on how much it cost to train a sailor, including numbers that demonstrated how much better a sailor would fare economically to remain in the service. Then there were other benefits, such as thirty-days paid leave, technical training, twenty-year retirement, and opportunity to see the world. But he realized that statistics in themselves were not enough, and that the benefits were not always significantly better than what could be offered in civilian occupations. Indeed this was no longer the navy of the Depression era when men were more than willing to be placed on waiting lists, and after enlisting find the best meals and living conditions of their life. Most of all, he understood that the biggest problems were separation of families and the pervasive feeling within many sailors—and other servicemen—that they had little or no control over their lives in the military. Consequently, Jimmy nearly always closed his articles on navy retention with a final appeal to God and country.

Ever alert to improving performance and efficiency, Jimmy wrote articles that were interesting, informative, plus mentally and spiritually stimulating. Above all, he made his articles relevant to his readers. As with the education program, he demonstrated initiative that could not help cause observers to wonder why others had not done the same earlier.

In the many years prior to Jimmy's tenure as commanding officer and regrettably in some periods since, the relationship between the navy and the Norfolk community—the "Navy Capital of the World" whether or not it wanted to be—was not and has not been positive. Former sailors can cite exact sites where their welcome was documented with signs reading, "No dogs or sailors on the lawn." In fairness to the citizens of that city, their unwelcome signs were placed due to public drunkenness of naval personnel, and other acts of poor conduct. But Jimmy had addressed sailors' responsibilities while in the community, and his efforts had not gone unnoticed by city officials and the media who in turn communicated the news to the citizenry. When an announcement was made in the late spring of 1955 that Jimmy would soon leave Norfolk to assume command of another carrier, city fathers in Norfolk moved to honor Jimmy for promoting better relations between the navy and city. The navy also recognized the importance of Jimmy's public relations efforts both on and off the base.[13] Even retired flag officers took time to write and commend him for "honest and forceful public expressions and your great interest in public relations in the best sense of that term."[14]

As important as community public relations was attention to needs aboard the station. Always leading by example, he moved to improve recreation and club facilities just as he had at Olathe. Knowing that leisure time on the station could be used to advantage or detriment, he took visible measures for improvement. Happily, Norfolk already had an active recreation program: participation in sports was encouraged with instructors, equipment, and facilities readily available. Jimmy particularly enjoyed visiting with station athletic teams during their practices and games. But win or lose, as often as possible Jimmy was there after the game to help celebrate or console.

USS Lake Champlain (CVA-39)

Just before becoming commanding officer at the Norfolk Naval Air Station, Jimmy and Dotty sold their home on Algonquin Road for what they paid for it and moved into quarters aboard the station. When orders arrived assigning Jimmy to a carrier based near Jacksonville, the decision to sell in Norfolk appeared even wiser. Still, time at Norfolk had been good to him and for him. It had been good for his health, particularly after he decided to cut back on smoking. A pipe replaced the formerly omnipresent cigarette in his hand and mouth, and he was able to keep his weight up. For the first time in his adult life he did not have to alter uniforms to fit. Now slightly over 140 pounds, the forty-nine-year-old captain was on the threshold of another assignment for which he was more than prepared. It was no accident that he would receive numerous compliments from superiors for his ship handling during task force operations. Certainly it was no surprise for anyone who remembered that Jimmy had helped design such operations during World War II.

As Jimmy prepared to move south down the Atlantic coast in June 1955, he was excited to hear that two-star Rear Adm. Arleigh Burke had been nominated by President Eisenhower to jump scores of senior flag officers and succeed Adm. Robert B. Carney as chief of naval operations. Also to Jimmy's delight, the president nominated Adm. Arthur Radford for a second two-year term as chairman of the Joint Chiefs of Staff.

Jimmy's new command was the USS Lake Champlain (CVA-39), one of the last members of the *Essex*-class to be completed. Commissioned 3 June 1945, "The Champ" was too late to see action during World War II but did earn one battle star for service off Korea. In September 1952 the carrier emerged from mothballs with her straight flight deck and open bow intact, but she had been refitted with a streamlined island, 5-inch flight deck gun mounts removed and new 3-inch gun sponsons on the starboard side. This was her configuration when Jimmy took command, and for the remainder of her active service no other major changes were made. The last straight-deck attack carrier in the navy, she was reclassified as an antisubmarine (CVS) carrier in August 1957 and served until decommissioned 2 May 1966.

A formal change of command ceremony was held on 22 June 1955 on the flight deck of the carrier while it was docked at Mayport, Florida. While very pleased to have command of an attack carrier, Jimmy was not equally happy about the carrier's mission with the Sixth Fleet or a cruise to the Mediterranean lasting between 23 August 1955 and 10 March 1956. At the end of the cruise Jimmy wrote, "The professional benefits accruing to an individual carrier from six months in the Sixth Fleet are not commensurate with the cost of the effort in terms of time, dollars, material and pilots lives." Specifically, Jimmy recommended more air defense and antisubmarine training plus joint operations with other NATO forces.[15] Nor was he satisfied with the navy's handling of security for either the Sixth Fleet or his ship. Recalling that the Japanese used the routine schedule of the Pacific Fleet to plan their attack on Pearl Harbor, Jimmy noted that his carrier's schedule was well known in the "fishbowl" Mediterranean. On the day prior to port call Jimmy observed that vendors began raising prices and that over five hundred prostitutes assembled. The bottom line was that he worried those who might endanger the ship had too much knowledge of navy policies.[16]

Jet aircraft aboard "The Champ" during Jimmy's year in command were comprised mostly of Grumman F9F-8 Cougars and marine-piloted McDonnell F2H-4 Banshees. These planes served as both fighters and attack aircraft, but the attack function was handled primarily by propeller-driven AD-4 and AD-6 Skyraiders. Although the single engine Skyraider, "the flying dump truck," could carry a small nuclear weapon, the special-weapons function was assigned to the North American AJ

Savage, a twin-engine propeller plane soon to be replaced by larger, faster jet aircraft. Squadrons operating aboard "The Champ" included VF-33; VF-74; VA-25; VC-4; VC-12; VC-33; VC-62; VAH-9; VAH-7; and Marine squadron VMA-324. While on the Mediterranean cruise—31,173 steaming miles—the carrier recorded 15,300 flight hours, completing 5,645 day and night landings with only three major and four minor accidents. Four fatalities were suffered, all at sea or over land well away from the ship, but there were no deaths among ship's company and the accident rate was less than one percent.

"The Champ" could not land many of the planes aboard the new *Forrestal* (CV-59), which was beginning to team with the older *Essex*-class carriers. The straight deck on CVA-39 was not the primary impediment. To have handled the higher speed and weight of newer aircraft, the flight deck required strengthening and other modifications. Jimmy's time aboard was during a period of great transition and marked advances in both aircraft and aircraft carriers. Some of the newer planes simply did not measure up to expectations or needs. The first Vought F7U-3 Cutlass jets to come aboard had to be quickly returned to shore. And there were problems aboard ship associated with operation of jet and piston aircraft. Jets burned fuel five times faster than propeller aircraft, and jet fuel could not be used in piston engines. Further, personnel trained to maintain propeller aircraft were not always equally proficient with jets.

Even though Jimmy was not overly happy with the purpose of his carrier's protracted cruise in the Mediterranean, his year on the bridge was rewarding both personally and professionally. Quickly adapting to his new ship, he rapidly appraised its strength and weakness as a fighting ship and took constructive action to improve its readiness. Marked improvement in the ship's appearance and operating capability were rapid.[17]

Jimmy got off to a running start with the crew by reassigning to shore duty enlisted men that had been at sea for two or more Christmas holiday periods. He took "Flatley High" aboard CVA-39, and by the end of the year the ship showed an improvement of 400 percent on diplomas earned. The number of men earning USAFI high school equivalency certificates exceeded any other ship in the U.S. Navy. Too, he carried aboard previous "Captain's Corner" articles for "The Champ." And the crew's church attendance, always voluntary, rose about 25 percent.

Both *Block Island* (1953) and *Lake Champlain* (1956) earned the coveted Battle Efficiency "E" Pennant under Jimmy's command. To that time he was the only commander known to have won the award twice on different carriers. Conduct of his CVA-39 crew ashore in the Mediterranean was "a credit to the naval service that will be difficult to equal [less than one percent]." Absenteeism was reduced to one-fourth previous figures, and the number of men advanced in rating (over two thousand) constituted a record for CVAs of the Atlantic Fleet. Reenlistment rates were so favorable as to educe a commendatory letter from the commander of the air force in the Atlantic Fleet. Further official recognition of his inspirational leadership while on the bridge of *Lake Champlain* came in a fitness report after he left the carrier for a new assignment on 27 July 1956: "He [Jimmy] has an expert knowledge of Task Force operations and his ship handling ability is a joy to observe. He has sold the value of a Navy to many . . . [while] constantly demonstrating original and constructive work reflected in his efforts to improve training and operations."[18]

It is logical to expect that the keys to Jimmy Flatley's success, and shortcomings, as a commanding officer be identified. Below, leadership positives are weighed against negatives, and an assessment is offered to note practices that could, or could not, have application in the contemporary navy.

Command Assessment: Leadership Positives

A Courageous and Committed Inner Man
Communicating a Sense of Purpose

Jimmy demonstrated courage not only when he was "unflappable in combat," but also in speaking up when he thought principle demanded him to act. Frequently speaking up when his voice was not always welcome or appreciated was nonetheless a display of commitment.

Jimmy was driven and motivated from within. Most who knew him realized he was a man of great depth, "low key, kind and compassionate," dedicated to convictions resting on a solid foundation.[19] Never described as complex, Jimmy had fully matured within himself and was cognizant of his strengths and limitations. For the second half of his life he viewed the family, country, and navy as one indivisible, sacred entity. But, as will be seen below, Jimmy, the inner man, on occasion encountered problems by not being more "other" or outwardly motivated. In contemporary language, he was not always politically correct by living and responding according to societal expectations. He was not and did not desire to be a rebel. But he was his own man and he marched along a religiously defined path always seeking others to walk with him.

Jimmie Thach defined low morale as being "when you're worried about breaking down from within rather than defeat."[20] Jimmy Flatley believed similarly and conveyed the message frequently in talks with pilots aboard his carriers and to all sailors in his "Captain's Corner" articles. Although a realist, Jimmy knew how important it was to present strength and a positive attitude regardless of the challenge or duress. Swede Vejtasa visited Jimmy in the hospital only days before his death and remembers that "Reaper Leader" displayed "only optimism and no sign of depression."[21]

Thach related one of the best stories documenting Jimmy Flatley's inner security. Thach recalled in his oral history that even late in life people would recognize him and say, "I remember you because I've looked at your training films so often . . . I wanted to meet you because you saved my life." Thach thought this very flattering, but as flattering as it was, he also recalled who pointed him toward his extensive work regarding training films. According to Thach, he lamented to Jimmy Flatley while they were together briefly at San Diego in July 1942 that he did not know how new pilots could be taught to fight by so few like themselves who had combat experience. Flatley replied, "You know, I've been talking to Walt Disney. I think he would like to help us." As aerial combat photography was all but impossible to use, Jimmy Flatley noted that training films using animation could solve the problems of clarity and distance in teaching tactics. The result was Thach—then in the advanced training command at Jacksonville—narrating a number of thirty-to-forty-minute Disney-produced films. Jimmy Flatley did not feel he had to "run the show" or take credit for meaningful contributions. Had Thach not recalled the story, Jimmy Flatley's role would have been forgotten, as he left no record of it in his own papers. But most significant, Jimmy Flatley's willingness to share, along with his concentration on the greater good, contributed to making him a particularly effective staff officer. Not burdened by having to prove himself to others or himself, he could address problems in a cooperative spirit as a member of a team. Here again, he knew the ultimate goal of his life and did not allow natural impulses to distract him.

Having matured within and knowing his own course provided Jimmy with confidence to reach out and provide direction to others when needed. Reinforced with the painful memory of youthful indiscretions, he knew what goals needed to be set in the lives of individual sailors. That addressed, he could move on to the collective goals of greater productivity and higher morale. Teaching one or more how to do something technical was relatively easy. Having a sense of purpose within and then conveying it to others in a manner so that they would incorporate it into their own lives was the hard part. Rear Adm. Robert Goldthwaite wrote, "Captain Flatley is an original thinker far advanced in comparison with the majority of his contemporaries . . . [initiating] original measures and recommendations for improving morale."[22] Such "original measures and recommendations" was a matter of achieving goals identified through a sense of purpose more than unusual or brilliant insight.

Passing a sense of purpose to juniors was a process recognized and appreciated by Jimmy's superiors. They understood it was critical for leadership qualities to be demonstrated and verbalized to help educate subsequent leaders. Then-Rear Adm. Marc Mitscher wrote in a 4 January 1944 fitness report that Jimmy "possesses a brilliant war record, and even more important, he possesses the ability to convey the lessons he has learned to his juniors . . . [and] achieves excellent results by personal example." Rear Adm. W. K. Harrill on 29 August 1944 echoed the same thought writing "excellent leader combining knowledge and experience with tact and determination . . . inspires juniors." And Vice Adm. Felix Stump also noted Jimmy's "influence which he has upon younger naval aviators who look to him for leadership."[23]

Jimmy's sense of purpose had benefits beyond helping him serve the navy and nation. Dotty recalls that Jimmy suffered as many losses as most other people both on and off the job. With his ultimate goals well known within and ever before him, he took his loss as a temporary condition, let it go, and resolved "to get them in the next round." Always it was resolution, not revenge.[24]

Competence and Compassion—the Basis of a Transformational Leader

Knowledge, as critical as it is for a leader, is not synonymous with competence, especially at the command level. Neither is experience nor being a prodigious worker, as Jimmy was. Sufficient ability to accomplish announced goals requires more. Jimmy's superiors recorded numerous comments attesting to his competence, and in so doing listed some of the qualities relevant to competence. Rear Adm. Ira Hobbs wrote

> He is an emotional type [of] leader that keeps his officers and men at an unusually high pitch of enthusiasm and energy. It has been an inspiration to observe his ship in operation. He does not know the reason why things can't be done. A fine seaman who knows the capabilities of his ship as well as its limitations. He possesses the ability to inspire others with his "can do" attitude. . . . I would particularly desire to have him with me in time of war or in an emergency.[25]

Rear Adm. Ingolf N. Kiland thought Jimmy's success could be attributed, in part, to him being "intensely interested" and being "well informed on all facets of his command." Kiland was sufficiently impressed to alter one fitness report so he could give Jimmy the highest rating possible on "cost consciousness."[26]

Kiland's observations were similar to those written 16 years earlier by Captain W. L. Lind. On Jimmy's 15 April 1938 fitness report Lind wrote that Jimmy was "keenly interested in all branches of the naval profession in addition to his own specialty."[27] Certainly, not every aspect of naval knowledge was as interesting to Jimmy as some others, but he nonetheless exerted himself to learn beyond what was expected. That trait, developed early in his career, paid great benefits in later years and serves as a consideration of desirable characteristics for contemporary success.

Jimmie Thach was charismatic. Jimmy Flatley was not. But both were transformational leaders. Both encouraged participation, shared power, shared information, enhanced the self-worth of others, got others excited about their responsibilities, and included others in the development of unit goals. By doing these things, peers and juniors were transformed beyond what they might otherwise have achieved.

The opposite type of leader was, and is, the transactional leader. Such a leader offers punishment as an incentive. Goals are more immediate and involve achievement of an objective in spite of the will or betterment of an individual. Stanhope Ring—also a courageous "inner man" with his own strong sense of purpose but with more experience than competence for what was required at Midway—was cited as a model of this type of leader. Another decorated warrior also cited earlier was Capt. Miles Browning, perhaps the penultimate example of a transactional leader. Cdr. Hal Buell was aboard *Hornet* (CV-12) with Air Group Two during the short periods when Browning was commanding officer. Buell recalls Browning "as a scowling, chain-smoking martinet . . . [whose] every order was a snarl, and his subordinates reacted to him with fear and hatred." In the summer of 1944 Browning's fatal character flaw—inability to delegate authority—ended his career. With one sailor known to be overboard, Browning countermanded an order of a subordinate and declined the recommendation of his immediate superior to search for others. When the body of a sailor surfaced two days later, Browning's career went overboard as well and did not recover.[28]

Jimmy was very much aware of these two methods of leadership as evidenced by speeches and short papers (written for courses) still extant. Although he did not use the terms "transformational" or "transactional," he did identify the two as "persuasive leader" and "authoritarian leader." Especially when speaking to junior officers, Jimmy detailed the differences between the two. The persuasive leader (transformational) "coaches, depends on good will, inspires enthusiasm, says 'we,' fixes breakdown, shows how and makes it a game." To the contrary, according to Jimmy, the authoritarian leader (transactional) "drives his men, depends on authority, inspires fear, says 'I,' fixes blame for breakdown, knows how it is done and makes work a drudgery."

For a transformational leader to succeed in this manner of leadership, he or she must delegate. Before one can delegate, however, one must first trust those to whom responsibility is given. Rear Admiral Dan V. Gallery touched on this when he wrote that Jimmy "Inspires confidence and loyalty in his subordinates and insists on a high standard of performance from them."[29] Adm. Ralph W. Cousins recalls that as a junior officer Jimmy "rescued" him from a safe but boring job and gave him "carte blanche" to put the new rocket-training program together.[30] But perhaps Joe Eggert, who served on Mitscher's staff as an intelligence officer while Jimmy was operations officer, offers the best testimony regarding Jimmy's attitude on trust and policy of delegation. According to Eggert, Jimmy "knew the book but once he knew his man, whether a regular officer or reserve, he was liberal in trusting him with the necessary latitude to get the job done. He let a man know exactly what he expected, not in any bashful manner but also not overbearing. One was not trusted until one had demonstrated he could do his job. Early on there would be soft questioning, then you were accepted when you knew the answers and could back up your perspectives."[31]

Eggert also recalls that Jimmy could be both forceful and sensitive at the same time. By virtue of his competence others were pleased to have the benefit of his knowledge and justly positive attitude. "Able to meet others at many levels, Jimmy was a living definition of empathy."[32] Eggert's statement on empathy does not contradict an earlier assessment that Jimmy was given to sympathy but not empathy. The earlier statement was primarily directed to aerial combat and Jimmy's relationship with pilots in his squadron and air group. Eggert's interaction with Jimmy was during the relatively tranquil days when both were on Admiral Mitscher's staff. Regardless, both empathy and sympathy are synonymous with compassion.

Empathy, sympathy, and compassion to the contrary notwithstanding, Jimmy did not expect to motivate others with just expressions of concern. He understood that for a commanding officer, whether squadron, ship or station, it was expected that everything would run smoothly and when *anything* went wrong, it was the commanding officer's fault. He differed from Jimmie Thach on pilot performance, believing that expectations for a squadron should be built around what the ordinary pilot could do rather than try to bring everyone up to the level of a Flatley or Thach.[33]

Jimmy recognized that it was possible, even highly desirable, to combine compassion and discipline to simultaneously meet the needs of the navy, the nation, his command, his career, and an individual sailor. Before the Mast and in other settings wherein Jimmy had to deal with a problem, he developed a habit for dispassionate questioning. This was unnerving to some but it got the job done without either party becoming angry or emotional.[34]

As Jimmy evolved into the few "they" at the top of the command structure, he did not leave the many "we" at the lower levels. He did not confine his interests, time, and communication to peers; a common practice often vigorously defended by high-level managers. Constantly visible throughout his commands at places of work and play whether ashore or aboard his two carriers, he demonstrated sincere interest by his presence. Arguably the pain of early personal and career failures lifted him off his bridge seat to walk throughout the ships he commanded, and the memory of early career training crashes kept him on the bridge until all planes were safely aboard. While watching carrier operations away from the bridges of *Block Island* and *Lake Champlain*, he usually said nothing: his mere presence making the most eloquent statements of concern or support. As a manager of people he may have been well ahead of his time.

Initiatives such as writing articles throughout his four major commands from Olathe through *Lake Champlain* were borne of similar epistles shared years earlier with the Grim Reapers during the darkest days of World War II. The only difference was the larger audience from 1952 through 1956. Here again the key was his ability to speak to even the lowest rating within his command as though everything depended upon that one sailor. To touch that lowest rating and everyone above, Jimmy presented the essence of the message he wanted to convey—God, country, and navy—with explanations of how this foundation directly affected that person in everyday life. A sailor might not have agreed with Jimmy's pleas for good conduct, dedication, and re-enlistment; but there was an understanding and appreciation that someone at the top cared. Creation of "Flatley High" and almost forcing young sailors to continue their education to have a reasonable chance for success in the navy and civilian life was a tangible expression of compassion. The abundance of statistics Jimmy used in his written and oral presentations demonstrated he had done his homework in knowing the real and true needs of his people. Again, his own vested interests merged with the vested interests of the ones he led.

Equally important to not leaving the "we" behind, Jimmy did not compromise his status by attempting to be one of the "we." As commanding officer he was the "they" and he made no attempt to relinquish the required role or any of its responsibilities. In short, his approach as commanding officer was inclusive rather than reclusive.

The above helps unlock whatever secret for success that Jimmy Flatley had as a leader. However, it does not necessarily reveal the legend among enlisted men that emanated from his era as a commanding officer. That secret lies primarily with sessions before the Mast. One example will suffice for countless others. A young sailor was unable to pay several bills and as a result was brought before the Mast. At that time it was revealed that the sailor had sent his money home to help pay medical bills for his ailing mother. Jimmy reprimanded the chief petty officer who brought the sailor before the Mast for not first determining the facts, and dismissed him. Then Jimmy emptied his own pockets of cash, thrust it into the hands of the sailor and sent him home to care for his mother.

Thoughts expressed by enlisted men in respective ship and station newspapers as Jimmy was departing for new assignments document the attributes of leadership and command that endeared Jimmy to his crew. At the farewell dinner at Olathe, the principal speaker was an apprentice airman, Phil Wyne (who got five minutes instead of everyone else's three). Wyne said, "To us he's not just a commanding officer, he's a human being. . . . He's the kind of commanding officer who'll see you no matter how many admirals are waiting in line behind you. If you want to see him, he'll see you."[35] Upon Jimmy's departure of *Block Island,* an enlisted man stated in an editorial that Jimmy "transmitted in his own unique way . . . the feeling of being a friend . . . sincerely interested in and concerned about the welfare and problems of each of us. Captain Flatley has acted as a father and counselor to many of us. He was never too busy to listen and never too overwrought to give his honest and sincere impression of our problems—he has laughed with us in times of joy and sympathized when . . . needed.[36]

Jimmy even drew praise for competence and compassion from sailors he never met. In a 23 July 1951 letter from Cdr. D. C. Lyndon to Adm. Lynde D. McCormick, vice CNO, Lyndon reported at length on the performance of the crew of the USS *Saint Paul* (CA-73) while off Korea. Digressing at the end of his letter he wrote the following:

> There is one other matter that so impressed me that I felt a need to comment on it to higher authority. I have been in the mid-west, specifically the Kansas City area, at approximately two-year intervals since leaving there in 1931. I was always conscious of the lack of interest, understanding and sympathy existing there for the Navy. This year I was pleasantly surprised by a very marked change for the better, amounting to enthusiastic support. It was widespread in that it extended to the smaller towns 60 miles away and covered educators, prominent businessmen, filling station attendants, etc. Part of the improvement can be accounted for as resulting from the Navy's actions in Korea, but I believe that the local response above that [is] noticeable nationwide is due to the efforts of the CO of the Naval Air Station, Olathe, Kansas, Captain J. H. Flatley. I have never met Captain Flatley, but it appears that almost everyone within a hundred miles of Kansas City had met him, admired him personally and respected the service he represents. I was so impressed by the impact of one officer upon an inland community and the sound and effective public relations benefits accruing from the officer's collateral efforts that I felt compelled to mention it.

Command Assessment: Leadership Negatives

Joe Eggert, a decorated reserve intelligence officer on Mitscher's staff, recalled that "academy people kept a finger on their number," but observed that Jimmy was not preoccupied by that practice.[37] Although

Jimmy was interested in ascending as high as possible, he was not occupied or driven solely by actions that could help his career. Had his priority been himself, he would have been more willing to lose some battles to help him win his career war. He was definitely familiar with the concept as evidenced by his last letter to the Grim Reapers. Therein he reminded the Reapers that they were still fighting too many individual battles instead of thinking and fighting as a team. Still, in the postwar years Jimmy appeared just as interested in winning battles as a war. For the most part he seemed not to distinguish between battles and wars. It was all war.

It was seldom necessary for others to apprise Jimmy of negatives that could affect his career, as he himself was fully aware of certain habits that did not sit well with peers and superiors. "Sometimes I am a little bit too impetuous," he wrote to a friend.[38] And he would not have disagreed with anyone who decried his impatience with those who did not agree with him.[39]

Impatience resulted from high expectations, a trait understandable and perhaps forgivable especially when sufficient evidence warranted a change in his thinking or actions. However, his tendency toward impetuousness was less easily forgotten. Always taking on issues by speaking clearly and directly, he sometimes became especially indignant when policies seemed absurd. Impatience and impetuousness were expressed frequently in personal letters and arguably more than necessary in official correspondence. Several examples attest to these continuing traits. Unhappy with the amount of time his carriers and the Sixth Fleet spent in the Mediterranean, Jimmy offered his unsought opinion to the chief of naval operations, referring to the Mediterranean as "that Roman lake over there."[40] In a required response to the Navy Department concerning special character guidance for "youngsters who need special attention," Jimmy let his emotions leak when he referred to the navy's "*non-sensical [sic]* attitude." Again he had the strength of fact on his side that a uniform was not always an indicator of maturity, but he might have hurt his argument by using one hyphenated word in the otherwise well-written, logical, and rational letter.[41] Another example was his reaction to an official letter on commissioned officers' messes that stated, "Officers are expected to display and exercise a high sense of responsibility in the conduct of both personal and official business. Prompt payment of bills is an obligation of every officer in the Naval service. Accordingly, the extension of credit to members is prohibited." In a written response, again not requested, Jimmy wrote, "Now, I ask you if that paragraph makes any sense?" Further, he pointed out that staff decisions made at distant headquarters often did not address realities at respective naval air stations. Continuing, he noted that linen costs varied from one location to another. Although allowed to charge officers on cross-country missions, his station actually stood to lose money by not being allowed to charge actual cost as opposed to the maximum amount set at distant headquarters. In sum, Jimmy had a strong argument to make, but the letter's tone detracted from the message by reminding the reader (or readers) they might not be very smart.[42]

In addition to impatience and impetuousness Jimmy, noted for nearly all his prewar career as a quiet officer, "talked too much" in his later years according to Admiral Burke.[43] Burke was only one of many to observe Jimmy's willingness to speak, the term "outspoken" evident in nearly every fitness report from the middle of World War II through the end of his career. Talking too much was only half the consideration of being outspoken among contemporaries who saw this tendency as a negative. Some thought Jimmy's protracted correspondence and contact with editors and politicians were "end runs." Here again, Jimmy would not have taken issue with detractors as he acknowledged this practice: "maybe the best way to get it done was through the politicians. I don't like to do that but I will certainly try it if nothing else works."[44] Aware that his methods were not universally appreciated, Jimmy was often careful to request recipients of his written opinions to maintain confidentiality. One of many examples was a letter to E. P. Scrivner, a congressman. Enlisting help to get approval from the Armed Services Committee for acquisition of land necessary to expand NAS Olathe, Jimmy ended his epistle stating, "I feel free to make this request on you directly, however, please don't use my name."[45]

Being outspoken was a contributing factor to Jimmy not being selected for rear admiral in 1956. Upon learning Jimmy was not selected, personal friend Orrin W. Shepherd went straight to his congressman, who then talked with the secretary of the navy. Afterward, Shepherd wrote Jimmy on 26 July 1956 "with a request that it not go any further . . . [that] during your career you might have been outspoken . . . and that as a result it might have been embarrassing either to a Naval officer or sister service." Rear Adm. George Anderson, a personal friend as well as professional colleague, addressed a contributing factor to Jimmy in a 25 July 1956 letter asking him "to realize that while it is always a great virtue to be frank, it is not the best thing to . . . be too critical of people . . . who . . . are trying to do the best they can within their own limitations." CNO Adm. Arleigh Burke wrote on 14 May 1956—just before the selection process—that although Jimmy's insights regarding the Sixth Fleet were mostly correct that "perhaps you have been tactless in your criticism." In the same letter, however, Burke noted Jimmy's "paternal fondness" and acknowledged "you are such a good leader." Thoughts of the traits that contributed to Jimmy's pass-over were still on the minds of friends a year later when his promotion was announced. Capt. H. S. "Sid" Bottomley Jr., a heavily decorated dive-bomber pilot, wrote, "It is comforting to know that some of the people who won't back down under fire can still get ahead."[46] And Vice Adm. Robert Goldthwaite wrote, "Congratulations . . . never any question in my mind of your inevitable selection in spite of the wrist slapping you suffered last year." Continuing Goldthwaite said, "Obviously one can slow down but never stop an officer of your caliber who says the right thing in the wrong way to the right people."[47]

The combination of being outspoken and honest did not always serve Jimmy in the manner he intended. Few appreciate a mirror being held in front of them to document less than perfect performance or ability. Not surprisingly, Jimmy was undaunted by such an argument as he believed there was a responsibility to state a high standard and then work to achieve it.[48]

Jimmy often quoted Ernie King and Marc Mitscher's dictum, "I tell people what to do, not how to do it." Mitscher lived by that quote, but King was not at all above violating it and neither was Jimmy. In fact, Jimmy was often quite detailed in telling or showing someone else, at all levels, how to do something. This habit was not necessarily a negative because many appreciated his demonstrated interest and saw it as an example of going above and beyond. Whether "telling how to do it" was regarded as a positive or negative by others, Jimmy either never realized he was not always in concert with his dictum or chose to ignore it in favor of practicality. He was clear enough on the subject to note, "Perhaps we spend too much time on the principles of good leadership and not enough on the techniques."[49]

Although Jimmy fought hard and spoke clearly for the things he believed, he was sometimes wrong. Because he had often committed his thoughts to paper, contemporaries could not help but know and remember when he had advocated a policy not adopted or had championed a view that did not materialize. In addition to having to scrap early World War II fighter tactics and not initially appreciating all-weather and night radar operations, he had to step back from some views on Korea. Within days of the outbreak of the fighting in Korea, Jimmy's boss, Admiral Doyle, thought the conflict could be kept isolated. Jimmy, however, advocated mobilizing industry and manpower: "It's about time the public opinion takes charge and demands this world mess be cleaned up regardless of the cost involved."[50] And when it appeared MacArthur's Inchon victory and rapid push north in the fall of 1950 signaled the end to the conflict, he wrote to the chief of staff of naval forces in the Far East, "If another fire breaks out over your way [get me an assignment to the combat zone]."[51] Like many others, Jimmy did not foresee the Chinese intervention in Korea and the fire that did break out. Of course many worried that the conflict would spread. But most did not have to step back from forceful, written statements that proved incorrect. And despite his voluminous appeals for carrier aviation over many years, he predicted that carrier construction would end with about two nuclear-propelled carriers sometime in the 1960s.[52]

It could be argued that Jimmy sometimes had a propensity to get too close to things to see the whole picture clearly. Perhaps the best example was his 8 June 1955 letter to CNO Burke complaining about the role of carriers and the Sixth Fleet spending so much time in the Mediterranean. Burke was probably surprised that his friend, who so often saw the big picture regarding geopolitics, had stated such a limited vision on this occasion. Burke realized the presence of the Sixth Fleet reassured friendly countries in the region of support from the United States and restrained the Soviet Union. Too, Sixth Fleet presence allowed the U.S. Navy to observe Soviet naval maneuvers.[53]

Dedication was nearly obsession for Jimmy, and this contributed in some degree for him to speak too much too soon. Flag officers who served with Jimmy realized that the higher he rose in prominence, the more this tendency had potential to threaten his career. Admiral Burke, however, best describes why Jimmy's speed of speech did not hurt him earlier and why it was tolerated later. Jimmy's boss during their task force days with Mitscher and his boss at the Pentagon from 1956 into 1958, Burke noted that war does not offer time for indecision. When in combat a commander must make a decision immediately whether that decision is right or wrong. To delay, according to Burke, is to automatically make the wrong choice. At least a quick response provides a fifty-fifty chance of being right.[54] Anyone who knew Jimmy recognized he was always at war. And for those who did not know him, he was quick to remind them that he and they were already participants in World War III, his often-stated definition of the Cold War.

In moments of retrospect Jimmy regretted only the impetuous tone in some of his letters. Everything else was moot, as they were yesterday's battles. And like most other middle-class Americans, there was too much to think about for tomorrow.

Then and Now

In the last year of Jimmy's career, the navy was encountering its usual number of problems. The difference in 1957–58 was that introspection and interviews revealed the navy, again, was its own worst enemy. The AWOL rate had risen from 1,000 a month for 1956 to 1,352 in 1957; venereal disease increased; nearly 18 percent of sailors separated in the past year failed to receive an honorable discharge; and the 1957 courts-martial count was 52,000. Particularly troublesome was a survey of 10,000 enlisted men wherein two-thirds reported that officers were not interested in their personal welfare. As a consequence of these problems, Secretary of the Navy Thomas S. Gates moved the subject of leadership to the forefront.[55]

The subject of leadership has remained on the front burner since 1958. Jimmy had emphasized the subject for years and had a long relationship with Secretary Gates, but the degree of his influence is speculative. What is clearer is that some of Jimmy's practices in the 1950s could have application for leaders at the beginning of the twenty-first century, but others would not work as well, especially in the military. Consequently, Jimmy Flatley's approach to leadership and command must be viewed primarily in the frame of reference of his time.

Upon leaving the *Block Island* in July 1953, Jimmy's last "Captain's Corner" message clearly stated his motivation for his periodic messages in the ship's newspaper. "I have tried to present . . . information that I felt would be of value to you in the day to day struggle for happiness on earth and at the same time help you to eventually achieve eternal happiness in Heaven."[56] Jimmy's honesty was widely recognized by those who knew him. Former chairman of the Joint Chiefs of Staff, Adm. Thomas Moorer recalls, "You could take anything Jimmy Flatley said to the bank." But Moorer also noted that Jimmy's inspirational leadership would have been handicapped in later years when religion as a basis for ethical conduct was largely replaced with political correctness. Too, Moorer noted Jimmy's honesty would not help his career in today's politically correct world.[57] Had Jimmy lived to learn about the events at the infamous Tailhook convention, he would have condemned the actions of pilots involved but would also have been livid in regard to the political decimation policy of punishment. And he would have been even more livid to hear the overwhelming silence of flag officers that did not protest the policy.[58]

Without his religious foundation, Jimmy would have been disarmed in the politically correct years at the end of the twentieth century and dawn of the twenty-first. In countless speeches and articles throughout his years as a commanding officer, he based everything on spiritual means, as he believed only this type of base could successfully resist international communism. Noting the considerable variance of societal mores and folkways between his era and that of the end of the century, he would especially regret that religion is often discounted as the foundation for moral emphasis in leadership and command. He would find that the leadership structure of the navy is still intact (admirals order captains who order commanders, and down the chain of command), but would wonder how effective the structure and its process (how it works, particularly its effectiveness toward defined objectives) could be without moral emphasis in leadership. Indeed, some retired navy officers in recent years have openly questioned whether a nonreligious standard would be able to provide an ethical foundation for contemporary officers.[59]

Legacy of Leadership and Command

In July 1942 Jimmy began corresponding with editors of newspapers and national magazines. In the following fifteen years he had considerable success in sharing his thoughts with the public through newspaper editors, primarily due to their proximity to his duty station or command. Relationships with editors of national publications—particularly Henry Luce (*Time-Life-Fortune*), Eric C. Lambert (*American Magazine*) and Hanson Baldwin (*New York Times* military editor)—evolved from professional to personal relationships but with mixed results in presenting Jimmy's perspectives. As noted earlier, the heaviest volume of correspondence between Jimmy and magazine editors centered on national policy with special emphasis on the conflict between the navy and air force. In these exchanges the subject of leadership and command was peripheral.

In the last year of his career, however, Jimmy found a conduit to spread concepts of leadership and command. Having written over a hundred articles for his station and ship command newspapers, Jimmy began to direct his thoughts to the entire navy. While station and ship commands propelled him to address a number of personal, professional, and moral concerns, he fully understood that the one subject applicable to all ranks, rates, and commands was leadership. Having prepared a lengthy paper for use in a two-to-three-day indoctrination seminar for prospective commanding officers at the Pentagon, he looked for another process for communicating his views about leadership and command when the proposed course was not established. Talks and correspondence in late 1957 with Frank Uhlig, editor of *Our Navy,* immediately proved beneficial. Uhlig edited Jimmy's protracted "Command Objectives" paper and solicited other contributions. A series of articles by Jimmy and others was intended to raise leadership awareness and begin a navy-wide dialogue. Although Jimmy soon fell ill, Uhlig carried through with the project. Articles written by Jimmy and edited by Uhlig appeared for years after Jimmy's untimely death. Also appearing years later was "Command Objectives" in its original form, distributed by the commander in chief of the U.S. Atlantic Fleet. The introductory letter cited Jimmy as "one of the more dynamic leaders produced in our generation."

Jimmy's final efforts on leadership and command were directed to both officers and enlisted men in *Our Navy* publications.[60] A new title, "What Makes a Good Skipper," replaced "Command Objectives" as a title. Another article, "That's The Way Buck Does It," was as much intended for the enlisted reader as officers while another article, "Suppose a Stranger Came Up," was directed primarily to enlisted men. Like his ship and station newspaper articles, Jimmy clearly identified both the problem and the audience to which it was intended. Having made countless forays as a commander into his ships and around his stations to see, speak, and listen, he knew what made his crew unhappy. Consequently his articles acknowledged problems and offered reforms. Convinced that chief petty officers were the heart of the navy, Jimmy encouraged CPOs to be ever mindful of their salient leadership role. Officers were admonished to first earn their CPOs' trust, then state clear expectations, and finally recognize that their proficiency and effective leadership depended on how they related and listened to their CPOs.

It is apparent that Jimmy, like countless others since the beginning of time, was attempting to state a formula that promised successful leadership. He knew, of course, that such a formula had historically proven elusive.

It is no surprise that the issues of leadership and command are complicated and complex because human beings are complicated and complex. Understanding this, Jimmy never devised a motto type of formula for universal application. Still, his legacy was built around a raised awareness of leadership and command by virtue of sharing concepts with peers and juniors. Jimmy believed in and demonstrated courage, commitment, competence, compassion, effective communication, and a transformational approach to leadership. But even this formula invites challenge when an officer has demonstrated all these attributes but has nonetheless left a legacy with less than unanimous agreement on success. The career of the late Adm. Elmo R. Zumwalt Jr. is one example. Zumwalt exhibited courage during the Battle of Savo Island in August 1942 and the October 1944 Surigao Strait phase of the Battle of Leyte Gulf. He was unquestionably committed to his nation and navy, was sufficiently competent to earn four stars plus appointment as chief of naval operations during the Vietnam War. The youngest CNO to that time, he was particularly noted for his communication process (the "Z Grams") that rifled a message to all commands rather than allowing a change to be slowed or modified as it filtered down. Compassion was either his greatest strength or weakest trait according to his supporters or detractors as he initiated numerous changes in navy tradition. Jimmie Thach, among others, was upset with Zumwalt's changes and feared that Zumwalt was destroying the navy.[61] Others, however, believe the changes promulgated by Zumwalt may have actually saved the navy by his response to cultural changes.[62]

Occasionally, seasoned leaders are too far removed in time and experience to remember that young students of leadership and command could use an inspiration for a starting point. Perhaps such inspiration could be based on knowledge that Vice Adm. Jimmy Flatley, Adm. Jimmie Thach, and Butch O'Hare—the transformational leaders who devised and implemented successful fighter tactics in the most difficult days of World War II—graduated in the bottom quarter of their respective academy classes. Flatley and O'Hare stated that leaders were not born, and Thach agreed in principle that effective leadership was a learning process. If still living at the beginning of the twenty-first century, all three would be pleased that their experiences in leadership and command are being reviewed and assessed for practices that others can incorporate or reject.

15

Last Assignment

IN JULY 1956 Jimmy became the director of the Special Weapons Branch, Strategic Plans Division, in the Office of the Chief of Naval Operations. Concerned with strategic planning involving the employment of nuclear weapons, he could speak only in general terms when addressing the matter as his work was classified. Not classified in the mid-1950s was thinking at influential levels that a limited nuclear war was a possibility.[1] And a limited nuclear war might see the introduction of nuclear weapons that could be delivered by carrier aircraft.

Despite the significance of his new assignment and satisfaction of settling into a normal family routine in the outskirts of Washington, D.C., the summer of 1956 was not one of the happiest periods in Jimmy's career. In late July the list of thirty-three captains promoted to rear admiral was announced. Eleven, one-third of those selected, were graduates of Jimmy's Naval Academy class of 1929. But Jimmy's name was not on the list. While he was hurt and disappointed, his friends in and outside the navy were incensed. Rear Adm. George W. Anderson Jr., a future CNO, wrote Jimmy on 25 July that he was "very distressed [and] most disappointed." Rear Adm. Robert B. Pirie expressed the same sentiments in a 10 August letter, as did a number of active, retired, and future flag officers. Some also expressed their disappointment with several who had been advanced. Adm. Felix Stump, Jimmy's boss during the late 1940s while Jimmy was with the Atlantic Fleet, served as president of the 1956 selection board. Stump wrote Jimmy on 19 July 1956 that he "could give . . . a lot of advice which I think you might take, but would probably be as mad as a wet hen," but did urge him to be patient for another year. It was good advice as the shorter list (twenty-five) announced in late July 1957 included Jimmy's name. On 2 August 1957 he passed his physical examination and then went shopping for some new uniforms. On one of his first occasions to wear the new rank, he pinned wings of gold on his oldest son who had graduated from the academy in 1956 and was in the final phase of pilot training at Corpus Christi.

Within weeks of his promotion, Jimmy received another assignment within the Pentagon. Effective 9 October 1957 he became director of the Air Warfare Division. This work was also classified, but Jimmy could speak directly to the navy's concerns of threatened freedom of the seas by the Soviet Union's 450 submarines and the rapid advance in missile technology. The Soviets were rapidly building a large navy and as their ships were being commissioned, many World War II–era U.S. Navy ships were wearing out. A second constant theme for Jimmy when speaking in public or writing articles was that rather than nuclear war with the Soviets, the United States should be more concerned about the possibility of the Soviet Union acquiring additional land and the minds of its population.

While international matters and helping prepare the navy counter the Soviet threat required more time than a day offered, Jimmy nonetheless made time to prepare a document for commanding officers. Wanting to complete the document while his experiences on the bridge were still fresh, he wrote a long paper intended to be the basis for a two- or three-day symposium he hoped to teach at the Pentagon for all officers selected to command a ship. Getting his thoughts down was not difficult, but finding the right title proved to be a challenge. The idea for a symposium or class was lauded but not approved. Having already shared correspondence with *Our Navy* editor Frank Uhlig in regard to a series of articles on command at sea, Jimmy converted his symposium notes into a lengthy article. As it turned out, this project was his last.[2]

At age fifty-one Jimmy Flatley was not on top of the world, but he was on his way. Flag rank was as challenging as he had been told it would be by friends also wearing stars. But for an all-navy person it was a wonderful challenge, and there was much to be accomplished both personally and professionally.

With son Brian at his side on New Year's Day, Jimmy was in a duck blind waiting for a good target, hopefully one better than usually offered by Japanese pilots during a war that now seemed to have been centuries before. Suddenly the beautiful scenery disappeared as he blacked out and fell from his stool. Rushed to a hospital, he recovered sufficiently from what was thought to be a back injury to be moved home. Tests, however, revealed the problem was more than an injured back. His younger brother John, by then an experienced physician, could not believe the difference in the 2 August 1957 X rays taken during Jimmy's required physical for promotion to rear admiral and what he saw on X rays in late January 1958. In those five short months, a tumor the size of a golf ball had grown on one of Jimmy's lungs. With trembling hands, Dr. John Flatley laid down the X rays. He did not need to be told it was cancer, and he held no illusions as to his brother's fate.

For six months Jimmy alternated between denial and acceptance of his condition. On 4 February he underwent surgery at Bethesda Naval Hospital to remove the tumor, and for the next few months his home became his office. Friends paid for Jimmy to take a quick trip to the Lourdes Shrine—famous among Catholics for its miracles—where he and longtime friend Ch. Maurice S. Sheehy, USNR, "put our case before the Supreme Court of prayer."[3] Like the insidious character of many cancers, Jimmy's cancer gave him little pain, though he suffered mostly from weakness following radiation treatments. By April he was advising friends that he had "licked this cancer thing and am on the way to complete recovery."[4] Despite Jimmy's optimism and pronouncements to friends that he was proving the medical profession wrong, navy doctors had made the same diagnosis as Dr. John Flatley, and on 2 June the navy placed Jimmy on the Temporary Disability Retired List. In the same correspondence, Jimmy was notified that since he had been specially commended by the president of the United States for performance of duty in actual combat, he had been advanced on the retired list to the rank of vice admiral, effective 2 June 1958. Before his fifty-second birth-day on 17 June, Jimmy was back in the hospital at Bethesda. Having fully accepted the will of God, on 9 July 1958 he gave up his will to remain on duty in this life. Burial in Arlington on the eleventh was "fit-ting that his mortal remains rest . . . among those to whom security of life was not an obsession."[5]

Honors and Remembrance

Immediately upon Jimmy's passing, tributes flooded into the Flatley home in Chevy Chase, Maryland. Particularly moving were comments from longtime friends Chief of Naval Operations Arleigh Burke and Secretary of the Navy Thomas S. Gates Jr. Six months later Gates, sur-rounded by dozens of flag officers and high ranking civilians, hosted a ceremony in his office on 23 December 1958 to present the Distinguished Service Medal (posthumously) to Dotty Flatley. The medal recognized Jimmy's inspiring leadership and exceptional contribution to the suc-cessful growth of naval aviation from July 1953 to June 1958.

Actually, tributes to Jimmy began before his death. Invited to be the guest of honor and to receive an award from the *Yorktown* (CV-10) Association at its eleventh annual reunion 3–5 May 1958, Jimmy was too ill to attend. However, a telephone hookup was arranged in the ball-room of the Hotel Roosevelt in New York City, and Jimmy was thereby enabled to hear the presentation at his home.

In 1959 the navy accepted an offer from the Columbus Division of North American Aviation to sponsor an annual award to the naval air unit or units that excelled in safety during an annual operation. Further, North American requested that the trophy be designated the "Admiral James H. Flatley Memorial Award for Naval Aviation Safety." The navy announced in an OpNav instruction that the award, enthusiastically supported by CNO Burke, would be made each fiscal year to one attack carrier and one antisubmarine carrier in recognition of outstanding achievement in accident prevention during aircraft carrier operations. Selected carriers received temporary custody of a large plaque and per-manent custody of a miniature replica. First awards in 1959 went to

USS *Ranger* (CVA-61) and USS *Antietam* (CVS-36). Several miniature plaques are on permanent display aboard the museum carrier *Yorktown* —Jimmy's ship in 1943—having been donated by either the curator of the navy or reunion groups after recipient carriers were decommissioned and scrapped.[6]

After Jimmy left Olathe in 1952, Kansas City area newspapers continually reported on his assignments, promotion to rear admiral, and his final battle. Many of the same friends who had sponsored his gala farewell party gathered again with navy officials to plan a memorial for Jimmy. Agreement was reached and the previously unnamed flight operations area of NAS Olathe—runways laid over the historic Santa Fe and Oregon trails that opened the West—was officially designated Flatley Field on Armed Forces Day in May 1962. A year earlier the Johnson County Navy League—remembering that Jimmy had championed the idea of naming streets within the complex for naval aviators from the region lost during World War II—had sponsored a monument outside the main gate. The monument designated the main street of the naval air station as Flatley Road in remembrance of the admiral and in recognition of his interest and participation in civic and community affairs.

As at earlier events, Dotty was the center of attention when the navy honored Jimmy at Norfolk Naval Air Station. And like earlier events, this one became a family reunion with sons Lt. Brian A. and Cdr. James H. III in attendance along with other family and friends. In a ceremony conducted by Vice Adm. Robert L. Townsend and Capt. E. M. Cooke Jr., the Fleet Airborne Electronics Training Unit was dedicated on 7 December 1970. The three-building training center is still known as Flatley Center.[7]

With a formal dedication ceremony on 26 June 1976, Green Bay, Wisconsin, honored Jimmy's memory by creating the Admiral Flatley Memorial Park in the downtown area at the eastern foot of the Main Street Bridge. At the river's edge of the park, two large weatherproof bronze plaques, one a bas-relief of Jimmy with an inscription, adorn a ten-foot-high, two-and-a-half-ton monument of precast concrete. Easily viewed from the Fox River as well as from inside the park, Green Bay not only honored a hometown boy but also upgraded the Bay Beach waterfront area with new trees, flowers, benches, and a circular lighted water fountain.

On 15 May 1980 at Bath, Maine, Dotty Flatley—with one of the all-time great swings of the champagne bottle—christened the new *Oliver Hazard Perry*–class guided missile frigate USS *Flatley* (FFG-21). Just over a year later on 20 June 1981 Rear Adm. (select) James H. Flatley III read the commissioning directive for the forty-one-hundred-ton ship named in his father's honor. Other ships of the class named in honor of Jimmy's friends included *Clark* (FFG-11), *Crommelin* (FFG-37), *Doyle* (FFG-39) and *Thach* (FFG-43). The *Flatley* served until 11 May 1996 when it was decommissioned and transferred to Turkey.

Although friends in Kansas City, Green Bay, Norfolk, and other cities considered Jimmy "their own," perhaps no group was as regular in their remembrance of him as the *Yorktown* (CV-10) Association membership. James T. Bryan Jr., a former ordnance officer and Wall Street business-man who founded the association in 1948 and served as its leader for nearly fifty years, considered Jimmy the patron saint of *Yorktown* even before it became a museum. Organizing a Carrier Aviation Hall of Fame aboard the museum ship, Bryan enlisted retired flag officers Arleigh Burke, George W. Anderson Jr. (who succeeded Burke as chief of naval operations), and Bill Martin to serve as the selection committee. Not surprisingly Jimmy, along with old friend Jimmie Thach, was named in the first group selected and inducted in 1981. In 1986 the association acquired an F6F Hellcat for permanent display and dedicated it to Jimmy.

Three years later on 4 May 1984 Jimmy again appeared in bronze, this time as one of the first two (Thach was the other) World War II fighter pilots to be inducted into the Hall of Honor within the National Museum of Naval Aviation, NAS Pensacola. A committee appointed by the deputy of naval operations (air warfare) based enshrinement on sus-tained performance in or for naval aviation; superior contributions in the technical or tactical development of naval aviation; and unique and superior flight achievement in combat or noncombat flight operations. Jimmy had indeed qualified on all three. Several retired officers on the museum's Foundation board that served with Jimmy during World War II and afterward, approved the wording for his plaque. His record appears on this plaque as it does on the others placed in his honor, but Jimmy would have greatly appreciated his peers recognizing the essence of his career with the words thereon. The plaque's concluding line reads, "Exercised outstanding professional ability and inspiring leadership throughout his career and contributed significantly to the moral standards of the Navy by his understanding, experience, advice and example."

Though proud of all his family, Jimmy would have smiled broadly upon viewing the naval service rendered by his oldest son. After graduating from the academy in 1956, James H. Flatley III made unprecedented test landings of a C-130 Hercules transport plane on a carrier (USS *Forrestal*) in 1964 before serving three combat tours in Vietnam flying the F-4 Phantom. He later broke the record for most carrier landings, commanded carrier USS *Saratoga* (CV-60), earned most of the same combat and meritorious service medals earlier awarded to his father, and served five years as a rear admiral before retiring in 1987. Jimmy would also have been happy to know two grandsons, Cdr. James H. "Seamus" Flatley and Cdr. Joseph Francis Flatley, became fighter pilots. And, he would not have been surprised to know that Dotty has continued to support naval aviation. Sponsored by the *Yorktown* Association, the "Dorothy M. Flatley Award" has been presented annually—often by Dotty personally—since 1988 to women exemplifying her inspirational support as a carrier aviator's wife, mother, or grandmother.

Security of Life Was Not an Obsession

Years before World War II Jimmy Flatley knew a time would come when all he would have was that which he had given away. He lived his life accordingly, living each day as though it was his last, giving his best, and attempting to persuade others to live as he lived, but without the mistakes he had made as a young man. During his last years he became even more intense in trying to teach others how to lead both in theory and by example. In the summer of 1958 his time came. Though never rich materially, his sense of purpose and daily exercise of practicing the Golden Rule made him a very rich man in the memories of those with whom he served.

Appendix

Combat and Command Decorations

Navy Cross

"For extraordinary heroism and conspicuous courage as pilot of an airplane of a Fighting Squadron in action against enemy Japanese forces in
the Battle of the Coral Sea on May 7 and May 8, 1942. As leader of the
fighter escort for our own planes attacking an enemy Japanese carrier on
May 7, Lieutenant Commander Flatley fearlessly engaged enemy fighters,
destroying one and assisting in the destruction of another with no loss to his
escort group. That evening, he led a seven plane division on combat air patrol
in a fierce attack and resultant dispersal of a formation of enemy scouting
planes, assisting in the destruction of two of them. On May 8, fighting per-
sistently and at great odds, he again led a division of the combat air patrol
in a courageous attack against enemy aircraft attacking our surface forces
and destroyed an enemy fighter harassing our anti-torpedo plane patrol and
assisted in the destruction of two others. On all these occasions, Lieutenant
Commander Flatley displayed the highest qualities of leadership, aggressiveness and complete disregard for his own personal safety."

(Permanent citation signed by James Forrestal, then Acting Secretary of the Navy.)

Distinguished Service Medal (Posthumous)

"For exceptionally meritorious service to the Government of the United
States in diverse duties of great responsibility from July 1953 to June 1958.
Exercising outstanding professional ability and inspiring leadership throughout this period, Vice Admiral Flatley skillfully carried out his varied and
exacting assignments. As Officer in Charge, U.S. Naval Aviation Safety
Activity and later, Commander, U.S. Naval Air Bases, Fifth Naval District,
he administered the responsibilities of his command with astute judgment

and foresight. A strong advocate and a relentless worker in support of aviation safety, he developed sound aviation training programs producing results which will remain forever an integral part of the evolution of naval aviation. As Commanding Officer of two aircraft carriers, the U.S.S. BLOCK ISLAND (CVE-106) and, later, the U.S.S. LAKE CHAMPLAIN (CVA-39), Vice Admiral Flatley succeeded in winning two highly coveted Battle 'E' pennants. In July 1956, he moved to the office of the Chief of Naval Operations as Head, Special Weapons Plans Branch, Strategic Plans Division; and, in October 1957, he became Director, Air Warfare Division. In both of these positions, he displayed broad capability and sound judgment in planning, coordinating, and directing the development of improved aviation weapons systems, thus assuring greater readiness of naval combatant forces. Throughout his entire naval career, he had contributed, by his understanding, experience, advice and example, to the moral standards of the Navy. During the later months of 1957 and the early months of 1958, his advice concerning the Navy's moral leadership program was frequently sought and used. Vice Admiral Flatley's distinguished record as a senior naval officer reflects the highest credit upon himself and the United States Naval Service."

(Permanent citation signed by Thomas S. Gates Jr., Secretary of the Navy.)

Legion of Merit

"For exceptionally meritorious conduct in the performance of outstanding service as Operations Officer on the Staff of Commander FIRST Carrier Task Force, Pacific, from 6 December 1944 through 28 May 1945. Charged with the responsibility for planning and conducting air operations in support of amphibious landings for the conquest of Iwo Jima and later of Okinawa, which included two large scale strikes against Tokyo, as well as strikes on the Kure Naval Base, enemy installations in Kyushu, support missions in the vicinity of our landings, and an air attack on major units of the Japanese Fleet on 7 April 1945, he consistently demonstrated high professional skill, initiative, and resourcefulness. During a protracted series of bitterly fought air engagements he set an inspiring example of calmness and courage, particularly on two occasions when hits by suicide dive bombers of the flagship required the Task Force Commander to shift his flag, when in spite of the difficulties involved, he quietly, quickly, and efficiently reestablished control of operations. His outstanding professional skill was at all times inspiring and in keeping with the highest traditions of the United States Naval Service."

(Initial and permanent citations signed by Vice Admiral M. A. Mitscher.)

Distinguished Flying Cross

"For heroism and extraordinary achievement in the line of his profession as a Fighting Squadron Commander attached to the U.S.S. ENTERPRISE while engaged with enemy Japanese naval forces in the Solomon Islands Area during the period from November 13 to 15, 1942. In the face of heavy anti-aircraft fire and enemy fighter opposition, Lieutenant Commander Flatley repeatedly led his squadron against Japanese surface and air forces, destroying at least ten enemy aircraft and inflicting heavy damage by strafing enemy combatant ships, transport, and shore installations. His outstanding leadership, great courage, and resolute determination were an inspiration to his command and in keeping with the highest traditions of the United States Naval Service."

(Permanent citation signed by Frank Knox, Secretary of the Navy.)

Distinguished Flying Cross (Second Award)

"For meritorious achievement as Commander of Fighting Squadron TEN, attached to the U.S.S. ENTERPRISE, during action against enemy Japanese forces east of Rennell Island on the afternoon of January 30, 1943. Sighting a formation of twelve hostile torpedo bombers maneuvering into striking position for an attack upon the U.S.S. CHICAGO, Lieutenant Commander Flatley, diving from an altitude of 14,000 feet, sped his patrol to the rescue of the threatened cruiser and engaged the enemy in an area already under vigorous fire from our own anti-aircraft batteries. Undeterred by a stream of blistering shells from Japanese planes, he fought to his last round of ammunition, shooting one hostile bomber down in flames and driving another into destructive range of a wing mate's guns. His superb flying skill and relentless devotion to duty were in keeping with the highest traditions of the United States Naval Service."

(Initial citation signed by Frank Knox, Secretary of the Navy.)

Distinguished Flying Cross (Third Award)

"For heroism and extraordinary achievement in aerial flight as Commander of an Air Group in action against enemy Japanese forces on Marcus Island, August 31, 1943. Exercising forceful leadership and tireless effort, Commander Flatley trained his air group efficiently and expeditiously prior to the actual operations and, subsequently effecting an extremely hazardous night take-off, promptly rendezvoused his planes and proceeded with his group to the objective, delivering the first attack before dawn. Courageously remaining over the target area for four hours, he skillfully directed and coordinated other attacks of the striking group and later the same day accompanied another flight and again directed a daring bombing and strafing raid on this important island. Commander Flatley's superb airmanship, aggressive fighting spirit and valiant devotion to duty contributed materially to the success of these vital missions and were in keeping with the highest traditions of the United States Naval Service."

(Permanent citation signed by James Forrestal, Secretary of the Navy.)

Bronze Star

"For meritorious service as Operations Officer on the staff of the Commander of the First Carrier Task Force, during action against enemy Japanese forces in the vicinity of the Philippine Islands, Formosa and the Nansei Shoto from September through October 1944. Discharging his duties with great professional skill and efficiency, Captain (then Commander) Flatley aided in the support of amphibious landings, thereby contributing materially in the success of many hazardous missions. His initiative and zealous devotion to duty throughout were in keeping with the highest traditions of the United States Naval Service."

(Initial citation signed by Vice Admiral M. A. Mitscher; permanent citation signed by James Forrestal, Secretary of the Navy.)

Commendation Ribbon

"For distinguishing himself by meritorious service on the Staff of Commander FIRST Carrier Task Force, Pacific on 11 May 1945. When the ship on which he was embarked was hit by two enemy aircraft, he voluntarily led parties below decks to rescue personnel who had been overcome in the smoke filled compartments. His coolness and leadership were at all times inspiring and in keeping with the highest traditions of the United States Naval Service."

(Initial and permanent citations signed by Admiral R. A. Spruance.)

Notes

Where the information was available, day, month, and year have been cited for personal conversations, interviews, fitness reports, and other unpublished material of that nature. In cases were the day was unknown, just month and year are shown. Unless otherwise stated, all interviews and conversations are with the author.

Chapter 1. *A Little Rogue*

1. Olynyk, *USN Credits for Destruction of Enemy Aircraft,* published by the author October 1982. In the absence of an official listing by the U. S. Navy, Olynyk's work serves as perhaps the best objective research into determination of how many planes a naval aviator may have destroyed in the war.

2. Blackburn, *Jolly Rogers,* 260; and conversation, July 1989.

3. Boyington, *Baa Baa Black Sheep.* When Rear Adm. James W. "Pop" Condit was asked in May 1996 about Pappy Boyington's story about him, Pop stated that Pappy embellished remembrance of him. Pop said he did defend Boyington's reputation verbally but he never dove across a table to attack another officer on the matter. Also, Pop recalled that Boyington intentionally misspelled his name and that of some others so that no one could challenge him in court.

4. Vice Adm. James H. Flatley Jr. (abbreviated as JHF in further citations), letter to Vice Adm. Gerald F. Bogan, 14 January 1950.

5. *The Pride,* Green Bay, Wisconsin, 9 June 1966, 3.

6. Dr. John Flatley, Jimmy's youngest brother, provided the story of Jimmy Flatley's youth. Also contributing was a sister, Mrs. Ruth Early.

7. All flight notations are derived from Jimmy Flatley's flight logs. All seven are well preserved but like those of many other pilots, bureau numbers do not always match the aircraft type. In his first log book Jimmy occasionally listed F4B-4 for bureau numbers that were actually F4B-2s. Determination of error is based on observations that the F4B-4 was not assigned to his squadron (VF-5B) in 1931–34 and was not yet in service on the dates of certain flights. In 1939–40

Jimmy flew the later F4B-4 model with a 550 hp Pratt and Whitney 1340-16 engine that could reach 188 mph.

8. Mrs. Dorothy Flatley, interview, 25 November 1997, and personal diary written in 1989. At the time of this writing ninety-three-year-old Dotty Flatley enjoys good health.

Chapter 2: *Flying in the Depression-era Navy*

1. Grossnick, *U.S. Naval Aviation,* 448.

2. *Congressional Record,* Senate (5 August 1958) 14778.

3. Reynolds, *Admiral John Towers,* 238.

4. JHF, letter to his mother, Joan Flatley, 14 February 1934. Jimmy's attitude changed in the late 1930s as he constantly volunteered to return to Hawaii, specifically requesting a billet as commanding officer of a patrol squadron or seaplane tender.

5. The P2Y-3 had both engines mounted at the leading edge of the upper wing: the lower wing for all versions of this plane had a smaller wing mounted on the hull to which the floats were attached.

6. Lt. Cdr. Joel J. White, Medical Corps, USN, by direction of Rear Adm. W. W. Johnson, commander of aircraft, Base Force, "A Brief History of the Fleet Patrol Plane Squadrons from the Organization of the first Squadron in 1919 to the Present Organization in 1935," 91–93, National Archives (abbreviated NA in further citations). An excellent general source is Lawson, ed., *History of U.S. Naval Air Power,* 31–35.

7. Lt. Cdr. Harold J. Brow on JHF fitness report, 30 October 1934.

8. Brow on JHF fitness report, May 1936.

9. Brow on JHF fitness report, 10 April 1935.

10. Comprising the 162 were 54 F3F-1s; 81 F3F-2s; and 27 F3F-3s.

11. Bureau of Aeronautics, Navy Department, *News Letter,* No. 63 (1 December 1937) and No. 47 (1 April 1937).

12. Commander of aircraft, Battle Force, letter to COs of VF-2, VF-3, VF-4, VF-5, VF-6, VMF-2, subject: aircraft tactical instructions, compilation of 29 July 1937, 2–3, NA.

13. Ibid.

14. Ibid., 3–4.

15. Ibid.

16. Adm. John J. Hyland, letter to David Flatley, 24 September 1986.

17. ComAir, Battle Force, letter to carrier squadron commanders, 29 July 1937, 4, NA.

18. Hyland to David Flatley.

19. Ibid.

20. Ibid. Also see Gates, "Track of the Tomcatters," 15.

21. Commander of aircraft, Battle Force, letter to CV squadron commanders and representatives, 17 March 1937, 1, NA.

22. ComAir, Battle Force, letter to CV squadron commanders and representatives, 4 August 1937, 34–35, NA.

23. Ibid., 100.

24. Ibid., 70.

25. Ibid., 35.

26. Ibid., 100.

27. Ibid., 101.

28. Despite the many positives, when reading the final compilation, Jimmy probably wished he had advocated a training carrier at NAS Pensacola as did another of the respondents.

29. Some sources, including the Fall 1984 *Hook* article, indicate a direct transfer to the F3F-2s, but all bureau numbers—9627 through 9674—in Flatley's log book match the F2F-1 "type of machine." Also see O'Leary, "Roll Out the Barrels!" 31–43. This is an interesting article on the development of the F3F Grummans with outstanding pictures.

30. From the Adm. John "Jimmie" Thach oral history: "We had a wonderful thing called a camera gun, and this camera was synchronized with a firing trigger so that you could go up and fight each other with a camera gun, and it had a little stop watch in it. That showed up in the corner of every frame of the film. Before you left the ground all the watches in the camera gun were synchronized, and you could go up and practice fighting and then come back and look at the film and you could tell exactly, there was no argument about who shot first. . . . [It was] unique in the U.S. Navy. . . . No other aviation squadron had it . . . it was a tremendous trainer . . . solved all arguments."

31. Interview with Cdr. Perry W. Ustick, USN (Ret.), who was aloft in a SOC-1 during the Battle of Tassafaronga when his cruiser, USS *Northampton* (CA-26), was sunk. He commented in November 1984 that no matter what official speed the Navy listed for the SOC-1, it could reach 150 mph only in a fatal crash dive.

32. JHF, letter to Bureau of Aeronautics, 7 February 1938.

33. Capt. W. L. Lind, letter to Bureau of Aeronautics, 26 August 1938.

34. Dorothy Flatley, letter to family, 30 March 1939.

35. Lind, letter to Bureau of Aeronautics, 16 September 1938.

36. Ewing, *American Cruisers,* 135.

37. Lind, letter to Bureau of Aeronautics, 10 February 1939.

38. Dorothy Flatley, letters to family, 27 February and 30 March 1939.

39. Lind on JHF fitness report, 20 October 1939.

Chapter 3: *Preparation for War*

1. CNO Adm. Harold Stark, letter to commander in chief, U.S. Fleet, subject: emergency procurement of naval aircraft, 10 October 1939, NA.

2. Churchill, *Their Finest Hour,* 288–91. (Figures from the Battle of Britain

were announced in the summer of 1940 and further documented in 1948 after researching German figures.)

3. There were slight differences in training phases between 1931 and 1939. In 1931, 40 percent was ground school and 60 percent flight training; but the five squadrons carried different evaluation totals and three had different names: Squadron One, 16 percent; Two, 16 percent; Three (then named Observation planes), 16 percent: Four (then named Instructional Flying), 5 percent; and Five (then named Fighting planes), 7 percent.

4. Grossnick, *U.S. Naval Aviation,* 96.

5. Ibid., 108.

6. Butch flew five different F4Bs for five hours on this day while Jimmy flew three different F4Bs for a total of 2.6 hours. All were F4B-4 or an F4B-4A. Information derived from the flight log books of both pilots.

7. Capt. A. W. Fitch on JHF fitness report, 25 April 1940.

8. Fitch on JHF fitness report, 10 October 1939.

9. Capt. A. C. Read on JHF fitness report, 14 January 1941.

10. Outlaw, conversation, June 1994.

11. Clark and Reynolds, *Carrier Admiral,* 74.

12. Ibid., 75. (The document was actually 160 pages including maps rather than the 350 Clark stated but no doubt it seemed more like 350 pages.)

13. Ibid.

14. Capt. Charles Mason on JHF fitness report, undated but circa April 1941.

15. Clark and Reynolds, *Carrier Admiral,* 73–74.

16. Lt. Cdr. Jimmy B. Taylor Jr., USNR, letter to chief of the Bureau of Aeronautics, "Report on Training Facilities at Pensacola, Corpus Christi and Jacksonville," 26 March 1942. One of the greatest of all World War II–era test pilots, Taylor was killed in 1942 testing a modified F4F Wildcat. The Test Pilot Hall of Honor, aboard the museum ship *Yorktown* in Charleston Harbor is named in his honor.

17. Ibid.

18. Ibid.

19. Mason on JHF fitness report, 15 September 1941.

Chapter 4: *Pearl Harbor*

1. VF-2 on *Lexington;* VF-3 on *Saratoga;* VF-41 and -42 on *Ranger;* VF-5 on *Yorktown;* VF-6 on *Enterprise;* VF-71 and -72 on *Wasp;* and VF-8 on *Hornet.*

2. In the contemporary navy the terms *squadron* and *section* still find use, but the term *division* is long gone as is the tactic of flying large numbers of fighters from a carrier together in formation to attack the same target.

3. Capt. Marc A. Mitscher (then acting as chief of the Bureau of Aeronautics), letter to commander of aircraft, Battle Force, subject: proposal for assignment of carrier-based aircraft, 2 October 1940, NA.

4. Ibid.

5. Cdr. H. S. Duckworth, letter to the chief of the Bureau of Aeronautics, 23 Dec. 1940, NA.

6. JHF, letter to Dotty, 16 October 1941.

7. JHF, memo to heads of departments, 18 November 1941.

8. Cdr. Paul Ramsey, letter to JHF, March 1942; an interesting letter with Ramsey alternating personal jibes with official instructions.

9. JHF, letters to Dotty, 22 and 28 October 1941; 4 November 1941.

10. JHF, letter to Dotty, 17 November 1941. "We are staying behind to do more extra work on our landing gear which isn't any too strong."

11. Ramsey, memo on "Engine operation," undated but circa July 1941.

12. JHF, letter to Dotty, 4 December 1941.

13. To Dotty, 8 November 1941.

14. To Dotty, 22 October, 5 and 28 November 1941.

15. To Dotty, 31 October 1941 (mail cost three cents by boat and twenty cents by Pan–American Clipper).

16. To Dotty, 16, 17, and 18 October 1941.

17. To Dotty, 18 October 1941.

18. To Dotty, 22 October 1941.

19. To Dotty, 25 October 1941.

20. To Dotty, 28 October 1941.

21. Ramsey, memo, undated but circa October 1941.

22. JHF, letter to Dotty, 19 November 1941.

23. To Dotty, 20 November 1941.

24. CO of USS *Saratoga,* letter to the commander of aircraft, Battle Force, regarding fighting planes, 30 November 1939, NA.

25. Gillette, "Fortunate Blunder," 66 (although not discussed herein, this interesting article is recommended reading).

26. Considering the significance of air operations since 7 December 1941, Jimmy evidently did not consider the short flights to and from Pearl on the thirteenth and fourteenth of December worthy of entrance into his log book. Given his meticulous attention to the log and especially the exact number of carrier landings, these omissions are unusual.

27. Given the demands of the new war, Jimmy was unable to take his oath until 14 March 1942 in San Diego.

28. The XF4F-4, BuNo. 1897, had hydraulic folding wings, but later F4F-4s wings were folded manually. More important, future F4F-4s had six guns, not four like the experimental 1897.

29. Rear Adm. James H. Flatley Jr., "What Makes a Good Skipper?" 20.

30. Dorothy Flatley, interview, 20 November 1995; and Vejtasa, letter to author, 20 April 1996.

31. Callan, interview, 14 April 1994.

32. Thach, interview at Bureau of Aeronautics, 29 August 1942.

33. Capt. W. L. Lind on JHF fitness report, 15 April 1938.

34. Potter, *Bull Halsey,* 139–40.

35. Moorer, interview, 3 May 1996.

36. Vejtasa, letter, 20 April 1996.

Chapter 5: *Battle of the Coral Sea*

1. JHF, letter to Bureau of Navigation, 4 April 1942.

2. Thach, interview, 5. In a conversation with John Lundstrom, Thach said that he preferred the "Jimmie" spelling. That preference is used herein to better distinguish Jimmie Thach from Jimmy Flatley.

3. Thach oral history.

4. Johnston, *Queen of the Flattops,* 28.

5. It was "so bad we had to open the cockpits to see anything." Vejtasa, letter to author, 30 March 1998.

6. CTC 17.5, dispatch to *Yorktown* and *Lexington,* 6 May 1942, NA.

7. Lundstrom, *The First Team: Pearl Harbor to Midway,* 204.

8. Time, altitude, and other specifics for the 8 May 1942 battle is derived directly from Jimmy's action report for that day. Consequently, readers may note a slight but not significant variance from other sources.

9. Lundstrom, *The First Team: Pearl Harbor to Midway,* 269–70.

Chapter 6: *"The Navy Fighter" and Fighting Squadron Ten*

1. Fourteen pilots were assigned on 3 June, but eight were on detached duty with USS *Long Island* (CVE-1).

2. Foss and Simmons, *Flying Marine,* 20–21.

3. Foss was thinking of Jimmy on 18 December 1992 when Joe wrote on an inscription for Dotty, Rear Adm. James H. Flatley III, and his two navy fighter pilot sons in *A Proud American: The Autobiography of Joe Foss,* written by Foss and his wife, Donna Wild Foss. Foss inscribed the following: "To the Flatley Family, Three generations of great fighter pilots. My best wishes and thanks for being my friends and instructor . . . God Bless you.

4. Adm. Chester Nimitz, message to Adm. Ernest King, 21 June 1942 (courtesy of John Lundstrom).

5. Lt. Cdr. Dale Harris, letter to JHF, 4 July 1942.

6. Ibid.

7. In a 29 July 1940 confidential memo from Cdr. Miles R. Browning, OinC, Fleet Aircraft Tactical Unit, to Vice Adm. William F. Halsey, Browning recommended a program for the employment of fleet aircraft tactical units. Therein Browning stated, "Recent and repeated instances in which British VF are reported to have achieved amazing successes with small VF forces attacking

large masses of German aircraft . . . indicate the strong possibility that relatively small VF units are more effective due to lack of interference, identification difficulties, etc. Recent conversations with U.S. naval aviators having extensive VF experience have divulged the opinion that a 6-plane VF unit is the optimum number to be simultaneously engaged, no matter what the numbers of the larger formation," NA.

8. "The pilot should approach from astern and slightly to the left so that when contact is made the propeller will be cutting down on the enemy elevator. This will tend to separate the planes and dump the enemy VT into the water. At the instant of contact the speed differential should be small and the movement relative to the enemy should not be rapid. The nose of the fighter should move in to make contact, across to the right, up and away." This quote comes from the undated four-page Thach letter noted in the text.

9. Dotty Flatley, interview, 24 March 1998.

10. Thach's original notebooks are currently held in the archives at the National Museum of Naval Aviation, NAS Pensacola.

11. JHF, letter to Cdr. F. W. "Spig" Wead, 24 June 1943.

12. Vejtasa, letter to author, 20 April 1996.

13. Thach oral history.

14. Carmody (VS-10 1942–43), letter to author, 26 March 1996.

15. Ramage (VS-10 1942–43), interview, 27 April 1996; and comments in Lawson and Tillman, *Carrier Air War,* 7.

16. Carmody, letter, 26 March 1996.

17. Vejtasa, letter, 20 April 1996.

18. Carmody, letter, 26 March 1996.

19. Vejtasa, letter, 20 April 1996.

20. Johnston, *Grim Reapers,* 49–50, and Vejtasa, letter, 20 April 1996. The original drawings are extant in the Flatley papers.

21. Vejtasa, letter, 20 April 1996.

22. Ibid.

23. Ibid.

24. U.S. Naval Air Forces, Pacific Fleet memorandum, 2 September 1942, NA.

25. Aces and credits recognized by American Aces Association: Flatley (6); Billo (6.25); Blair (5); Harris (9.25); Vejtasa (10.25); Leppla (5); Voris (7); Reiserer (9); Gordon (7); Harman (6); Kane (6); and Feightner (9).

26. Johnston, *Grim Reapers,* 81; and Vejtasa, letter, 30 March 1998.

27. Vejtasa, letter to author, 30 March 1998.

28. Cdr. F. W. "Spig" Wead, Navy Department Office of Public Relations, memo to JHF, 10 July 1943. Wead had "recently encountered a statement quoting you (JHF) indirectly to the effect that Stanley Vejtasa is the greatest of the fighter pilots . . . if fact . . . could we have your reasons . . . to be used in a publicity story." An inductee into the Yorktown Carrier Hall of Fame, Vejtasa's

plaque records his unique experience of having been awarded the Navy Cross for dive-bombing and as a fighter pilot. Swede received a total of three Navy Crosses for World War II among other decorations.

29. Vejtasa, letter, 30 March 1998.

30. Feightner, interview, 14 March 1996.

31. JHF, letter to Mr. and Mrs. George W. Leppla, 22 November 1942.

32. Vejtasa, letter, 20 April 1996.

33. The final third of his hours were divided between administrative flights, ferrying, and field and carrier landings.

34. Vejtasa, letter, 20 April 1996.

35. Feightner, interview, 14 March 1996. Jimmy was aware that VF-6 squadron commander, Lt. James Gray (three kills early in the war), for his relative youth arguably made the correct decision at Midway to return VF-6's fuel-starved F4F-4 Wildcats to his carrier rather than ditch them into the water like some of those from VF-8. Such instances only heightened Jimmy's interest in a matter of long-standing concern.

36. Vejtasa, letter, 20 April 1996.

37. Thach oral history.

38. Palmer, interview, 2 November 1993.

39. John Lacouture, interview, 29 April 1996.

40. Ibid.

41. Johnston, *Grim Reapers,* 102.

42. Feightner, interview, 14 March 1996.

Chapter 7: *The Grim Reapers and the Battle of Santa Cruz*

1. Rear Admiral John G. Crommelin was a nearby neighbor in the Montgomery, Alabama, area during the early 1980s. He often visited my office while I was a professor at Faulkner University. While he was comfortable in an old recliner I dubbed "The Crommelin Chair of History," he would relive his days on *Enterprise* and other assignments. Although aware of the deep respect and admiration *Enterprise*'s crew held for him during and after the war, he nonetheless occasionally felt compelled to downplay his unofficial title of "Mr. *Enterprise.*" During the Battle of the Eastern Solomons, he said he was standing at the rear of the carrier's island timing the attack of Japanese dive-bombers (seven seconds) during the bombing runs on the carrier. He correctly announced to those standing nearby that one of the bombs would hit the ship, then announced that a second would hit. But contrary to the legend assigned to him, he stated he did not intend to wait to see where the third would hit because it was apparently heading straight for him. According to "Uncle John," the only reason he did see it strike just below him on the edge of number two elevator was that there were too many sailors already heading through the small door he wanted to use.

2. Ramage, interview, 27 April 1996.

3. Feightner, interview, 14 March 1996.

4. Masse, "Prayers for Grim Reapers." Also, note that Johnston's version in the *Grim Reapers* is slightly different, but the essence is the same.

5. Feightner, interview 14 March 1996.

6. Buell, interview, 29 February 1996.

7. Crommelin gave all credit to navigator Cdr. Richard W. Ruble rather than to Hardison.

8. Lundstrom, *The First Team and Guadalcanal,* 437, 585.

9. Feightner, interview, 14 March 1996.

10. Ibid.

11. Mott, conversation, August 1984 (date missing because the conversation took place long before I ever thought I'd use the comments in a book). A further note: it was a convention for many Naval Academy graduates to take their swords along with them, but it proved to be a bad idea for combat. By 1944 most officers realized how bad an idea it was, particularly in the close confines of ships at war.

12. Buell, interview, 29 February 1996.

13. JHF, letter to CO CV-6, CO TF16, and the secretary of the navy, 12 February 1943.

14. Lundstrom, *The First Team and Guadalcanal,* 423.

Chapter 8: *The Grim Reapers at Guadalcanal and Rennell Island*

1. Feightner, interview, 14 March 1996.

2. Voris, conversation, 9 May 1996.

3. Feightner, interview, 14 March 1996.

4. Crommelin, conversation, March 1985.

5. Feightner, interview, 14 March 1996.

6. Coffin, conversation, August 1986.

7. In log books during World War II, the letters *K* and *J* were entered for tactics and scouting, respectively. There was no letter designation for combat or combat air patrol.

8. Feightner, interview, 14 March 1996.

9. Carmody, letter to author, 26 March 1996.

10. It is not clear from Jimmy's log book entry whether he was speaking just for himself or his division, but he recorded an attack on two destroyers.

11. Feightner, interview, 14 March 1996.

12. Carmody, letter, 26 March 1996.

13. Lundstrom, *First Team and Guadalcanal,* 505. Lundstrom credits Carmody with a bomb hit, but his assessment differs pertaining to the Zero credits during Carmody's pullout.

14. Vejtasa, letter to author, 20 April 1996.

15. Foss and Foss, *A Proud American,* 156.

16. Johnston, *Grim Reapers,* 186–87.

17. Burns, *Then There Was One,* 155–56; and JHF, letter to Bobby's parents, 15 February 1943.

18. Feightner, interview, 14 March 1996.

19. Capt. Joe Foss, USMCR, interview, in the Marine Corps Public Relations Office, 28 April 1943.

20. Rennell Island action report, 31 January 1943, 7, NA.

21. Maj. John Smith, USMC, VMF-334, interview, in the Bureau of Aeronautics, 10 November 1942 (interviewer not identified).

22. Reynolds, *The Fast Carriers,* xix.

23. JHF, letter to Dotty, 20 January 1943.

24. In Jimmy's section of the 31 January 1943 Rennell Island action report, he expressed an opinion that the Japanese may not have seen *Enterprise* at all, NA.

25. Feightner interview, 14 March 1996.

26. JHF, letter to Mr. and Mrs. Edwards, 15 February 1943.

27. Lundstrom, *The First Team and Guadalcanal,* 526. Lundstrom's research with Japanese records indicates seven of eleven land attack planes from the 751 Air Group were lost.

28. "VF-10 Report of Action and Medal Recommendations," 5 February 1943. Herein Jimmy differed from his earlier 31 January 1943 report indicating the Japanese didn't see *Enterprise.* Apparently, he had more complete information on 5 February than he had on 31 January, NA.

29. Feightner, interview, 14 March 1996.

Chapter 9: *Air Group Five Commander on Yorktown (CV-10)*

1. Naval Examining Board, letter to the secretary of the navy, regarding permanent promotion of officers eligible, 16 January 1943.

2. These were the exact words expressed to President Roosevelt by Medal of Honor recipient Butch O'Hare during the brief 21 April 1942 ceremony in FDR's office.

3. Duncan, "History of Fighting Squadron Five" (unpublished monograph). The reader should also see Reynolds's *Fighting Lady* for more detailed discussion. A number of documents used by Reynolds are in the Flatley papers.

4. Duncan, "History of Fighting Squadron Five."

5. This statement is based on numerous interviews during which it became apparent that after fifty years some carrier pilots were not aware of this policy for air group commanders. Evidently, this was due to some inconsistency in policy application by COs and air officers.

6. JHF, letters to Navy Department, 11 May and 20 May 1943.

7. In a 26 December 1943 letter to Fr. Ben Masse, Jimmy wrote, "Stanley Johnston writes a book on the fly. He can sit down and knock out 10,000 words. The results are not too bad. I believe that if he took it more seriously, he could be a great writer. If you get a chance, meet him. He's a very interesting guy."

8. JHF, letter to Dotty, 26 August 1943.

9. To Dotty, 24 August 1943.

10. To Dotty, 26 August 1943.

11. To Dotty, 28 August 1943.

12. Commander (JHF) of Air Group Five, action report of attack on Marcus Island, 31 August 1943, to commanding officer, 3 September 1943.

13. JHF, letter to Dotty, 7 September 1943.

14. Marcus Island action report, p. 2.

15. Ibid.

16. Ibid.

17. Duncan, "History of Fighting Squadron Five."

18. Marcus Island action report, p. 11.

19. JHF, letter to Dotty, 1 September 1943.

20. To Dotty, 6 September 1943.

21. To Dotty, 7 September 1943.

22. JHF, speech in San Diego, circa winter 1944.

Chapter 10: *Task Force Operations Officer: Battle of Leyte Gulf*

1. JHF, letter to Dotty, 3 and 6 September 1943.

2. Dotty Flatley, interview, 20 November 1995.

3. JHF, letter to Fr. Ben Masse, 26 December 1943.

4. Naval Aviation Confidential Bulletin, April 1944, p. 11.

5. Leonard, interview, 12 March 1996.

6. Ibid.

7. "History of Fleet Air Command, West Coast" (monograph), 22 January 1945, 28.

8. Ibid.

9. Collier, "Tiny Miracle: The Proximity Fuze," 43–45.

10. Leonard, interview, 12 March 1996.

11. Pyzdrowski, conversation, circa 1991, and undated letter to Rear Adm. James H. Flatley III.

12. Thach oral history.

13. Taylor, *Magnificent Mitscher*, 171.

14. Leonard, interview, 12 March 1996; Eggert, interview, 26 February 1996.

15. Taylor, *Magnificent Mitscher*, 189; and Potter, *Admiral Arleigh Burke*, 110–23.

16. Potter, *Admiral Arleigh Burke*, 181; Burke, interview by J. Bryan and D. Flatley, 17 July 1986.

17. Burke, interview by J. Bryan and D. Flatley, 17 July 1986.

18. Ibid.

19. Taylor, *Magnificent Mitscher*, 251.

20. Reynolds, *Fast Carriers*, 258.

21. Potter, *Admiral Arleigh Burke*, 189, 195.

22. Taylor, *Magnificent Mitscher*, 257.

23. Winters, *Skipper*, 124; and interview, 1 November 1996.

24. Potter, *Admiral Arleigh Burke*, 202.

25. Ibid., 207.

26. Winters, *Skipper*, 68; and interview, 1 November 1996.

27. Winters, *Skipper*, 133–34. (Many other scholarly sources reverse the order in which *Chiyoda* and *Chitose* were sunk.)

28. In fairness, many critics of Halsey at Leyte Gulf have not failed to note that he deserved major credit for leading Allied forces to victory in the South Pacific from October 1942 through the summer of 1944.

29. Inoguchi, Nakajima, and Pineau, *Divine Wind*, 6.

Chapter 11: *Task Force Operations Officer: Iwo Jima and Okinawa*

1. Riera, interview, 28 February 1996; and conversations dating from 1980.

2. Jimmy's impatience is treated elsewhere in this story, but this attribute was seldom evident with air group and squadron commanders during his tenure as operations officer.

3. Riera, interview, 28 February 1996.

4. On 10 December 1944, Vice Adm. George Murray, then commander of the air force in the Pacific Fleet, forwarded a letter to the commander of aircraft in the Seventh Fleet (logistics), and the commander of naval air bases in the Pacific, who was stationed in Guam. His subject was the maintenance of combat efficiency of reserve carrier groups and replacement pilots in forward areas. Outlined were flight requirements—forty hours a month—for the anticipated one to two months a pilot would wait before assignment to a carrier. Arleigh Burke noted "facilities are optimistic—if they are not available air groups may deteriorate rather rapidly." Jimmy, however, was not favorably disposed to Murray's letter. "This looks very good on paper," he wrote in the Remarks section of the routing form, "but the war will be over before it's functioning. It takes months to get a setup like this going . . . air groups in the forward area will go to pot. They are over-trained now . . . I think we should fight this and insist on rotation at four months."

5. Thach oral history (Operation Jack was named for his young son).

6. Ibid.

7. Ibid.

8. Thach was referring to Clark Reynolds's comments in *The Fast Carriers,* 300. *Fast Carriers* was first published in 1968 before Thach's death (1981).

9. McCain, letter to the commander of the Third Fleet, 24 January 1945, 4.

10. Reynolds, *Fast Carriers,* 292.

11. Books on Mitscher credit him with writing this letter while Burke's biographers credit him. Mitscher did add a significant, positive sentence, he did sign it, and Burke did approve it; but Jimmy's name is clearly printed on the five-page original as the writer. Further, it is not difficult after reading volumes of letters and other papers to find a pattern of writing and speech for an individual. Burke was more concise in his writing and less given to emotional passages than Jimmy.

12. Recommendations forwarded to Mitscher included one to have fighters level off attacks at two thousand feet. Mitscher, after hearing Jimmy strongly oppose the idea, rejected this proposed change to USF 74-B. "Such a procedure would require breaking off the attack at about 2,800 feet . . . [resulting in] little or no damage to the enemy anti-aircraft position, and much danger from that AA position to the attacking plane [commander of the First Carrier Task Force, Pacific, to the commander of the air force, Pacific Fleet, 21 April 1945]."

13. This damage to CV-3 did not involve her inability to turn quickly. Pictures taken from a catwalk along the large island structure within seconds of the first crash clearly show that only the photographer was aware of the kamikaze's approach. Most crewmembers shown in the photograph were intent on watching the movement of aircraft on the flight deck.

14. Burke, memo to all officers of the staff, 24 February 1945.

15. JHF, memo to all officers of the staff, 22 February 1945.

16. Inoguchi, Nakajima, and Pineau, *Divine Wind,* 211.

17. Initially, 724 was the accepted number for those killed, but research into the 1990s by members of the *Franklin* Reunion group determined the number to have slightly exceeded 800. The exact number was and is difficult to determine as so many died on other ships and the status of missing is difficult to resolve. Also, some sources report *Franklin* as being too badly damaged to be worth repairing. If fact, she was completely rebuilt from the hangar deck up, and after the war was determined to be in the best material condition of any *Essex*-class ship when the Korean War began in 1950. That neither she nor repaired *Bunker Hill* ever returned to active duty was doubtless due more to their tragic losses than material deficiency.

18. Commander of the air force, Pacific Fleet, re: *Yorktown* action report, 14 March–11 May 1945, to Pacific commands, 29 June 1945, NA.

19. Events during the kamikaze attacks on *Bunker Hill* were pieced together from a number of sources including *Summary of War Damage, 8 December 1944 to 9 October 1945;* Taylor, *Magnificent Mitscher* (290–94); Potter, *Admiral Arleigh Burke* (253–56); an unpublished letter written by Lt. Cdr. R. E. Hill (VF-84) in the Flatley papers; and in Commander Flatley's Legion of Merit

and Commendation citations. Also quite beneficial were walks through the museum carrier *Yorktown*. Although the carrier has been greatly modified—frame numbers, ladders, and original compartment identification labels enable one to retrace Flatley's actions.

20. Not all in the task force accepted this commendation in a magnanimous spirit. While acknowledging Air Group Eighty-four's effective performance, at least one task group commander questioned why other air groups were not similarly cited. Mitscher noted in his 6 May 1945 letter to Nimitz that he "reserves the right to make commendatory remarks concerning units under his command without being criticized for it by a subordinate."

21. When the *Essex*-class carriers were modernized in the early and mid-1950s, many ready rooms were moved below the hangar deck.

22. Although Mitscher's action and statement have been popular knowledge and reprinted many times, it was a pleasant surprise to discover that the original source was a letter from Jimmy Flatley written to *The Saturday Evening Post* on 18 December 1947 soon after Mitscher's death. Jimmy's exact wording was "As staff watch officer, just before it (kamikaze) struck, I ordered all crew on the bridge to hit the deck. After the explosion, I cautiously looked around from my prone position. There stood the Admiral in the midst of all of us with his arms folded and perfectly calm. As I rather sheepishly got to my feet he said to me laconically: 'Son, if the radio is working tell the Task Force that my flag is still flying but that if the Japs keep this up they are likely to grow hair on my bald head yet.' This was typical of the greatest combat Admiral of World War II."

23. Thanks to researcher-writer Henry Sakaida, the record was corrected in 1987.

24. JHF, letter to Lt. Herman Rosenblatt and Lt. (jg) Robert Reynolds, 23 May 1945.

25. Commander in chief, Pacific Ocean Areas, for distribution, "Estimate of Enemy Strength," 25 June 1945, NA.

Chapter 12: *From Combat to Cold War*

1. Cousins, letter, 11 March 1996.
2. Feightner, interview, 14 March 1996; Buell, interview, 29 February 1996.
3. Feightner, interview, 14 March 1996.
4. Johnston, *Grim Reapers,* 81.
5. Miller, *CACTUS Air Force,* 150.
6. Santa Cruz action report, 175–78, NA.
7. Ibid., 176.
8. Johnston, *Grim Reapers,* 29; confirmed by McCuskey, in conversation, 4 June 1992.
9. Leonard, interview, 12 March 1996.
10. Calvert, *Silent Running,* 93–94.

11. Marcus Island action report, 3 September 1943, 8, NA.

12. "To involve his pilots in the details of the air plan, Jimmy Flatley solicited ideas from them at squadron meetings" (Reynolds, *Fighting Lady,* 32).

13. Vejtasa, letter to author, 20 April 1996.

14. Leonard, interview, 12 March 1996.

15. Carmody, letter, 26 March 1996.

16. Adm. Arleigh Burke, letter to Crane Murphy, 18 July 1966.

17. Buell, interview, 29 February 1996.

18. Feightner, interview,14 March 1996.

19. Putman, interviews, November 1994. I spoke with him several times that month.

20. Clark G. Reynolds had opportunity to discuss Fairlamb, Pownall, Ginder, and Ghormley's problems either with the principals and/or with others who directly witnessed the events noted. The most extensive accounts in Reynolds's books for Fairlamb, Ginder, and Pownall are *Fast Carriers, Fighting Lady,* and *Carrier Admiral,* the latter co-authored with Clark. For Ghormley, see *Admiral John H. Towers,* 423–24.

21. Lundstrom, *The First Team: Pearl Harbor to Midway,* 313. The original source was the diary of Lt. Smokey Stover.

22. Leonard, interview, 12 March 1996.

23. An article in *Proceedings* (Linder, "Lost Letter of Midway," 29–35) pertaining to a recently discovered letter written by Ring does not mitigate his actions on 4 June 1942 at Midway. A response to the article (Tillman, "Comment and Discussion," 12, 14) corrects several salient assertions offered in the article. It also offers the comment that some of Ring's pilots "regarded their CAG as a stiff disciplinarian unfamiliar with current fleet aircraft or operating procedures." Too, students of World War II naval history may have noted that the late George Gay in his 1979 privately printed book, *Sole Survivor,* refers several times to "Group Commander" (1986 printing) but did not use Ring's name. When questioned about this in 1987, Gay—always a friendly, helpful man for all our other time together while working on several projects—offered an adamant scowl with equally adamant comments.

24. Vejtasa, letter to author, 20 April 1996.

25. Carmody, letter, 26 March 1996.

26. Clark, *Carrier Admiral,* 248. Jocko wrote in his autobiography, "Since my duties as basic training commander were not heavy . . ."

27. Voris, interview, 9 May 1996.

28. Scheuer, "The Birth of the Blues," 14; Voris, conversation, 9 May 1996.

29. Dees, "A Billion Dollar Blunder?" 75–77. The desire for economy and "cheap victory" is as current at the end of the century as it was throughout.

30. JHF, letter to Frank A. Tickenor, editor of *Aero Digest,* 22 July 1942.

31. JHF, letter to Bogan, 14 January 1950.

32. Ibid. Also, conversations with John Crommelin, 1982–1987. Further, see Barlow, *Revolt of the Admirals,* 235–37, 244. Barlow's "martyr" comments on

pages 282–83 are correct based on my conversations with John Crommelin as he adamantly believed to the end of his life (1996) that the extremes to which he went were necessary. As a result of his actions he was furloughed and retired (and advanced to the rank of rear admiral on the basis of his combat decorations).

Chapter 13: *Commanding Officer: NAS Olathe and USS Block Island*

1. JHF, letter to Rear Adm. Felix B. Stump, 18 July 1950.

2. JHF, letter to Rear Adm. A. K. Morehouse, chief of staff of naval forces in the Far East, 9 October 1950.

3. Rear Adm. L. A. Moebus, letter to Naval Air Reserve Training Commands (NARTC), 31 August 1951.

4. Cain, conversation, 6 May 1997.

5. Rear Adm. Arthur K. Knoizen, USN (Ret.), commented in an October 1993 conversation that he and three other AD Skyraider pilots of VA-45 spent three weeks in April 1953 at a training facility for nuclear weapons in New Mexico. The purpose of their secret training was preparation to launch from *Lake Champlain* (CV-39) and drop an atomic bomb on North Korea if an armistice was not soon signed. It was signed three months later.

6. Rear Adm. Arleigh A. Burke, personal and confidential letter to Capt. Alexander McDill, Office of the Secretary of the Navy, 9 October 1950, NA.

7. JHF, letter to Capt. Roy Johnson, 22 July 1950.

8. JHF, letter to Roy Grumman, 8 September 1950.

9. JHF, letter to Roy Roberts, military editor, *Kansas City Star*, 3 December 1951.

10. Letters from the deputy chief of naval operations (air), 13 August 1951; Governor E. F. Arn, 2 August 1951; Lawrence, Kansas, Chamber of Commerce, 24 July 1951; American Red Cross, 26 July 1951; Maj. Gen. George R. Acheson, USAF, 24 July 1951; and Lt. Col. L. W. Nicol, USAF, 19 May 1952.

11. JHF, letter to John F. Hallett, 17 August 1950.

12. JHF to Rear Adm. A. K. Doyle, 9 October 1950.

13. JHF, letter to Admiral Moebus, 17 January 1952 ("I would make it mandatory that every officer in the command be required to take a public speaking course conducted after working hours at the Naval Air Stations").

14. JHF, letter to Roy Roberts, military editor, *Kansas City Star*, 25 July 1950.

15. *Kansas City Star*, 3 September 1950.

16. *Olathe Mirror*, 15 May 1952.

17. JHF, letter to Capt. William Sutherland, Op-54, Naval Operations, Navy Department, Washington, D.C., 6 March 1951.

18. JHF, letter to Capt. G. A. Dussault, CNO (Op-54), Navy Department, Washington, D.C., 29 April 1952.

19. JHF, letter to Hanson Baldwin, military editor, *New York Times*, 12 October 1953.

20. When the ship was in port, the paper was called *The Fighting Block Island,* and when at sea, *The FBI Daily Press.*

21. JHF, letter to Rear Adm. Daniel V. Gallery, commander of the Hunter-Killer Force, 3 December 1952; and JHF, letter to Rear Adm. Frank Ward, commander of the Hunter-Killer Force, 14 May 1953.

22. *FBI Daily Press,* 7 June 1953.

23. Ibid.

24. *Kansas City Star,* 29 June 1953, 7.

25. Rear Adm. Ira E. Hobbs on JHF fitness report, 21 May 1953; Hobbs, message, 23 June 1953; Vice Adm. John J. Ballentine, message, 10 July 1953.

Chapter 14: *Commanding Officer: Safety Activity, NAS Norfolk, and USS Lake Champlain*

1. Unless otherwise cited, all information for the discussion on safety was taken from the original "Review of Naval Aviation Accident Prevention Methods" by the Naval Aviation Safety Activity to CNO, 3 September 1953, which included sixty-three pages plus three prefatory pages.

2. JHF, letter to Vice Adm. Felix B. Stump, 20 February 1951, and 6 March 1951; JHF, letter to Vice Adm. John Cassady, 20 February 1951; and JHF, letter to Lt. Col. John L. Smith, USMC, 7 March 1951.

3. Roemer, "The Flatley Report Which Saved Naval Aviation," *Wings of Gold,* 28–31; also in *Foundation,* 56–61.

4. *Norfolk Virginian-Pilot,* 17 June 1953 and two other articles from the same newspaper, undated but circa 1954–55.

5. *Dope Sheet,* 28 May 1954.

6. *Dope Sheet,* 23 April 1954.

7. *Dope Sheet,* 7 May 1954.

8. *Dope Sheet,* 28 January 1955.

9. *Dope Sheet,* 14 May 1954.

10. *Roanoke World-News,* 29 January 1955, 4.

11. *Dope Sheet,* 4 June 1954.

12. Ibid.

13. Rear Adm. Ingolf N. Kiland on JHF fitness report, 4 October 1954.

14. Vice Adm. Ralph O. Davis, personal letter to JHF, 22 May 1955.

15. JHF, confidential letter to the commander of the air force, U.S. Atlantic Fleet via the commander of Carrier Division Two, 21 March 1956.

16. JHF, letter to Rear Adm. A. A. Burke, 8 June 1955.

17. Rear Adm. Robert Goldthwaite, the commander of Carrier Division Two, on JHF fitness report, 1 October 1955.

18. Rear Adm. F. T. Ward, commander of Carrier Division Two, commendation letter to JHF 12 January 1957; and Rear Adm. D. Harris on JHF fitness report, 21 March 1956.

19. Cousins, letter, 11 March 1996.

20. Thach oral history.

21. Vejtasa, letter to author, 20 April 1996.

22. Rear Adm. Robert Goldthwaite on JHF fitness report, 2 September 1955.

23. Vice Adm. Felix B. Stump on JHF fitness report, June 1950.

24. Dotty Flatley, interview, 20 November 1995.

25. Rear Adm. Ira E. Hobbs on JHF fitness report, 6 April 1953.

26. Rear Adm. Ingolf N. Kiland on JHF fitness report, 15 March 1954.

27. Capt. W. L. Lind on JHF fitness report, 15 April 1938.

28. Buell, "Death of a Captain," 92–96. This article also presents outstanding lessons about combat leadership.

29. Rear Adm. Daniel V. Gallery on JHF fitness report, 22 December 1952.

30. Cousins, letter to author, 11 March 1996.

31. Eggert, interview, 26 February 1996.

32. Ibid.

33. Riera, interview, 28 February 1996.

34. Cdr. Richard Best, letter, 14 April 1996, and conversation, May 2000.

35. *Olathe Mirror,* 15 May 1952.

36. *FBI Daily Press,* 22 July 1953.

37. Eggert, interview, 26 February 1996.

38. JHF, letter to Capt D. E. Wilcox, chief of staff, NARTC, NAS Glenview, 11 March 1951.

39. In their book on Adm. Arleigh Burke, the authors noted that Jimmy "was impatient with those who disagreed with him." Jones and Kelley, *Admiral Arleigh (31-Knot) Burke,* 122.

40. JHF, letter to Burke, 8 June 1955.

41. JHF, letter to Rear Adm. Henry Crommelin, Office of Chief of Naval Operations, 4 December 1955.

42. JHF, letter to Wilcox ,11 March 1951.

43. Adm. Arleigh Burke, interview by Bryan and D. Flatley, 17 July 1986.

44. JHF, letter to Rear Adm. R. F. Hickey, Navy Department Office of Information, 13 September 1951.

45. JHF, letter to Congressman E. P. Scrivner on 18 May 1951, and again to Scrivner "Please protect my name on this matter," on 14 September 1951 in regard to the possible loss of flight pay.

46. Captain H. S. Bottomley Jr., letter to JHF, 5 August 1957.

47. Vice Adm. Robert Goldthwaite, deputy commander in chief, U.S. Atlantic Fleet, letter to JHF, 9 August 1957.

48. Von Mann, interview, 3 June 1997.

49. JHF, letter to Rear Adm. F. A. Brandley, 3 March 1958.

50. JHF, letter to Rear Adm. A. K. Doyle, 15 July 1950.

51. JHF, letter to Rear Adm. A. K. Morehouse, 9 October 1950.

52. JHF, letter to Capt. John S. McCain Jr., 25 November 1957.

53. Demetracopoulos, "Muzzling Admiral Burke," 65.

54. Burke, interview by Bryan and D. Flatley, 17 July 1986. Jimmy Flatley is not a classic example of Burke's thought. Jocko Clark, however, might be. Upon assignment to command *Yorktown* (CV-10), Jocko the warrior wisely chose Cdr. Raoul R. Waller, a quiet man and very efficient administrator, to be his executive officer and counterweight.

55. Vice Adm. H. P. Smith, chief of naval personnel to all flag officers, 20 May 1958, in reference to Secretary of the Navy Thomas S. Gates 17 May 1958 General Order No. 21 to all ships and stations on the subject of leadership.

56. *The Fighting Block Island* (CV-106 ship's newspaper), 17 July 1953.

57. Moorer, interview, 3 May 1996.

58. See Connaughton, "Revolt of the Admirals: Part Deux," 77.

59. See Patch, "Teaching Military Ethics Within a 'Moral Operating System,'" 66–67.

60. Original drafts extant in Flatley papers.

61. Admiral Thach, interview by John Lundstrom, October 1974.

62. Zumwalt recognized his controversial place in U.S. Navy history by commenting that "I have a wonderful list of friends and a wonderful list of enemies, and am very proud of both lists" (Cutler, "Hero and Heretic?" 10–12).

Chapter 15: *Last Assignment*

1. Thomas E. Murray, United States Atomic Energy Commission before the subcommittee on Disarmament of the Committee on Foreign Relations, 12 April 1956.

2. Series of letters beginning in mid-1957 between JHF and Frank Uhlig ending 13 June 1958. Jimmy's article, "What Makes a Good Skipper?" was titled by Uhlig and appeared just before Jimmy's death. Upon Jimmy's death Uhlig wrote a glowing editorial tribute.

3. Funeral sermon conducted by Vice Adm. Maurice S. Sheehy, USNR, 11 July 1958.

4. JHF, letter to Vice Adm. Robert B. Pirie, commander, Second Fleet, 9 April 1958. To a family friend he wrote in the same month that for someone who was supposed to be sick, he felt very good. This same message and tone was shared with many others.

5. Funeral sermon.

6. North American Aviation, letter to Dorothy Flatley, 1 September 1959; *Approach*, NAVAER 00-75-510, October 1959; and *Our Navy*, 15 September 1959, 8.

7. *Norfolk Virginian-Pilot*, 11 December 1970.

Bibliography

Note: Personal and official navy correspondence to and from Vice Adm. James H. Flatley Jr. are in the Flatley papers (FP) along with all of his flight log books, career and command files, orders, health records, fitness reports, and commendations. Copies of documents from the National Archives (NA), Library of Congress (LC), and the Operational Archives Branch of the Navy Historical Center in the Washington, D.C., Navy Yard (NHC) are denoted as having been in these archives before being copied and added to the Flatley papers. Also included in the Flatley papers are letters written to the author in response to requests for information and the audio tapes of face-to-face and telephone interviews conducted for this book. At the time of this writing (1996–2001), the Flatley papers are aboard *Yorktown* at Patriots Point Naval and Maritime Museum, Mt. Pleasant (Charleston Harbor), South Carolina. Also at Patriots Point through 2002 are the Enterprise Collection (EC) and Yorktown Association files.

Books

Barlow, Jeffrey G. *Revolt of the Admirals: The Fight for Naval Aviation, 1945–1950.* Washington, D.C.: Naval Historical Center, U.S. Government Printing Office, 1994.

Blackburn, Tom. *The Jolly Rogers: The Story of Tom Blackburn and Navy Fighting Squadron VF-17.* New York: Orion Books, 1989.

Boyington, Col. Gregory, USMC. *Baa Baa Black Sheep.* New York: G. P. Putnams' Sons, 1958.

Brown, Capt. Eric, RN. *Wings of the Navy.* London: Jane's, 1980.

Bryan, J., III. *Aircraft Carrier.* New York: Ballantine Books, 1954.

Buell, Cdr. Harold L., USN. *Dauntless Helldivers.* New York: Orion Books, 1986.

Buell, Thomas B. *The Quiet Warrior: A Biography of Raymond A. Spruance.* Boston: Little, Brown, 1974.

Burns, Eugene. *Then There Was One: The USS* Enterprise *and the First Year of War.* New York: Harcourt and Brace Company, 1944.

Calvert, Vice Adm. James F. *Silent Running: My Years on a World War II Attack Submarine.* New York: John Wiley and Sons, 1995.

Churchill, Winston S. *Their Finest Hour.* New York: Bantam Books, 1962.

Clark, Adm J. J., with Clark G. Reynolds. *Carrier Admiral.* New York: David McKay Co., 1967.

Cressman, Robert J. *That Gallant Ship USS* Yorktown *(CV-5).* Missoula, Mont.: Pictorial Histories Publishing Co., 1985.

Cressman, Robert J., Steve Ewing, and others. *A Glorious Page in Our History: The Battle of Midway 4–6 June 1942.* Missoula, Mont.: Pictorial Histories Publishing Co., 1990.

Dessler, Gary. *Management: Leading People and Organizations in the 21st Century.* New Jersey: Prentice Hall, 1998.

Ewing, Steve. *USS* Enterprise *(CV-6): The Most Decorated Ship of World War II.* Missoula, Mont.: Pictorial Histories Publishing Co., 1984.

———. *American Cruisers of World War II.* Missoula, Mont.: Pictorial Histories Publishing Co., 1986.

Ewing, Steve, and John B. Lundstrom. *Fateful Rendezvous: The Life of Butch O'Hare.* Annapolis: Naval Institute Press, 1997.

Foss, Joe, with Donna Wild Foss. *A Proud American: The Autobiography of Joe Foss.* New York: Pocket Books, 1992.

Foss, Joe, and Walter Simmons. *Flying Marine: The Story of His Flying Circus.* New York: E. P. Dutton and Co., 1943.

Frank, Richard B. *Guadalcanal.* New York: Random House, 1990.

Friedman, Norman. *U.S. Aircraft Carriers: An Illustrated Design History.* Annapolis: Naval Institute Press, 1983.

Gay, George. *Sole Survivor.* Naples, Fla.: Privately printed, 1979; revised 1986.

Grossnick, Roy A. *United States Naval Aviation 1910–1995.* Washington, D.C.: Naval Historical Center, U.S. Government Printing Office, 1997.

Gunston, Bill. *Grumman: Sixty Years of Excellence.* New York: Orion, 1988.

Inoguchi, Capt. Rikihei, Cdr. Tadashi Nakajima, and Roger Pineau. *The Divine Wind: Japan's Kamikaze Force in World War II.* New York: Bantam Books, 1960.

Jensen, Lt. Oliver, USNR. *Carrier War.* New York: Simon and Schuster, 1945.

Johnston, Stanley. *The Grim Reapers.* New York: Dutton, 1943.

———. *Queen of the Flattops.* New York: Dutton, 1942.

Jones, Gareth R., Jennifer M. George, and Charles W. L. Hill. *Contemporary Management*. Boston: Irwin McGraw-Hill, 1998.

Jones, Ken, and Hubert Kelley Jr. *Admiral Arleigh (31-Knot) Burke: The Story of a Fighting Sailor*. New York: Chilton Books, 1962.

Karig, Capt. Walter, USNR, Lt. Cdr. Russell L. Harris, USNR, and Lt. Cdr. Frank A. Manson, USN. *Battle Report*. New York: Rinehart and Company, 1948.

King, Admiral Ernest J., USN, and Cdr. Walter M. Whitehill, USNR. *Fleet Admiral King: A Naval Record*. New York: W. W. Norton, 1952.

Lawson, Robert L. *The History of U.S. Naval Air Power*. New York: The Military Press, 1985.

Lawson, Robert L., and Barrett Tillman. *Carrier Air War in Original WWII Color: US Navy Air Combat 1939–1946*. Osceola, Wis.: Motorbooks International, 1996.

Lundstrom, John B. *The First South Pacific Campaign: Pacific Fleet Strategy, December 1941–June 1942*. Annapolis: Naval Institute Press, 1976.

———. *The First Team: Pacific Naval Air Combat from Pearl Harbor to Midway*. Annapolis: Naval Institute Press, 1990.

———. *The First Team and the Guadalcanal Campaign: Naval Fighter Combat from August to November 1942*. Annapolis: Naval Institute Press, 1994.

Mersky, Peter. *The Grim Reapers: Fighting Squadron Ten in WWII*. Mesa, Ariz.: Champlin Museum Press, 1986.

Miller, Thomas G. Jr. *The CACTUS Air Force*. New York: Harper and Row, 1969.

Morison, Rear Adm. Samuel E. *History of United States Naval Operations of World War II*. Vol. 3, *The Rising Sun in the Pacific, 1931–April 1942*. Boston: Little, Brown, 1948.

———. *History of United States Naval Operations of World War II*. Vol. 12, *Leyte, June 1944–January 1945*. Boston: Little, Brown, 1958.

———. *History of United States Naval Operations of World War II*. Vol. 13. *The Liberation of the Philippines: Luzon, Mindanao, the Visayas, 1944–1945*. Boston: Little, Brown, 1963.

———. *History of United States Naval Operations of World War II*. Vol. 14, *Victory in the Pacific, 1945*. Boston: Little, Brown, 1960.

Morrissey, Lt. Thomas L., USNR. *Odyssey of Fighting Two*. N.p.: Privately printed, 1945.

Olynyk, Frank J. *USN Credits for the Destruction of Enemy Aircraft in Air-to-Air Combat, World War II*. Aurora, Ohio: privately printed, 1982.

Potter, E. B. *Nimitz*. Annapolis: Naval Institute Press, 1976.

———. *Bull Halsey*. Annapolis: Naval Institute Press, 1985.

———. *Admiral Arleigh Burke*. New York: Random House, 1990.

Rearden, Jim. *Koga's Zero: The Fighter that Changed World War II.* Missoula, Mont.: Pictorial Histories Publishing Co., 1995.

Reynolds, Clark G. *Famous American Admirals.* New York: Van Nostrand Reinhold, 1978.

———. *The Saga of Smokey Stover.* Charleston: Tradd St. Press, 1978.

———. *The Fighting Lady: The New* Yorktown *in the Pacific War.* Missoula, Mont.: Pictorial Histories Publishing Co., 1986.

———. *History and the Sea: Essays on Maritime Strategies.* Columbia: University of South Carolina Press, 1989.

———. *Admiral John H. Towers: The Struggle for Naval Air Supremacy.* Annapolis: Naval Institute Press, 1991.

———. *The Fast Carriers: The Forging of an Air Navy.* New York: McGraw Hill, 1968. Rev. ed. Annapolis: Naval Institute Press, 1992.

Solberg, Carl. *Decision and Dissent: With Halsey at Leyte Gulf.* Annapolis: Naval Institute Press, 1995.

Stafford, Cdr. Edward P., USN. *The Big E: The Story of the USS* Enterprise. New York: Random House, 1962.

Stockdale, James B. *Thoughts of a Philosophical Fighter Pilot.* Stanford: Hoover Institution Press, 1995.

Stern, Robert C. *The* Lexington-*Class Carriers.* Annapolis: Naval Institute Press, 1993.

Sudsbury, Elretta. *Jackrabbits to Jets: The History of NAS North Island.* San Diego: San Diego Publishing Co., 1992.

Swanborough, Gordon, and Peter M. Bowers. *United States Navy Aircraft since 1911.* Annapolis: Naval Institute Press, 1982.

Taussig, Betty Carney. *A Warrior for Freedom.* Manhattan, Kans.: Sunflower University Press, 1995.

Taylor, Theodore. *The Magnificent Mitscher.* Annapolis: Naval Institute Press, 1991.

Tillman, Barrett. *Corsair: The F4U in World War II and Korea.* Annapolis: Naval Institute Press, 1979.

———. *Hellcat: The F6F in World War II.* Annapolis: Naval Institute Press, 1979.

———. *The Wildcat in World War II.* Annapolis: Nautical and Aviation Publishing, 1983.

———. *U.S. Navy Fighter Squadrons in World War II.* North Branch, Minn.: Specialty Press, 1997.

U.S. Naval Academy. *The Lucky Bag.* Annual of the Regiment of Midshipmen. Annapolis: U.S. Naval Academy, 1923, 1926–29.

U.S. Navy, Naval Historical Center. *Dictionary of American Naval Fighting Ships.* Washington, D.C.: U.S. Government Printing Office, 1959–70.

Winters, Capt. T. Hugh. *Skipper: Confessions of a Fighter Squadron Commander 1943–1944.* Mesa, Ariz.: Champlin Fighter Museum Press, 1985.

Wooldridge, E. T., ed. *Carrier Warfare in the Pacific: An Oral History Collection.* Washington, D.C.: Smithsonian Institution Press, 1993.

Y'Blood, William T. *The Little Giants: U.S. Escort Carriers against Japan.* Annapolis: Naval Institute Press, 1987.

Yukl, Gar A. *Leadership in Organizations.* Englewood Cliffs, N.J.: Prentice-Hall, 1981.

Articles

Adams, Capt. John P., USN. "The First Use of the 'Thach Weave' in Combat." *Foundation,* spring 1988, 40–41.

Buell, Commander Harold L., USN (Ret.). "Death of a Captain." *Proceedings,* February 1986, 92–96.

Barnes, Hampton. *Congressional Record,* July 1958, 14778.

Cagle, Vice Adm. M. W., USN. "Arleigh Burke—Naval Aviator." *Foundation,* September 1981, 2–11.

Collier, Midn. Cameron D., USN. "Tiny Miracle: The Proximity Fuse." *Naval History,* July/August 1999, 43–45.

Connaughton, Lt. Cdr. Sean T. "Revolt of the Admirals: Part Deux." *Proceedings,* February 1999, 77.

Cutler, Lt. Cdr. Thomas. "Hero and Heretic?" *Proceedings,* February 2000, 10–12.

Dees, Ens. D. S. USN. "A Billion Dollar Blunder?" *Proceedings,* July 1997, 75–77.

Demetracopoulos, Elias P. "Muzzling Admiral Burke." *Proceedings,* January 2000, 65.

Flatley, Rear Adm. James H. Jr., USN. "What Makes a Good Skipper?" *Our Navy,* 1 May 1958, 20–21, 34–37.

Flatley, Vice Adm. James H. Jr., USN. "That's The Way Buck Does It." *Our Navy,* 1 October 1958.

———. "Suppose a Stranger Came Up." *Our Navy,* 1 March 1959.

Gates, Thomas. "Track of the Tomcatters, A History of VF-31, Part One: Fighting Six—The Shooting Stars 1935–42." *The Hook,* fall 1984, 15.

Giangreco, D. M. "The Truth about Kamikazes." *Naval History,* May/June 1997, 25–29.

Gillette, Capt. R. C., USN (Ret.). "Fortunate Blunder." *Proceedings,* December 1997, 66.

Jensen, Milinda D., USN. "Flatleys: Three Generations of Aviators." *Naval Aviation News,* May/June 1991, 21–23.

Kellar, Lt. Gen. Robert P., USMC. "First Class at NAS Jax." *Foundation,* spring 1998, 66–73.

Lacouture, Capt. John E., USN (Ret.). "Maui Aviation." *Wings of Gold,* spring 1989, 45–47.

Levy, Deed. "The Origins of a Great Navy Training Plane—the NS/N2S (and How Jerry Bogan Made It Possible)." *Foundation,* fall 1985, 10–15, 18.

Linder, Capt. Bruce R., USN (Ret.). "Lost Letter of Midway." *Proceedings,* August 1999, 29–35.

Masse, Benjamin L. "Prayers for the Grim Reapers." *America,* 2 August 1943, 545.

McCuskey, Captain Scott E., USN, and Bruce Gamble. "Time Flies: The Oral History of Captain E. Scott McCuskey, USN (Ret.)." *Foundation,* spring 1992, 56–61.

O'Leary, Michael. "Roll Out the Barrels!" *Air Classics,* March 1996, 31–43.

Patch, Lt. Cdr. John P., USN. "Teaching Military Ethics Within a 'Moral Operating System.'" *Proceedings,* October 1999, 66–67.

Roemer, Capt. Charles E., USN. "The Flatley Report Which Saved Naval Aviation." *Foundation,* spring 1985, 56–61.

Scarborough, Captain W. E., USN (Ret.). "Fighting Two—The Flying Chiefs, Part One, 1927–1941." *The Hook,* summer 1991, 16, 19–21, 23–28, 30–35.

———. "Fighting Two—The Flying Chiefs, Part Two, Pearl Harbor to Coral Sea." *The Hook,* fall 1991, 13–18, 20–24.

Scheuer, Dave. "The Birth of the Blues." *Foundation,* spring 1996, 8–20.

Stillwell, Paul. "John Smith Thach, Adm., USN, 1906–1981." *Navy Times,* 25 May 1981, 21.

Tillman, Barrett. "Comment and Discussion." *Proceedings,* October 1999, 12, 14.

———. "Night Hookers, Part One, 1942–1945: A History of Carrier Night Operations." *The Hook,* spring 1988, 41–52.

Voetsch, Capt. Stephen S., USN. "VF-101—The F-14 FRS: The Grim Reapers Train Tomcat Pilots and RIOs for Fleet Duty." *Wings of Gold,* winter 1999, 8–12, 15.

Newspapers

The Champ.
Dope Sheet.
Honolulu Advertiser.

The FBI Daily Press.
Kansas City Star.
New York Times.
Norfolk Virginian-Pilot.
Olathe Mirror.
Pensacola News Journal.
The Pride, Green Bay, Wisc.
Roanoke World News.
San Diego Tribune-Sun.

Official Records

National Archives, Washington, D.C.
National Museum of Naval Aviation, Pensacola, Fla.
National Personnel Records Center, St. Louis, Mo.
Naval Historical Center, Washington, D.C.
Nimitz Library, U.S. Naval Academy, Annapolis, Md.
Patriots Point Research Library, Charleston Harbor, S.C.
Summary of War Damage, 8 December 1944 to 9 October 1945. Patriots Point
   Research Library, Charleston Harbor, S.C.

Action Reports

Battle of the Coral Sea, 1942.
Battle of Santa Cruz, 1942.
Battle off Rennell Island, 1943.
Air Raid on Marcus Island, 1943.
Battle of Leyte Gulf, 1944.
Iwo Jima, 1945.
Okinawa, 1945.
Air Raids on Japan, 1944–45.

Unpublished Documents and Monographs (FP)

"A Brief History of the Fleet Patrol Plane Squadrons from the Organization of
   the First Squadron in 1919 to the Present Organization in 1935." Prepared
   by Lt. Cdr. Joel J. White, Medical Corps, USN, by direction of Rear Adm.
   A. W. Johnson, USN, commander of aircraft, Base Force.
"Current Tactical Orders and Doctrine, U.S. Fleet Aircraft." Vol. 1, "Carrier

Aircraft, USF-74B." Prepared by the commander of the air force, Pacific Fleet, November 1944.

Duncan, Robert W. "History of Fighting Squadron Five." Submitted to the Yorktown Association, 23 September 1975.

Flatley, Lt. Cdr. James H. Jr. "The Navy Fighter." Memorandum later forwarded to Commander, Carriers, U.S. Pacific Fleet, 25 June 1942.

———. "Combat Doctrine: Fighting Squadron Ten." July 1942.

Flatley, Capt. James H. Jr. "Introduction to Leadership." Undated but circa 1947.

"History of Fleet Air Command, West Coast." 22 January 1945. Original at NHC.

Ramsey, Lt. Cdr. Paul H. "Memorandum for all VF-2 Pilots." Undated but circa 1942.

"Station Regulations, U. S. Naval Air Station, Jacksonville, Florida." Undated but circa 31 December 1940.

USS *Enterprise* (CV-6). War Information Bulletin, 28 October 1942. EC.

U.S. Naval Institute Oral Histories

Martin, Vice Adm. William I., USN.
Thach, Adm. John S., USN.

Diaries, Personal Narratives, and Private Collections

The *Enterprise* (CV-6) Collection.

Flatley, Vice Adm. James H. Extensive personal papers. Courtesy of the Flatley family.

Thach, Lt. Cdr. John S. Thach Papers. National Museum of Naval Aviation, Pensacola.

Yorktown Association Collection. Extensive records, papers, diaries, and unpublished books/monographs aboard *Yorktown* (CV-10) at Patriots Point Naval and Maritime Museum.

Author Interviews, Correspondence, and Conversations

Abbot, Rear Adm. Lloyd J. Jr., USN (Ret.). Interview, 13 March 1996.

———. Interview, 26 April 1996.

Adams, Capt. John, USN (Ret.). Conversations, dating from 1977.

———. Interview, 28 February 1996.

Balden, Bill. Letter, 3 September 1994.

Best, Cdr. Richard H., USN (Ret.). Conversations, dating from 1988.

———. Letter, 14 April 1996.

Blackburn, Capt. Tom, USN (Ret.). Telephone conversation, July 1989.

Bryan, Cdr. James T., USNR. Conversations, 1984–1996.

Buell, Cdr. Harold L., USN (Ret.). Conversations, dating from 1984.

———. Interview, Mt. Pleasant, S.C., 29 February 1996.

———. Interview, Orlando, Fla., 20 April 1996.

———. Letter, 15 October 1996.

Cain, Capt. James, USN (Ret.). Conversations, 1987–1997.

———. Interview, Mt. Pleasant, S.C., 29 April 1997.

Callan, Capt. Willie A., USN (Ret.). Telephone interview, 14 April 1994.

Carmody, Rear Adm. Martin D., USN (Ret.). Interview, Orlando, Fla., 26 April 1996.

———. Letter, 26 March 1996.

Coffin, Rear Adm. Albert, USN (Ret.). Conversations, 1984–1988.

Condit, Rear Adm. James W., USN (Ret.). Conversations, dating from 1987.

———. Interview, Mt. Pleasant, S.C., 3 May 1996.

Cousins, Adm. Ralph W., USN (Ret.). Letter, 11 March 1996.

Crommelin, Rear Adm. John G., USN (Ret.). Conversations, 1982–1996.

Early, Mrs. Ruth. Telephone interview, June 1996.

Earnest, Capt. Albert K. "Bert," USN (Ret.). Conversations, dating from 1987.

Eggert, Lt. Cdr. Joseph R. Jr., USNR. Telephone interview, 26 February 1996.

Elder, Capt. Robert M., USN, (Ret.). Conversations, dating from 1987.

———. Interview, Mt. Pleasant, S.C., 25 March 1996.

Feightner, Rear Adm. Edward L. Conversations, dating from 1993.

———. Interview, Mt. Pleasant, S.C., 23 April 1994.

———. Interview, Mt. Pleasant, S.C., 14 March 1996.

Flatley, Mrs. Dorothy. Conversations, dating from 1987.

———. Interview, Mt. Pleasant, S.C., 20 November 1995.

Flatley, Rear Adm. James H. III, USN (Ret.). Conversations, dating from 1987.

Flatley, Dr. John. Telephone interview, 6 March 1996.

———. Interview, 21 March 1996.

Gaskill, Lewis. Conversation, 12 May 2000.

Gay, George. Conversations, October 1987–4 June 1992.

Gayler, Adm. Noel A. M., USN (Ret.). Telephone interview, March 1994.

Gray, Capt. James S. Jr., USN (Ret.). Conversation following his Battle of Midway remarks at a Naval Aviation Museum Symposium, Pensacola, Fla., May 1987.

Hawkins, Capt. Ray, USN (Ret.). Conversation, Orlando, Fla., 27 April 1996.

Knoizen, Rear Adm. Arthur K., USN (Ret.). Conversation, Mt. Pleasant, S.C., October 1993.

Lacouture, Capt. John E., USN (Ret.). Conversations, dating from 1993.

———. Letter, 29 April 1996.

———. Letter, 6 May 1996.

———. Letter, 30 March 1997.

Leonard, Rear Adm. William N., USN (Ret.). Telephone interview, 12 March 1996.

Lundstrom, John B. Conversations, dating from 1988.

McCuskey, Capt. E. Scott, USN (Ret.). Conversations, Mt. Pleasant, S.C., June 1992.

———. Conversations, Mt. Pleasant, S.C., April 1996.

Moorer, Adm. Thomas, USN (Ret.). Telephone interview, 3 May 1996.

Mott, Capt. Elias B., USN (Ret.). Conversations, Milwaukee, Wis., 1982–1985.

———. Correspondence, 1982–1985.

Newbegin, Ed. Conversation, Mt. Pleasant, S.C., 19 December 1999.

Outlaw, Rear Adm. E. C., USN (Ret.). Conversation, Mt. Pleasant, S.C., 20 June 1994.

Palmer, Patricia O'Hare. Conversations, dating from 2 November 1993.

Putman, Capt. Charles F., USN (Ret.). Interviews, Scottsdale, Ariz., November 1994.

Pyzdrowski, Henry A. Conversations, dating from 1987.

———. Letter to Rear Adm. James H. Flatley III, undated.

Quinn, Charles H. Jr. Letter, 20 January 1999.

———. Letter, 6 July 1999.

Ramage, Rear Adm. James, USN (Ret.). Conversations, dating from 1988.

———. Interview, Orlando, Fla., 27 April 1996.

Reynolds, Clark G. Conversations, dating from 1984.

Riera, Rear Adm. R. Emmett, USN (Ret.). Conversations, dating from 1980.

———. Interview, Mt. Pleasant, S.C., 28 February 1996.

Sharkey, Joe. Conversations, dating from 1987.

Sillivant, Gordon. Letter, 19 September 1996.

Stockdale, Vice Adm. James B., USN (Ret.). Conversations, Mt. Pleasant, S.C., October 1993.

———. Letter, 13 March 1996.

———. Letter, 26 March 1996.

Strean, Vice Adm. Bernard M., USN (Ret.). Interviews, Mt. Pleasant, S.C., November 1994.

Sutherland, Cdr. James, USN (Ret.). Conversations, 1990–1998.

Tillman, Barrett. Conversations, dating from 1987.

Ustick, Cdr. Perry, USN (Ret.). Conversations, 1984–1992.

Von Mann, Milton Ludwig. Interview, 3 June 1997.

Vejtasa, Capt. Stanley, USN (Ret.). Conversations, dating from 1987.

———. Letter, 20 April 1996.

———. Letter, 30 March 1998.

Voris, Capt. Roy M., USN (Ret.). Conversation, 9 May 1996.

Vraciu, Cdr. Alexander, USN (Ret.). Conversations, dating from October 1993.

Winters, Capt. Hugh, USN (Ret.). Letter, 25 March 1996.

———. Interview, Mt. Pleasant, S.C., 1–2 November 1996.

Ziglar, Don, USS *Yorktown* (CV-10) crew. Conversations, dating from 1987.

Interviews and Correspondence (Not by Author)

Burke, Adm. Arleigh A., USN. Interview by James T. Bryan Jr., and David Flatley. Tape recording, Washington, D.C., 17 July 1986.

Foss, Capt. Joe, USMC (Ret.). Interview in the Marine Corps Public Relations Office, 28 April 1943.

Foss, Brig. Gen. Joe, USMC (Ret.). Interview by David Flatley. Tape recording, n.p., 1 January 1987.

Harkness, Don. Letter to James H. Flatley III, 23 February 1996.

Hyland, Adm. John, USN. Letter to David Flatley, 24 September 1986.

Smith, Maj. John, USMC, VMF-334. Interview at the Bureau of Aeronautics, 10 November 1942.

Thach, Lt. Cdr. John S., USN. Interview at the Bureau of Aeronautics, 29 August 1942.

Thach, Adm. John S., USN (Ret). Interview by John Lundstrom, October 1974.

Index

Steve Ewing is the author of several books on naval history including *Memories and Memorials: The World War II U.S. Navy 40 Years after Victory; American Cruisers of World War II: A Pictorial Enclyclopedia; USS Enterprise (CV-6): The Most Decorated Ship of World War II—A Pictorial History; The Lady Lex and the Blue Ghost: A Pictorial History of the USS Lexingtons CV-2 and CV-16;* and *In Remembrance.* With Robert J. Cressman he co-authored *A Glorious Page in Our History: The Battle of Midway, 4–6 June, 1942,* and with John Lundstrom he co-authored *Fateful Rendezvous: The Life of Butch O'Hare,* published by the Naval Institute in 1997. Dr. Ewing was a college professor for twenty years, and in 1988 he became senior curator at Patriots Point Naval and Maritime Museum, Charleston Harbor, South Carolina.